GARDEN

TICKET OFFICE.

Going to America

Going to America

BY

TERRY COLEMAN

Stephanie Wilks

January 10, 1976

Pantheon Books

A DIVISION OF RANDOM HOUSE, NEW YORK

Manufactured in the United States of America

FIRST AMERICAN EDITION

Library of Congress Cataloging in Publication Data

Coleman, Terry.   Going to America.

London ed. (Hutchinson) has title: Passage to America.   Bibliography: p.
1. Gt. Brit.—Emigration and immigration—History. 2. Ireland—Emigration and immigration—History. 3. Canada—Emigration and immigration—History. 4. U.S.—Emigration and immigration—History.

I. Title.   JV7618.N7C58   1972   301.3′28′42073   79-39602
ISBN 0-394-47988-2

For Cat

Contents

	List of illustrations	**9**
	Acknowledgements	**13**
	Foreword	**15**
1	The Lands of Promise	17
2	Who Should Go, and Why	28
3	America in the Mind of the Time	42
4	Leaving Home	56
5	Liverpool and the Last of England	63
6	Hard-driven Ships and Brutal Crews	85
7	The Voyage	100
8	Washed Away; Drowned Altogether	119
9	1847, the Plague Year	128
10	New York	155
11	Quarantine, Runners, and Rackets	169
12	Colonising and Shovelling Out	189
13	The Breaking of Lieutenant Hodder	205
14	America for the Americans	218
15	Steamships and Castle Garden	236
	Sources and Bibliography	251
	Appendices	
	A. The Passenger Acts (British and American)	287
	B. Emigration from the United Kingdom in the Years 1835–60	295

C.   The Proportion of Emigrants who were Irish   297

D.   Occupations of Emigrants to the U.S.A.   299

E.   Emigrants Helped by the New York
       Commissioners   301

F.   Emigrants' Stated Destinations   302

Index   305

Illustrations

Departure of the *Nimrod* and *Athlone* steamers from Cork for Liverpool. *Illustrated London News*, May 10, 1851

The parish priest blesses Irish emigrants. *Illustrated London News*, May 10, 1851

Emigrants on the quay at Cork, 1851. *Illustrated London News*, May 10, 1851

A scalpeen at Kilrush. *Illustrated London News*, December 19, 1849

Brigid O'Donnell and children. *Illustrated London News*, December 22, 1849

A Dorsetshire labourer's cottage, 1846. *Illustrated London News*, September 5, 1856

Lime Street, Liverpool, in the mid-1850s. From a lithograph by W. G. Herdman, in the Brown, Picton, and Hornby Libraries, Liverpool

Waterloo Dock, Liverpool. Lithograph by W. G. Herdman, in *Views of Modern Liverpool*, 1864

Emigrants embarking at Liverpool. *Illustrated London News*, July 6, 1850

Irish emigrant reading wall posters at Dublin, *c.* 1855. Original watercolour by Richardson Fox, done for a lithograph later published by Currier and Ives. From the Edward W. C. Arnold collection lent by the Metropolitan Museum of Art. Photograph courtesy of the Museum of the City of New York

The medical officers' office at Liverpool. *Illustrated London News*, July 6, 1850

Emigrant sailing packet about to be towed out into the Mersey. *Illustrated London News*, July 6, 1850

'Departure from Home,' an engraving from *Harper's Weekly*, New York, 1858. This was an example of American plagiarism. The original was 'Eastward Ho,' a painting by Henry Nelson O'Neil, which was exhibited at the Royal Academy, London, in 1858 and showed the departure of British soldiers for the Indian Mutiny. The engraving in Harper's altered one or two details, turned the soldiers' caps into civilian hats, deleted a sergeant's stripes, and thus changed the figures into emigrants. *Harper's Weekly,* June 26, 1858. Museum of the City of New York.

Emigrants in the steerage. *Illustrated London News,* July 6, 1850

Sailors searching an emigrant ship for stowaways. *Illustrated London News,* July 6, 1850

The Black Ball packet *Isaac Webb. Gleason's Pictorial,* Boston, May 17, 1851

Emigrants, sailors, and the Yankee captain on board the American ship *Cambridge,* 1844, drawn by one of their fellow passengers. From the manuscript, diary and drawings of T. Hibbert Ware in the Toronto and Early Canada Collection, Metropolitan Toronto Central Library

Emigrants dancing between decks. *Illustrated London News,* July 6, 1850

Wreck of the brig *Charles Bartlett. Illustrated London News,* July 7, 1849

The Train packet *Ocean Monarch* on fire in the Mersey, 1848. Lithograph in the Brown, Picton, and Hornby Libraries, Liverpool

A Train packet speaking a Collins steamer. *Ballou's Pictorial,* Boston, March 10, 1855

A passenger left to drown by lifeboat crew. From *Yankee Notions,* New York, Vol. 4, Number 1, 1855. The magazine was commenting on the wreck of the Collins steamer *Arctic* the previous September. She was not carrying emigrants, but it was not unknown for the crews of emigrant ships to save themselves before their passengers. There was not enough room for all

———————————

The *City of Glasgow,* run by William Inman for Richardson's of Liverpool, was the first steamer to carry steerage passengers regularly. *Gleason's Pictorial,* September 6, 1851

Panorama of New York, 1852. From a lithograph by K. Th. Westermann published in Weissenberg, Germany. Edward W. C. Arnold Collection lent by the Metropolitan Museum of Art. Photograph courtesy of the Museum of the City of New York

The quarantine grounds and hospital at Staten Island. *Frank Leslie's Illustrated Newspaper,* September 13, 1856

Castle Garden, New York, 1851. *Gleason's Pictorial Drawing Room Companion,* Vol. 1, 1851

South Street, New York, in the 1850's. Museum of the City of New York

Monument to 5425 emigrants who died at Grosse Isle quarantine in the St. Lawrence. Courtesy Public Archives of Quebec

Emigrants landing at New York. *Harper's Weekly,* June 26, 1858

Paddy O'Dougherty, emigrant who made $100,000. *Illustrated News.* New York, November 5, 1853

'Paddy's Ladder to Wealth in a Free Country.' *Yankee Notions,* New York, 1853, page 254

Arrival of the packet *Kossuth* at New York. *Gleason's Pictorial,* Boston, June 14, 1851

A Runner's Progress. John Morrissey as emigrant runner, prizefighter, gambler, and State Senator. Woodcuts from John Morrissey. *His Life, Battles and Wrangles, Etc.* by William E. Harding, sporting editor of the *Police Gazette,* New York 1881

Baggage smashers at New York, *Yankee Notions,* New York, 1853, page 254

Runners at New York. *Harper's Weekly,* June 26, 1858

Canal barges on the North River at New York. *Gleason's Pictorial,* Boston, December 25, 1852

A pair of engravings, *As I Was* and *As I Am,* from *Work and Wages* by Vere Foster, an emigrants' pamphlet sold in London in 1855.

The emigrant's Christmas dinner in the Far West. *Yankee Notions,* New York, 1853, page 254

ILLUSTRATIONS IN THE TEXT

Advertisement for the packet ship *Yorkshire, Liverpool Mercury,* May 21, 1847   *page* 67

Advertisement for Tapscott's, one of the biggest emigrant brokers. From the *Liverpool Mail,* May 21, 1851   69

Cholera poster in Liverpool. Colonial Office Papers, C.O. 384/92; Public Record Office, London   79

Map showing New York, Boston and the St. Lawrence   139

Advertisement by Richardson's for their emigrant steamships, 1853. Colonial Office Papers, C.O. 384/93 Public Record Office, London   239

Foreword

This book does not set out to be a history of emigration. It is the story of emigrants—who they were, and why they left, and how, and what happened then. It is not a history of the political or other movements which caused emigration, though these movements must be understood. Because it is about people, it must be about particular people. There is no sense in taking, say, the whole of the nineteenth century, because in such a long time the people get lost in an accumulation of letters, newspapers, books, State Papers, and other documents which are too many to read let alone understand. So this is a history of the emigrants who left Great Britain and Ireland in 1846–55. These ten years saw by far the greatest emigration from the United Kingdom to America known till then. The period starts with a year of ordinary emigration; then takes in the Irish famine; then includes the years of the early 1850s when, without famine or any other extraordinary cause, emigration from England and Ireland was at its height; and ends quietly with only a small emigration, because of war in Europe and a slump in America. In the mid-1840s many emigrants still sailed in old brigs. By 1850 they were mostly crossing on the big American sailing packets out of Liverpool. By 1855 substantial numbers were travelling by steamship, and it was the steamship, and not the reforming, humanitarian, or self-interested motives of any government, which made the Atlantic passage in steerage for the first time tolerable.

Acknowledgements

I owe a great deal to the staff of the following libraries. In England: the British Museum Reading Room; the British Museum Newspaper Library, Colindale; the Public Record Office, London; the National Maritime Museum, Greenwich; Holborn Public Libraries; the Brown, Picton, and Hornby Libraries, Liverpool; the Liverpool Record Office. In the United States: the New York Public Library; the New York Public Library Manuscripts Room; the New York Historical Society; the Museum of the City of New York; the Library of Congress; the National Archives, Washington D.C.; and Boston Public Library and its Rare Book Department. In Canada: the National Library and Archives, Ottawa; La Bibliothèque de la Ville de Montreal, and particularly to Marie Baboyant, librarian in charge of Canadiana; Metropolitan Toronto Public Library, and particularly its manuscripts room; les Archives de la Archevêché de Québec and particularly to Father Armand Gagner, archivist; and les Archives du Séminaire de Québec. In Ireland: the National Library of Ireland, Dublin; Limerick City Library; and the Galway County Library, Galway.

I am grateful to Philip Hope-Wallace and to the Canadian government, who between them enabled me to see more of Canada than I should otherwise have seen, to Mr. Freddy Masson, the director of Grosse Isle, for letting me see the cemetery and memorials on the island, to Nancy Poland, who did a great deal of research in the National Archives in Washington, and to John Rosselli, of the University of Sussex, who read the American chapters. Last, I thank my wife Lesley for reading, correcting, suggesting, and encouraging; and for making the index.

I

The Lands of Promise

Julia, a domestic servant holding a superior position in a gentleman's family, wrote in December 1849 to an emigrant journal in London saying she earnestly desired to emigrate, and asking advice. She wanted to know if the provisions on board ship were such as a person might eat who had been accustomed to decent living in England, what clothes she should take, and how to avoid seasickness. The magazine, which printed a column of such letters each month, replied that she should not go at all if she was afraid. To help out the rations on board ship she should take a little good tea and a few other comforts. For clothes, she should take a warm grey cloak with loose sleeves, cotton peignoirs, and 'all other dresses made to close in front; it is very awkward to lie in your berth and try to hook-and-eye behind'. For seasickness there was no remedy: 'Get your digestion in good order before starting; keep your feet warm with woollen stockings while ill. We have found cayenne pepper in soup very comforting; but there is no rule.'[1]

Thomas Thompson and Son, chemists, of Liverpool, did offer a remedy sold by only the most respectable druggists in the principal seaports of the United Kingdom, 2s. 9d. a packet or 11s. a tin. It was a remedy whose sale, according to the advertisements, had exceeded the most sanguine expectation of the proprietors, and had, in extensive trials over two years in almost all parts of the globe, prevented or cured seasickness in ninety-three cases out of a hundred. It was also without the least unpleasant taste.[2]

An emigrant clergyman, writing in 1849 under the pseudonym of Pioneer of the Wilderness, did not think seasickness was much to be feared. He knew, because he had sailed to Quebec. On the voyage he had gone every morning before breakfast to the forecastle and had buckets of salt-water dashed over him, and derived benefit from it, he thanked God. This was early in the morning when, he said, the decks were pretty sure to be clear of females. He was thankful to add that he was none of the seasick sort, but by the way, he said, as regards seasickness, a vast deal depended on keeping up a good heart. Some people recommended wearing opium bags over the stomach; he recommended not looking at the yeasty waves, but eating and drinking as much as you reasonably could. Thick gingerbread cake, gingerbread nuts, and oranges and apples were good for you. Take medicines if you had to, but by no means make an apothecary's shop of your interior if you could help it. Pioneer went on to say it was no loss to bring out Cleveland Bay stallions, Durham bulls, and pigs of the Berkshire and Chinese breeds, but advised against bulky furniture, 'unless the ladies have a favourite pianoforte'.[3] Which showed that he knew as much about the Atlantic passenger trade, in steerage out of Liverpool, as Sidney Smith, who wrote a book in 1850 saying a sea voyage was by no means so formidable an affair as was imagined. Actors, singers, dancers, authors, took the trip, across the Atlantic and back, again and again, without the slightest repugnance. Nobleman and squires went for pleasure, and timid women sailed without scruple, two or three times. Mr. Smith said you should reassure yourself by looking at the thickness of the ship's sides, and never be alarmed until the captain was. As for seasickness—'indeed, by straining the system, and clearing it thoroughly out, it almost invariably renovates and invigorates the whole constitution'.[4]

William Chambers, magazine editor, who made the voyage from Liverpool to Halifax and Boston in 1854, was hearty too. At ten each night he made a supper of devilled legs of fowl and 'glasses of something to keep away that nasty squeamishness'. He was sick for only an hour on the second day, but even so he said, 'The slightest touch of seasickness takes away the poetry of the ocean.' He went by the Cunard steam packet *America*, twelve and a half days to Halifax, fare £25.[5] The emigrant went steerage, in a sailing vessel, fare £3 10s., passage usually four to seven weeks.

The Society for Promoting Christian Knowledge,[6] which from 1850 to 1852 published eighteen emigrant tracts, price 1d. each, also had an optimistic view of the steerage. Remarking that labour was the lot of fallen man, one tract advised the emigrant to pray; to read the Bible; to rise early like King Alfred, who had allowed only eight hours out of the twenty-four for sleep, recreation, and meals; to discourage indecent jests; to eat the best concentrated beef-tea which was made by Messrs. Brand, 11 Little Stanhope Street, Mayfair—because it was the pure juice of beef, full of flavour and not too gluey; and to submit to seasickness. 'This is a misery you must make up your mind to, for there is no preventing it; and, after all, unless very severe indeed, you feel rather better than worse afterwards.' The emigrant should lie down, tempt the stomach with a bit of toasted fat bacon, and the surgeon would give him some essence of peppermint on a lump of sugar, or, if the passenger was still tormented, a few drops of ether in water. Nine ships out of ten had no surgeon, and what surgeons there were had no ether. And if Samuel Cartwright, M.D., of New Orleans, had been surgeon on board an emigrant ship he would not have given his patients even peppermint. In 1854 Cartwright wrote eight long letters on moral hygiene to a United States Senate Committee on sickness and mortality on emigrant ships. His cure for seasickness was sea-water, which he said was emetic, aperient, and tonic. 'Seasickness caused by it rarely troubles the patient again', he said. He also thought constipation at sea was caused by the rocking of the boat, and that a rocking chair had the same effect on land. Emigrants would be much healthier if they were compelled to come on deck and promenade in regular order, like soldiers on the march, holding one another up if the sea was rough. If there were no surgeon on board, the sick should be handed over to the care of some old, discreet, and faithful sailor. 'The patient, after going through a course of sea-water and afterwards promenading the deck in the fresh air, supported by one or two of the crew, or some friendly arm, will soon be well.' Dr. Cartwright also prescribed gaiety. The emigrants should be encouraged to enjoy themselves on deck with music and dancing, under a power, however, to enforce order and decorum as strict as that over soldiers on parade, otherwise such amusements would become a nuisance. He said gaiety was the natural remedy for sadness. He was the kind of doctor who also thought that New Orleans, in 1854, standing as it did on the soil of five separate cypress forests, was one of the healthiest cities in the world.[7]

In rough weather, when passengers were most likely to be seasick, they could not safely have come on deck at all, and would often have been battened down. In calm seas, when they would not have needed his remedy, they could not in any case have come on deck, or not more than a few at a time. The biggest emigrant ships carried a thousand steerage passengers, and most of the deck space was kept not for them but for the few cabin passengers.

Herman Melville had been to sea as a sailor on the New York passage out of Liverpool, and in 1849 he described an emigrant ship, with 500 aboard, encountering its first squalls in the Irish Sea. From under the two hatches came the steady drum of a subterranean wailing and weeping. 'That irresistible wrestler, seasickness, had overthrown the stoutest of their number, and the women and children were embracing and sobbing in all the agonies of the poor emigrant's first storm at sea.' It was bad enough for the cabin passengers, who had privacy and stewards. 'How then, with the friendless emigrants, stowed away like bales of cotton, and packed like slaves in a slave ship; confined in a place that, during storm time, must be closed against both light and air; who can do no cooking, nor warm so much as a cup of water; for the drenching seas would instantly flood their fire in their exposed galley on deck? We had not been at sea one week, when to hold your head down the fore hatchway was like holding it down a suddenly opened cesspool.'[8]

The emigrants had nowhere but their berths to be sick, and in almost all emigrant ships, and in all those of any size, the berths were set up in two or three tiers, each tier holding four people. Those below were the least fortunate. Afterwards the passengers could not be induced or bullied to clear up, even if the crew was diligent enough to try to make them.[9]

In 1853, 947 emigrant vessels sailed from Liverpool for North America.[10] The average vessel was of 890 tons, smaller than the *Cutty Sark* clipper preserved at Greenwich, and half the size of the frigate U.S.S. *Constitution* preserved at Boston, Mass. To a vessel of 890 tons, the North Atlantic, at any time of the year, is not a lake. Notwithstanding cayenne pepper, a little good tea and other comforts, Thomas Thompson's remedy at 2s. 9d. a packet, opium bags over the stomach, essence of peppermint on lumps of sugar, seawater purges and forced marches on deck, most emigrants in small sailing vessels were seasick the first few days out, and in storms afterwards. The steerage stank from the first. And seasickness was the least of their troubles.

The emigration of 1846–55 was by far the heaviest ever known from Great Britain and Ireland. According to British government figures, which are generally inaccurate and generally an under-estimate, 2,740,000 people emigrated in these ten years. Only 430,000 altogether went to Australia, New Zealand, and the Cape, and more than 2,300,000 to America.[11] The emigration to the southern colonies, though it was what the British government really wanted to encourage, was small and untypical. To colonise Australia the government selected only the young and fit, and carried them out free in state-chartered ships. The North American emigration, on the other hand, was spontaneous, disorganised, and private. No emigrant was ever given a government-assisted passage to the United States, or, in the period 1846–55, to Canada. Emigrants to America went in ordinary commercial vessels, paying ordinary commercial fares. There was no selection. Anyone could go. The only qualification was the ability to find the steerage fare.

The British government concerned itself with the American emigration no more than humanity demanded. In London there were three emigration commissioners, paid civil servants, who consti-tuted the Colonial Land and Emigration Board. With a small staff of clerks, they did their best to regulate the trade, not only to the colonies but also to the United States. It was their business to ensure that emigrant ships were not more intolerably overcrowded than the law allowed—though the overcrowding permitted by law was intolerable anyway. Regulatory Acts of Parliament were passed now and again throughout the period, generally after yet another select committee had discovered once again how wretchedly emigrants were treated. But, strangely, emigration was never a political issue. Both Whig and Tory governments did as little as possible, thinking it wrong to interfere unnecessarily with trade, and anyhow lacking the resources to do much. The only time an emigrant to America came across government regulation in any form was at the ports, where a few emigration officers, half-pay naval officers in the employ of the commissioners, struggled against indifference and the paramount demands of commerce, and tried to enforce largely unenforceable laws.

In the middle of the century there was a sudden and huge increase in emigration to the United States. From independence up to the end of 1845 only 1,600,000 people, of all nationalities, had entered the republic. In 1846–55 more than 1,880,000 British and Irish came. So in those ten years a quarter of a million more people entered the U.S.A., from the United Kingdom alone, than had gone there from all parts of the world in the previous seventy years.[12]

In these ten years nearly all immigrants were from the United
Kingdom or from Germany. The Germans do not concern this book,
except that many of them did not sail direct from Germany but first
crossed to England and sailed from London or Liverpool in English
or American vessels.[13] The London packets were often full of
Germans.[14] The majority of the United Kingdom emigrants were
Irish, but, again, most of them sailed from the English port of
Liverpool. Very few mid-century immigrants were of other nationalities. In 1846, to take a few examples, only four Poles, eighty-eight
Italians, three Greeks, and seven Chinese entered the U.S.A., and in
1851 only one Russian, ten Poles, and 423 Italians. In 1855, it is true,
there were more than 1,000 Italians and more than 3,000 Chinese,[15]
but these were still small numbers compared with those of the 'old
immigrants' from western Europe. A substantial Asiatic immigration was still years away, and so was the 'new immigration' from
southern and central Europe and Russia.

Since independence, the United States had welcomed emigrants.
As Benjamin Franklin drily put it, 'The only encouragements we
hold out to strangers are—a good climate, fertile soil, wholesome air
and water, plenty of provisions, good pay for labour, kind neighbours, good laws, a free government, and a hearty welcome.'[16] And
the policy of the United States towards immigrants was stated in
1817 by John Quincy Adams, when he was Secretary of State, and
still held good in the middle of the century. He said America invited
none to come, but would not keep out those who had the courage to
cross the Atlantic. They would suffer no disabilities as aliens, but
could expect no advantages. Both immigrants and native Americans
would have the same opportunities, and their success would depend
on their activity and good fortune.[17]

Not until 1835 did emigration to the United States become
consistently greater than to British North America. After that the
flow to the U.S.A. became greater and greater until in 1852 eight out
of nine were going there.[18] And this is according to British government statistics, which do not point out that many thousands only
sailed to Canada because the fare was cheaper and the passage shorter,
and then walked south across the border. As trade between Britain
and North America grew, there were more ships to carry emigrants.
British and American vessels brought to England cotton and tobacco
from the States and timber from British North America. They needed
a return freight, if only of steerage passengers, and competed for
them. In 1816 the fare was as much as £12, but by the 1840s it was

rarely more than £3 10s. The ships wanted the passengers, and the passengers could find the lower fares.

Jesse Chickering, writing a statistical summary of immigration in 1848, said that it was obviously immigrants, coming 'with a view to live and die here', who had made America what it was. The first settlers, when they came, had found nothing but wilderness, wild beasts, and savages. By the middle of the nineteenth century, the privations and mortality of immigrants were less than they had been, and Chickering regarded this as one of the evidences of an improvement in the condition of mankind, but still emigrants suffered anxiety, sickness, and death before they planted themselves. Whole families died before they reached their destination. Often the immigrants themselves did not live to have any taste of prosperity; sometimes it was only the children who enjoyed what their parents had spent their lives to get.[19]

One emigrant who did not live to enjoy much for himself was Henry Johnson,[20] who on July 7, 1848, at the age of twenty-eight, sailed with 500 other steerage passengers from Liverpool to New York. On the third day out he took his provision box from the hold, but found the ham alive with maggots and threw it overboard. The rest of the stuff he ate sparingly, but could not spin it out for more than four weeks and then had to subsist on the ship's allowance of two pounds of meal and five pounds of biscuit a week. Writing afterwards to his wife, he said: 'The pigs wouldn't eat the biscuit so that for the remainder of the passage [of eight weeks altogether] I got a right good starving there was not a soul on board I knew or I might have got a little assistance, but it was every man for himself.' Six days before they arrived at New York another storm blew up. He said: 'Anything I have read or imagined of a storm at sea was nothing to this. . . . One poor family in the next berth to me whose father had been ill all the time of a bowel complaint I thought great pity of. He died the first night of the storm and was laid outside of his berth the ship began to roll and pitch dreadfully after a while the boxes, barrels &c began to roll from one side to the other the men at the helm were thrown from the wheel and the ship became almost unmanageable at this time I was pitched right into the corpse, the poor mother and two daughters were thrown on top of us and there corpse, boxes, barrels, women and children all in one mess were knocked from side to side for about fifteen minutes pleasant that wasn't it. Jane Dear Shortly after the ship got righted and the captain came down we sowed the body up took it on deck and amid the raging of the storm he read the funeral service for the dead and pitched him overboard. When I got into New York I eat too freely and the second day I took dysentry, a very common complaint here, which lasted fourteen days. I went to a doctor & he gave me a small bottle, told me to use with it a glass of burnt brandy three times a day this I done but it still continued untill I was scarcely able to stand on my feet.'

Johnson stayed in New York for ten days looking for a job, but then reckoned he could stay till doomsday before getting one, and, feeling his money slipping away fast, started off for Canada. There, from Hamilton, he wrote to his wife, saying he could not send any money yet.

'Don't be discouraged Dear Jane I am at present in right good health and determined to do all that lies in my power for you and if possible to redeem some of the past errors of my life as I intend writing again soon I need say little more except this I don't wish this letter to be shown it is only for yourself as there are few others care anything for me so I wish to be forgotten by them. God bless you! I am as ever My Dear & beloved Jane your faithful and devoted husband for ever

Henry Johnson'

On January 9, 1849, his wife wrote from County Antrim saying that if he wished she would bring the children out.

'Dear Henry I am sure you are thinking great long to see me and the children Mary can call Dada and is a sweet child. Little Alexander talks a great deal about you. excuse this writing as I could hardly tell you the state my mind is in. As soon as you receive this write
I am as ever,
Yours faithful and Affectionate
until Death
Jane Johnson

Dear Henry—You might write oftener than you do.'

On March 3 Henry wrote again, this time from the township of Gainsborough, Canada West, saying, and underlining the words, '*Bring the gun.*' On May 22 Jane wrote from Dungonnel, near Antrim, saying that she had taken passage with her two children in the ship *Riverdale,* of Belfast. She ended the letter: 'PS. Dear Henry do not neglect to meet us at Quebec.'

He did not meet her. He had for some reason returned to New York and died there of cholera on July 5, leaving £1 13s. 5d. His widow married again. Alexander and Mary, her two children by Henry, lived long lives, both dying in 1919.

Others were luckier than Henry Johnson. Andrew Carnegie left Dunfermline in Scotland with his parents in May 1848, when he was thirteen, and sailed from Glasgow in the *Wiscasset,* an ex-whaler, of 800 tons. During the seven-week voyage he came to know the sailors and the names of the ropes, and was able to tell the passengers how to answer the calls of the boatswain: the ship was undermanned and the passengers' help was needed. He left the ship with regret, and found his arrival at New York bewildering. He had been taken to see the Queen at Edinburgh, but that had been the extent of his travels before. He was overwhelmed by the bustle and excitement of New York. To the end of his life he remembered that at Bowling Green, down on the Battery at the south tip of Manhattan, one of the *Wiscasset*'s sailors called Robert Barrymore took him to a refreshment stand and gave him a glass of sarsaparilla. Carnegie became messenger-boy in a telegraph office at $2.50 a week, and then salesman, broker, railwayman, owner of an iron-and-steel combine which dominated American industry, and also an exploiter of immigrant labour. In 1901 he sold out, and for the rest of his life, until 1919, became what he called a 'distributor of wealth for the benefit of mankind', giving away $350,000,000 of his own money.[21]

Another, smaller, success story was that of Paddy O'Dougherty, which was told in the *Illustrated News* of New York in 1853. It sounds an embellished story, but there it is, complete with a picture. He had been a stevedore, and arrived in America a pauper, but was taken on bridge building, probably on railway works, at 40 cents an hour. He spent nothing on drink or tobacco, but saved every cent of his first earnings to bring out his wife and children. 'And now,' says the *Illustrated News*, 'pursuing the even tenor of his way, minding his own business, working hard, but his wages being gradually raised, we see Paddy fairly afloat in the New World. Six months after, Paddy remitted home the money for the passage of his wife. Nine months from the day he landed he moved his wife and family into an humble little dwelling, entirely paid for by his earnings. . . . Eight years from the time he first engaged himself to Timothy Brown at forty cents a day, Paddy O'Dougherty was worth one hundred thousand dollars, owned a country seat within sight of his first day's labours, and employed Timothy Brown as superintendent of it at two dollars a day; and, though rough be the name, few gentlemen more affable, polite, or intelligent, or more gentlemanly in appearance, can this day be seen in Water street than this same Paddy O'Dougherty.' It reads like an advertisement for emigration and Self-Help. Perhaps there was some truth in it.[22]

Among the many other Irish men, women, and children to come over about the same time as gentlemanly Paddy O'Dougherty were Nancy Riley, aged 24, Thomas Comer, 40, Edward Riley, 30, all on the bark *Syria*; Ellen Murtilly, 50, another Ellen Murtilly aged 46, John Colville, 84, all from the *Perseverance*; James Managhin, 55, Patrick Fagin, 13, Patrick Jordan, 8, Mary Mack, 2, Eliza Whalen, 3, all of the *Wandsworth*. All died of ship fever in May 1847 at quarantine in the St. Lawrence.[23]

Then there was Patt Waters, aged 16 or 17, who on September 6, 1851, told the gentlemen of a select committee inquiring into emigrants that she and her brother Michael, aged 15, had arrived in New York City from Ireland two days before. She said, 'I have had only some bread and meat which a lady gave me today. I have no place to go to tonight . . . we had no luggage except a little bundle with some shirts and socks, which I carried under my arm; I can read middling well and can write my name middling too.' On the same day Maria Campbell, who had come from Scotland by way of Liverpool, said her husband had left her in New York to go to Connecticut. She had tried to pick up something by peddling apples. She had sold her blankets. She was destitute.[24]

Catherine Haggerty from Castletown, County Mayo, had come to America in search of a sister who had sent for her. She knew her sister had been 'somewhere in the States six years'. On the docks at New York the trunk containing all she had was placed on a cart, and while she was talking to a woman the cart drove off. She cried with despair, and was taken to a charitable home in the city. The *New York Tribune* said: 'She is industrious and well disposed, but subject to violent paroxysms of grief, at the recollection of her parents who endeavoured to dissuade her from leaving them and the helplessness of meeting her sister for whom she had braved all the hardships of a long voyage to a strange land.'[25]

Or there was Thomas Garry, of Sligo, by profession a beggar. He stowed away on an emigrant ship and was discovered, but his fellow passengers subscribed to pay his fare. He was emaciated, with thin hands like a woman's. In 1847 he arrived at St John, New Brunswick, came south to the United States, and wrote to his wife

saying he was working on the railway at 8s. a day and would send £6
later on. 'Be on the watch at the Post office day after day I wont delay
in Relieveing yous as it is a duty Encumbered on me by the laws of
Church and I hope God will Relieve me . . . I long to see that long
wished for hour that I will Embrace yous in my arms there is nothing
in this world gives me trouble but yow and my dear Children whoom
I loved as my life.'

He asked his wife to let him know how his two sons Patrick and
Francis were, and ended his letter in this way:[26]

'. . . you will shortly be in the lands of promise and live happy with
me and our children.

No more at Preasent

From your Faithful husband till death

Thos. Garry

I was ready to go to work to pay Passge for you and the children but i
consider yous would not stand the wracking of the sea till yous be
nourished for a time.'

2

Who Should Go, and Why

William Cobbett, agriculturalist, agitator, and radical, lived in America for a year in 1817, and continued to edit his *Political Register* from Long Island. 'You know', he wrote, 'that I have never *advised* any body to emigrate.' He had always said America was no place for men to live without work; no place for a farmer who did not work himself—'no place, in short, for any one, who is not able and *willing* to work at the *ordinary sorts of work*, but, for such men, there is every where a plentiful, happy, and easy life. None should come however, who have any views of idleness; and, even for the industrious poor, I see no reason why they should expend their last shilling, and undergo all the miseries of a sea voyage, in order to save those who eat the taxes, the expense of their share of poor rates.'[1]

Everyone agreed America was no place to go unless you could work with your hands. People did not ask of a stranger what he was, but what he did. Samuel Sidney, who was best known as a writer on horses and hunting, also brought out a monthly magazine, price 6d., which gave frequent advice to intending emigrants. In March 1849 a man signing himself C.O.B. wrote, describing himself in this way: 'Four years a teacher in a school; four years at sea; three years on railway work as a superintendent; then a year farming in Ireland; can plough, dig, and sow; have only £40; think of going to the United States.'

'Just the man to go and prosper,' said Sidney;[2] adding, in reply to another correspondent: 'A *valet de chambre* had better remain where he is.' And: 'On a bell-hanger's prospects we cannot speak.'[3] Every man, before setting out, should be sure that he had a good reason for going. He should not leave his native country for ill-temper, or to be pitied, or to be regretted, or because he was a poet, but because he had not enough to eat in England and was sure of abundance where he was going.[4] To any Englishman of education, unless his position in England had been destitute, a residence in America would be excessively disagreeable. An English settler was the mark for all the vulgarity of the district to insult, and all the roguery to swindle. Nor was there any point in Englishmen going to the western frontier and pioneering: 'It will be as well to let the Americans take the rough edge off the country. There are no pioneers equal to them.'[5]

In spite of his view of the United States, which was probably as sour as it was because, as a loyal Briton, he prefererd Canada, Sidney gave forthright and sensible advice. Action was the first requisite, the ability to do anything, to have a talent for making shift. Discontented dispositions had better stay at home, and so had all the stars of society, wits, diners-out, the leading lights of literary institutions and of provincial debating societies. Furthermore, drunkenness was the bane of British emigrants of all classes.

There were few vacancies for accomplished governesses. 'A Draper's Assistant, Bath' was told that persons of his class could not be recommended to go unless they were prepared, in default of a situation, to saw wood, drive a team, shepherd, cook, or do something useful, and that was an answer that would do for all clerks and gentlemen without capital. 'Two Youths, Gloucester, 18 and 19', fond of farming and able to handle a gun, meaning to go west and farm fifty acres, were told to join some people who had a little capital—and daughters about their age. In Tennessee, Scottish shepherds would do well: 'Their dogs would also be required, being none of the breed there.' A man from Whitby was told that a writer to an attorney would be out of place as an emigrant, but that a cook accustomed to the sea would be all right. A saddler in the prime of life, married to a farmer's daughter and with two children, a good amateur carpenter, able to mend shoes and sing sacred music, and something of a phrenologist, was told: 'Your place, without question is in one of the rising towns of the Western States . . . you can travel cheaply, working at your trades, giving lectures on phrenology, &c, as you go on.' Sidney said London tradesmen had been found even more unfitted than ruined country gentlemen, officers, and the like;

but, on the other hand, town-bred wives, if under forty, soon adapted themselves.[6]

William Chambers, another editor, was much more sympathetic than Sidney towards America. It was a country which had been made by ordinary men. 'No one can forget that, except in the case of Virginia, and one or two other places, it has been peopled by the more humble, or, at all events, struggling classes of European society. The aristocracy of England have shrunk from it. Instead of acting as leaders, and becoming the heroes of a new world, they have left the high honour of founding communities throughout America to groups of miscellaneous individuals, who at least possessed the spirit to cross the Atlantic in quest of a fortune, rather than sink into pauperism at home.'[7]

But the magazine *Punch*, perhaps anxious that the new world should not be deprived altogether of the qualities of aristocratic leadership, was proposing in 1846 that instead of sending strong working men out of the country, large premiums should be offered to the English dukes, to induce them to emigrate. Two years later it printed another item entitled 'Emigration for the Upper Classes', which said: 'The Lords have been bitterly complaining of having nothing to do in their own House, in consequence of the work that has been cut out for them this Session by the Commons. . . . We recommend their Lordships to try emigration, the great remedy of the day, which, during the recess, they might resort to very beneficially. They have been lately merely dummies in the game of life; but if they were to suit themselves with spades, they might turn up regular trumps in some distant colony.' Two woodcuts showed first a dispirited House of Lords, and then a distant part of the forest, with three peers hacking happily at a tree.[8]

Perhaps one or two peers even thought of going. Chambers, writing in 1852, said the tide of emigration was working so powerfully through the land that not only the labourers and artisans but many of the gentry were beginning to think of going. But unfortunately for them these young ladies and gentlemen had been taught dependence as a duty of civilised life, so Chambers proposed that before breaking up their life here they should submit themselves to the ordeal of six or twelve months in a labourer's cottage deep in the English countryside. A few pounds would buy a cottage infinitely more comfortable and healthy than the log cabin they thought they wanted to go to. So, he suggested, let the gentleman who wanted to try himself out engage one farm servant, and a country-girl to do the rough work of the house. The ladies of the family would have to do the rest, wash all the fine linen, iron, make the beds, help with the cooking, the poultry and the pigs, and would thus by degrees have their bodies and minds strengthened and their habits formed—or else discover that it was all beyond them. Or, if a man had to live cheaply, it would be better for him to join with ten, twenty, or thirty people and take a large old-fashioned house in the English countryside, dress plainly, and eat wholesomely; this would be better than all the risks and privations of expatriation. There were spots in England, Ireland, and Scotland as wild, solitary, and healthy as any in the far west.[9]

Sidney would have agreed with all this; he dissuaded not only the gentry from emigrating but anyone with a bit more than enough to live on:

'*Pater familias* would be a lunatic if he gave up his pension of £400 a year for land anywhere . . . there's no place like England for a man with £400 a year, unless he has an army of daughters.'[10]

Some Scots farmers did go out with capital, but that was different: Scots farmers were not gentlemen. One took a steerage passage and yet had £700 or £800 with him, on his person. A party of Scots who left from Campbeltown had as much as £14,000 between them.[11]

Sidney kept a list of the people who wrote to him asking for advice, and in October 1848 made this analysis of 100 letters addressed to him. Of the women, seven had been governesses, five dressmakers, and three domestic servants, and four did not describe themselves. Of the men with some capital, there were five tailors, drapers, or hosiers; four clerks; three engineers; five medical students; four architects or surveyors; two farmers or graziers; two attorneys; a country smith, a grocer, a painter, a bookseller, a general dealer, a country gentleman, six young gentlemen of no profession, and four miscellaneous. Of the men without capital, nineteen were labourers, domestic servants, and hard-working youths; eight were clerks and shopmen, three painters and paper-hangers, two gardeners, two schoolmasters, and one a nightwatch-man. He gave this list purely as a matter of curiosity and did not suggest that it was typical. He was sure that the people most anxious to emigrate read very little, and that some were unable to read.

He was right. Many thousands of emigrants were not grocers, or nightwatchmen, or domestic servants, or useful people of any kind at all. Many were like Bridget O'Donnel, who had lived near Kilrush, a small seaport on the Shannon estuary in the west of Ireland.

In December 1849 she was destitute, and the landlord wanted the land, and to be rid of his wretched tenants. Her husband used to have four and a half acres of land and three acres of bog. They had been put out because they owed rent, and their crop of oats had been taken. Her husband had gone and she was alone with two children. She was about to have another baby and had gone back to the cottage. This is what happened then:

'Dan Sheedey and five or six men came to tumble my house; they wanted me to give possession. I said that I would not; I had fever, and was within two months of my down-lying; they commenced knocking down the house, and had half of it knocked down when two neighbours, women, Nell Spellesley and Kate How, carried me out. I had the priest and a doctor to attend me shortly after. Father Meehan anointed me. I was carried into a cabin, and lay there for eight days, when I had the creature born dead. I lay for three weeks after that. The whole of my family got the fever, and one boy of thirteen years old died with want and with hunger while we were lying sick. Dan Sheedey and Blake took the corn into Kilrush, and sold it. I don't know what they got for it. I had not a bit for my children to eat when they took it from me.'[12]

The likes of Bridget O'Donnel went out of despair and destitution. Many others who were not destitute went out of fear that they might become so if they stayed at home. They went for three meals a day, or because they thought they stood a better chance of getting them in America: it was a tradition among the English poor that you ate in America. There were stories about it. There was the one about the Yorkshireman travelling from New York to Zanesville, who said: 'It is a main queer country, for I have asked the labouring folks along the road how many meals they eat in one day, and they all said three and sometimes four. We have but two at home and they are scanty enough.' What American, asked the journalist who reported this, would have thought of enquiring how many meals the working people eat in a day; but it was the first thing the poor Englishman thought of, and he asked it all along the road.[13] That was back in 1816, and the journalist who quoted it was American, perhaps with a bias towards representing his own country as prosperous. But in 1848 another journalist, this time a Scot visiting America, told the story of a poor emigrant's first morning walk in the new country. The emigrant thought to himself that he had passed twenty-six houses, and heard the hiss of the frying pan at seventeen; there were fewer meat breakfasts at home.[14]

Or women went to save themselves from prostitution. In 1850 *Punch* was not the cosy publication it later became, but a radical and at times campaigning magazine. That year it printed a poem called 'The Needlewoman at Home and Abroad'.[15] Here are two stanzas:

And so we strove with straining eyes, in squalid rooms, and chill
The needle plied until we died—or worse—oh, Heaven, have pity!
Thou knowest how 'twas oftener for want we sinned than will—
Oh nights of pain and shameful gain, about the darkling city!

Now speed thee, good ship, over sea, and bear us far away,
Where food to eat, and friends to greet, and work to do await us—
Where against hunger's tempting we shall not need to pray—
Where in wedlock's tie, not harlotry, we shall find men to mate us.

Two years before, Captain P. L. Macdougall, of the Royal Canadian Rifles, wrote in London that England had no *political* grievances, at least none such as would create any political discontent among the lower classes if their labour could earn them a proper living. There were grievances, of course, but he thought they were not the kind that could be put right by legislation. 'The contrasts of this great country, as has very often been remarked, are startling— they are appalling; Dives and Lazarus elbow each other in our crowded thoroughfares.'[16] The captain was premature in saying there were no political differences: 1848 was a year of discontent in England. The revolution in France was welcomed at many meetings of working-class men. The Chartists, asking among other things for universal suffrage, prepared a petition of five and a half million signatures and assembled on Kennington Common in south London on April 10, intending to march to the House of Commons to present the petition. Troops were posted all over London, and 120,000 special constables were sworn in, but there was no need. The crowd of Chartists was much smaller than expected and was not allowed to cross the Thames bridges to Westminster. The Commons rejected the petition, which was found on examination to contain fewer than two million signatures. There was little violence. It was a fiasco, and it was the last of the great Chartist marches and petitions. After that Captain Macdougall would have been right in saying that the great grievance was not strictly a political one, simply that of an enormous disparity between needlewomen and gentlewomen, between rich and poor—the disparity that Benjamin Disraeli, then a young Member of Parliament but twenty years later to become

Prime Minister, wrote about in his novel *Sybil: or Two Nations*, which was published in 1845.

Vere Foster, a philanthropist, who had given away 250,000 copies of his pamphlet *Work and Wages; or, the Penny Emigrant's Guide to the United States and Canada, for Female Servants, Laborers, Machanics, Farmers etc.*, and thereafter, running out of money, sold them for 10d. a dozen, wrote that in the United Kingdom there were a million paupers whose daily life was a succession of privations and miseries and a mere struggle for existence. 'The poorer classes of this country should emigrate *now*, for the sake of all who are dear to them, and whom they wish to shield from future suffering.' He saw emigration as a more effectual means of raising wages and bettering the condition of the working classes than strikes or any probable parliamentary reform.[17]

The repeal of the Corn Laws in 1846 made bread a little cheaper, but it also gave the farm labourers a new fear. They heard their masters the farmers grumbling that this new free market in foreign corn would ruin the English farmers. This did not happen, but the farmers believed it would, and their labourers believed them, and left. Their emigration could be construed any way you liked. The emigration commissioners said: 'In effect, the labouring classes were in former years [before 1847] driven to emigrate only by the presence or the immediate fear of destitution; they are now induced to do so by the hope also of advancement.'

Some hated England. In one ballad called 'Sons of John Bull' the singer addresses the mother country.[18]

> Thy vurkhouses built for the poor, lame, and silly,
> O who is the covey wot from 'em would part?
> The fine suits of grey, and the nice soup and skilly,
> The pride & the boast of an Englishman's heart.
> O isn't thy vurkhouse a palace of pleasure?
> Your poor for amusement, pick oakum, break stones.
> O vare is the country can equal your treasures?
> Can boast an assortment of such rags and bones,
> Then hail, happy country, bright gem of the ocean,
> Such brave sons of freedom the world never saw?
> Thy prisons are full, and your treadmills in motion,
> Then jolly good luck to Old England, hur-raw!

Many people emigrated just in hope. An American who had been to Ireland gave evidence to a United States Senate committee in 1854, and said: 'There is nothing unnatural in the desire of the unfortunate Irish to abandon their cheerless and damp cottages, and to crawl inch by inch, while they have yet a little strength, from the graves which apparently yawn for their bodies.' At Dublin he had met a young wife many of whose family had died of hunger. She had gone aboard an emigrant ship, but only the night before sailing had given birth to a child. He suggested she should wait for another vessel, but she declined. 'She would rather start with the hope, however delusive it might prove, of arriving soon in America, than to remain under the positive certainty of speedy recovery.'[19]

The emigrants themselves, then, left for three meals a day, or if they were Irish for any meals a day, or to advance themselves, or just in hope. Those whose business it was to write about emigrants, or to preach to them, discovered higher reasons. William Chambers saw emigration as a gift to the world, as the exporting of Britain's industrious energy. The Neapolitan Lazaroni lay basking in the sun; the Hindoo worked on his paddyfield only as hard as his ancestors had a thousand years before, and no harder; the Chinaman was content to turn his little wheel and irrigate the paddock that satisfied all the wants of his frugal household; the Red Indian despised work; the black man, though offered a fair percentage of the fortune which a little exertion from him would draw out of a cotton plantation, would work until he had earned a red handkerchief, and no more. There was only one boundary to the influence of free trade, and that was the boundary of contented poverty. 'The enterprising English subduing the soil, and adapting it to their objects, are sometimes looked on, and openly spoken of, as people having the mixed elements of the madman and the fool: the madman prompting them to a restless energy in the cultivation of the earth, the building of houses, and the fabrication of clothing—the fool prompting them to make a boast and exultation of this diseased propensity instead of concealing it.' It seemed to Chambers that all this industry was divinely inspired: 'The highest intellects of Europe are looking with breathless wonder at the spread of the Anglo-Saxon race, impelled by their instincts, and led by the hand of GOD over the vast continent of America.'[20] There spoke the Protestant ethic. Chambers rather forgets that a good half of the emigrants were Irish Celts, not by nature industrious, and, if led by God, then by a Roman Catholic one.

William H. G. Kingston, the author of a penny pamphlet published in London by the Society for Promoting Christian Knowledge, also believed in the hand of God. He acknowledged that there was much poverty, wretchedness, sickness, and pain in Britain, but he was confident, and so he trusted would his readers be, that the great and beneficent Ruler of the World would not have allowed these evils to exist without also providing the means of remedying them. 'I think it is very evident that these lands were given us for that object; that when more people were born in England than England could support, the surplus should cheerfully leave the old country and go to occupy them.' Every year another 300,000 people were born in Britain. Think of that, he said; there were too many already, what number would there be the next year, and the year after that, and the year after that? 'The choice given us is either to stay and push and shoulder our neighbours, we keeping them back [and] they keeping us from—we will not say getting on, but from—even getting bread to put into our children's mouths; or to bid farewell to the dearly beloved little island, which is, after all, only part of England, and to go across the wide seas to another part of England.'[21]

Thomas Rawlings, who once owned and edited the *Cheltenham Chronicle* but by 1845 was editor of *The Old Countryman, and Emigrant's Friend* in New York City, was a great encourager of emigration. He had stumped Wales addressing meetings, saying, through a Welsh interpreter, that the West was emphatically the country for the poor man: there were rich people there now, but they had once been poor. He hoped to attract at least 50,000 to West Virginia. He also published, in New York, an address to the clergy of England, Ireland, Scotland, and Wales on the condition of the working classes. Every day brought another thousand more human beings to be fed, and he would endeavour conclusively to show that the only effective remedy for this national disease, if he might so express himself, was emigration. He suggested that the Poor Law commissioners of Britain should be given power to assume that a certain number of able-bodied men were likely to become a burden on the parish, and to ask them if they would like to emigrate to the United States or Canada, giving them a choice, and also making them a gift by way of encouragement, of the sum which might have been paid them if they had gone on relief for, say, three to five years. In New York City he had met Harriet Whitmore, with five children. In October 1844 she had been living with her husband at Ashley Paivey, Leicestershire. The husband asked the parish guardians to help him to emigrate to America, and they declined, although they offered him £25 if he would go to New Zealand. So he went on his own to America, leaving behind his wife and children, who received 7s. 6d. a week parish relief from October 1844 until July 1845, when the husband paid their passage over.[22] Altogether the parish spent about £11, which could have paid the passage of the man and his family to America in the first place.

Emigration was the manly choice made by the author of a long poem published in London in 1856. He was apparently an English-man who had fought in the Army, and, as he said, had never from the cannon shrunk, but had then found himself with no money or work, and was ashamed to go on the parish. Here are a few lines:[23]

> Bread of dependence never would be sweet,
> Even were it mine, which it is not, to eat;
> With God's good blessing on me I will go,
> And manly independence I will show.
> There is no room in this o'ercrowded land
> For men to rise, nay, hardly room to stand;
> Men packed and jostled are, too tight, too close
> And hence grow selfish, savage, and morose.
> No, I will seek a wider scope and sphere,
> Than industry and genius can find here—
> Will forfeit luxury and ease, and press,
> My way into the distant wilderness.

Rawlings and the poet, with their assumption that an increasing population was an evil to be exported if possible, were accepting the classical Malthusian doctrine. Thomas Malthus was a clergyman and political economist who in 1798 published his *Essay on Population*, in which he contended that population increases in geometrical progression, but the means of subsistence only arithmetically, and that checks on population were therefore necessary to reduce vice, misery, and want. He died in 1834 at the age of sixty-eight. The inscription on his memorial tablet in Bath Abbey extols 'his admir-able writings on the social branches of political economy'. The rising population of Great Britain did give colour to his views. In 1811 the census showed the population was 12,597,000, by 1831 this had risen to 16,539,000, and by 1851 to 20,960,000.

The influence of Malthusian doctrines was great, but they had their opponents, notably in Cobbett and, later, in the Chartists. One writer against Malthus was Amicus Populi,[24] who under this name addressed a letter to the philanthropic seventh Earl of Shaftesbury in 1848 saying that the expressions 'superabundant population' and 'overproduction' were in almost daily use by political economists, but were not properly understood. The real wealth of a nation consisted in its having a large, intelligent and industrious population, occupying a fruitful soil rich in ores and minerals; a good climate; the most perfect kind of machinery for the abundant supply both of raw materials and manufactured articles; and good communications by land and water with all parts of the world. Any increase in population was an increase in wealth, because every individual, however humble, created wants. Provided the labour of this extra population was properly used, the result would add to the national stock of goods. The evil of over-production would be alleviated if not removed if the labourers were paid a proper wage for their work; they could then buy more goods, and this would not only prevent the stock of commodities from increasing but would increase the manufacturers' profit. Some theorists no doubt believed themselves to be acting kindly when they helped the labouring classes to emigrate, but others seemed to want to get rid of the excess on principle, whatever the cost. Amicus Populi then quoted Malthus as having said:

'A man born into a world already possessed, if he cannot get assistance from his parents, and if society does not want his labour, has no claim of right to the smallest portion of food, and, in fact, has no business to be where he is. At Nature's mighty feast there is no vacant seat for him; she tells him to be gone . . .'

The admirers of this doctrine were, said Amicus Populi, numerous and a disgrace to mankind.

These opinions, if they were disgraceful, were also held by the mildest and most charitable, like the 112 members of the Emigrants' Employment Association which helped to publish *The Emigrants' Penny Magazine* at Plymouth.[25] This magazine printed knitting recipes for emigrant knitters and needlewomen: one pattern for coarse cotton gloves needed two needles, knit three and purl three and so on, and recommended 'leaving the ribbed end open for the admission of the hand'. The ladies sent out, prepaid, for the use of emigrants, flannel, old linen, cast-off garments, old collars for transferring, and 'Games, most of Chance'. Collections of money were made at branches in Bath, Bristol, Camberwell, Cheltenham, Croydon, Darlington, Dorsetshire, Falmouth, Hitchin, and fourteen other places, and the most generous contributions were £5 from the Countess of Mount Edgecumbe, and £6 from Miss Willyams, said to be part of the proceeds of *The Young Emigrants*, a children's book.

The magazine reprinted bits of advice, including a warning by the New York Commissioners of Emigration that 'What is called a shilling in America is not worth more than sixpence sterling'.

In September 1850 the magazine set out 'The Three Objects of Emigration'.

First, to reduce excess population at home. 'The garden wants weeding, the flowers by springing up so thickly are incommoding each other.'

Second, the bettering of the individual condition. 'We believe that no person is philanthropic or patriotic enough to quit his native country merely for the purpose of relieving it of one of its surplus population, and thereby advancing its prosperity: no, this would be expecting too much from human nature. All emigrants then, must be actuated by the grand motive self advantage, or the system of colonisation will fall to the ground.'

Third, to people 'those vast tracts of our globe as yet lying waste and desolate, and so fulfilling the original command—"be fruitful, multiply, and replenish the earth, and subdue it"'. This third object, that of carrying out what appeared to be the original design of the Creator, was, said the magazine, in whatever light it was viewed, a grand one. But 'the immense valley of the Mississippi, capable, it has been calculated, of maintaining, if properly cultivated, all the inhabitants of Europe, was not surely meant by the great Architect of Nature, who forms nothing in vain, to lie idle from century to century. Emigration then, whilst it meets the necessities and advances the interests of man, may be said to have the sanction of Heaven. . . .'

Emigration might also have been said to have the sanction of profit. Edward Young, of the Bureau of Statistics in Washington, compiling in 1871 an official report on the emigration of the previous fifty years, reckoned that the emigrants of all those years had enriched the United States by the sum of at least $6,243,880,800.[26] He arrived at that figure by calculating the worth of each emigrant as $800, and this $800 itself was a sum he arrived at by long and apologetic explanation. He said the difficulty of ascertaining the pecuniary or material value of a foreigner coming to the States was not inconsiderable, as there was no accessible data. 'Indeed, the very attempt to do so may appear derogatory to the dignity of human nature. To regard a man merely as an automatic machine, computing his productive power, minus his running expenses, places a low estimate on a being made in the image of his Maker, and seems an insult alike to the Creator and the created.' Nevertheless, Mr. Young made the attempt. One thousand dollars had usually been regarded as the average worth of each permanent addition to the population; he thought this was too much, and made his own more exact computations. If a labouring immigrant with a wife and two children earned $400 a year, and spent it all, $160 of this would go one way and another in taxes or in profits to retailers and producers, who also contributed to the wealth of the country. Each of a family of four was therefore worth $40 to the country, and if this $40 were capitalised at 5 per cent, it gave $800 as the average annual capital value of an immigrant. But it was impossible, he said, to make an intelligent estimate of the value to the country of emigrants who brought their educated minds, their cultivated tastes, their skill in the arts, and their inventive genius.

Emigration certainly had the sanction of commerce. 'The colonial ships would go out in ballast if it were not for the emigration', said T. F. Elliot, assistant under-secretary at the British Colonial Office.[27] Dr. Thomas Rolph, an English surgeon who became emigration agent for the Canadian government and toured Scotland drumming up emigrants, quoted Lord Brougham, the statesman and judge, as saying that every axe driven into a tree in British North America set in motion a shuttle in Manchester or Sheffield, and explained that there were essentially three elements to be considered. They were, first, the unremunerative capital of England; second, the unemployed population of the United Kingdom; and, third, the unproductive lands of British America. Bring those together and you would have a most useful and profitable scheme—'it is in their mere conjunction only where the difficulty lies'.[28]

In 1848 Robert Bowne Minturn, an American owner of emigrant ships and one of the Commissioners of Emigration for New York, came to London and told a House of Lords' committee that emigration had become one of the great supports of commerce. In 1847 emigrants had paid $5,000,000 in fares, and this greatly reduced the cost of carrying freight to and from Europe in these ships. American cotton and grain were therefore cheaper in England than they would otherwise have been. Freight carried on the New York packets to Liverpool and London was, in effect, subsidised by emigrants.[29]

Minturn gave evidence to the committee at length and plainly, and without trying in any way to mislead. He was a shipowner and said nothing about the dangers of the voyage, but he did not have to:

he was not asked. As a commissioner, he was in sympathy with emigrants, but he was a successful man, and by his nature saw the best of things. The Irish Emigrant Society of New York, which was a voluntary society of Irishmen who tried to look after the interests of their countrymen, saw things differently. In an address to the People of Ireland made in 1849[30] the society said: 'We desire, preliminarily, to caution you against entertaining any fantastic idea, such as that magnificence, ease, and health, are universally enjoyed in this country. . . . It is natural for persons who have adventured to leave home and to seek their fortunes in a foreign and distant country, to give highly coloured accounts of a success, which in reality, has been but the obtaining a laborious employment; and it is equally natural for those who send you money to wish rather that you should suppose it a reckless gift from the lavishness of wealth rather than a charitable donation from the sympathy of poverty.' An emigrant might do well, or he might not: and then the society made this strong point, so obvious that many in their enthusiasm might have overlooked it:

'We therefore conclude by saying, that you must never forget that when you emigrate, you leave home.'

3
America in the Mind of the Time

Hark! Old Ocean's tongue of thunder
Hoarsely calling, bids you speed
To the shores he held asunder
Only for these times of need.
Now, upon his friendly surges,
Ever, ever, roaring come
All the sons of hope he urges
To a new, a richer home.[1]

The only thing that matters about these lines is that they are by
Martin F. Tupper, English versifier and philosopher and recipient of
a gold medal for literature from the King of Prussia. And the only
thing that matters about Tupper—although he did have some
ancestors who sailed to America with the Pilgrim Fathers, while
other Tuppers stayed home and joined the British Army, with the
consequence that there were two Major Tuppers at Bunker Hill,
one on each side—is that Queen Victoria once said he was her
favourite poet. He was an enormously popular author who sold
more than a million copies of one collection of platitudes called
Proverbial Philosophy.[2] He was only one of the many authors who
wrote about emigration and America. It was one of the great topics.
America was in the mind of the time. People may not have had an
accurate idea of what America was going to be like, but so much had
been written and talked about the United States and Canada that

would-be emigrants could hardly have avoided carrying in their heads people's stories, enthusiasms, and myths.

Dickens went to America in 1843 to write about the country for money. Alexis de Toqueville went in 1831–2 to write a report for the French government. De Toqueville liked what he saw and said Americans were one of the happiest people in the world: what he wrote was very much liked in America.[3] What Dickens wrote was not. In *American Notes* he said that pigs roamed the streets. There was no privacy. The press was licentious, with ribald slander as its stock-in-trade. The women attended elevating lectures, but the men hawked and spat everywhere. Americans could not stand a hint of criticism; furthermore, they were dull. He was oppressed by the prevailing seriousness. 'This is not the republic I came to see; this is not the republic of my imagination. . . .' The hero of his next novel, *Martin Chuzzlewit*, was an innocent Englishman who emigrated to America among privations, sickness, and swindles, bought a tract of land called Eden, and arrived to find he had been sold a bit of Illinois swamp.[4]

Two Englishwomen, Harriet Martineau and Frances Trollope, both wrote books about visits to America, and both sold many thousands. Mrs. Martineau went there in 1824 and liked a lot she saw. She said it was striking for a stranger to see, for the first time in any country, the absence of poverty, of gross ignorance, of all servility, and of all insolence of manner. America had much to learn—and some disgraceful faults, like slavery, to put right—but she thought the day might come when America, if it attained its democratic *ideal*, would be as superior to other nations, which just acted out of *expediency*, as a great poet was superior to common men.[5] Mrs. Trollope was an unsuccessful immigrant. She went to America in 1827 and started a bazaar in Cincinatti. It went bankrupt, she had to work her way back to England, and when she got home she turned to writing as another way of making a living. Her *Domestic Manners of the Americans* was a best-seller, and was the first of more than fifty novels and travel books she wrote. She was very downright about the Americans she had met. 'I do not like them. I do not like their principles, I do not like their manners, I do not like their opinions.' She did not like democracy. She said it was all very well for the theory of equality to be discussed by English gentlemen in a London dining-room, when the servant, having placed a fresh bottle of cool wine on the table, respectfully shut the door and left them to their walnuts and their wisdom; but it would soon be found less palatable when it presented itself in the shape of a hard greasy paw, and was claimed in accents that breathed less of freedom than of onions and whiskey. 'Strong indeed, must be the love of equality in an English breast if it can survive a tour through the Union.'[6]

When Anthony Trollope went to America he had to be tactful about his mother's book. He said it was essentially a woman's book, and that she had described with 'a woman's light but graphic pen' the social defects and absurdities she saw. All she said had been worth the telling, but what she had not done was to explain that the absurdities of social custom were the natural result of newness, which would pass, but that the political system, if good, would remain. But he found it difficult to be always so placid himself. He carried a writing desk with him everywhere. One day a railway porter tossed it carelessly on to a pavement and smashed it. Trollope wrote: 'Knowing it was smashed I forgot my position on American soil and remonstrated. "It's my desk, and you've utterly destroyed it," I said. "Ha! Ha! Ha!" laughed the porter. "You've destroyed my property," I rejoined, "and it's no laughing matter." And then all the crowd laughed. "Guess you'd better git it glued," said one. . . . This was very sad, and for the moment I deplored the ill-luck which had brought me to so savage a country.'[7]

These accounts are remembered now because their authors are still remembered. There was a great deal more written about America, by people who are now forgotten. It is without exception enthusiastic, one way or the other. Anyone who visited America was decidedly for the country or against it. Sir Francis Head, said in 1847:[8]

'The heavens of America appear infinitely higher—the sky is bluer—the clouds are whiter—the air is fresher—the cold is intenser —the moon looks larger—the stars are brighter—the thunder is louder—the lightning is vivider—the wind is stronger—the rain is heavier—the mountains are higher—the rivers larger—the forests bigger—the plain broader . . .'

And so on. Head had once opposed emigration, but after he became lieutenant-governor of Upper Canada in 1835 he took the grand, religious view. While every backwoodsman in America imagined that he was working solely for his own interest in clearing his own place, every tree which fell to his axe admitted a patch of sunshine to the earth, and softened and ameliorated to an infinitesimal degree the climate of the vast continent around him. This was a familiar idea; but Head did not want to take it too far. Though the assiduity of the Anglo-Saxon race had, he said, no doubt affected the climate of North America, the axe by itself was too weak an instrument to produce any *important* change. Head also told the story of an emigrant bird, a lark, which had done well in America. This bird had been taken to Quebec, wrecked in the St. Lawrence, and then given to Head. When it died he took it back to England with him, had it stuffed at the British Museum, and wrote these memorial lines:

THIS LARK
taken to Canada by a poor emigrant
was shipwrecked in the St. Lawrence,
and after singing at Toronto for nine years,
died there on the 14th of March, 1843
Universally regretted.
Home! Home! Sweet Home.

The *Illustrated London News* in 1849 was also celebrating the rise of the New World, and in doing so lamenting the fall of the Old. In the Christmas number of 1849 a leading article entitled 'Signs of Decay' said that the sons of Britain had founded a new empire. In fifty or twenty years, or even sooner, Great Britain would no longer be the principal seat of the vigorous race of the Anglo-Saxons. Although that race would continue to rule the world, it would not be from the banks of the Thames. An empire twenty, thirty, or fifty times as extensive and as rich as Britain had already arisen on the other side of the Atlantic, and was enticing to its bosom the best British blood, the young, the hardy, and the persevering young men and women of England. Britain could not say to its sons, as the New World could, that every man was a man and welcome, for the sake of his manhood, to the great feast of nature, where there was enough and to spare. These young people were daily invited to leave an effete Europe and settle in a vigorous America. 'We must, sooner or later, yield our place to the more prudent, the less embarrassed, and the more vigorous offshoots of our race, and consent to occupy the easy chair of our senility. Nor is there anything to regret in this. What is there in our own corner of the globe that it should for ever expect to give the law to all others? The civilisation that is removed is not destroyed; and the genius of our people can exert itself as well on the banks of the Ohio, or the Mississippi, as on the banks of the Thames; and rule the world from the White House at Washington, with as much propriety as from the Palace of St. James.'[9]

This was prophetic stuff, but it is very strange that it appeared only

eighteen months before the Great Exhibition of 1851 at the Crystal
Palace in London, when the mood in England could not have been
more imperially self-confident. Not only Englishmen, but also
foreign visitors, noticed that things were more prosperous in Britain
than before. Lamartine, French poet and statesman, writing in the
autumn of 1850, said that twenty years before he had found the
English masses emaciated, and inflamed by a great hatred against the
propertied class. The *proletaires* were brutish, and degraded by
ignorance and hunger. But in 1850 he found the people cleaner and
healthier, and fewer of them drunk: it appeared to him that a superhuman hand had carried away during that sleep of twenty years all
the venom which had racked the social body of England.[10] Frederika
Bremer, Swedish novelist, whose principal purpose in life was to
prepare for a Christian millennium, saw a more sudden change. In
1849, in a solitary walk of ten minutes through Hull, she had seen
ten times more want than she had seen in ten months in Denmark.
But by 1851 there was a new spirit, a new mental atmosphere.
'The Crystal Palace was its full blown, magnificent blossom . . . I
perceived more clearly every day of my stay in England, that this
period [was] one of a general awakening to a new, fresh life.'[11]
Perhaps what happened was that many Englishmen, awakening to
this new, fresh, life, saw a still newer and fresher one across the
Atlantic. They could also more easily than before find the fare to
America. For whatever reason, 1851 was the year of quite the largest
emigration up to then from Britain to America.

At this time Herman Melville was seeing the United States as
something more than a new country, and as a force for keeping peace
in the world, but not with guns. He said: 'Settled by the people of
all nations, all nations may claim her for their own. You cannot spill
a drop of American blood, without spilling the blood of the whole
world. . . . We are not a nation, so much as a world.' More down to
earth, he noticed that in Liverpool the beggars were white. In
America only the Negroes were destitute. To see white beggars
reminded him more than anything else that he was not in his own
country: to be born an American citizen seemed a guarantee against
pauperism.[12]

Eulogies of America are easy to come across. The toast at the St.
Patrick's Day meeting in 1854 of the Friendly Sons of St. Patrick of
New York City was as follows: 'The United States—Land for the
friendless, home for the homeless—for worth, honor; for labor, its
reward.' The toast was drunk to the music of 'Yankee Doodle'.[13]

Jacob Harvey, an Irishman in New York who worked hard to help emigrants in that city, wrote home to his friend Lord Monteagle, a beneficent landowner, saying what a blessing it was that there was in America such an immense wilderness to fill; how the country was teeming with prosperity; and how in America even rogues would find they could easily earn an honest living without roguery. He said: 'I wish you would come over and look at this young Giant—with all her faults, England may well be proud of her eldest daughter.'[14]

Everyone who travelled at all in America was struck by the size of the country. Vere Foster computed that the thirty-one states and nine territories which existed in 1854 had ninety-five times as much space as Ireland, and sixty times as much as England; it was a fair boast that there was room to give every man a farm. By 1854 there were already 17,000 miles of railroad and another 12,000 were being constructed, more of either than in all the rest of the world put together.[15]

William Chambers saw hurry everywhere. American minutes seemed worth almost English days. Even the climate was faster. Newly plastered houses were dry enough to be lived in a day or two after being finished. Clothes dried more quickly, and ink in half the time it took in England. He saw energetic industry, temperance, and independence of thought, and everywhere English was spoken well. The whole tendency of living was to evoke self-reliance. 'If I may use the expression, there is a spontaneity of well-doing in America.'[16]

One woman traveller found herself very much at home, and said any English traveller would—more so at New York than at Ostend or Calais. There was the common language, and there was also Christianity, which she called the electric chain which united communities. 'This is the band which to the British Christian renders America a second native land.'[17] This was unusual praise of the United States, which few thought really Christian. The author of one English tract insisted that emigrants must prefer British North America, and gave as one reason that there were no clergymen in the States. 'For years people live on in a state bordering on heathenism. I do not say this is always the case, but I may safely assure you that it is so generally, and nearly always.' He was generous with his assurances and went on to give his readers another big one. The climate of other countries was generally inferior to that of British colonies, and people who were rosy and healthy in England became, in the United States, sallow and racked with pain.[18]

The writer of an emigrants' guide started by enumerating the many good qualities of Americans: they were brave, sober, in-

dustrious, enterprising, admirable in domestic relations, and
hospitable in the rural districts; but then added that to all foreigners
they were the most disagreeable people on the face of the earth.
They had all the prejudices of the Frenchman without his civility,
and all the love of money of the Englishman without his sense of
honour. They were swindling rogues, and the result of an exciting
climate and a state of society in which an accumulation of dollars was
the only social distinction.[19] This was in 1848, but it was a view
traditionally held. A guide published in London much earlier, in 1816,
objected to the United States on similar moral grounds. The
author, who wrote under the pen-name of An Old Scene Painter,
said emigrants who had been dazzled by the infatuating sounds of
democracy, independence, liberty and equality, had been led to see
America as the only happy spot on earth, where the necessaries,
comforts, and luxuries of life flowed spontaneously or were to be got
without that effort and industry required for their attainment in other
civilised nations. 'Flattered, or rather misled, by this chimera,
thousands have inconsiderately emigrated to the new world; and
have experienced that disappointment which always attends premature conclusions drawn from false reasoning. . . .' Every nation, he
said, had some peculiar characteristic, and that of America had been
very justly called low cunning. The inhabitants of the five New
England states were known as Yankees, and noted for every species
of dishonourable traffick and chicanery; so much so, that all unfair
dealings, swindlings, and artful evasions, were called Yankee tricks.
He thought it would be unjust to include all American citizens in one
indiscriminate mass of censure; the inhabitants of the southern
states, for instance, were not Yankees; they were just luxurious,
indolent, and proud.[20]

One Yankee trick, perfected in the mid-1840s, was to sell emigrants
bad seeds. According to the wife of a Canadian emigration officer
who had travelled in the States, Yankee seeds were sad trash. 'Moreover, they are pasted up in packets not to be opened till paid for,
and you may, as we have done, pay for little better than chaff and
empty husks, or old and worm-eaten seeds.' She said emigrants
should bring their own, British, seeds.[21] This was a good, loyal
English view, almost as loyal as the British sailors of H.M.S.
Belisarius, who, just before the 1812 war, stopped an emigrant ship
and shanghaied the emigrants into the Royal Navy. 'Come along,'
said the sailors, 'you shan't go into that damned republican country;
we are going to have a slap at them one of these days, and you shan't

be there to fight against us . . . we shall suffer no more emigration to that damned democratic country—into the boats.'[22]

This sounds like boasting, which some travellers seemed to think was solely an American quality. One said that when at an American hotel he was told there was handsome accommodation he expected to find the rooms at one remove from very bad; if elegant entertainment he expected it to be tolerable; if a person was a clever man, that he would turn out to be not an absolute fool; and if a factory was said to be the first in the world he expected to find, and generally did find, about six men and three boys employed there. This account appeared in the same issue of a magazine which went into greater detail about the way emigrants could expect to be racked with pain in America. There was consumption at all the eastern seaports, though it was hardly known in the West. The American diseases were generally neuralgic, the effect of nerves, and were common to almost all the Union. The *tic douloureux* was another common complaint all over America. One out of ten suffered from it more or less, the majority being women.[23]

Englishmen in the States were frequently irritated by three all-American customs—slavery, democracy, and deference to women.

As for the women, *Chambers's Journal* said they always had to have the best seats and the best of everything, and reported this incident one night in a New York theatre. An Englishman had paid for the best seat in the house and was sitting in it. An American entered, accompanied by a woman, said, 'The lady, sir,' and motioned to the Englishman that he should give up his seat. The Englishman refused. 'Some words ensued, which attracted the attention of the sovereign people in the pit, who magisterially inquired what was the matter. The American came to the front of the box and said, "There is an Englishman here who will not give up his place to a lady." Immediately their majesties swarmed up by dozens over the barriers, seized the offender—very gently though—and carried him to the entrance . . . They placed him carefully on his feet again at the steps, one man handing him his hat, another his opera-glass, and a third the price he had paid for his ticket for admission, then quietly shut the door upon him, and returned to their places. The shade of the departed Judge Lynch must have rejoiced at such an angelic admin-istration of the law.' The writer said it was curious that women in modern America were treated much as they had been in Europe in the middle ages, as beings to receive an external homage which lifted them to the rank of mortal divinities.[24] He also reported, with disgust, that when New York horse-buses were full, the men would take women on to their knees.[25]

Slavery disgusted the English press even more. *Punch* said in 1847 that the American Eagle, that bird of liberty, laid rotten eggs. It reported that when two anti-slavery men went to Harrisburg, Long Island, to preach liberty to the benighted citizens of the freest nation on earth they were met with foul eggs, crackers, and brickbats, 'the arguments of the good and the wise'. *Punch* at this time was generally critical of the United States. In 1851 it said America only needed a few square feet at the Crystal Palace: if she displayed Colt's revolvers over the soap, and piled the Cincinatti pickles on top of the Virginia honey, this would concentrate in very small space all the treasures of American art and manufacture.[26]

Chambers, when he was at Washington, managed to be equally scathing about both American slavery and American equality. He went to the White House, which he called a gentleman's residence in a quiet rural district, sent up his card, and was received by President Pierce. This pleased him. But he also saw a young Negro auctioned off for $945, and three Negro children playing at auctioning one another. A boy of five was selling a girl about a year younger to a third child. 'Fifty dollars for de girl—fifty dollars—fifty dollars—I sell dis here fine girl for fifty dollars.' Chambers was also grieved, though not quite so much, that American railway conductors affected a dash of the gentleman, and off duty passed for respectable personages at any of the hotels, and could be seen lounging round in the best company with fashionable wives. No one would be surprised to find that they were colonels in the militia.[27]

But in the mind of the truest haters of American ways the principal charge against the United States was disloyalty to the British crown, as if the War of Independence had been fought five years before, not seventy. In the middle of the century there was some fear that Canada might be annexed by the United States, but mostly the anti-American view was held not out of reason but instinctively, and often by those Anglican clergymen who expressed noble, Hand-of-God views on emigration. One clergyman advised emigrants to take out a lot of religious and loyal prints, pictures of the Queen, Prince Albert, Wellington, Nelson, Windsor Castle, English cathedrals, and men-o'-war, to counteract as far as possible the influence of the tawdry pictures, found all over America, of the Signing of the Declaration of Independence, and of George Washington. He thought the question of settling in the United States in preference to

Canada was hardly one that could trouble a loyal churchman for a moment. 'Give me I say the cross-emblazoned flag of my glorious country for my banner,—and the mild sway of my Gracious liege lady Her Most Excellent Majesty Queen Victoria for my government, and I cannot but be content; and I think he who prefers the "stars", richly deserves to have the "stripes" into the bargain.' This patriot also feared disaffection in British North America, and in the telling of one story showed himself an ultra-loyalist. In 1837 the French Canadians had rebelled against the British. The rebellion was put down, but then, after Lord Durham's report, Canada was given what amounted to self-government of her domestic affairs. This was bad enough, but then, as a deliberate act of policy, the rebels were not penalised. This was too much for the British loyalists, who burned down the Parliament buildings in Montreal, on the principle 'that the house where treason had been sanctioned must be PURGED BY FIRE'. So they set fire to the place, and the Members of Parliament rushed from the building. 'When, suddenly, a shout arose amongst the multitude—"The Queen's Picture!" The words struck like an electric spark. The foremost of the rioters darted forward at the sound—rushed into the blazing pile,—and at risk of their lives bore the portrait of their beloved sovereign . . . almost uninjured from the flames; the act gilding with a sort of rainbow glory the popular tempest as it loured.'[28]

Loyalty could also be expressed in verse, though never in good verse. The author of *The Arrival*[29] saw himself and his colleagues, when they landed in Canada, as

> Pioneers of civilisation,
> Founders of a mighty nation.

He was glad to camp by spruce and cedar trees, which he called monarchs of the solitude, and said:

> O rather would I pursue
> The wolf and the grisly bear,
> Than toil for the thankless few,
> In those seething pits of care.

The seething pits were back home in England.

Then there was the author of *The Emigrant's Dream*, who in an epic poem addressed both Britannia and America. First Britannia, who was said to be fully conscious that her flag unfurled, had given law supreme to half the world. And then America, who was apparently masculine:

> One word to you, America, to you my son,
> One parting word to you—and I have done;
> Swear to me, ere we part, that ne'er again,
> Your offspring ye unnatural will train
> To hate the Mother land—to curse the earth
> That gave their fathers and their grandsires birth.[30]

In other words, emigration to the States was all right as long as there was never another war of 1812. The author also bade Americans re-mould their language in that tongue, in which his Johnson wrote and Goldsmith sung. He bade them Cowper as their model take, and love old England for old Wordsworth's sake.

Apart from disloyalty, and the way of speaking English, one of America's great drawbacks, to any middle-class English emigrant was the difficulty of getting servants. T. Hibbert Ware of Cheshire, a barrister who sailed to Canada in July 1844 and went to Orilla, near Toronto, stayed only a few months and by November was booking his passage back home. He wrote in his diary that the greatest inconvenience under which a family of respectability had to labour in Canada was the difficulty not only of getting female servants but of keeping them. Wives were in such great demand that servants frequently left to get married, giving no notice. Another disagreeable thing was the notion of equality which the lower orders imbibed from the American air they breathed.[31]

The wife of a Canadian officer, the same woman who advised emigrants against buying Yankee packets of seeds, wrote advising female servants in America to avoid the error of a too free-and-easy manner, bordering on impertinence, towards their masters. These servants should bear in mind that they were commanded by the Bible to render honour to whom honour was due. Good breeding was a charming trait in a servant, and if a more kindly feeling existed between the upper and lower classes, a bond of union would be established which would last through life. How much more satis-factory that would be than the unloving strife where the mistress was haughty and the servant insolent.[32] The officer's wife had not realised that in America there was not the same sharp distinction as in England between the upper and lower classes. Her book, like so many other books and magazines on emigration, was read widely in Britain, and may have encouraged emigration in a way she did not count on.

The uppitiness of servants in America, and the difficulty of getting any at all, may have been a great encouragement to those who were servants in England, and wanted something better in America.

There was also the view, not altogether rational and perhaps even a bit mystical, that the spirit of America altogether changed the character of the men and women who went there.

Nathaniel Hawthorne, the novelist, held something like this view. In 1853 at Liverpool he saw a multitude of young girls who had been taken from workhouses and trained at a charity school to be domestic servants. Their figures and features were mean, coarse, and vulgar and betrayed unmistakably, so he said, their low origins and brutal parents. There was scarcely a trace of beauty. They did not appear wicked, but stupid, animal, and soulless. All America could not have shown the like. Two years later, in August 1855, he was looking at schoolgirls again in a park near Liverpool. He said it struck him to observe how the lower orders of England showed their birth and station by their aspect and features. In America there would have been a great deal of beauty in 150 children and budding girls of whatever rank of life, but in Liverpool they were evidently plebeian, stubbed and sturdy, coarse and snub-nosed, the brown bread of human nature. It would have been impossible to make a lady of any of them. 'Climate, no doubt, has most to do with suffusing a slender elegance over American young womanhood; but something, perhaps, is also due to the circumstance that classes are not kept apart there, as they are here; they cross-breed together, amid the continual ups and downs of our social life; and so, in the lowest stratum of life, you may see the refining influence of gentle blood.'[33]

This would have amused many Englishmen who did not see in America much of the refining influence of gentle blood. It was fashionable to attack America in one way or another, and Americans were very touchy about this and defended themselves when attacked. In the mid-1850s an English clergyman, the Rev. Mr. Conybeare, wrote a novel called *Perversion*, in which he described one emigrant in this way:

'He transported himself to New York. He professed his intention of devoting himself to political life in his adopted country, and, with his talents, energy, and unscrupulousness, there can be little doubt that he will become a distinguished member of Congress. . . . Nor is it impossible that we may one day see him representing the United States of America at the Court of St. James.'

This incensed a New York magazine, which said here was an

English clergyman who had suggested that the United States could send as ambassador to London a man who, in the novel, was not only a perjurer, a gambler, and an adulterer, but also an atheist. 'Of all the lies that have ever been lied about America, this last lie, lied by an English parson, is the most vile and profligate. Let the author of *Life and Epistles of St. Paul* [the same man] put that in his pipe and smoke it.'[34]

There were plenty of entertaining ballads about America too. Not the likes of *The Emigrant Ship and Other Poems*, an epic of fifty-five pages, whose author said he hoped to 'inculcate energy in overcoming obstacles, and a reliance on Divine support to endure misfortune',[35] but short verses mostly printed on one side of a sheet of paper and sold in London for a penny.[36]

'Happy Land! Comic Version' was very ironic:

> As emigrants, pray tell me who would roam,
> When they can stay and starve at home.

'Rouse, brothers, rouse!'—which was illustrated by a woodcut of young men and women, evidently the servants of the estate, dancing in a park with a stately mansion in the background, probably rousing themselves to get up and go to America—said America needed emigrants and courted their labour, so why should they stay like men forlorn. Across the sea there was fair elbow-room for men to thrive in, and if cities followed them into the wilderness, they could go on still further west. The last four lines read:

> And new-born states in future years
> Shall own us fathers of a nation,
> And bless the hardy pioneers.
> Rouse! Brothers rouse! the way is long before us.

'To the West' begins:

> To the west, to the west, to the land of the free,
> Where mighty Missouri rolls down to the sea.

The words are not much, but might have sounded fine if they were sung hopefully, by people who really believed that away, far away, was the land of the west, where the young could exalt and the aged could rest.

These ballads were published by tatty printers in the Seven Dials part of London, a notorious slum a few hundred yards north of Trafalgar Square. There are all sorts. Along with 'Sufferings of the

British Army in the Camp and Sebastapol', and 'The Jenny Lind Mania' ('But I never saw a singing bird wear petticoats before'), are 'Gold in California', 'The Irish Emigrant', 'Carry Me Back to Old Virginny', and 'Come Into My Canoe'.

> Come into my canoe, ah come along Dinah, do
> Step into my canoe, but not without boot or shoe . . .
>   De riber am wide,
>   Down we shall glide
>   Down de Ohio—
>   Away let us go.

It is an ordinary, vaguely erotic song, only it is set on the Ohio. Another song like this was 'A Maiden's Wants', which had a bit of spirit.

Oh, here I am a blooming maid who long have single tarried,
And no one knows a maiden's woes who wants for to be married.

I want—nine dozen pairs of sheets, I don't intend to plank it,
I want two bedsteads and two beds, six pair of Witney blankets.

Lots of music too I want, for I'm very fond of singing,
I want a piano and a harp, and a sofa with a spring in.

If I find a man who's to my mind, with pleasure I'll bewilder him
For I want a husband who can get me half a dozen children.

Emigration and America were in the mind of the time. The river to take a girl down was the Ohio. The tune of 'A Maiden's Wants' was 'Yankee Doodle'. At no time before had so many people been aware of America and what it offered. Emigration, even on penny broadsheets, was the fashion.

4
Leaving Home

Throughout the British Isles posters from the emigration commissioners and advertisements from passenger brokers were stuck on cottage walls as decorations. Whole families and groups of families emigrated together. The *Illustrated London News* printed an engraving showing two emigrant carts on a country road. Both were covered hay waggons, painted yellow, one from a parish in Buckinghamshire, and the other from near Northampton. They had joined company on the road. The men walked. The women rode.[1]

The posters were stuck up in Irish villages too, though many of the Irish could not speak English, let alone read it. One reporter, who was a Scot and therefore could read, said it was sadly clear that the inmates of the cottages on which the posters appeared knew little more of their meaning than if they had been Chinese notices on a tea-chest.[2] Often the priest translated and explained. And before they left, the emigrants waited for the priest's blessing. They cried as they left their villages, but went confidently believing in the blessing they had received. In the most wretched times they had extraordinary faith. An English clergyman who saw a lot of Ireland said that the people were Roman Catholics, and he was a Protestant, but he recognised the depth of their faith. He once saw a girl and her dying mother waiting by the roadside for a priest to come and give the last sacraments. As they waited, the girl held before her mother's face a cross made of two pieces of stick tied with rush.[3] A French Catholic priest said Irish emigrants carried with them the double treasure of a faith tempered by persecution, and an habitual virtue. But, he said, they bore these treasures in vessels of clay, and would need strength of soul, perseverance, and courage to preserve them from the multiplied shocks of a life of travel and adventure. He quoted II Corinthians 4:7, 'Weep sore for him that goeth away: for he shall return no more, nor see his native country.'[4]

Richard Cobden, leader of the anti-Corn Law league, who had great sympathy with those forced to emigrate and particularly with the Irish, believed that of all created beings Man was the hardest to sever from the place of his birth. It was more difficult to tear him from his country than to tear an oak up by its roots. He had seen people, on the point of leaving, cling on to the last moment. 'Oh, you would not need to ask their feelings, for their hearts spoke out in their faces.'[5]

Many Irish sailed directly from Irish ports, particularly from Limerick and Galway in the west, and Cork in the south, but a far greater number always sailed from Liverpool, and first had to reach that port on board small steamboats from Cork or Dublin. From Cork the passage to Liverpool took twenty-two to thirty-six hours, according to the weather. John Duross, a constable of the Cork Constabulary whose duty it was to see emigrants on board, had known as many as 800 statute adults travel on one steamer, and since two children counted as one statute adult according to the Passenger Acts, he said there might have been as many as 1,200 people aboard a steamer of 800 tons. The average number was 500 to 700. The emigrants stayed on deck all voyage. Duross had never known a steamboat which provided any shelter for them, 'with the exception of a tarpawling, which they have in very stormy weather thrown over; but that does not save the emigrants from the storm; it keeps the tremendous blast off some of them, but it is impossible to cover them all. . . .'[6]

John Besnard, who also came from Cork, told the same story. He was general weighmaster of the city, and presided over the Cork Butter Market, which he presumed was the largest in the world. He had gone to Liverpool expressly to watch the arrival of the Irish steamers, and had seen as many as 1,100 on board. For the 10s. passage money the steamship company found no provisions, and in any case the emigrants were so crowded that it was impossible for them even to get a drink of warm water. He thought the way they were conveyed was disgraceful, dangerous, and inhuman. They were as wet as if they had been dipped in the sea. The people were prostrated by the voyage and scarcely able to walk. The pigs carried between decks were taken better care of: somebody had an interest in their lives, but nobody seemed to care about the poor emigrants.[7]

A journalist who made the passage from Dublin to Liverpool said the emigrants crowded round the funnel. If they were not used to the sea—and most were not—they were seasick, and became helpless and covered with each other's vomit. He came over one stormy night. The boat heaved about, seas washed over her, and the 250 deck passengers were drenched. Fifty or sixty were stiff and cold, and he took them into the saloon and made them take their wet clothes off. One boy was apparently dead, but they laid him in front of the fire and rubbed him in hot water and he revived. A girl of about twenty was so bad that she was unconscious from five in the morning until the boat arrived at Liverpool at seven in the evening.[8]

In the twelve months before June 1, 1854, more than 100,000 passengers, probably about half of them emigrating to America, were carried to England by the Dublin and Liverpool Steam Packet Co.[9] William Watson was managing director of this company, and when he gave evidence to a Parliamentary committee he brought along a model of one of his company's steamers to show them. He said it was of *The Princess*, 636 tons gross, eight or nine knots, and licensed by the Board of Trade to carry 350 deck passengers. About 150 of these could get under cover, and the directors' orders were that as far as possible the women and children should be sheltered and the men left outside. He was then questioned further about the deck houses on the model, and asked if they were not really intended for cattle. He said they were.

The committee pressed him:

Those covered places on the deck are intended for cattle if you have any?—Yes.

If you have not any cattle they are intended for passengers?—Yes.

If you have both cattle and passengers you give the cattle the preference?—We cannot have them both in the same places.

But the cattle would be sheltered, and the deck passengers would not be sheltered?—Yes.

Mr. Watson said he might mention that the idea of the stalls had been suggested in this way: when Queen Victoria visited Ireland in 1849 his company had to take the horses, and put up the stalls on deck, and had left them there.[10]

Once they had left home, even before they had boarded the ships for America, emigrants were helpless and almost without resources.

In the restrained language of a Parliamentary report they were described as people whose ignorance and consequent helplessness made them the easiest prey to fraud and the least able to obtain redress for ill-usage.[11] If they were not destitute, they were very poor, but this was often not realised even by those who professed to know about emigration. In 1852 a man called Widder wrote a pamphlet offering advice to emigrants arriving in Canada and possessing from £300 to £800 a year. This provoked a Mr. Montamis, who knew emigrants better, to write to the provincial government of Quebec saying this surmise was entirely preposterous. People earning that much had never left Europe. Neither the United States nor Canada possessed the least inducement to make them leave home. Things in Europe were not so bad as the newspapers made out. It was true that in Europe many things ought to be changed, but the same was true of America or anywhere, and always would be as long as men remained selfish and sinful. Mr. Montamis doubted if half a dozen emigrants to America in the previous sixty years had possessed £300 a year.[12]

Emigrants were described by various people—who all knew emigration thoroughly and were sympathetic to emigrants—as disorderly, unbelievably innocent, and lower than civilised. Frederick Sabel, one of the only two honest lodging-house keepers in Liverpool, said he kept coming back to this point, that if only they were orderly you could do something for them, but they were not.[13] A reporter of the London *Morning Chronicle* who went to Liverpool in 1850 noticed that very few emigrants seemed even to know whether Canada was or was not a British possession.[14] The Unitarian mission in Liverpool came to the conclusion that in their attire, their manners, their habits, their wildness of look and their gestures and language, many emigrants had more savagery about them than could be included within the lowest definition of civilised life.[15] Liverpool did not like the Irish: the only good quality about them was ingenuity, and that was often dishonest. In 1847 Thomas Maguire was brought before the Liverpool magistrates charged with stealing rum from a ship in dock. Mr. Shaw, a shipping clerk, had noticed that puncheons of rum on board ship had been broached, and the rum poured out and taken away. He offered a reward of 10s. for information. Maguire took his offer and his 10s. and then said, 'You see the thief before you. I am the man. Me own four bones broached the cask and drank the rum . . . It's not my saying alone; all the neighbours in the street will tell you the same thing, for they all had a nip.' Maguire was arrested. Sir Joshua Walmsley, a magistrate, said he never heard of a more barefaced act in his life, and ordered Maguire to pay a 5s. fine and 4s. 6d. costs. Maguire paid this out of the 10s. reward for information, and was left with 6d. over. Mr. Shaw then asked for his 10s. to be restored to him but the magistrates said they had no power to order this.[16]

A land agent who had exported 4,600 pauper emigrants from the Irish estates of the marquesses of Lansdowne and of Bath, found the Irish very crafty. In Liverpool they broke loose and ran about the streets to the terror of the inhabitants. They hid the good new clothes he had given them and took delight in appearing almost naked and in their worst rags. They were a strange, wild, unmanageable crew.[17]

Very few defended emigrants as Mrs. Caroline Chisholm did. She was principally concerned with emigration from London and Plymouth to Australia, but she considered that the much larger Liverpool emigration to America had been neglected by the clergy and Parliament. If there were no washhouses or bath places for the emigrants to go to, and there were not, then it was impossible for them to be clean. 'So that before emigrants are considered and classed as a filthy set, and the blame is all put on pauperism, it should not be so, but on the neglect of those who do not provide the emigrants with proper accommodation.'[18]

Those on whom emigrants were a charge could not be expected to be so charitable. Five members of the Massachusetts House of Representatives reported to the House that the susceptibility, volitions, moral purposes, wishes, hopes, and fears of many emigrants were of a very low order. 'Their relations to their country have been proved, of course, too little satisfactory or intimate to keep them there; and those which they can be supposed to have formed here will not be of a higher grade. It may be said, without any purpose of depreciation, any sense of scorn, or any lack of humane commiseration, that the whole life and being of the confirmed pauper [this meant pauper emigrants] is almost purely animal, and often of a degraded character even in that classification.'[19] Another report, this time to the Massachusetts Senate, was particularly hard on the Irish, saying, 'The want of forethought in them to save their earnings for the day of sickness; the indulgence of their appetites for stimulating drinks, which are too easily obtained among us; and their strong love for their native land, which is characteristic with them, are the fruitful causes of insanity among them.'[20]

Friedrich Kapp, one of the Commissioners of Emigration for New York State, was more sympathetic. He said that to the shippers the emigrants were less than a box of goods, 'and handled with less care, as they did not break, nor, if injured, required to be paid for'.[21] Samuel Sidney, who watched emigrants embarking at Liverpool, thought the same as Kapp. He said: 'Emigrants are not to be compared to other persons; they are an exception; they are the most helpless people in the world.' He was asked if they were more helpless than a person shipping a bale of goods: the implication was that goods might also be delayed or knocked about. He replied: 'Yes; a person shipping a bale of goods is generally resident here [and therefore knew the reputations of the shipping companies], and understands his business, which emigrants do not.'[22]

Few emigrants had ever left home before, few had ever been to Liverpool, and fewer still had ever been to sea, so they could not know what they were about. They were on their own and had to look after themselves. They were offered kind advice which was little use. A charitable and Christian society suggested energy, patience, benevolence, and good sense, but first of all recommended emigrants to 'the Great Physician'. This society also suggested they should play word games to help pass the time. Out of the letters TAC, you could make the words CAT and ACT; and out of the word GRANDFATHER you could make 150 other words.[23] An emigrants' guide-book offered encouragement and recipes for

> Beans, Lima
> Coffee, substitute for
> Ducks, wild
> Pumpkins
> Partridges
> Pigeons
> Soup
> Squirrels.[24]

The Gutta Percha Company begged to call the attention of emigrants, or at least of those who could read, to the ease with which gutta-percha soles could be applied to boots and shoes in countries where no shoemaker could readily be found, and offered gutta-percha ewers, basins, and night pails, and cricket and bouncing balls. S. W. Silver of 4 Bishopsgate, London, offered floating mattresses as 'preventives to sinking'.[25]

William Chambers did offer some good advice, which was to

travel light. Emigrants with too much luggage could not move without carts to and from the ship, and had to look around for help in carrying their belongings, which put them at the mercy of swindling porters and runners. 'If an emigrant knew the consequences, he would prefer going without a change of underclothing for a month, rather than embarrass himself with baggage. I could not but pity the lot of many who fell in my way on the wharfs and in the railway stations; there they sat, each on a great box, unable to stir. They could not safely leave this precious encumbrance, and were as good as nailed to the spot, while all about them was bustle, and they ought to have been off on their journey, or helping themselves in some way. Oh these boxes.'[26]

This was important, as anyone arriving at Liverpool on an Irish steamer found out. Sabel often saw what happened, and described it like this:

'The runners watch the steamboats night and day. Suppose a ship arrives at one o'clock in the morning, and it rains as fast as it can; the passengers are all frightened; everything is strange to them; and the moment the ship arrives, however many passengers there may be, there come as many runners, who snatch up their luggage as quickly as possible, and carry it away; they are like so many pirates. If any of the passengers wish to keep on board the ship, they cannot; the police come and drive them away; they are afraid to smoke a pipe. No fire is allowed while a ship is in dock, although, at the same time, the chimnies of the steamers are spitting fire continually. Everything seems as if it were done on purpose to favour the runners and man-catchers; the people are actually driven from the ship with sticks into the hands of those people . . . It is really a horrible thing.'[27]

5
Liverpool and the Last of England

By the middle of the nineteenth century Liverpool was a great city,
with a population of 367,000.[1] It was the second-largest city in
England, and three-quarters the size of New York. Liverpool was a
port which had grown rich first with the slave trade and with privat-
eering, and then with the American trades of cotton and emigrants.
By the end of the eighteenth century, five-sixths of the English slave
trade belonged to Liverpool. In the last year before the abolition of
the slave trade in the British Empire in 1807, 185 Liverpool ships
carried 49,213 slaves.[2] In the nineteenth century the port received
timber from the American north, and cotton from the southern
States for the Manchester mills. When emigration started again after
the Napoleonic wars, Liverpool became by far the biggest emigrant
port, and always remained so. Today Liverpool is easily the grandest
English city outside London. The centre of no other English city is
planned on such a scale. The streets are wider and the public
buildings more massive. By the 1850s, when the city that once
had five-sixths of the slave trade had in its place two-thirds of the
British emigrant trade, many of these buildings were already there,
put up out of the profit from slaves, cotton, and emigrants; and then
they were new. Almost all had been built in the few years before.
Two of the grandest buildings, to give an idea, are St. George's Hall,
begun in 1839 and completed in 1854, and the Albert Docks, opened
in 1845. The hall, which is concert hall and law courts and a monument to lots of money, is one of the greatest classical buildings of the

nineteenth century, probably the finest neo-classical structure in
Europe, and, according to Norman Shaw, one of the great edifices of
the world. The style is Roman but the refinements are Greek. The
columns are polished granite, the balustrades marble, the doors brass
with foliated tracery, and the façade is 300 feet long. Very few
buildings in London are anywhere near so magnificent. It is a few
hundred yards from the docks where hundreds of thousands of
emigrants embarked. The Albert Dock, which was opened by Albert
the Prince Consort in 1845, was only one of the many docks built in
Liverpool, but for its time it was gigantic, and so were its warehouses
with their cast-iron Doric pillars.[3] Liverpool was opulent, and the
docks were a wonder.[4] Herman Melville said that the young mind
which had previously seen only the miserable wooden wharves and
slipshod shambling piers of the New York waterfront was filled
with wonder and delight at the Liverpool docks. In New York a
visitor could not help being struck by the long line of shipping and
tangled thickets of masts along the East River, but in Liverpool there
were Chinese walls of masonry, vast piers of stone, and a succession
of granite-rimmed docks as extensive and solid as the Egyptian
pyramids. In magnitude, cost, and durability the docks of Liverpool
surpassed all others in the world.[5]

Into these docks there came—apart from cotton and timber—
brimstone, cocoa, coffee, fustic, ginger, cowhides, jute, molasses,
palm oil, pepper, rice, rum, saltpetre, sugar, tar, tallow, tobacco,
and turpentine.[6] From them went not only emigrants but also the
cotton goods of Lancashire and the manufactures of the industrial
Midlands. In 1845, 20,521 vessels traded in and out of the port.[7] The
merchants who grew rich with this trade supported an elegant
society. In 1847 the city had ten daily or weekly newspapers. B.
Rogers and Sons, musicians, respectfully announced that they
supplied large and small quadrille bands for balls and assemblies, and
military reed bands for ship launches, regattas, and public dinners.
John Cripps, shawl manufacturer and cloak-man, ran the Maison de
Lyon in Bold Street, and had the honour of informing the nobility,
gentry, and strangers, that he had at all times an extensive and
superior stock of shawls, mantles, and cloaks in the first style of
fashion; indeed, it was the largest stock in the kingdom. Thomas
Henry Satchell was hatter to His Royal Highness Prince Albert.
W. Bennett, also by royal appointment, made Imperial Patent
Metallic Bedsteads.[8]

From August 1853 to June 1857 Nathaniel Hawthorne, the

novelist, was American consul at Liverpool. He had got the consulship, which was the most dignified in the gift of the United States, as
a piece of patronage from Franklin Pierce. When Pierce ran for
president in 1852 he asked Hawthorne, who was an old college
friend of his, to write a 'campaign biography' for him. Hawthorne
wrote it, Pierce was elected, and Hawthorne was sent off to the
Liverpool consulship which was supposed to be not only dignified
but a mine of wealth. When he got there, he kept complaining that it
did not produce as much as he expected, but still said in 1853 that he
would 'bag from $5,000 to $7,000 per annum'. In some ways
Hawthorne had a disappointing time in England. He did not meet
Thackeray, Dickens, Charles Reade, or George Eliot, and saw
Tennyson only in a picture gallery.[9] Neither did he write anything
while he was in England, except that in his journals he gave a detailed
day-to-day account of Liverpool. He said the Mersey had all the
colour of a mud puddle; and no atmospheric effect, so far as he
could see, ever changed this to a more agreeable tinge. A great many
steamers plied up and down the river to various landing places, and
so did steam tugs, and small boats mostly with dark red or tan-
coloured sails oiled to resist the wet; here and there was a yacht or a
pleasure boat, and ships rode at their anchors, probably on the point
of sailing. The river was not crowded, because the multitude of ships
were all in docks, where their masts made an intricate forest miles up
and down the shore. The small black steamers whizzing industriously
along, many of them crowded with passengers, made up the chief
life of the scene. When a Cunard transatlantic steamboat came in
with her red funnel whitened by sea spray she lay for several hours
after mooring with smoke and steam coming out of her, as if she
were smoking her pipe after the heavy Atlantic passage. Once a
fortnight an American steamer of the Collins Line passed a Cunarder
in the river, and they saluted each other with cannon, all the more
ceremoniously because they were rivals and jealous of each other.
Almost every day Hawthorne walked about the city, preferring the
darker and dingier streets inhabited by the poorer classes. Women
nursed their babies at dirty breasts. The men were haggard, drunken,
care-worn, and hopeless, but patient as if that were the rule of their
lives. He never walked through these streets without feeling he might
catch some disease, but he took the walks all the same because there
was a sense of bustle, and of being in the midst of life and of having
got hold of something real, which he did not find in the better streets
of Liverpool. Tithebarn Street was thronged with dreadful faces—

women with young figures but with old and wrinkled countenances, young girls without any maiden neatness, barefooted, with dirty legs. Dirty, dirty children, and the grown people were the flower of these buds, physically and morally. At every ten steps there were spirit vaults. Placards advertised beds for the night. Often he saw little children taking care of little children, and, it seemed to him, taking good and faithful care of them. At the provision shops, little bits of meat were ready for poor customers, little heaps and selvages and corners stripped off from joints and steaks. 'The people are as numerous as maggots in cheese; you behold them, disgusting, and all moving about, as when you raise a plank or log that has long lain on the ground, and find many vivacious bugs and insects beneath it.'[10]

Sailors loved Liverpool, and on long voyages constantly talked about its charms and attractions. It was a sailors' paradise. But as the seamen from hundreds and hundreds of ships went to dinner in town at mid-day they were pestered by an army of paupers, old women drying up with slow starving, young girls incurably sick, and puny mothers holding up puny babies. One cripple held a painted board on his knees intended to represent the man himself caught in the machinery of some factory and whirled about among the spindles and cogs. Another man said nothing but sat with one finger pointed silently down to a square of flagging at his feet which was swept, and stained blue, and bore the inscription in chalk: 'I have had no food for three days; my wife and child are dying.' In the evening, hand organs, cymbals, and fiddles played outside boarding houses which each displayed a sign outside—a crown, an anchor, a ship, a windlass, or a dolphin. The walls were covered with placards for ships to the United States and Canada, advertisements for Jewish clothesmen, ambiguous medical announcements, and inducements to all seamen disgusted with the merchant service to accept a bounty and join the Royal Navy. Few took the offer.[11]

Away from the handsome classical buildings and the houses of the merchants, the rich city of Liverpool was narrow, dirty, and infested, and itself a great inducement to emigration. Whole streets were given over to the business. Goree Piazza, which was where the slave trade once had its offices, and which took its name from Goree Island off Senegal where slavers took on their cargoes, contained in 1848 twenty-two shipbrokers, commission agents, provision merchants, emigration agents, or porters. In the same year in Waterloo Road, which runs from the city centre northwards, past the docks where the American packets lay, there were nineteen shipping agents or brokers, fifteen provision shops or eating houses, and sixteen public houses or spirit vaults.[12] Before the emigrants even got on board ship they had to have dealings with ship brokers, otherwise known as emigration agents or recruiters; with runners, otherwise called crimps, touts, and man-catchers; with boarding-house keepers, who overcharged them and delayed them as long as they had money to pay for more lodgings; and the keepers of spirit vaults and provision stores, who sold them bad food and drink at high prices. Runners were almost always boarding-house keepers, and boarding-house keepers often ran spirit vaults or food shops on the side. It was all confused and disorderly, and almost always a racket. Each man took his cut, and the first and biggest cut went to the broker.

The broker was a speculator. He did not own ships. He sold space in the packets and received from the shipping company a commission on each berth sold. Or he chartered whole ships, which did not belong to the packet companies and did not keep any regular sailing times. These were almost always inferior ships. When the broker chartered a ship he did not receive commission from the ship-owner, but bought the whole space in it for one voyage, and then packed into that space as many passengers as the law allowed, or, really, as many as he could get away with. The steady income was from the packet ships. The big money was made out of charter ships. Brokers advertised both kinds of ships as if they owned them. They

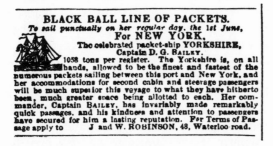

Advertisement for the packet ship *Yorkshire,*
the fastest of the Liverpool–New York packets

advertised ships as larger than they were, and as sailing on dates on which they did not sail. They acted through agents in English provincial towns or in Ireland, and often, when they had no space left on a ship or even no ship at all, the Liverpool brokers repudiated their agents' bargains. The shipowners also at times repudiated the bargains made by the brokers, as they could easily do, because there was no contract between shipowner and emigrant, only between emigrant and broker; and indeed there was in practice no enforceable contract even between emigrant and broker unless the emigrant could prove that the man who had acted as the broker's agent was in fact the broker's agent. Even if there was a provable contract, emigrants did not make successful litigants. They did not have the money to sue, or they did not know how, or they were in a hurry to get away and had no time to stay and sue, or were quite unable to wait because they had no money and would starve unless they got on board ship, any ship, whether or not it was the one they had contracted for. Samuel Sidney[13] said: 'It is just like taking a ticket on a railway in which you have never seen the carriage, you do not see anything of it until you are going in it, and then, under the present arrangements, it is too late to find fault.'

'In those cases [he was asked] the advertisement is an imposition from first to last?—Yes, that is the ordinary thing.

'In point of law, it is a fraud at the present time?—No doubt of it ... they [the brokers] are like recruiters, they collect emigrants; their ships are known in the trade by the name of paper ships.'

As a policeman[14] put it, there was a general impression that the emigrants were defrauded from the day they started from their houses. They had no remedy.

It was very big business. According to Lieutenant Thomas Hodder,[15] chief emigration officer at Liverpool, whose figures were always approximate in spite of their apparent accuracy, and always too low, the whole sum paid for passages in 1850 was £581,315. Of this sum the brokers took 12½ per cent on average. One of the biggest firms of brokers was that of W. & J. T. Tapscott, run by the brothers William and James Tapscott, who were both Americans, and both outwardly respectable. William worked from the Liverpool end and James in New York, and James was a bigger crook than William. Both claimed to be very kind to emigrants. William published a pamphlet called *Tapscott's Emigrant's Guide*, and said he had distributed 50,000. In 1851 he employed from twelve to twenty agents in Liverpool, and from the beginning of that year until June 13 sent out nearly 20,000 emigrants.[16] Assuming they paid the usual £3 10s. each, their fares would have come to £70,000, of which Tapscott took 12½ per cent. Tapscott would have had to pay his touts and runners anything between 5 and 7½ per cent, say

Advertisement of Tapscott's, one of the biggest emigrant brokers. The Tapscott brothers were systematic villains, whose frauds began with their advertisements. This one flagrantly exaggerates the tonnage of every ship named. The *Garrick*, here said to be 2,000 tons, was in fact 895 tons.

an average of 6½ per cent, thus keeping for himself 6 per cent of £70,000, or £4,200 from six months' business: £8,400 a year, or, by present-day values, at least £84,000 a year, untaxed. William got steadily more prosperous. In the 1847 Liverpool directory he had one office address. By 1848 he had two offices. By 1855 he had two offices, and a private house as well.[17] Compared with his brother he was a scrupulous man.

The principal business of James, the Tapscott brother in New York, was selling prepaid passages to emigrants who had already been in America a little while and had saved enough to bring their families or friends over.[18] The New York Tapscott then sent the money to the Liverpool Tapscott, who brought the new emigrant over on one of his ships. But another essential part of the business in New York, until mid-1847, was to bond passengers. It worked like this. Any shipowner bringing emigrants into the port of New York had to give the city a bond, which amounted to a written assurance that he would provide for any emigrant who became destitute and a charge on the city. This was a tedious responsibility, which the owners passed on to professional bondsmen. The ship-owners paid the bondsmen say 50 cents for each passenger brought in, and in return the bondsmen gave the city the necessary assurance, undertaking to look after emigrants who became paupers. Most bondsmen were also passenger brokers, and one of them was James Tapscott, who ran a second-rate workhouse at Williamsburg, Long Island, to receive the destitute. In 1847 three citizens of Williams-burg visited the workhouse and said in a letter to the *New York Sun* that they had found it 'exhibiting a state of misery and wretchedness not to be borne or countenanced by any civilized community'.[19] They called it a prison house. Tapscott replied, in a letter to another New York newspaper, the *Herald,* that it was insinuated that he had been instrumental in introducing people to emigrate to America by false representations. But though he and his brother published the *Emigrant's Guide*, which was given away free in England and Ire-land, they certainly would not advise anyone to emigrate who was likely to become a burden on the firm's workhouse.[20] He declined to spend anything more on the workhouse, which he did not seem to think was too bad at all. It almost certainly was. Anne Doyle came to New York in the *Republic* in 1846 and her husband then deserted her, forcing her into the Tapscott workhouse, where she stayed until Tapscott said she must leave or he would kick her out. She said: 'The biscuit was very bad, and generally given to the hogs, which were in the yard immediately beyond the house; the hogs, however, did not thrive, and many died.'[21]

Harnden and Co.[22] were another of the Liverpool brokers. The firm had been started by William Harnden, an American, and had other offices in New York, Boston, and Philadelphia. In Liverpool, from their offices at 60a Waterloo Road, they distributed posters saying they paid particular attention to emigrants. They certainly did; emigrants were their living. In 1847 a steward who sailed on one of the ships they chartered made a complaint against them, which rings true.[23] The steward, William Tansley, sailed in the ship *Triton*, 770 tons, from Liverpool to Quebec. By the list, there were 368 statute passengers. The government emigration officer came on board twice but the only thing he did was examine the provisions. On May 18 the *Triton* sailed with 415 statute passengers, forty-seven over the legal limit. Many had been put on board as under fourteen years old, and therefore counting under the Passenger Act as only half a statute passenger, but some of these halves were more than forty years old, and had paid the full fare. Tansley said that Harnden's had deliberately and wilfully, with the intention of defrauding, made out an incorrect list of passengers. In the Mersey a man from Harnden's came aboard. The steward saw a decrepit woman of about sixty who said her name was Eliza O'Neil. On the list she had been put down as under fourteen. He asked Harnden's man if he considered her a child, and the man said to say nothing about it and offered the steward a sovereign. Tansley said this was one instance out of many. One family called Bateman was put down as numbering four adults, and as entitled to rations for only four adults, but in fact there were thirteen of them, the youngest about twelve years old, and all had paid full fare. Tansley made this complaint to a Justice of the Peace at Quebec, and it found its way back to the Colonial Office in London, who asked the emigration officer at Liverpool to investigate. He did, and sent on to London a letter from Harnden's, which was all astonished innocence, inviting inspection of their ticket books at any time, though what this would have shown it is difficult to see. Harnden's said that Mr. Tracy, their man at Liverpool, had offered the steward one pound as an inducement to take good care of the passengers and provisions. They said it was customary on every chartered ship, as the emigration officer would know, to give the mate or steward a pound or two: it was so much a custom that they were angry if they did not get it. 'This was the bribe he [Tansley] mentions as being offered him. If he considered it a bribe he was rascal enough to receive it.' The only explanation Harnden's could think of for the steward's statements was that the captain had been sick and that in his absence the steward embezzled the provisions and concocted this story to account for their having been used. 'Or is it possible that this Steward might have clandestinely taken on board some passengers & received the pay without our knowledge or that of the Master—for he seems to have been the greatest personage on board the ship.'[24] Hodder took the broker's side. He said the *Triton* had been cleared by one of his assistants with 368 statute adults, and if the steward had known that any more had been put on board after the vessel was cleared, then he was therefore a consenting party. This was thin, but Hodder also said he had no reason to doubt the correctness of the passenger list, 'from the respectability of the Establishment—it being one of the leading American houses in Liverpool'.[25] A few years later this respectable establishment declared itself insolvent, leaving in the hands of the Commonwealth of Massachusetts alone many thousands of dollars worth of useless bonds.[26]

George Saul appeared to be an honest broker.[27] He handled about a fifth of the emigrant trade of Liverpool. Although there were many emigrants, there was great competition for them. If a broker chartered a ship he had to fill it by a certain time, or make a loss, so passengers had to be got, and the lodging-house keepers had to be bribed to push emigrants out of the lodgings. 'And our inducement must be greater than the emigrant pays for lodging. If a lodging-house keeper finds it his interest to keep a man he will do so, but if our inducement is greater than that, then he sends him away.' Lodging-house keepers were almost always runners, and he was so trammelled by them, and was so much in their power, that he dare not refuse to pay them. He and other brokers had tried refusing to pay runners for bringing passengers they could get themselves, but this attempt had collapsed when trade got short and other brokers began to pay the runners again to get preference. He had been the last to give way. He had to, for fear that the runners would fall in with passengers coming to his office and take them off to a broker who did pay. Runners came along with passengers who would have come anyway, and then demanded their $7\frac{1}{2}$ per cent commission. But he would destroy his trade if he withheld what he knew was not due to them.

These were the lodging-house keepers and runners whom Melville called a company of miscreant misanthropes leagued together, bent upon doing all the malice in their power. 'With sulphur and brimstone they ought to be burned out of their arches like vermin.'[28] They never were. There was never much chance of it. As another passenger broker, William Fitzhugh, put it, they were even more powerful than the Roman Catholic clergy.[29]

Sir George Stephen of Liverpool, a barrister and philanthropist who concerned himself with emigration, had seen runners set on emigrants and carry them away to brokers or provision stores. He said, 'Actually, I do not know how to describe it, except tearing to pieces, only they do not separate their limbs; but they pull them by the collar, take them by their arms, and, generally speaking, the runners who are successful enough to lay hold of the boxes are pretty sure of carrying the passenger with them.' They would also dollar the emigrant's money if they could persuade him; that is, change his English sovereigns into dubious dollars or worse. One emigrant who had forty sovereigns was persuaded that English gold would not be current in America, which it would have been, and that he must buy United States coin. For his forty sovereigns he received forty 'Californian pieces', worth the eighth part of a farthing each. Another emigrant, a Welshman, was more canny. For his £22 in sovereigns he at least got £16 worth of American gold.[30] Lieutenant Thomas Prior, an assistant emigration officer, said the runners would not allow a man to carry his own chest if he wanted to. There was one set of runners called the Forty Thieves, who snatched up luggage and would not let it go until they had been paid an exorbitant price for carrying it. They were so strong they generally got all they asked.[31] Sylvester Redmond, a journalist, called them man-catchers, who fleeced the emigrants in every shape and form. They were in league with the provision merchants, who allowed them 15 per cent on anything bought by an emigrant they dragged in, and with clothes merchants who also gave them a percentage. The emigrants were sold bad food, and unnecessary pocket mirrors, razors, bowie knives, rifles, pistols, and telescopes.[32]

What the runners got as commission on all this is impossible to reckon. But it is possible to get some idea of their main extortions, which were from passenger brokers for the emigrants they caught. In 1849, 146,162 emigrants sailed from the port, say at £3 10s. each. This makes £511,567, and the runners' 7½ per cent of this amounted to £38,368. Since there were about 400 runners, this came to about £1,000 a year each, or £10,000 untaxed today. This was the calculation of the London *Morning Chronicle*.[33] Lieutenant Prior arrived independently at much the same figure. He said he had known the runners get up to £20 a week.[34] Again, this assumes that, as far as their trade allowed them, they dealt honestly. Some, brighter than the others, did not just take emigrants along to passage brokers, but appointed themselves sub-brokers, sold passages direct to emigrants for up to £5, provided passages they then bought from the real brokers for £3 10s., and kept the difference.

There were many suggestions that runners should be licensed, made to wear badges, and give money guarantees for good conduct. The system was tried but never worked. The chairman of the emigration commissioners was asked what constituted a runner. 'I believe,' he said, 'a runner constitutes himself.'[35]

One of these self-constituted runners was Maurice Dalton, and a dubious fellow he was. He came forward to give evidence to a Parliamentary committee in 1851, whose members were very sceptical of his good faith.[36] He was written down in the report as treasurer of a 'society called the Liverpool Emigrants' and House-holders' Protective Society'. It is not easy to see in what way he and his colleagues even attempted to protect emigrants. Their main interest was to protect themselves against the idea of a large State-run boarding house, and against two large private boarding houses which had recently been set up. Dalton said emigrants could complain to the society, who would expel any offending member, but admitted that no member ever had been expelled, or, for that matter, no complaint ever heard. He said the society met at 'my place, No. 86 Waterloo Road'. According to the city directories for 1848, one M. Dalton, provision dealer, also had a place at 90 Waterloo Road. By 1855 his name was spelled Maurice d'Alton, he was described as victualler, and he had a place at number 82.[37]

He was asked if he ever warned emigrants against particular captains or particular ships. No, he said, because nearly all ships and captains were of a very good class. After a long examination, one of the committee members got very short with him and asked:

'You are a lodging-house keeper, are you not?—No.

'What is your calling?—I keep an hotel.

'Of how many persons does your society consist?—About one hundred lodging-house keepers and about thirty disinterested persons.

'One hundred runners?—Yes.'

Dalton insisted, though, that they were 100 respectable runners. The unrespectable runners were presumably the other 300 who were in competition with Dalton's society. The unrespectable lodging-house keepers, in his view, were those who kept the two new big hostels and had formed 'a huge monopoly, destructive to the interests of the large and respectable class of lodging-house keepers and tradesmen in the north end of the town'. No one except Dalton ever maintained that the tradesmen who dealt with emigrants were honest.

John Bramley Moore, who had been Mayor of Liverpool in 1848, said in 1851 that the emigrant was plundered at every stage and every step from the moment he landed.[38] Everyone tried to get in on the swindle. Ships' mates acted as runners or connived with them. In one case the mate of a ship did some running himself, took anything from 30s. to £3 each from twenty people and stowed them away. When the captain mustered the passengers at the beginning of the voyage the stowaways were discovered, had no tickets, and were landed. The mate said he had never seen them before and the captain, in spite of the passengers' protests, believed his mate could never have done anything so dishonest.[39]

Even priests were rumoured to take a cut, though this was little more than a rumour. The Rev. John William Welsh, who was Anglican chaplain to the emigrants at Liverpool, appointed by the rector of the city and licensed by the Bishop of Chester, said he visited about a third of all the emigrants who passed through the city, and that he had been offered a commission to tell runners of those he knew to be arriving. 'But it was not in my way', he said, 'and therefore I did not do it. It has been mentioned to me that Roman Catholic priests have been in the habit of receiving commissions for the consignment of emigrants. I have understood it from the statements of emigrants themselves, and have no reason whatever to doubt it. Of course, I never saw the money paid, but the emigrants did not conceal anything.'[40]

The only apparently honest boarding-house keepers in Liverpool were Frederick Sabel and Frederick Marshall, and they ran the two 'monopolistic' hostels which the respectable runners so disapproved of. Sabel[41] started his house in 1850, at 28 Moorfields, just across the road from the Lancashire and Yorkshire railway station.[42] It was a spacious, well-ventilated place, licensed to sleep 300, and in the first twelve months it was open 4,164 people stayed there. At first it was called the Union Hotel, and later the Emigrants' Home. Sabel at first catered for German emigrants who sailed from Rotterdam or Antwerp or Bremen to Hull on the east coast, travelled by rail to Liverpool, and sailed from there. But later he took everybody.

He charged 1s. a day for bed and three meals, as against 4d. for bed
only in the ordinary boarding houses, so he got the better-off emigrants, few Irish, but mainly English, Scots, and Germans. Even so,
he gave them only boards to sleep on, and no bedding. 'If we gave
them a bed we should be obliged to throw it away the next day . . .
they are so dreadfully dirty.' He was pestered by runners. 'There are
too many of them to be kept in proper order; it would require in
Liverpool at least 1,000 men to keep them in order; indeed, no force
could keep them in order; there would be a continuous fight.'
He had frequently been attacked by gangs of ruffians. He had also
innocently assisted a fraud. A New York clergyman had come over,
and Sabel agreed that this clergyman should receive emigrants when
they arrived in America, and send them up-country. The agreement
was signed by both and carried out by Sabel, but then he found that
the clergyman was only the head of a gang of thieves. 'I was for six
months printing and distributing cards, and sending people into the
lion's mouth, until, having heard complaints on the subject, I
caused enquiries to be made, and found out what was going on.
Yes, and I had a letter from the British Protective Emigration
Society [in New York] describing his character: he was a Methodist
preacher, and they said he had been driven away; he dedicated a
Hebrew dictionary to Her Majesty, and got himself made LL.D.
and with that he introduced himself.'[43]

Sometimes emigrants who wanted to go to Sabel's were prevented
by gangs of runners. One party of 1,200 emigrants from County
Wexford was due to stay there. Their priest had arranged for them
to come to Liverpool 300 at a time and sleep at Sabel's. They came,
and the priest tried to see them to the hostel, but the runners defied
and bullied the priest, and took the emigrants off.[44]

The other large hostel at Liverpool was run by Marshall,[45] who
had previously organised a similar place at Plymouth. He was asked
to open his Liverpool hostel by some of the Roman Catholic priests
in the city and in Ireland. He kept a Catholic chaplain there, though
he tried to avoid what he called a display of Catholic feeling. Half his
customers were Irish, but the other half were Welsh, who would have
been mostly nonconformists. His hostel, which was opened in 1851,
was in a warehouse by Clarence Dock, and was licensed for 650.
It cost him £1,000 to equip, and £400 a year in rent and rates.
He did not provide food, but since he only charged 4d. a night his
place was a better bargain than Sabel's. The 4d. included bed,
bedding, blankets, counterpanes, any quantity of writing paper, hot

and cold baths, and fire for cooking if people wanted to cook for themselves. He also gave them the use of maps and guide-books. Great violence was used to keep emigrants from coming to him. The emigrants themselves were assaulted and dragged away, and the carts carrying their luggage seized by runners. 'They will come and stand at the door of the house, and howl, and curse, and blaspheme by the hour together; they will take off their coats and offer to fight me, and call me all manner of names.'

What the emigrants got when they were dragged away was a good deal less than Sabel or Marshall offered. In 1850 a reporter of the London *Morning Chronicle* found eighty emigrants living in one small group of four houses, which had three rooms each. In all his experience of the filthiest streets in London, the most wretched closes of Edinburgh, and the purulent wynds of Glasgow he had never seen anything approaching the dirt, discomfort, and squalor of Liverpool. One keeper was brought before the stipendiary magistrate for having ninety-two lodgers in his home, which was only licensed for nineteen.[46]

The less fortunate got an even worse deal, and probably found themselves in cellars. In 1849 there were 7,700 cellars, occupied by 27,000 people.[47] Sir George Stephen found as many as thirty emigrants stowed away on the stone floors of one. He talked to a man called Doyle, who had lodged in the same room for several nights with four women. 'I asked him,' said Stephen, 'whether or not he meant that he had merely slept in the same room or slept in the same bed, on which his expression was, and I must speak out on such an occasion as this, "I could not manage more than two of them, I was not man enough", and turned round to one of these young women, standing at his right hand, as much as to ask her, if that was not the case, at which she laughed, and assented.'[48]

Even when the runners, crimps, touts, man-catchers, Forty Thieves, boarding-house keepers, and sharks had done the emigrant all the damage they could in Liverpool, they had not finished. The same reporter of the *Morning Chronicle* who was so disgusted by the cellars and boarding houses of the city wrote this: 'Even after they have drained him as dry as they can, they are loth to part with him entirely, and they write out, per next steamer, a full, true, and particular account of him—his parish, his relations, his priest, and his estimated stock of money—to a similar gang in New York.'[49]

Before the emigrant could board his ship he was given a medical inspection by government doctors. This was a farce. No evidence was ever given that it was anything else. In 1851 a doctor who had made many Atlantic crossings in American ships from Liverpool wrote to the *New York Times* saying that sometimes a thousand emigrants a day were examined at Liverpool. They were required to show their tongues, but no other notice was taken of their filthy bodies, which might be full of ulcers, itch [probably scabies], smallpox and other disagreeable diseases.[50] His letter sounded angry, but in fact he was putting his case very mildly. Sabel, the lodging-house keeper, often saw the examinations and called them a regular farce. On Monday, which was the busiest day, sometimes more than a thousand emigrants gathered outside what was known as the Doctors' Shop, where two doctors were employed looking at people's tongues and stamping their tickets as fast as they could. It amounted to no inspection at all. 'They [the doctors] stand behind a little window, and when the people come before them they say, "Are you quite well? Show your tongue," and in the meantime their ticket is stamped.'[51] One Liverpool shipbroker said as many as 2,000 or 3,000 emigrants were sometimes passed in a day, and thought if there was to be an examination at all it might as well be done properly.[52] An emigrant of the winter of 1850 described his examination by the government doctor in this way: 'I passed before him for inspection. He said without drawing breath, "What's your name? Are you well? Hold out your tongue; all right," and then addressed himself to the next person.'[53]

Mutterings did reach the commissioners of emigration, that a stricter examination might prevent much of the disease which broke out on shipboard. The commissioners replied that they did not think so. They believed that the greater part of the disease was produced by the inevitable change of diet acting on frames depressed by seasickness, and, perhaps, by alarm.[54]

The descriptions of the medical examination by the commissioners' own officers and doctors damned it. It was useless. If a man could stand upright he was fit. Lieutenant Lean, emigration officer at London, which was nothing like as busy as Liverpool and where the whole process should have been more thorough, said the surgeon looked at people, saw they were in health, and passed them.

Opposite: Warning poster put up in Liverpool by the emigration commissioners, 1853. From Colonial Office Papers, C.O. 384/92; Public Record Office, London.

TO EMIGRANTS.

CHOLERA.

CHOLERA having made its appearance on board several Passenger Ships proceeding from the United Kingdom to the United States of America, and having, in some instances, been very fatal, Her Majesty's Colonial Land and Emigration Commissioners feel it their duty to recommend to the Parents of Families in which there are many young children, and to all persons in weak health who may be contemplating Emigration, to postpone their departure until a milder season. There can be no doubt that the sea sickness consequent on the rough weather which Ships must encounter at this season, joined to the cold and damp of a sea voyage, will render persons who are not strong more susceptible to the attacks of this disease.

To those who may Emigrate at this season the Commissioners strongly recommend that they should provide themselves with as much warm clothing as they can, and especially with flannel, to be worn next the Skin; that they should have both their clothes and their persons quite clean before embarking, and should be careful to keep them so during the voyage,—and that they should provide themselves with as much solid and wholesome food as they can procure, in addition to the Ship's allowance to be used on the voyage. It would, of course, be desirable, if they can arrange it, that they should not go in a Ship that is much crowded, or that is not provided with a Medical Man.

By Order of the Board,

S. WALCOTT,
SECRETRAY.

Colonial Land and Emigration Office,
8, Park Street, Westminster,
November, 1853.

He said the men were not stripped, but that the doctor could see whether they had got the itch or any complaint of that kind by looking at their hands. The greater number of emigrants he had seen passed by one doctor in an hour was 400, or perhaps rather more. When this statement was received with surprise, he said he had not meant to say an hour; such a number would take between two and three hours.

'You think that in between two and three hours you have seen a medical man inspect 400 persons?—Yes; when I speak of inspection, I mean he has seen that their general appearance is such that there can be no doubt about their being in perfect health.' He said a medical man was paid one pound for every hundred persons, and agreed that this was a profitable occupation.[55]

Lieutenant Hodder explained the routine at Liverpool.[56] Sometimes there were sixteen ships to clear in a day. This was 1851, and most of these ships would have been large American packets carrying up to 1,000 emigrants each. The government doctors had an office near the dockside. Hodder said there was no great difficulty. The doctors judged from appearance, looked at tongues and felt pulses; the emigrants went through one door and came out the other, and the doctors were kept going from morning till night. Morning was ten o'clock, when the doctors began, and night was three in the afternoon, when they stopped. By 1854 there were three medical officers at Liverpool, C. A. Holcombe, W. J. Gruggen, and J. J. Lancaster, all M.D., and all paid, by that time, not £1 a hundred, but a fixed salary of £400 a year. This was nearly twice as much as the assistant emigration officers, who had an impossible job and worked all hours, and about £100 more than the chief emigration officer.

Dr. Lancaster described the inspections in his own words:[57]

'For what causes do you reject them?—Only for infectious disorders, such as typhus fever, and the ordinary eruptive diseases of childhood, and ophthalmia.

'Do you strip those persons you examine?—No; it is merely the same sort of inspection as that to which the troops and convicts are subjected; those in Millbank [a London military hospital] are drawn up in the prison-yard or wards; the medical man walks before them and looks at each individual, and if he sees anyone who looks disposed to sickness he looks at his tongue and feels his pulse . . .

'Do you reject for consumption?—No; it is not an infectious disease.'

Lancaster then went on to describe the way the emigrants got on board. It was not as simple as walking up a gangplank. It was a scramble. He said he did not mean it was any fault of the captains, but often they would not allow the passengers to go aboard until the last minute.

'In consequence of which we sometimes have dreadful scenes; sometimes the passengers have to watch their opportunity, and when the ship gets near the entrance to the dock you may see men, women, and children clambering up the sides of the ship.' Frequently people fell into the water and occasionally they drowned. This was all because the captains did not want passengers on board until the cargo was finally stowed in the hold.

'And then he [the captain] proceeds to move his vessel out of the dock before the people have time to get onboard?—Very often when she gets to the entrance to the dock where it is very narrow, she is detained there for a short time while other vessels are going out, and during that time the passengers are scrambling in; and I have seen 500 or 600 men, women, and children in a state of the greatest confusion, and their screams are fearful; on several occasions I have gone down and attempted to get on board, but I found it to be quite out of the question. . . .'

A passenger who had to climb on board one of the newest and largest of the American packets complained that there was no regularity or decency about the embarkation: 'Men and women were pulled in any side or end foremost, like so many bundles. I was getting myself in as quickly and dextrously as I could, when I was laid hold of by the legs and pulled in, falling head foremost down upon the deck, and the next man was pulled down upon the top of me. I was some minutes before I recovered my hat, which was crushed as flat as a pancake. The porters, in their treatment of the passengers, naturally look only to getting as much money as they possibly can from them in the shortest space of time, and heap upon them all kinds of filthy and blasphemous abuse, there being no police regulations, and the officers of the ship taking the lead in the ill-treatment of passengers.'[58]

Liverpool was so crowded that getting on board any ship, let alone an emigrant packet, was likely to be dangerous. A cabin passenger who went by Cunard steamer to Halifax, and was put on board the steamer from a small tender in a foggy river, said this was more dangerous than the whole voyage across the Atlantic. The tender was small and overcrowded, and was run down in the Mersey.

Her mast and cordage fell across the confused mass of baggage, some of which was broken in pieces and some lost overboard. And even to Cunard cabin passengers, Liverpool was rough enough. The night before he sailed he went to the office to collect his ticket and 'experienced such treatment as might be expected by a pauper emigrant who went to seek an eleemosynary passage'. He paid £25, the highest fare, for what was described as an excellent berth, but found it was nothing of the sort, and got wet every time he left his cabin to go to the saloon to eat.[59]

If you looked hard in Liverpool you could find uplifting scenes. Melville found it exalting to listen to the singing of some German emigrants, who had apparently been allowed on early, and were singing as their American ship lay in dock. Their fine ringing anthems reverberated among the crowded shipping and rebounded from the lofty walls of the docks; if you shut your eyes you could have thought yourself in a cathedral.[60]

Most emigrants would have thought themselves in no such place. Certainly not those who failed in the scramble to get on board as their ship left dock, and then had to hire a rowing boat to take them down the Mersey to catch up, which the boatmen would not do for less than half a sovereign.[61]

An American reporter described the fuss as one of the largest packets cleared Liverpool bound for Boston. The deck was thronged by steerage passengers.[62] 'Unlettered and inexperienced, everything seems dreamlike to their senses—the hauling of blocks and ropes, the cries of busy seamen as they heave round the capstan, the hoarse orders of the officers, the strange bustle below and aloft, the rise and expansion of the huge masses of canvas that wing their floating home, and will soon cover it with piled up clouds. Here are women with swollen eyes, who have just parted with near and dear ones; perhaps never to meet again; mothers seeking to hush their wailing babes. In one place an aged woman, who has nearly reached the extreme term of life, sits listless and sad, scarcely conscious of the bustle and confusion around her. She lives not in the present, but in the past. Her days of hope are over; she is almost done with the world, and yet clings with tenacity to a life of which the charms are gone. The voyage across the Atlantic is another dreary chapter of an existence made up of periods of strife with hard adversities. . . .'

An account in a London newspaper was more factual.[63] The American packet *Star of the West*, 1,200 tons, Captain Lowber, a new ship on her first voyage, left Waterloo dock at 8.30 one morning in

July 1850 with 385 passengers. Either she was half empty, which was unlikely in 1850, or she was carrying a heavy cargo as well as the emigrants. In the river the cook refused to sail, and a coloured steward leaped overboard and swam back to shore. In mid-river the ship dropped anchor to send back to Liverpool the orange girls, cap merchants, and dealers in Everton toffee, ribbons, laces, pocket mirrors, gingerbread nuts, and sweetmeats—nearly forty men and women in all—who had pushed their way on with the emigrants at the dock.

Then there was the roll-call for stowaways. Each passenger's name was called and he had to show his ticket. The mates did this in rhyming chant:

> Paddy Bile [Boyle]
> Come here awhile.
>
> Joseph Brown
> Come down.
>
> William Jones
> Show your bones.

Sometimes as many as a dozen stowaways were found.[64] The captain, or more likely one of the mates, together with the passenger broker's clerk and some of the crew, went below with lanterns and rummaged around with long poles, chisels, and hammers, breaking open suspicious-looking barrels. Occasionally the pole was tipped with a sharp nail to poke into dark corners. The men with hammers hammered the piles of bedclothes. If a stowaway was suspected to be in a barrel, he was assumed to have hidden himself head uppermost and the barrel was turned upside down. If a man was inside, he generally revealed himself after two or three minutes. Some of those discovered in the search contrived, after lamentations and protests that they had no money, to pay their fares with coins 'not infrequently found to be safely stitched amid the rags of petticoats, coats, and unmentionable garments'. Anyone who survived this search and was only found after two or three days out was liable to be tarred and feathered, and made to work his passage.

Hodder[65] said three or four people had died after stowing away in chests. 'There was a box, I believe, of three feet and a half, into which there was a rather large woman and a man crammed; how they existed there I do not know. They came out much exhausted, but they were alive.' He thought it was done by runners, who said they would get emigrants a cheap passage, and then put them into barrels or boxes.

It was imagined, by those who stayed behind and wrote verses about it, that emigration was, of course, both joyful and sad. It was sad, naturally, because it was the last of England.

> Farewell, England! Blessings on thee—
> Stern and niggard as thou art.
> Harshly, mother, hast thou used me,
> And my bread thou hast refused me,
> But 'tis agony to part.[66]

But it was joyful, also naturally, because those who left were carrying on God's work.

> Friends stood upon the shore in grief,
> And watched the bark dissolve and fade;
> And whom it bore, in their belief,
> Were lost to sight in endless shade.
>
> What think ye in that bark meanwhile,
> Chanced with the adventurous spirits there?
> Hope, joy, and triumph, jest and smile
> Laughter and mirth their voyage cheer!
>
> They scorn the pauper left behind,
> His scanty diet pining o'er;
> And feel themselves for sway design'd,
> Once landed on that other shore.[67]

They were probably just beginning to feel seasick. But the poet, in subsequent stanzas, went on developing an ingenious argument that to emigrate was really like going to heaven, and going to heaven was just like emigrating. When the body died the soul really just put off to angel-land in a Ship of Souls.

But if there was any joy, and spectators were often struck that there was no conspicuous sorrow, it was likely to have been for another reason. An Irish gentleman, watching Irish emigrants leave, said they were all in the most uproarious spirits. There was no crying or lamentation. All was delight at having escaped the deadly work-house.[68] An English reporter, watching another ship, said, 'What seemed most singular, there was nothing like sorrow or regret at leaving England. There was not a wet eye on board—there had been no fond leave-taking, no farewells to England, no pangs of parting.'[69]

6

Hard-driven Ships and Brutal Crews

Convict ships were at least second-class vessels, and much better than emigrant ships, which might be taken from any class or in fact from no class at all.[1] This at least was the view of an emigration officer at an Irish port, and it was probably strictly correct. Second class meant second class at Lloyd's. In 1851 there were three classes. Second-class vessels were 'unfit for carrying *dry* cargoes, but perfectly fit for the conveyance, *on any voyage*, of cargoes not in their nature subject to sea damage'. Third-class vessels were good for short voyages only, and not out of Europe.[2] It was in vessels good for short voyages only, or in vessels not considered by Lloyd's good enough for that even, that most emigrants embarking direct from Irish ports would have sailed across the Atlantic. The emigration officer's opinion probably held good for the smaller English vessels sailing from English ports as well, and this is not surprising, since these were private vessels and given only the most cursory survey, whereas convict vessels were chartered by the government. But the officer's view was certainly not true of the large American packets, and it was in these ships, after 1847, that by far the greatest number of emigrants sailed from Liverpool. Still, even the largest ships would not have been pleasant to sail in.

An emigrants' manual of 1851 told its readers they would be as entirely captive in their vessel as Africans in a slave ship, that the emigrant ship was a scarcely less horrible den for filth, foul air, and corrupt food, and that the slaver had a greater money interest in keeping his cargo alive.[3] A magazine article of 1853 said there seemed to be as little limit to the stowage of an emigrant ship as to that of the pit of a theatre: no money being returned in either case, you were left to survive the squeeze as best you might.[4] A journalist who went daily on board emigrant ships in Liverpool said he never saw a life-boat ready for clearing. They were always filled with lumber.[5]

This does not sound like the advertisements in Liverpool news-papers and on Liverpool walls. It does not sound like the Black Ball Line's description of 'the celebrated, fast-sailing, favourite American Packet ship *Montezuma* [1,100 tons]. Persons proceeding to the United States are particularly requested to inspect the various accommodations of this "floating palace".'[6] The advertisements of the biggest emigrant agents in Liverpool also gave their own ships good references. Harnden and Co. said all their ships were fast sailers, coppered and copper-fastened, departing punctually, and commanded by men of experience, who paid special attention to emigrants, protecting them from all fraud and imposition.[7] Tap-scott's said the twenty-five American packets they advertised were of the largest class, commanded by men who would take every pre-caution to promote the health and comfort of passengers during the voyage.[8] P. W. Byrnes and Co., of Liverpool, New York, and New Orleans, went further, saying its vessels were commanded by gentlemen, and referring 'with much satisfaction to the fact, as proving the superiority of the Ships, that out of upward of 30,000 Souls who have sailed during the last year [1850] from this Establish-ment, *not a single Life was lost* from Dangers of the sea'. A second advertisement by the same house in the same column of the same newspaper went further still, saying that Byrnes's, as the oldest established and most extensive house in the trade, could confidently assert that 'of the Hundreds of Thousands forwarded by them during the last QUARTER OF A CENTURY, not one has had any just cause of complaint'.[9]

This was far-fetched. The emigrant would have been very sensible to keep well away from any ship offered by Tapscott's, Harnden's, or Byrnes's, but he would not know that until too late.

But some ships were very fine, and not only their owners or agents said so. Nathaniel Hawthorne, as consul, became very critical of the emigrant trade. Nevertheless, he did write approvingly in his journal about some of the ships. In 1854 he was at a dinner on board the

James Baine, a new vessel built by Donald McKay of Boston. The passengers' berths had not yet been erected, and there was room for four or five hundred guests, principally Liverpool merchants and their wives, to sit down to dinner at tables spread between decks. The next year he had to go on board an American vessel in the Mersey to take depositions about a death on board. He wrote:

'There is no such finery on land, as in the cabin of one of these ships in the Liverpool trade, finished off with a complete panelling of rosewood, mahogany and bird's eye maple, polished and varnished, and gilded along the cornices and the edges of the panels. It is all a piece of elaborate cabinet-work; and one does not altogether see why it should be given to the gales, and the salt-sea atmosphere, to be tossed upon the waves, and occupied by a rude shipmaster, in his dreadnought clothes, when the finest lady in the land has no such boudoir.'[10]

How is it possible to reconcile this great difference between ships worse than slavers with lumber in their lifeboats, and floating palaces with gilded cabinets? The first distinction to make is between British and American vessels. British ships were usually smaller, and not specially built for the emigrant trade. *Chambers's Edinburgh Journal* said many were in the timber or general import trade, and seemed to export emigrants pretty much as a kind of ballast. 'In short, the emigration business is with them only a secondary or incidental consideration, not that primary object which, in a right system it ought to be.'[11] The vessels had a choice of sailing to North America empty to pick up their timber, or of taking emigrants on the way over, and emigrants, though they were a nuisance, paid fares. Robert Bunch, British vice-consul in New York, said the same: British vessels were not built for emigrants at all, but were large cargo ships.[12]

But American vessels were built expressly for passengers. John Bramley Moore, Mayor of Liverpool, said that though the American vessels would bring back to Britain anything they could get, they were constructed with the whole idea of taking emigrants and had found that to be the most profitable carrying trade.[13] Captain Charles Patey, R.N., emigration officer at Glasgow and Greenock, agreed that the great mass of the habitual passenger trade was in the hands of the Americans, and that they sailed much finer ships than the British.[14] Thomas Murdoch, chairman of the British Emigration Commissioners, said the Americans did have much the finer vessels, very much the largest, very high between decks, sometimes as much as eight or nine feet, and much better arranged than British vessels.[15]

Most of these vessels were Atlantic packets, and the packet was entirely an American vessel. The British merchant marine never made any real attempt to compete in this trade on the Atlantic. A packet is not any particular kind of vessel. She is just a liner, in the sense that she sails regularly between the same ports and to a regular timetable.[16] The first of the Atlantic packet lines was the Black Ball which began in 1818 to sail from New York to Liverpool, with passengers and mail, and fine freight. By 1849 several lines were sailing into Liverpool, all American. There was the Black Ball, sometimes called the Old Line because it was the oldest; the Red Star; the Blue Swallowtail; and the Dramatic, whose ships bore names like the *Garrick*, the *Siddons*, and the *Roscius*. All these were out of New York. Then there was Enoch Train's line from Boston. Apart from these, there were other lines, like the Black Star, which called themselves packet lines, but really sailed whenever they had a charter, or a shipful.

Packets were big business, and their owners were rich men. Among the packet owners of the late 1840s were Henry Grinnell, Robert Bowne Minturn, Edward Knight Collins, and Enoch Train. Henry Grinnell (1799–1874) was born into the shipping business. In the early 1830s he married Sarah, sister of R. B. Minturn, and Grinnell, Minturn and Co. became one of the strongest shipping and mercantile firms in New York. They ran the Blue and Red Swallowtail Lines, the Blue sailing to Liverpool and the Red to London. By 1846 Minturn was said to be worth at least $200,000, and by 1851 owned shares in the following packets: a quarter-share in the *New World*; with Moses Grinnell, half of the *Patrick Henry*; and with two partners, Henry and Moses Grinnell, seven-eighths of the *Constitution* and ten-sixteenths of the *Queen of the West*. E. K. Collins (1802–1878) had a more adventurous career than most, and eventually failed. His family had come over from Ireland as early as 1634. When he was fifteen he went to New York and became clerk in a shipping firm. In 1836 he started the Dramatic Line to Liverpool, and in 1848 the United States Mail Steamship Company, generally known as the Collins Line. His four paddle steamers were of 2,800 tons, bigger and faster than Cunard's, and he was given a Congressional subsidy of $858,000 a year. One of his four original steamers, the *Arctic*, was lost in 1854. The next year he launched the *Adriatic*, which was even bigger, 4,114 tons. But in 1856 the *Pacific*, another of the original four, disappeared, his subsidy was withdrawn, and two years later his ships were sold to pay creditors. Enoch Train (1801–1868) made his fortune in the Baltic and South American trades, and then in 1844 established his line of packets between Boston and Liverpool. This was generally known as the White Diamond Line from the diamond design on the house flag, and his ships also carried a large 'T' on their foretopsails.[17]

The Atlantic packets were the largest sailing ships of their day. A single vessel would cost the entire fortune of a very rich man. When the *Garrick* ran ashore in 1842 her insurance value was estimated at $70,000. By 1848–52 the average value of a packet was $80,000, and a big packet was worth about $100,000.

The American ships were better constructed, more ably commanded, and kept to their sailing dates: this built them a reputation and a monopoly. In a modern phrase they would be called passenger and cargo liners. Eastward from New York they sailed light, perhaps with a cargo of cotton, or corn, and a few passengers. Westward from Liverpool they were fully loaded, with many more passengers, and with iron, coal, salt, machinery, and manufactured goods. At first many of the passengers were prosperous enough to go in the cabin, aft of the mainmast. After 1840 two things began to happen. The cabin passengers began to prefer the steamships, which were much faster, and many more poor emigrants wanted steerage passages in the 'tween decks. West-bound packets began to carry less cargo, and many more people, who paid better than cargo. By 1850 the packets had become almost entirely emigrant ships, and new packets were particularly built for that trade.

Though the word packet does not describe a type of ship, a type did evolve, and the packet and the clipper became the best known kinds of American vessels. There was nothing to stop an Atlantic packet being a clipper, but she rarely was. Both clipper and packet were full-rigged ships, that is to say vessels with three masts, square-rigged. By the early 1850s the clipper had much influenced the design of the packet, but no extreme clipper was ever successful in the packet service. Clippers were too sharp-built and too loftily sparred for the North Atlantic. They were built for speed, but their sharp bows, made to cleave through the water, were also apt to cleave under it. Clippers shipped water. They were wet vessels, and too easily strained by the buffeting of the North Atlantic. The packet became typically more rounded in the bow, and more buoyant and dry. The characteristic packet bow was apple-cheeked, with a convex bulge rather than the slender taper of the clipper. The packets were given stouter hulls, and more room for passengers and cargo. Their masts were lower than the clippers', and they carried less canvas. Their absolute speed was deliberately reduced by this design, but in fact, because they rode the Atlantic weather more easily, they were, over a voyage, faster than clippers on that route. The clipper attracted the legends and the painters of ships' portraits. The packets more often made a profit.

To get a close idea of the kind of vessel a packet was, it is best to take two examples, both ships which were well known in the trade, the *Yorkshire* and the *Washington*.

The *Yorkshire* was launched in 1843 and became the crack ship of the old Black Ball Line, which also owned the floating palace of the *Montezuma*. A newspaper advertisement[18] of 1847 said the *Yorkshire* was, on all hands, allowed to be the finest and fastest of the numerous New York–Liverpool packets, and that her commander, Captain Bailey, had invariably made remarkably quick passages and secured a lasting reputation for his kindness and attention to passengers. This was the truth. The *Yorkshire* was the fastest vessel ever built on packet lines. In 1846 she sailed to America in sixteen days. On November 2 she left Liverpool, was off Sandy Hook on November 17, and in her dock at New York by noon on the 18th. This was the fastest west-bound passage ever made by a sailing ship of any kind. Between 1844 and 1862 her average time westbound was twenty-nine days. The clipper packet *Phoenix*, of New York, built for the Red Star Line, and built for speed, and a much bigger vessel (1,487 tons), took on average two days longer westbound than the *Yorkshire*, and her best passage was twenty-six days, ten days longer than the *Yorkshire*. The *Yorkshire*'s career ended in 1862 when she left New York for Liverpool and was never seen again. It was thought she struck an iceberg. Probably no ship in the packet trade ever earned more.[19]

She was the greatest of all the packets. A more typical emigrant ship was the *Washington*. She sailed for the Black Star Line, not to be confused with the Black Ball. Black Star did not run a packet line in the strict sense. Its ships sailed when they could, or when they were full. The several other lines carried thousands of emigrants, but had not started in the emigrant trade. From the beginning, Black Star's whole business was emigrants. This does not mean that some of its vessels were not very fine. They were, and the *Washington* was one of them. She was launched in New York in 1849, and was of 1,655 tons, compared with the *Yorkshire*'s 996. She was 205 feet 6 inches in length compared with the *Yorkshire*'s 166 feet 6 inches, and 41 feet in the beam as against 36 feet. The ships were growing to meet the trade. The *Washington* carried 1,000 steerage passengers at times. In 1850 the Black Star Line was circulating handbills in Liverpool. These bills listed eighteen ships in all, and said: 'They are all first class ships, *nearly all new*, built of the very best materials, and are remarkably fast sailers. Their commanders are men of experience and nautical judgment, and are well acquainted with the trade . . . The second cabin and steerages are lofty and airy, and are in every way adapted to promote the comfort and health of passengers.'[20] The *Washington* later got an evil reputation. In 1853 she put into New York, having lost ninety-four passengers from cholera on the voyage, and with another sixty-two ill on board. Three years before that her captain and crew were accused, with every appearance of truth, of great and unnecessary brutality. But, still, she was a fine ship.

By the late 1840s the Americans were carrying more than twice as many emigrants as English and Irish ships put together: in 1849, 134,657 passengers entered New York in 594 American vessels as against 62,403 in 371 British ships.[21] If the proportion of British ships seems higher than might be expected, it must be remembered that the British ships would have been much smaller. According to these figures, each American ship carried 227 passengers and each British ship 168, but the figures are for all vessels, including steamships, which carried only a few cabin passengers, and cargo vessels with occasional passengers on board, and so give no real idea of the average number of passengers in an emigrant vessel.

After 1850 the proportion of American ships in the trade grew even higher. In 1850, 568 different vessels sailed with steerage emigrants from British ports where there were emigration officers to record them, that is to say, from all the large ports. Of these, 182 were British and 386 foreign.[22] By 1853, although emigration as a whole had declined, and only 405 vessels were engaged in the trade, there were then 360 American vessels to 43 British, and two of other nationalities.[23] Vessels got bigger throughout the period too. In 1847 a London ship agent who had been in the business for years was saying that the average emigrant vessel was about 500 tons, that they varied from 300 to 800 tons, and that 300 was quite the smallest ship proper for emigration.[24] By 1851 few of the ships advertised in Liverpool newspapers admitted to being less than 1,200 tons register. But this is misleading. This was Liverpool, and it was from there that the largest ships sailed. There were many smaller vessels at the smaller ports. And of the Liverpool ships, those advertised were the best and biggest. It was a device of agents to book passengers for one such ship and then transfer them to older, smaller, unadvertised vessels. There was some confusion what the tonnage meant: was it tons register or tons burden? Of the Black Star ships, the *Lady Franklin* was 1,374 tons register, and 2,300 burden, and the *Kate Hunter* 731 and 1,279. The register tonnage approaches nearest to a modern figure. Most of all, the advertisements were misleading because they were meant to be. Tapscott's and Byrnes's were best at this. In one advertisement Tapscott offers twenty-two ships for New York, nineteen of 2,000 tons and more. Byrnes's, in a list of six to sail for New York, have nothing under 2,000, and three vessels of 3,000 tons: if these vessels had been what the agents said, they would have been by far the largest sailing ships in the world for their day. But the figures can be checked. The *Constitution*, Captain Britton, which is 1,600 tons in an advertisement by an agent called Rippard, achieves in a Tapscott advertisement a Tapscott tonnage of 3,000. She was really of 1,327 tons. The *Winfield Scott*, Captain Glidden, 1,240 tons in an advertisement by a small agent, becomes 3,000 tons in a Byrnes advertisement on the same day on the same page of the same newspaper.[25]

The average American vessel was probably of about 1,000 tons, and a good ship. She may have looked like a palace in dock, or at least the captain's cabin and the cabin passengers' saloon may have looked like pieces of a palace, but by the time anything up to 1,000 emigrants had been packed into the steerage she began to look more like a slaver. With a humane captain and a competent crew the voyage might still be tolerable. But it was not certain how often captain and crew were humane and competent.

American ships were known to be better than British ships, and not only that, it was the general opinion, even in England, that American shipmasters were better too. The emigration officer at Greenock said he never had any trouble with American ships, whose captains never resisted his authority; his trouble was with British ships. The American captains were 'a much better class of men' than British masters.[26] Robert Bunch, British vice-consul in New York, talking about the ill-treatment of passengers on board ship, said he did not see how any law could prevent it. If the captain of the vessel was a bully and a tyrant he could not help bullying and tyrannising, but Bunch thought that, taking the run of American captains, they were an exceedingly decent and good class of men. They were almost always part owners of their ships, which the British masters were not.

And American insurance offices, before they would insure a vessel, wanted to know the character of a captain. 'They know all about him, his history, where he comes from, and what his habits are; and they will not insure a vessel, except at a very high premium, unless they are satisfied that the captain is a decent man.' The result of all this was, in Bunch's opinion, that the American captains were certainly very much superior.[27] They also had flair. They had the reputation that at the hour of sailing, if the wind served at all, they would set all plain sail at the pier, lay their vessels flat aback, drive stern first into the stream, and then, while the spectators shouted themselves hoarse, send their ships rippling down to sea. It does not matter that this is probably legend, and that most captains towed out into the river and anchored. They had the *reputation* of flair.

Seventeen American captains out of Liverpool were even concerned enough about their passengers to send a petition in 1850 to Lord Grey, the Colonial Secretary, saying that a government depot for emigrants at Birkenhead would save a lot of hardship in embarking emigrants. Captains C. Knight of the *New World*, D. S. Shearman of the *Yorkshire*, T. B. Cropper of the *Isaac Webb*, and J. W. Russell of the *Empire State* signed, along with thirteen others.[28]

Nathaniel Hawthorne wrote in his journal after the death of one captain he had known: 'I have seldom been more affected by anything quite alien from my personal and friendly concerns. He was a sensitive man—a gentleman, courteous, quiet, with something almost melancholy in his address and aspect.' This was about Captain Luce, who went down with his ship, the *Arctic*, in 1854.[29] The *Arctic* was a steam packet, one of the Collins Line, and her master was likely to be distinguished in his profession, but Hawthorne also had a high opinion of four other masters he met at Mrs. Blodgett's boarding house in Liverpool. He said they were alive and talked of real matters, and matters which they knew. They were favourable specimens of their class, being all respectable men, in the employ of good shipping houses, and raised by their capacity to the command of first-rate ships. In his official duties he did not usually see the best side of ships' masters, as they seldom came before him except to complain or be complained against. But when, at Mrs. Blodgett's, he heard their daily talk, and listened to what was in their mind, and heard their reminiscences of what they had been through, then he found that they were men of energy and ability, fit to be trusted, retaining a hardy sense of honour and loyalty to their own country, which was the stronger because they had compared their own country with many others. 'Most of them are gentlemen, too, to a certain extent;—some more than others, perhaps;—and none to a very exquisite point;—or, if so, it is none the better for them, as sailors or as men.'[30]

Some of the common sailors were given a character at least as good. One American surgeon, who was telling a U.S. Senate Committee that sailors ought to be allowed to mix with virtuous women on board so that their seeming rudeness might be tempered with gentleness and delicacy, said that American sailors were not ferocious but humane, chivalrous, and generous. In shipwrecks they perished themselves sooner than let a woman drown. They made it a point of honour to be the last to leave a ship in flames or going to pieces on the rocks. They were never disobedient to orders when the tempest howled and danger threatened. 'It is not from fear of punishment that they are true to their profession under such appalling circumstances, but from a deeper principle radicated in that moral virtue which none knows so well as the American mother to instil into the human heart.'[31]

A tract published in London had no such faith in the ability of English mothers to produce tame sailors, but put its faith rather in God, and advised sailors to think of life as a voyage. At the end of that voyage, whether it was long or short, they would either find themselves in a country of great fertility, beauty, happiness, and holiness; or else they would be landed in a howling wilderness. So they should set their sails into the stream of life. For this they would need a chart. 'My friends, that chart is the Bible.' The tract went on to practicalities. They should not get drunk, because they might fall overboard if they did. They should not entice young women emigrants into the paths of sin. They should think of their own parents and sisters at home, and of the dishonour that seduction would bring to their own country, and of 'the harm done to the colonies'. Even should the women on board be so lost to virtue and delicacy as to seek the sailors' notice, the men should be firm, so that this firmness in repelling their advances might recall the women to a sense of their duty and save them from further infamy and degradation.[32] It was not until 1860 that the U.S. Congress passed an act 'for the better protection of female passengers', which provided that any officer or seaman of an American vessel who seduced a passenger under the promise of marriage, or by threats, or by solicitation, or by the making of gifts or presents, was liable, unless willing to marry the girl, to one year's imprisonment or a fine of not more than $1,000.[33]

There was very little explicit evidence to the various committees of enquiry into emigrant ships to suggest that the crews were not competent, or the vessels not adequately manned. But there were a few hints. It was strange that a shipbroker should say that passengers liked to help work the ship: if there had been enough crew the emigrants would only have got in the way and would not have been encouraged to help. But were some members of the crew sailors at all? In 1854 the chairman of the emigration commissioners was asked this, and said one of the emigration officers at Liverpool had been in the habit, when he doubted if a man was a seaman or not, of making him go aloft. But this was only in ships chartered by the commissioners to go to Australia. When he was asked whether this was also done in private ships, that is in those going to America, and whether it would not be best for the inspecting officer to demand to see the loosing and furling of sails to decide whether the men signed on as crew really were sailors, not merely men with blue jackets on, the witness said he did not know whether this was possible.[34] This meant no. There is no account of this ever being done, and the inspecting officers were already overworked. Another emigration officer said he would not allow men to be included in the crew where they were put down at the nominal pay of a shilling a month and were going really to work their passage and do as little as possible, but he did not say whether he did more than look at the roll of names and wages.[35]

There is no doubt at all that many sailors, Americans among them, were so ill-instructed by their mothers that they were brutal to passengers. A surgeon said he had seen frequent beatings. He had seen passengers kicked from sheer wantonness, without provocation, and deluged with water from a firehose on a cold, piercing night in the St. Lawrence, by sailors almost in a state of mutiny.[36] William Fitzhugh, a Liverpool passenger broker who had spent all his life in the emigrant trade, and acted for the Black Star Line, said: '. . . ours is one of the worst trades in the world for seamen, we get very bad sailors indeed; in fact, we get a class of men who go more to pilfer from the steerage passengers than for the purpose of going to sea.'[37]

Hawthorne, as consul, reported back to Washington the trial and sentence of a man called Campbell, an American citizen but by birth an Irishman, who was sent to transportation for life for shooting and wounding James Christie, a coloured seaman, on board the American ship *James L. Bogart*.[38] The ship had taken on a coloured crew at

Liverpool, where Campbell was also taken on as second mate. Hawthorne said that as usual the crew were not on board when the vessel left dock, and when they were got on board, in the river, were mostly drunk. Two refused to go on board at all, and to fill their places Christie and another were inveigled on board on a Sunday by a shipping agent under the pretence that the *Bogart* was an English vessel going to Antigua. When they discovered the truth they refused to work, but were compelled by the mates. Early on Monday, Hawthorne heard that one of the crew had been shot and the chief mate badly wounded. He sent police to the ship, and the crew were charged with mutiny and Campbell with shooting Christie. The Birkenhead magistrates dismissed the charge of mutiny, saying it did not come within their jurisdiction, but sent Campbell for trial for shooting Christie. At the trial the evidence of the pilot and others showed that from the time the vessel anchored in the river the crew had been driven to work and attacked by the mates with pistols and other weapons. Hawthorne said the severity of Campbell's punishment would have a salutary effect in staying the acts of violence common on board vessels. Campbell was well known for his brutality in previous vessels. On board the ship on which he came to Liverpool a man had been found hanging dead in the forecastle, in circumstances so suspicious that Hawthorne demanded Campbell's surrender on a charge of murder. He was arrested, the evidence proved gross cruelty, but the magistrates did not consider it was enough to commit him for trial, and discharged him.

Hawthorne came to have the lowest possible opinion of seamen on American ships out of Liverpool. In September 1853, less than two months after his appointment, an American captain came to him to say he had shot a seaman who had attacked him on board ship. In Hawthorne's opinion this was little short of murder, if at all, but then, he said, what would be murder on shore was almost a natural occurrence in such a hell on earth as one of those ships in the first hours of her voyage. The men would be all drunk, some of them in delirium tremens, and the captain felt no safety for his life except in making himself as terrible as a fiend: it was the universal testimony that there was a worse set of sailors between Liverpool and America than in any other trade whatever.[39] Two years later he wrote: 'I am sick to death of my office;—brutal captains and brutish sailors,—continual complaints of mutual wrong, which I have no power to put right, and which, indeed, seem to have no right on either side. . . .'[40]

He sent frequent despatches to Washington about this brutality.

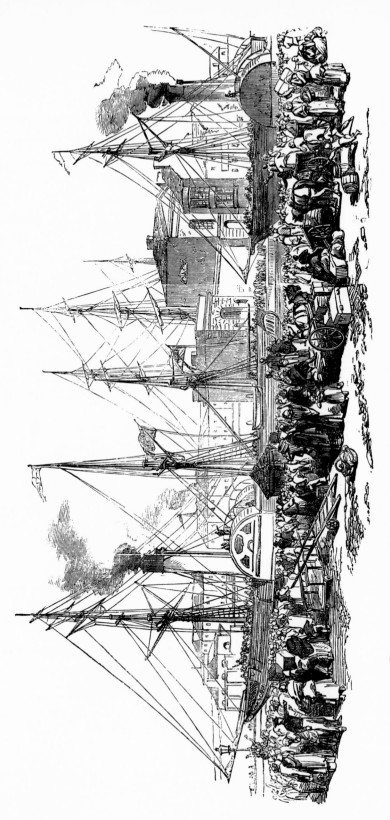

Departure in 1851 of the *Nimrod* and *Athlone* steamers from Cork for Liverpool, where their passengers embarked on sailing packets for the transatlantic voyage. As many as 1,000 emigrants crowded on the open deck of the Irish steamers for the 36—hour passage.

The parish priest blesses emigrants as they leave
home in 1851 to walk to the emigration port.

Emigrants on the quay at Cork, waiting to embark, 1851.

A scalpeen at Kilrush, made from bits
of timber and thatch salvaged from
a tumbled cottage, 1849.

Brigid O'Donnell and children, after
being evicted from their cottage at
Kilrush in 1849. December 22, 1849.

What the emigrant was leaving behind:
a Dorsetshire labourer's cottage, 1846.

The grandeur of Lime Street, Liverpool, in the mid-1850s.

Waterloo Dock, Liverpool, where many packets sailed from.

Emigrants embarking on an American packet at
Waterloo Docks, Liverpool, 1850.

Irish emigrant reading wall posters
at Dublin, c.1855.

The medical officers' office at Liverpool, 1850. The inspection
was a farce. Emigrants went in through one door and out by
another. As many as 3,000 were examined by three doctors
in a day.

Emigrant sailing packet about to be towed
out into the Mersey, 1850.

Departure from Home, 1858,
a plagiarized American version
of a famous English picture,
Eastward Ho! See note on page 9.

The Black Ball line packet *Isaac Webb,*
1,300 tons, a typical large emigrant ship
on the Liverpool–New York run, 1851.

The steerage where, on an average packet, 700 or so emigrants
would be herded together for thirty-five days or more.

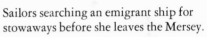

Sailors searching an emigrant ship for
stowaways before she leaves the Mersey.

Emigrants on board the American ship
Cambridge, 1844, drawn by one of their
fellow passengers.

Sailors on board the *Cambridge.*

Dennis O'Brien, Irish emigrant on
board the *Cambridge.*

Emigrants dancing between decks, 1850.

The Yankee captain of the *Cambridge*.

The Train packet *Ocean Monarch,*
1,300 tons, which burned in the Mersey
in August 1848 with the loss of 176 lives.

Wreck of the brig *Charles Bartlett*,
run down by the Cunard steamship *Europa*
in 1848, with the loss of 134 lives.

A Train packet loaded with emigrants
speaking a Collins steamer, 1855.

A cartoon of 1855.
MAN IN WATER: Help, help, or I perish.
ONE OF CREW IN BOAT: Row on Jem, neve
mind him; he's only a passenger.

In September 1855 he had trouble with the ship *Cultivator*, on which
one man had stabbed another. When she returned to New York, the
newspapers there carried reports of more brutality on board her.
These reports were reprinted in English newspapers, and to make his
point Hawthorne took one cutting and sent it off to Washington
with a covering despatch. The report, from the *New York Evening
Post*, said that when the *Cultivator* docked in the city the appearance of
her sailors was shocking.[41] One sailor had been singing the Bowline,
and put in the words 'The captain is growling', whereupon the third
mate knocked him senseless with a bucket, and the second mate fell
on him and pounded him with another bucket. He had been knocked
down and whipped about every day since they left Liverpool.
Patrick McCoy, an Irishman, aged twenty-one, said the second mate
hit him on the head with steel knuckles, and then, some days afterwards, hit him on the head with a weapon called a crown-cracker—
he could not say how many times—and nearly knocked him overboard. John Johnson was so lame from continual beatings that he
could hardly walk, and was covered in sores and bruises. He said the
first mate often hit him with a belaying pin. 'I don't know how many
times I must have been knocked down and mauled; and my coat was
almost cut off me with a dirk.' William Smith said: 'It was nothing
but knock down and knock down and maul with that fellow; and
none of the men could look at one of those officers without getting
knocked down. I have been eight years on the sea, and I never saw
such rascality in my life.' William Thomas said: 'Two days before
we came in—that is, on Saturday—the first mate ordered John
Johnson to be taken forward to shave his whiskers and disfigure
him. I was ordered to get grease and slush him down till the mate
shaved him. I dare not do any other way, or have it done to me.
Then he sent the boy Jim to get a bucket of tar. While I slushed him
down with grease, the mate shaved all the whiskers off his left side
and part off his right, but left some on the right. He then ordered me
to run tar on the whiskers that were left, and I took and covered
them over with tar.'

In an earlier despatch that year, reporting the death of yet another
American seaman, Hawthorne said that he again earnestly called the
Secretary of State's attention to the evils arising from a system
under which American citizens were stolen and expatriated from
their country and put on board vessels to do duties they knew
nothing of.[42] Another time he sent to Washington papers from the
Liverpool Society of Friends of Foreigners in Distress which said

that some American sailors had been carried on board by force or stratagem, leaving behind parents, wives, and children. Of those destitute sailors the society had lately seen in Liverpool, only thirty-seven had shipped of their own accord, and sixty-nine had been brought over against their will. It would have been difficult for any of these men to pass themselves off as sailors even if they had wanted to. On the *Ocean Monarch* men had been forced to draw with their teeth iron nails driven into the deck, for that purpose, to a depth of two inches. They had been compelled to lick up the dust from the cabin floor.[43]

No notice was taken of anything Hawthorne sent, or wrote himself. In one of his last despatches to Washington before he left Liverpool[44] he went further than he had ever done before, and urged the Secretary of State, Lewis Cass, to believe that the laws for punishing crime on board ship were ineffectual, and went on to survey the whole state of the American mercantile marine. He said there was a supposition that the United States really possessed a body of native-born seamen and that its ships were chiefly manned by American crews. 'It is unfortunately the fact, however, that not one in ten of the seamen employed on board our vessels, is a native-born or even naturalised citizen, or has any connection with our country beyond his engagement for the voyage . . . It is not an exaggeration to say, that the United States have no seamen. Even the officers, from the mate downward, are usually foreigners, and of a very poor class, being the rejected mates and other subordinates of the British commercial navy. Men who have failed to pass their examinations, or have been deprived of their certificates by reason of drunkenness or other ill conduct, attain, on board of our noble ships, the posts for which they were deemed unworthy in their own.'

Having given his low opinion of the seamen and mates, Hawthorne went on to the masters, saying: 'On the deterioration of this class of men [the mates] necessarily follows that of the masters, who are promoted from it. I deeply regret to say, that the character of American shipmasters has already descended, many degrees, from the high standard which it has held in years past; an effect partly due, as I have just hinted, to the constantly narrowing field of selection, and likewise, in a great degree, to the terrible life which a shipmaster is now forced to lead. Respectable men are anxious to quit a service which links them with such comrades, loads them with such responsibility, and necessitates such modes of meeting it.'

Now Hawthorne, in this letter, was writing at such length (thirteen foolscap sheets), and so passionately, because he believed that the Secretary of State in Washington had impugned his honour. It is a complicated story, but, broadly, what had happened was this. Lord Napier, the British Minister in Washington, had complained about the treatment of some seamen on American ships. Cass had replied, and this reply had been published in English newspapers. It said that the laws of the United States were adequate for the protection of seamen, but that the execution of those laws devolved mostly on American consuls, some of whom, in British ports, may have been 'delinquent in the discharge of their duty'. Hawthorne retorted that he had investigated all cases, and punished those he was empowered to punish, but that most of the worst brutality was not punishable by the existing law because it was not committed by the master or at the master's orders, but by subordinates acting on their own. Hawthorne said he had done his duty. If he had failed to do this, he would consider himself guilty of a great crime. If he was innocent, he said, then unquestionably the Secretary of State had wronged him. It was unfortunate that Hawthorne had already placed his resignation in the hands of the new President, James Buchanan, because, as he said, he would now be supposed to have committed official suicide, and to have resigned to avoid being dismissed. Hawthorne's views in this letter certainly differ from those he had earlier expressed on the respectable masters he found at Mrs. Blodgett's lodging house, but he did say those men were favourable specimens.

The emigrant trade, particularly when it was at its most flourishing, was a trade likely to be brutal. To carry more people and cargo, the lines of a packet's hull were not made so fine as the shipbuilders could have made them, and to make up this deficiency the ships were always driven hard night and day by master and mates, who drove their seamen hard to do it. Line competed with line, and the ships within each line competed with each other. The North Atlantic was not the easiest sea, and emigrants were not the cleanest cargo. The better sailors chose other ships. The forecastles of American packets had to be filled with riff-raff, convicts, dive-sweepings, and foreigners, and bucko mates and bullying captains were needed to handle them. Most American captains were not brutal, but they were busy with the responsibility of their ships' safety, and with driving their crews. Many skippers never visited the steerage the whole voyage long. In even the best American ships the emigrants' welfare was left to the mates and to the dive-sweepings.

7
The Voyage

'Before the emigrant has been a week at sea he is an altered man. How can it be otherwise? Hundreds of poor people, men, women, and children, of all ages, from the drivelling idiot of ninety to the babe just born, huddled together without light, without air, wallowing in filth and breathing a fetid atmosphere, sick in body, dispirited in heart, the fevered patients lying between the sound, in sleeping places so narrow as almost to deny them the power of indulging, by a change of position, the natural restlessness of the disease; by their agonised ravings disturbing those around, and predisposing them, through the effects of the imagination, to imbibe the contagion; living without food or medecine, except as administered by the hand of casual charity, dying without the voice of spiritual consolation, and buried in the deep without the rites of the church.'[1]

These are the words of Stephen de Vere, a landowner and philanthropist from County Limerick, a distant relative of the former Earls of Oxford, a convert to Rome, and a poet who translated Horace's Odes. He saved Irishmen from the gallows, taught in Irish schools, charged his tenants less than a fair rent for his lands, and for more than twenty years abstained from wine to encourage temperance among the poor.[2] In 1847 he went out to America not in the cabin but as a steerage passenger, to see for himself how poor emigrants were treated.

He sailed from London, in a ship which he said was better regulated and more comfortable than many others. But the food was seldom cooked enough, because there were too few stoves. The filthy beds were never brought on deck to air. The narrow space between the sleeping berths and the piles of passengers' boxes was never washed or scraped, but stank until the day before the ship came to quarantine, when all hands were ordered to scrub up to clean the ship for the doctor and government inspector. 'No moral restraint is attempted, the voice of prayer is never heard; drunkenness, with its consequent train of ruffianly debasement, is not discouraged, because it is profitable to the captain, who traffics in the grog.' The meat was of the worst quality. There was plenty of water on board, but the passengers were given so little that they sometimes had to throw overboard their salt provisions and rice because they did not have enough water both to cook the food and satisfy their raging thirst afterwards. They could wash only if they used their cooking water. The master refused to listen to complaints. The food and water was served out by false gallon measures which contained only three quarts. Once or twice a week spirits were sold to the passengers, producing what de Vere called unchecked blackguardism. Lights were prohibited because the ship—although she had open fire grates on deck and although matches were struck in the steerage and pipes secretly smoked in the berths—was freighted with gunpowder.

At the end of the voyage a clerk came on board, questioned the captain or mate, and ended by asking whether any passenger meant to make a complaint, but this was a farce, because the captain took good care to 'keep away the crowd from the gentleman'. And few passengers would try to start a prosecution anyway: they were ignorant, friendless, penniless, disheartened, and anxious to get on to their destination.

Herman Melville has a similar account in his first novel, *Redburn*.[3] In his ship, out of Liverpool, the bunks were rapidly knocked together with coarse planks, and looked more like dog kennels than anything else. The emigrants talked of soon seeing America. The agent had told them that twenty days would be an unusually long voyage. Suddenly there was a cry of 'Land', and the emigrants crowded on deck expecting America, but it was only Ireland, which they had left three or four weeks before in a steamboat for Liverpool. They were the most simple people. They seemed to have no idea of distance, and to them America was a place just over the river. One old man would stand for hours together looking straight ahead as if he expected to see New York City every minute, when they were 2,000 miles away and steering into a head wind. After a while the emigrants began to think they had been cheated, and that the ship was bound for the East Indies or some other remote place. A malicious sailor set a rumour going that the captain proposed to take them to Barbary and sell them for slaves. The emigrants were under a sort of martial law. The captain was a despot. Perhaps at sea this was necessary, but there was no appeal, and too often the captain was unscrupulous. And as for going to law with him after the voyage, said Melville, you might as well go to law with the Czar of Russia. The steerage was like a crowded jail. From the rows of bunks, hundreds of thin, dirty faces looked out. Scores of unshaven men, seated on chests, smoked tea-leaves and created a suffocating vapour which was, still, better than the fetid air of the place.

These two accounts, by de Vere and Melville, cannot be taken as typical. De Vere sailed in 1847, by far the worst year to be a steerage passenger on the Atlantic, and he sailed in a British ship, and British ships were notoriously worse than the Americans. On the other hand, he did not sail from Liverpool but from London, whose ships' crews were on the whole less practised in brutality. And as for Melville, although he had sailed in the Liverpool trade as a seaman, and his account was very nearly documentary, it does appear in a novel.

But there are many authentic accounts of emigrant voyages. One is by Robert Garnham,[4] who sailed to New York in the *Northumberland* as a cabin passenger, because he wanted a trip abroad, and also to help a friend see that an emigration contract was carried out. He was an English gentleman, of a kind emigrant ships' masters disliked. He said the universal complaint of the passengers was that they were treated like dogs by the captain and crew. In the Quebec trade the emigrants were looked on as a bore. All the captain wanted was to get to Quebec, get rid of the emigrants as soon as possible and then take on his cargo of timber. One day Garnham went to the aid of a German emigrant hit by the mate, and the captain ordered him not to interfere again. 'I told him very plainly, and the whole of the passengers supported me in what I said, that of course I had nothing to do with the ship, and should not interfere with anything relating to the management of it; but that if I saw any person, never mind who he was, struck down and ill treated, I, as an English gentleman, should of course go to his assistance.'

The most detailed account of all is by an Irish gentleman, Vere Foster, who was no relation of Stephen de Vere, and must not be confused with him. Foster sailed in the *Washington* which left

Liverpool for New York in October 1850.[5] This was not a year of
great disease. The passage was not stormy, although it was winter.
The *Washington* was no hulk, but one of the finest American emigrant
ships. She was new, strong, and dry. Her two passenger decks were
each over seven feet high, and bulwarks more than six feet high
protected the deck from sea spray. She had a crew of thirty-one
sailors, three boys, four mates, and a captain. She carried a surgeon.
She was a great deal better in all ways than the average run of
emigrant ships. She left Liverpool on October 25 with 934 passengers
and anchored in the Mersey to take on supplies. Next day Foster
went on board to sail as one of the cabin passengers. He was the
man who had given away 250,000 copies of his *Emigrants' Guide*.
He was a philanthropist, and a relative of Lord Hobart, who was
with the Board of Trade in London.

One of the first things Foster saw on board was the doling out of
the daily water ration. All 900 or so passengers were called forward
at once to receive the water, which was pumped into their cans from
barrels on deck. The serving out was twice capriciously stopped by
the mates, who cursed, abused, kicked, and cuffed the passengers
and their tin cans and, having served about thirty people, said there
would be no more water that day. Foster gently remonstrated with
one of the mates, observing to him that such treatment was highly
improper and unmanly, and that the mate would save himself a great
deal of trouble and annoyance and win, instead of alienating, the
hearts of the passengers, if he would avoid foul language and brutal
treatment: the mate replied that if Foster said another word he would
knock him down. By October 30, no food at all had been served to
the passengers although the contract tickets stated they were to be
fed each day. The poorer steerage passengers had brought nothing
with them, and for five days had nothing to eat except what they
could beg from their better-off companions. Foster began to write a
letter of complaint addressed to the captain on behalf of the
steerage passengers. He began 'Respected Sir', and had got as far as
courteously enquiring when they might expect to be fed, when the
first mate knocked him flat on the deck with a blow on the face.
'When the mate knocked me down,' Foster said, 'which he did
without the smallest previous intimation or explanation, he also made
use of the most blasphemous and abusive language.' Foster went to
his cabin, the mate remarking that if he found him in the 'tween decks
again he would not hit him but throttle him. Next day Foster did
manage to get to the captain, Page, to present his letter. The captain

told him to read it aloud. Foster had read a third of it, when the
captain said that was enough; he knew what Foster was—he was a
damned pirate, a damned rascal, and he would put him in chains
and on bread and water for the rest of the voyage. The first mate
added more foul abuse and blasphemy, and was later found heating a
thick bar of iron in the kitchen fire and saying he intended to give
Foster a singeing with it.

That same day provisions were issued for the first time. Foster had
brought with him a weighing machine to check the amounts given
out. He and his colleagues in the cabin got 2¾ lb. of wheat flour,
which was ¾ lb. more than their due; 2½ lb. of biscuit instead of
5 lb.; and 6 oz. of tea instead of 12 oz. They were given short
measures of rice, oatmeal, and molasses, and no pork or vinegar,
although they should have received both. When one of the occupants
of berth 180 came for pork, not knowing that another man from the
same berth had already received all the rations for that berth, the first
mate laid about him with a rope's end, saying, 'If any other b——
annoys me, God damn his soul, I'll smash his head for him.' The
captain never bothered to visit the steerage, and the first and second
mates, the cooks, and the surgeon seldom opened their mouths
without prefacing what they had to say with, 'God damn your soul to
hell', or 'By Jesus Christ, I'll rope's end you'. Those who gave the
cooks money or whisky could get five meals cooked a day. Others
who had no money to give, or chose not to give, had one meal a
day, or one every other day.

Foster frequently talked to sailors, and asked them if this was their
first time on the *Washington*. All said it was, and all that it would be
their last. Some said the first and second mates would get a good
thrashing as soon as they reached New York. About three weeks out
Foster asked the third mate where the ship was, and got the usual
reply, that he did not know. Except for the captain and first mate no
one ever knew where the ship was, and they kept it a deep secret.
On November 17 the surgeon hurled overboard a great many
chamber pots belonging to the women passengers, and told them to
come to the privies on deck, which were filthy. Foster heard him
say: 'There are a hundred cases of dysentery on the ship, which will
all turn to cholera, and I swear to God that I will not go amongst
them; if they want medecines they must come to me.' The same
morning, the first mate played the hose on the passengers who were
in the privies, drenching them. The fourth mate had done the same
four days before. One of the passengers, who was himself a doctor,

went round canvassing for a testimonial to the ship's surgeon, collecting money for a gift to placate him. Nobody wanted to give. The ship's doctor, hearing of this, muttered that the steerage passengers had plenty of money on them, which they would not know what to do with when they got to New York, and that if they would not look after him he would not look after them. Some passengers said they would not mind contributing a shilling each if they thought it might be used to buy a rope to hang him.

The first mate kneed John M'Corcoran, an old man, who afterwards passed blood whenever he went to the privy. The doctor, now he was getting no gift, decided to charge for his services, and extorted half a crown from one passenger and a shilling from another, and charged sixpence for a glass of castor oil. On November 25, a month out, when it had been very cold, another child, making about twelve in all, died of dysentery and from want of proper food. He was thrown into the sea sewn up in a cloth weighted with a stone. No funeral service was conducted: the doctor said the Catholics objected to a layman conducting any such service. The sailors were pulling at a rope, and raising their usual song:

Haul in the bowling, the Black Star bowling
Haul in the bowling, the bowling haul—

and the child was thrown overboard at the sound of the last word of the song, which became a funeral dirge.

On November 30, two days off New York, Foster wrote in his diary: 'The doctor came down to the second cabin in company with the first mate, and to display his authority, drew himself up and swelled himself up excessively tremendous, roaring out, "Now then, clean and wash out your rooms every one of you, God damn and blast your souls to hell." ' On December 2, a beautiful day and a favourable breeze, they took a pilot aboard. Foster drew up a second letter, testifying as a warning to future emigrants that the passengers had been treated brutally by the officers and had not been given one half of the proper rations laid down by Act of Parliament and stipulated for in the contract tickets. Next day, in the afternoon, the *Washington* docked. Foster wrote: 'The 900 passengers dispersed as usual among the various fleecing houses, to be partially or entirely disabled for pursuing their travels into the interior in search of employment.'

In New York, Foster met passengers he had sent out in the *Washington* on her previous voyage, and was told no food was served out during the first two weeks of that voyage, and no meat at all for the whole of it. He met passengers he had sent out on board the *Wm. Rathbone*, who were treated the same. He also met some friends who had come out two months before in the *Atlas*; as they described it, the 415 passengers on board that ship had been even worse treated than the *Washington*'s. Both the *Wm. Rathbone* and the *Atlas* belonged to the Black Star Line, the same line that owned the *Washington*.

Foster wrote a long account of the voyage and sent it to Lord Hobart. He sent it on to the emigration commissioners in London, adding that the commissioners would perceive that the treatment undergone by the emigrants was considerably worse than that ordinarily experienced by brutes, and that from what Foster said at the end of his letter, about other ships, the case seemed by no means an exceptional one.[6] The commissioners, in return, said they were sorry Foster had not prosecuted the *Washington*'s officers in New York, because if he had they would doubtless have been punished 'for their misconduct'.[7] The commissioners did tell Lieutenant Hodder, emigration officer in Liverpool, to look out for the *Washington* when she returned there. He went to see the master when she docked, and then wrote to London that, as might be expected, his detail differed widely from the complainant's, and that in the absence of all evidence he could go no further. The commissioners wrote again to Hobart telling him this was what they had expected. In England nothing could be done until Foster arrived back, and even then it seemed very doubtful whether an English court would have jurisdiction over acts done in a foreign ship on the high seas.[8]

In February 1851 the House of Commons called for the papers on the *Washington*, and Foster's letter and others were published. Later that year a Parliamentary Committee learned a bit more about the voyage, but not much. Murdoch, chairman of the emigration commissioners, said he did not think the American laws were enforced unless there was a flagrant case. From the tone of what he said, he did not seem to count the *Washington* as a flagrant case. When he was asked if he supposed Foster's account was correct, he said very likely it was. The committee asked if any inquiry had been instituted into the case from London. Murdoch said no, because there was no power to do so.[9] This answer was accepted without demur, though the commissioners could at least have asked for the British consul in New York to look into things.

As it was, Robert Bunch, the British vice-consul in New York, happened to be in England at the time of the select committee, and he came along and explained why there had been no prosecution.[10] At the time of the *Washington*'s arrival he had been acting consul, and Foster came to him, showed him his journal of the voyage, and said he would like to prosecute if there was a chance of success. Bunch told Foster he believed the consul had a sort of discretionary power, which had never been acted on, to prosecute any very gross case of ill-treatment of emigrants. He sent Foster to Edwards, solicitor of the consulate, saying that if Edwards thought it worth while prosecuting, then he (Bunch) would pay the expenses himself and take his chance of ever getting them back from the Treasury. Edwards made a report full of solicitor's caution: he thought on the whole it was not worth while, that no charge lay against the captain, and that though a case of common assault might lie against the mate it would hardly be worth while, particularly as Foster wanted to get away from New York. Bunch put this report to Foster, asked him what he thought, and repeated his offer to pay the expenses. But Foster was discouraged and did not think it worth while to go on. There the matter dropped. There was no prosecution. According to Bunch, Foster did go to see the owners of the vessel two or three times, and was treated civilly, but that was all. Most of the passengers had by then dispersed.

When the committee wanted to know if there was not another side to the matter, and if Foster had not perhaps gone among the steerage passengers haranguing them and exciting them to complain, Bunch said he did not know, but that Foster's actions, though founded perhaps in strict justice and right, would not tend to create a good feeling towards him in the ship; Foster had told him that the captain had said, 'We know who you are; you are a bloody pirate, and we mean to serve you out for it.'

What emerges from this is that it was true, as Melville had said, that as for going to law with the master of a ship, you might as well go to law with the Czar of Russia. According to Bunch, only four complaints were made to the British consul by emigrants in the whole of 1850, and Foster's was the most glaring. No prosecutions were brought at all, and this is not surprising. It seems plain that the consulate had no idea how to go about a simple prosecution, even when a substantial complaint was made. Foster was the sort of man who might have been regarded as an interfering radical, but his account is so circumstantial that it must either be substantially correct or else a fabrication. If half of what he said was true, the officers of the *Washington* would have been guilty of breaking every other clause in both the American and British Passenger Acts. And if a literate, concerned, and determined man like Foster, who was moreover the relation of an English peer and knew how to go about things, was still unable even to get his case to court, what hope was there for most immigrants, who were poor, illiterate, afraid, and without connections?

Of course there were pleasant voyages. In the summer of 1845 Martin Donald Macleod[11] emigrated to Canada with his wife and eight children, and settled as a farmer at Oak Ridges near Toronto. In a letter home he wrote: 'We had a most pleasant passage from Greenock to Montreal, we never had a reef paint tied, indeed, we carried Royals all the way, a lighted candle could have been carried on the deck until we saw land on the side . . . the Master was particularly civil & we were as comfortable as we could desire.' The master was perhaps civil because Macleod was a captain in the British Army. And Macleod sailed from Greenock where the emigrant trade was nothing like so heavy as Liverpool's, and the weather he met was a miracle.

An Atlantic voyage, and the whole business of emigration, was easy to idealise, and this was done in *The Young Emigrants*, a children's book published in 1851 in New York and two years later in London.[12] It is the story of three children, Tom Lee aged twelve, Annie aged eleven, and George aged seven, who go with their father to join an uncle in Cincinatti. They travel by ox-cart to the interior, they try to ride on pigs in the streets of Cincinatti, one of the children escapes from drowning by leaping from a boat caught in a cataract, and another fights a rattlesnake and wins. But the most idealised description is of their voyage to New York. The good ship *Columbia* is crossing the Atlantic towards the end of April on her way to the great western world, 1,000 miles from land with the blue waves dancing merrily in the bright sunlight. The ship's motion is steady. Some of the grown-ups are sad, but not the children, who watch porpoises playing and flying fish landing on deck. Their father comes on deck and addresses the children: 'I promised to show you some sights this evening, and is not this ship bounding over the heaving ocean, with its white sails spread, and its tall masts bending to the wind, a most striking one! Is it not a great specimen of man's skill and power?'

The Lee children were fortunate in the ship their author invented for them. It was not the kind of ship that Mr. J. Custis, a surgeon from Glasnevin, Dublin, was used to.[13] He worked as surgeon in six emigrant ships and wrote, in one of a series of newspaper articles, that the torments of hell might in some degree resemble the sufferings of emigrants, but crime was punished in hell, whereas in an emigrant ship it flourished without check or retribution. 'No! take all the stews of Liverpool, concentrate in a given space the acts and deeds done in all for one year, and they would scarcely equal in atrocity the amount of crime committed in one emigrant ship during a single voyage . . . I have been engaged during the worst years of famine in Ireland; I have witnessed the deaths of hundreds from want; I have seen the inmates of a workhouse carried by hundreds weekly through its gates to be thrown unshrouded and coffinless into a pit filled with quicklime . . . and revolting to the feelings as all this was, it was not half so shocking as what I subsequently witnessed on board the very first emigrant ship I ever sailed in. In the former instance every exertion was made to save life,—in the latter to destroy it.'

Mr. Custis had a gift for the vivid, and for the lurid. The emigration commissioners, though not apparently taking the trouble to check what he said, which would have been difficult because he said nothing until some of the voyages were several years old, were inclined to say he exaggerated.[14] But even if Mr. Custis's accounts, particularly when he is talking about sexual depravity, read like fiction, there are plenty of circumstantial accounts which show that the general tone of his articles was not far from the truth.

A good, cheerful voyage was made by an unnamed emigrant from Bristol to New York in 1848.[15] He sailed in a well-managed vessel, in which the printed articles were read out loud by the captain, and the rules nailed up to the mainmast. Most emigrant ships had no rules to nail. He was one of only four passengers who were not seasick, but for the first few days he had no appetite for anything but gruel. His provision chest was lashed on deck, and it was pretty well known that he had apples, cheese, and butter.

'Pray, sir, when are you going to open your chest? I hear you have some nice cheese; should like to beg a bit.'

'Have you any apples to spare? I hear yours is fine fruit.'

'How I should like to taste your bacon. I am told it is the best on board.'

As the ship rolled, plates were smashed, and hot water from kettles showered about. Beefs and hams were suspended overhead, and the gangway between the bunks was cluttered with boxes and reduced to a zigzag of ten inches. Three fiddles played on deck. After nine days out the captain ordered the vessel to be fumigated, which shows his was an exceptionally well-run ship. The emigrant opened his food chest, and found the oranges and bread spoiled and the plum cake spoiling. A storm came up and he jammed himself between two boxes, but even this would not always do and he often got his food within an inch of his mouth when the ship rolled and the food went one way and himself another. Fifteen days out they tried to catch a shark, but it would not take the bait they offered. The sailors ate red herrings for breakfast, which they called old soldiers. Passengers and crew drank 'coffee royal'—brandy mixed in boiling coffee and sweetened. After twenty-seven days out they met an American fishing vessel, and exchanged two bottles of rum and some pork for fresh cod. The captain sold it to emigrants at 3d. a pound, which was reckoned dear. After thirty-seven days tobacco had run out. Good water was scarce, and there was none to cook in. 'Mem. Potatoes boiled in salt water with the rinds on; ate good; but bad if pared—secret worth knowing. Fresh meat and pudding good if boiled in half-salt water.' Here was a healthy, sanguine, strong man, who sailed in an unusually well-run ship and had the luck not to be seasick at all. But even he wrote, fifteen days out, when he was given some soup but the ship's rolling upset it, 'Job verily would have complained had he been here.'

The Atlantic passage in a sailing vessel must by its nature have been an ordeal for most landsmen. Many ships, even the bigger ones, were not dry, particularly when they had a part cargo of iron or railway lines. Captain Schomberg, emigration officer at Liverpool, tried to superintend the loading, not only to make sure the ship was safe but also to look after the passengers' health. 'A deep ship will very probably, under ordinary circumstances, be very wet and uncomfortable, and the people will live up to their knees in water . . .'[16] Even the cheerful emigrant from Bristol complained that 'two holes, cut for air, often admit water upon us, through the ship's heaving'.

The crowding itself made decency and comfort impossible. When the emigrant bought a ticket he imagined he had bought a berth, but he had not. He had bought a quarter. Berths were almost always six feet square, and into each berth four people were fitted. There was not space to contain half of them in comfort.[17] The Rev. John Welsh of Liverpool found in one vessel that three women and an infant had been put into one berth three feet three inches wide, to go to Quebec. In more than half the American ships the berths were suspended from the beams by rods: these were good, and strong, but in many other vessels the berths were rickety, and he had frequently, by a shake, brought down some of them. Four people to three feet three inches was unusual, but even the six feet square berths, taking four persons, as provided for in the Passenger Acts, were very bad.[18] Lieutenant Hutchinson, R.N., harbour and pilot master at Kingstown, who had seen thousands of Irish immigrants packed in, said, 'I should recommend that the berthing of passengers below should be fitted up in quite a different manner. I think it is most indecent to have four persons sleeping in a compartment of six feet by six feet; they have not more than their coffin.'[19]

On board most ships, men and women were indiscriminately berthed together. Sir George Stephen once asked a ship's mate how he managed with marriages at sea; how did he manage to bed the couple on board? To which the mate replied: 'There is no difficulty as to that; there is plenty of that work going on every night to keep them all in countenance.'[20] George Saul, passenger broker, said that if people wished to be improperly berthed, he shut his eyes to it, thinking he could not make people virtuous if they were disposed to be immoral.[21] Thomas Murdoch, chairman of the emigration commissioners, was once asked whether women were ever berthed together with men against their will: he replied that this happened only very rarely, and that it did not matter so much on board Atlantic ships because the voyage was shorter than on the Australian run.

'Surely [he was asked] when persons of different sexes are berthed together it does not require forty days to produce a bad result?'— 'No,' he said.[22]

Sylvester Redmond, journalist, was asked if he thought indiscriminate intercourse took place. He said: 'I saw on two occasions, in the daytime, persons in very indelicate positions.'

'Of different sexes?'—'Yes.'[23]

This is risible; as it was when a captain in the Royal Navy was solemnly questioned about unmarried men on board being able to 'view the married women dressing or undressing, and see what is going on'. He had to agree that there was 'use given to the eyes'.[24] But this berthing together must have been intolerable for a modest woman. Sometimes women had to sit up all night on boxes because they could not think of going to bed with strange men, under the same blanket.[25]

An emigration officer was asked: 'The single men and women all sleep alongside of one another . . . ?—Yes, there is no privacy whatever.

'But supposing an emigrant comes and finds that there is no room on board the vessel, except in a berth holding four, one half of which is already occupied?—He would have to go into that; his contract is, that he shall have eighteen inches space.

'And if that is occupied by a married couple, the emigrant, whether a single man or a single woman, would be put into that berth alongside the married couple?—I do not see anything to prevent it.'[26]

The officer was speaking in 1851. The Passenger Act of 1848 forbade the berthing together of single men and women, but though the spirit of this would have prevented the berthing of a single man or woman with a married couple, the letter did not; and the law, such as it was, was disregarded anyway. In 1852 a new Act required all single men to be berthed together in a separate part of the steerage.

In many ships there were no water closets, and never more than one for every hundred passengers. They were little use in any case. If they were on deck, the emigrants could not get to them in rough weather. In high seas they were sometimes washed away. Thomas Murdoch said, 'The people who are put on board, the labouring classes, are not in the habit of using that form of convenience, and they use it very ill, and throw bones and all sorts of things down it. They are the greatest nuisance that can possibly be on board ship. I believe on board men-of-war they are bad enough, and they are much worse on board emigrant ships . . . In fact, I confess, we are at our wits' ends on the subject of water closets.'[27] On the other hand, it was trying, particularly for the women, when there were none. Welsh, the chaplain, came across a family who had been round their ship in port, and the women, when they saw there were no lavatories, were in great distress and did not know what was to become of them on the voyage. 'They said that if they had known this, they would not have left home on any account.'[28]

The women got the worst of it in other ways. Those who had no men to look out for them found it difficult to get any food at all. A doctor[29] who had made many voyages from Liverpool to America said that on rough days he had often been obliged to go into the steerage with buckets of water and a bag of biscuits to feed the women to save them from starvation. Women and feeble men went days without a bite.[30] A boarding-house keeper at Liverpool who had made one voyage on a ship with about 400 passengers, said that there was only room for six people to stand and cook at the same time, and there was incessant cooking and fighting from six in the morning till six at night. 'The women particularly, who were alone, must have wanted their food.'[31]

The food, anyway, was nothing like Cunard food. That, if you had the appetite to eat it, was an incessant banquet. Breakfast at 8.30 was Irish stew, cold meat, ham, mutton chops, fish, eggs, tea, coffee, and hot rolls. Lunch at twelve was a light meal—soup, cold beef, and roasted potatoes. Dinner, at four, was iced water, soups, fish, meat, fowls, game, side dishes in the French style, pastry, and dessert of fresh fruit. At seven in the evening there was tea and coffee, with supper to come at ten.[32]

The steerage passengers in sailing ships got their food uncooked and not enough of it. Dr. William O'Doherty,[33] who had made nine or ten voyages with emigrant ships, was asked if the ration laid down in the Passenger Acts was enough. He said: 'I do not think it is; I know it is not what you would give your servants.' Speaking for himself, as a professional man, eating in the cabin and at the captain's table, he found the American ships better. They had tasty delicacies as well, for females and children. In a British ship, even in the cabin, the captain sat down to 'a miserable junk of beef'. But in both English and American ships the steerage passengers did badly. He had never seen a potato given out on board any ship since he went to sea. The biscuits were generally very bad and not fit to be eaten. On many Irish ships the staple diet was a coarse concoction of wheat, barley, rye, and pease, which became saturated with moisture on board ship, where it fermented and became baked into a solid mass 'requiring to be broken down with an axe before using'.[34]

Many emigrants would not eat unaccustomed food, though it might have been perfectly good. The Irish, although preferring potatoes, which they never got, would eat oatmeal. The English, thinking it food for horses, would not. One passenger said he had seen it thrown into the St. Lawrence. He had seen the river covered with oatmeal.[35] Many emigrants were too poor and ignorant to know what to do with the food they were given. One captain said a third of them did not know what tea was. 'It is no uncommon thing to see an Irishman survey his allowance of tea for a while, and then fill his pipe with a portion, and smoke it with evident satisfaction.'[36]

The sensible emigrant, if he could afford it, bought extra rations to take with him—biscuits, a few pounds of fish and bacon, and, if he had enough money, a little coffee, tea, and sugar.[37]

But even if passengers had their own food, they sometimes found themselves at the mercy of a cruel cook. In August 1853 the packet ship *George Canning*, Captain Jacobs, docked at New York City. Eighteen passengers had died on the voyage. Soon after landing, a four-year-old girl, a perfect skeleton, died of diarrhoea, and an inquest was held on her, at which all sorts of accusations were made about the treatment of the *George Canning*'s passengers. The *New York Times* published a leading article entitled 'Inhuman Treatment of Passengers on Shipboard'. It said in part:

'Once at sea their anticipations were cruelly mocked, as they found themselves under the rule of a brutal captain, and at the mercy of a greedy cook. The latter, when they wished to prepare, for their sick friends, any little delicacy which they had furnished, out of their own private store, packed in their chests before they quitted the fatherland, [charged] a dollar for the use of the fire with which they cooked it—a dollar for the cooking of an invalid's meal—a bowl of arrowroot for instance! And the same cook made coffee for the whole ship-load of emigrants, with water taken from the Atlantic! When the captain was told of things, and told, too, that the emigrants were sick and dying, he expressed the wish, that they might all die! The *George Canning* . . . had two kinds of water for her passengers—fit, drinkable water for the captain, the cabin-passengers, and the crew; and bilgewater, or water taken from the ocean, for the steerage emigrants.'[38]

Even if few captains and cooks were villains, it is impossible to be certain how pure a ship's water was. According to official returns in 1847, the water for Liverpool ships was taken from Bootle waterworks and was 'abundant and excellent'. For Cork ships it came from that city's waterworks, and was also probably good. But from Limerick it was 'taken from the river when the tide answers'; at Waterford casks were filled 'at proper times of tide from the river four miles above the bridge'; and at Castletown and Berehaven casks were 'filled from a pure stream'. Even if the water was good, the casks could contaminate it. Some were old wine and whisky casks, and unless they had been well charred the water would be bad.[39]

Any emigrants who had been used to a decent diet on land would have found themselves badly off at sea. A short description of steerage food was given by William Philipps, a London shipowner and ship-broker whose packets sailed weekly to America and carried 15,000 passengers a year. He said: 'It is sufficient to stave off starvation, but it is not enough to live upon and fructify; you cannot live well upon it.'[40]

Most did not live well upon it. Many became ill, and then they were in trouble. Even on those ships that carried surgeons they were unlikely to be the best of doctors. Dr. George Douglas, who was medical superintendent at Grosse Isle quarantine station in the St. Lawrence, said ships' surgeons were certainly not competent. It was exceptional if the medical gentlemen who came out in charge of emigrant vessels were regularly educated. Sylvester Redmond, who saw emigrant vessels leave Liverpool every day, knew a man called Murphy who was surgeon on an American ship, but was neither surgeon nor apothecary.[41] 'I knew him in Dublin,' he said, 'and I know that *Beck's Medical Jurisprudence* is the most he ever read on medecine.'

Redmond was asked, 'Was he an English practitioner?'—'He was no practitioner at all.'

Dr. Isaac Wood, who worked in the quarantine service at New York, said the persons who had been taken on board vessels that came to the port were nothing but apothecaries. For ships' captains to put emigrants' lives in the hands of men they would not trust to treat any domestic animal they valued, was a crying evil.[42]

Surgeons who were willing to work aboard ship sometimes had strange and impractical ideas. In November 1851 a Dr. Doherty called unasked on the emigration commissioners' office in London and said all passengers should be compelled to take a bath every day. When he was asked how they should be compelled, he said that if the men refused they should be put in irons, and the women on short rations.[43]

The surgeons on the Australia run were better. They had to be qualified, and they were paid by the government and supervised by the commissioners in London. Even so, many of them were pretty doubtful doctors. Of the seventy-eight surgeons sent out on Australian ships in 1849, twenty-two were found to be either inefficient or wanting in energy. Here are short reports on five of them:

'Surgeon died on the voyage from a disease brought on by intemperance.'

'Surgeon efficient, but guilty of gross misconduct after landing, with respect to a female emigrant.'

'The surgeon extremely inefficient, apparently from intemperance. He was mulcted £48.'

'Great neglect of his duties on the part of the surgeon, owing, apparently, to his having become insane on the voyage.'

'Surgeon inflicted improper punishments on some single females.'[44]

And these were from the pick of ships' surgeons. The Liverpool ships got the leavings. It was no great loss that most of them carried no surgeons of any kind. The 1848 British Passenger Act laid it down that all ships carrying more than 100 passengers should either carry a surgeon or allow each emigrant twelve instead of ten square feet. Most ships allowed the extra space, but then took on extra passengers after clearing, putting things back where they had been before. The truth was that this clause in the Act was unworkable, because there were not enough qualified men to be found.

The commissioners knew this quite well. In 1847 they asked the opinion of several eminent medical men, and found that if they were to attempt to lead Parliament to enact, without alternative, that no ship could carry 100 passengers without a surgeon, they would virtually be forbidding a large part of the emigration of the year.[45] The President of the Royal College of Surgeons said enough men could be found only if they were better paid. The Master of Apothecaries Hall thought enough could be found in Scotland and Ireland but he did not know about England. The President of the Royal College of Physicians in Edinburgh considered that to a young physician 'the appointment of Surgeon to an Emigrant ship bound for North America would be no object of desire, both by reason of the low pay which could be afforded, and because the appointment would very seldom lead to anything better'.

After 1855 the new British Passenger Act demanded that each ship carrying more than 300 passengers should carry a surgeon, no matter what space each emigrant was allowed. By then, emigration had fallen off so much that there were enough surgeons to be had. The same year, the new American Act tried a new way of protecting the health of passengers—not by insisting on doctors but by fining ships' masters $10 for every steerage passenger who died on the voyage.[46] The idea for this came from a Senate committee which was convinced that the surest motive for humanity was self-interest, and quoted the precedent of British convict ships. At first the British government had paid shippers for the number of convicts embarked. The shippers were, of course, honourable men, but saw no reason why convicts should not be inconvenienced on the passage, and unfortunately a tenth of them were so inconvenienced that they died. The government then decided to pay according to the number of convicts delivered in Australia alive, whereupon the inconveniences to the convicts became less severe, and only one in forty-six died.

Up to the mid-1850s most emigrants had either to doctor themselves or be practised upon by the crew. Robert Garnham said after
his voyage, 'You may have access to the medecine chest, and sometimes it is used pretty freely. If anybody is ill, the mate goes to him
and gives him what he thinks will do him good, and then laughs if it
produces a more powerful effect than the one intended.'[47]

The emigration commissioners made regulations saying what
medical instruments a vessel should carry. They included:

A pocket dressing case, containing scalpel, two bistouries (blunt-
pointed and sharp), gum-lancet, tenaculum, spatula, scissars, two
probes, silver director, and curved needles of different sizes.

Case of tooth instruments.

Midwifery forceps and trachea tube.

Set of silver and gum elastic catheters, including female catheter
and some bougies.

One amputating knife and catlin, one amputation saw, one
Hey's saw, tourniquet.

Silk of different sizes for ligatures and other sutures.

'Desirable additions' were cupping apparatus, trocar and canula,
trephine and elevator, craniatomy forceps, perforator, and blunt
hook.

The vessel should also carry the following remedies:

Blue pill, calomel, balsam of Capivi, castor oil, cream of tartar,
Epsom salts, spirit of hartshorne, jalop in powder, laudanum,
peppermint, Friar's balsam, and rhubarb in powder.[48]

The passengers often took their own medicaments, which were
widely advertised at the ports. Liverpool newspapers carried
advertisements for Holloway's Pills, 1s. 1½d. to 33s., which were said
to have the Greatest Sale of Any Medecine in the Globe, and to
have cured the Earl of Aldborough of a liver and stomach complaint.
A testimonial letter from the earl said this had been a cure 'which all
the most eminent of the Faculty at home, and all over the Continent,
had not been able to effect: nay, not even the waters of Carlsbad and
Marienbad. I wish to have another Box and a Pot of the Ointment.'

After quoting this testimonial the advertiser said his pills could
cure any of a list of thirty-six ailments, including scrofula or King's
Evil, tumours, venereal diseases, and 'weaknesses from whatever
causes, etc., etc.'[49]

Tracts published in London by the Society for Promoting Christian
Knowledge also offered temporal and medical advice:

'Do not be anxious to go aloft, else you may go overboard.'

'For drunkenness. Bathe the head well with cold water, or vinegar and water, and if the patient cannot sleep, give him thirty drops of laudanum four times, an hour apart.'

'Rules useful in any illness:—The smell of soap is a great enemy to all fevers.'[50]

Soap would not have been much good against cholera. On September 3, 1853, Delaney Finch, a farmer, sailed from Liverpool to Quebec in the *Fingal*, with 200 other passengers and 1,100 tons of railroad iron. She was lost on the return voyage. Finch said she was a good ship, though the berths broke down. On the voyage of seven weeks, thirty-seven or forty-one passengers died: he could not remember which. Later he was asked what happened.[51] He said: 'I should not like to give an opinion, but my impression is, that Epsom salts and castor oil are very improper medecines to administer to persons labouring under the cholera.'

'Is that what they gave?—Yes.'

'Epsom salts and castor oil?—Yes, and thirty-five drops of laudanum, and then rubbing a man's face with vinegar.'

He was asked if any record was kept of the deaths: 'When we got to Quebec, I and Mr. Liefchild, a gentleman who was in the second cabin, had to put down the names of the parties who died on the voyage, but it was more guess-work than certainty.'

Then he was asked how the burials were carried out, and he said the bodies were thrown overboard, not covered up or anything.

'Did he [the captain] give directions to have the corpse sewn up in canvas, and thrown over?—No, he did not use his jurisdiction in that matter, because he said in the cabin, "We are not bound to do it; it is only according to courtesy."'

8

Washed Away; Drowned Altogether

In the first week of May 1847 *The Liverpool Telegraph and Shipping Gazette* carried a paragraph saying the King of Holland had strongly recommended the Emperor of Japan to throw open his country to the Europeans so as not to run the risk of being bombarded into civilisation like the Chinese, and a letter, on something nearer home, from a correspondent who signed himself as One Long Connected with the Shipping Interests of Liverpool. He wrote: 'Another emigrant ship has foundered and 248 of our fellow creatures have been launched, unshrived, into eternity. And another, and another, will share the same fate unless a strict and searching inquiry be instituted to ascertain if man is not guilty in some measure of causing so great a sacrifice of human life. The tale of one unfortunate vessel is the tale of many . . . A few days and the circumstance is forgotten—it is only the foundering of an emigrant ship—remembered but by relatives. Of the 251 passengers (the supposed number on board) only three escaped. The rest were drowned "between decks" or washed from the wreck. No agonising cry was heard—no piercing scream for help arose above the howling of the waves—all were silent, speechless, and sank into the sleep of mute death . . . O God! it is a most harrowing picture.'[1]

The ship was the *Exmouth*, out of Londonderry bound for Quebec, and wrecked on the west coast of the Scottish island of

Islay. She was an old vessel, launched in 1818, but she was in good repair. She foundered in a chasm. Later 108 bodies were recovered, hooked up by men who were lowered by ropes from the summit of the rocks on either side. Most of the dead were women and children, who were naked and mutilated, some without faces, others without heads or limbs. They were separately wrapped in sheets by two men named Campbell, who saw to their decent interment in a spot near the cliffs.[2]

Fifty-nine emigrant ships to America were lost in the years 1847–53,[3] and the Foundering Emigrant Ship was a classical Victorian disaster, much reported. The *Powhattan*, bound for Philadelphia, was wrecked on April 16, 1854, off the coast of New Jersey. She was stranded within eight yards of the low-water mark, so near that the passengers and crew could hear and reply to the suggestions made by those on shore, and though she did not break up for nearly twenty-four hours after she struck, no one from her reached the shore alive.[4] The *California Packet*, a brig of 292 tons carrying pig iron, advertised to sail on August 29, 1853, finally did sail on October 6, put back the next day, sailed again only on November 3, and was abandoned the next day when she began to leak. The boats were not provisioned, the master abandoned the passengers seventy miles off the coast of Ireland and made off. Three adults and fourteen children died.[5] The summer of 1849 was a bad one. The brig *Hannah*, 287 tons, having had large repairs, and a new deck, sailed from Newry for Quebec, and struck an iceberg; 129 passengers were saved but fifty or sixty were crushed by the ice.[6] In mid-July the *Maria*, with 111 passengers from Limerick to Quebec, also struck an iceberg, and there were only nine survivors.[7] That same month the brig *Charles Bartlett* of Plymouth, Mass., bound from London to New York, was run down by the Cunard steamer *Europa*, 1,918 tons. Forty-two of the brig's 142 passengers were saved, and the steamship company 'voluntarily intimated to the Mayor of Liverpool their intention of forwarding, free of charge, by their next two steamers to America, the persons saved from the wreck'.[8]

The best-documented wreck of all was that of the *Ocean Monarch*,[9] which burned and sank in the Mersey, barely out of Liverpool, with a loss of 176 lives. She was a ship of 1,300 tons, a three-decker, launched at Boston in June 1847, owned by Enoch Train and Co., and put into their White Diamond Line. She was no ancient, under-manned, and leaking vessel, but one of the sharpest of the Liverpool packets. Nor was she overloaded, or even loaded to capacity. On her fourth voyage she sailed from Liverpool on August 24, 1848, with iron, dry goods, salt, earthenware in crates stuffed with straw, light merchandise, and twenty-eight cabin and 322 steerage passengers. In the estuary she caught fire, the flames ran from stern to stem, and spars crashed on the mob herded on deck. The captain later said he believed one of the steerage passengers had been smoking. Or a seaman who had been searching for stowaways was said to have left a burning candle under one of the after-cabins. The passengers jumped overboard or clustered in the bows as the fire swept forward. By the time the flames had taken hold, the upper deck was covered with the whole mass of passengers. Many had run from below naked, and were searching for husbands, wives, and children. An eyewitness on board said: 'While some were standing in resignation, or insensibility, others were yielding to the most frantic despair. Some on their knees were earnestly imploring, with noisy supplications, the mercy of Him whose arm, they exclaimed, was at length outstretched to smite them; others were hastily crossing themselves, and performing the external acts required by their peculiar persuasions. Several of the emigrants' wives and children, who were in the after cabins in the upper decks, were engaged in prayer and in reading the Scriptures with the ladies, some of whom were enabled, with wonderful self-possession, to offer to others those spiritual consolations, which a firm and intelligent trust in the Redeemer of the world, appeared at this awful hour to impart to their own breasts.'

The Brazilian steam frigate *Affonso* and the yacht *Queen of the Ocean* were lying nearby, and rescued 192 people between them. Two other vessels took off another thirty. Thomas Littledale, of the *Queen of the Ocean*, said that as the fire gained, the men and women crowded still further forward until they clung to the jib as thick as they could pack, even one lying over another. At last the foremast burned and fell, carrying with it the fastenings of the jib, which, with its load of human beings, dropped into the water. When only half a dozen women and children remained, paralysed with fear, clinging to the remains of the hanging jib, an Englishman, Frederick Jerome, a native of Portsmouth and a seaman of the American ship *New World,* stripped himself, swam through the heavy sea and the wreckage, climbed a rope up to the last emigrants, lowered them into boats, and was himself the last to leave the sinking ship.

All the first-class cabin passengers were saved. A long list of the dead steerage passengers was published, including Jas. Drumy, Andrew Outlaw, and Margaret, Ellen, Mary, and Thomas Smith. There was a much shorter list of the steerage passengers saved, who included 'Donaghan, Mary (a child, its mother lost)'.

The survivors were taken to Regent Street, in the north end of Liverpool. Most were women, some with burns on their necks and shoulders from the blazing masts and timbers, others with black eyes and contused wounds caused by their being dashed, in a heavy sea, against the hull of the burning vessel. A girl from County Leitrim, who was almost dead when she was brought in by the *Affonso*, said that long after the fire had broken out, while she was standing on deck, she was thrown overboard by another woman, who perhaps thought it better for the girl to drown than to burn, or perhaps was just mad with fear. In the water the girl floated. 'Sometimes she was ascending, and at others descending. At length she caught hold of a hand. It was the hand of a dying woman. They seized each other with a sort of death grasp, and for some time it was a kind of struggle with them as to who should be the conqueror or last survivor of the two. The dying woman, however, who had been shattered about the head, from having been no doubt frequently driven against the hull of the burning vessel, breathed her last. Her head sank but her body floated on the water. [The girl] held on by that dead body, and was absolutely saved by it. It bore her up for a considerable length of time, until, at length she was taken on board the *Affonso*, where she was put into a warm bed, and had brandy and other restoratives administered to her.' The Brazilian crew of the *Affonso* gave the survivors meat, brandy, wine, coats, trousers, and whatever they had to give. At least three accounts of the disaster were published in pamphlet form to help raise a subscription fund for the survivors, and *The Ocean Monarch, A Poetic Narrative*, an indifferent poem of sixty-five pages in two cantos, was dedicated to Queen Victoria and Prince Albert and the proceeds of the sale given to the fund.

One of the most lucid accounts of a voyage and shipwreck was written by R. C. Walters, a poor boy, probably a petty criminal or fancied to be a petty criminal in the making, who was sent to Canada with eleven other boys by the benevolent gentlemen of the Ragged School Union, which ran eighteen schools in London for the destitute and delinquent poor.[10] Walters was shipped off in the *Annie Jane*, 1,013 tons. She foundered, with the loss of 287 of her 351 passengers.* Of the eleven ragged boys, two survived and returned to London, and a clergyman said it was pitiful to behold those whom they had formerly seen in all the energy of life and activity, going forth with hope and prayer to another land, return a mere case of bones. Walters wrote his story while he was recovering. 'At our request,' said the gentlemen, 'he employed a part of his leisure time in writing an account of his sufferings. We thought it would be a good lesson for him in composition and orthography, as well as an easy lesson during his weakness.'

Walters wrote that he embarked on the *Annie Jane* at Liverpool on August 23, 1853, and sailed for Montreal on the 24th. It was the ship's maiden voyage. On the third day out a hurricane carried away the fore, main, and mizzen masts, with the spars and rigging. The boatswain refused to serve any food to the passengers. They were in darkness. The ship rolled, the passengers' sea-chests flew about, children screamed, and seamen cursed. The French-Canadian crew did not understand their orders, which were shouted in English. The passengers petitioned the captain to turn back to Liverpool, and they did return there, after nine days out, on September 2. After repairs they sailed again on the 9th, and again, two days out, a gale carried away bits of the ship, but this time only the foretop mast and main topgallant mast. The ship, which was carrying a cargo of railway iron, once again began rolling. Some spare spars were rigged up, and the ship turned again towards England; but then, during the night, the captain changed course towards the St. Lawrence. Next morning the passengers formed themselves into a council and went to the captain and demanded to know where they were going. The captain thereupon called out to one of his mates to hand him his revolver, levelled it at the deputation, and threatened to shoot the first man who interfered between himself and his duty. The ship kept her course. The passengers had to help man the pumps. Then on September 21 they ran into another storm, the lifeboat was washed overboard, and the captain at last turned back towards England or Ireland. They got as far as Iceland, and then drifted south-east to the Hebrides. One night a rumour spread through the ship that they were approaching a reef of rocks, but Walters paid little attention to it, having become so used to seeing danger. Then another boy said he had seen some of the sailors shake hands, and they became afraid.

---

* These are the figures of the emigration officer at Liverpool. In his account, Walters says 350 were lost out of 452. For various reasons (see Chapter 13) his figures are likely to be as near the truth as the emigration officer's.

The vessel struck sands, the water rose in her, and they clung to their berths. One of the other boys put out his hand and said, 'O! Walters, we shall all be drowned!' The steerage passengers crowded forward, towards the partition which separated the first cabin from the after part. A sailor with a hatchet broke through into the cabin, and the boy heard some people ask the captain if there was any hope. He replied to them: 'Let me go upon deck and attend to my duty.' Walters and a friend shook hands with the captain, who said, 'God bless you, my dear boys.' The water rose to their waists; they got on a table which floated up to the sky-light, and saw that the ship lay in three pieces. Walters said: 'I heard poor G—— calling out to me for twenty minutes; I answered him, and told him which way to come, but it seems he was jammed with the broken timbers, and the water rising gradually to his mouth gave the poor fellow a lingering death.' It must have been eleven at night when they struck, and they did not get off until 6.30 the next morning. 'The place where we were was strewn with broken fragments of the wreck, which kept floating about inside the cabin, maiming a great number of us. The deck above our heads was bending like a sheet of paper, and threatening to fall and crush us every instant.' As daylight broke, Walters was on the beach, sitting on a pile of broken timber. Just at his feet a man lay half buried in rubbish, and a little further off lay another. Walters was pulling off the timber, thinking they might only have been stunned, when one of the sailors called out to him to leave them alone. Groups of half-naked men and women were sitting about half dead with cold and fright.

The wreck was widely reported in Britain and America. The *New York Times*[11] carried a long account which has only one detail not mentioned by Walters. 'While the passengers were clustered round the boats, and within a very few minutes after the ship had grounded, she was struck by a sea of dreadful potency, which instantly carried away the dense mass of human beings into the watery waste, and boats and bulwarks went with them . . . It is the opinion of our informants that at least one hundred of our fellow-creatures perished by this swoop.'

They were on Barra, the southernmost of the Hebrides. Nine of the eleven ragged boys were gone. Six Barra men came and helped them. Then they sailed to the Isle of Skye, two days and two nights in a small boat, and lost all their canvas on that short voyage too. They went by packet to Glasgow, Walters spent a week there in hospital, and was back in Liverpool on October 27, two months and four days after he first embarked on the *Annie Jane*. He returned to London, and after all this ended his account by saying he was hoping soon to sail again, this time for Australia.

The editor of the Ragged School magazine who published this account added that there was reason to hope that the awful scenes witnessed by Walters had made a deep and salutary impression on his mind, which, with God's blessing, might result in a change of heart and life. Mr. William Locke, the secretary of the union, further added that it was well known that the Bible was the foundation of all their teaching, so he had been delighted to find, on questioning the lad Walters, that he and his companions had not, even amidst such dangers as he described, omitted to read their Bible, and that they had been found by the captain several times reading the Scriptures to each other.

For every vessel that foundered there were several that at one time or another came near it. In the summer of 1848 a Protestant Irish emigrant was in the steerage of one of these vessels. On the third day out of Liverpool it came on to blow very hard. He was in his berth when he was wakened with cries and shouts of 'The ship's lost'. He started up, and found men and women rushing to the upper deck, some praying, some crossing themselves, others with faces white as a corpse; gathered, he said, like sheep in a pen crying on the captain to save them. The emigrant was a northern Irishman, from County Antrim, and even in danger he was unable to forget it. He seems proud that his own righteous Protestantism shone out among the distress of his fellow passengers, who were mainly southern Irish and Roman Catholic. He asked some of them what was wrong but they were so frightened they could not speak, so he went to see for himself. Water was coming in through one of the portholes at the bows as thick as a large barrel. The sailors and two mates tried to stop it up, but then gave in and told the captain to lower the boats. He cursed and told them to try again. There were four or five hundred emigrants on board, almost all Catholics; the Protestant said that a more cowardly sect of hounds he never saw; they would do nothing but 'sprinkle holy water, cry, pray, cross themselves and all sorts of tomfoolery instead of giving a hand to pump the ship and then when danger was over they would carry on all sorts of wickedness and they are just the same you meet them at home or abroad'. Thanks no doubt to Protestant piety, the ship weathered the storm and reached America.[12]

John Ryan,[13] of Limerick, a Roman Catholic, never got that far. At Limerick in November 1853 he bought a ticket from an agent for £3 14s., to take him from Limerick to Dublin, from Dublin to Liverpool on the steamer, and from Liverpool to New York on board the *Commerce*. He got to Liverpool with two days to spare, but the *Commerce* had sailed a fortnight before, so he was put on board the *E.Z.* She was a 'short ship', not a packet or properly an emigrant ship at all, one which took only a few passengers and therefore did not have to be inspected by the emigration officers. Ryan was one of the many thousands of emigrants who sailed this way, and so never got into anybody's tables of statistics. He was a labourer, illiterate, and nothing would have been heard from him if he had not been wrecked and brought back to Liverpool. By the spring of 1854 he was back in Limerick, having been repaid his passage money and 25s. compensation besides from the shipowner, because he had lost everything he had on the *E.Z.* He was called to London to appear before a Parliamentary committee on emigrant ships, and these are some of the questions he was asked and the answers he gave. Nothing else shows so clearly the simplicity and helplessness of the ordinary emigrant:

Did you come across from Dublin to Liverpool?—Yes.
Upon the deck of the steamer?—Yes.
Was it a bad night?—It was a very bad night indeed.
Had you any shelter?—None, except as a man can shelter himself.
Then you were taken to the *E.Z.*?—Yes.
And then you were given sleeping places, where; on the upper deck?—Yes, on the upper deck, in the bows . . . We had a house made with boards over the hatchway.
There were fourteen of you?—There were.
And several were of one family?—There was eight of one family, and another girl who joined them, which made nine.
What was the name of that family?—Fitzgerald.
Now, when you were some time out, it happened that those houses were knocked away by a sea?—Yes, quite away.
And there were persons carried away with them and drowned?—There were; drowned altogether.
You saw no more of them?—I saw no more of them than of a man that was at Cork.
Were you all washed overboard?—Thirteen were washed away; every one but myself.

Had you good food?—They gave me no drink but water, and the biscuit was too hard for me.

Do you know the tonnage of the vessel; what size it was?—There were three masts in it.

Were you ever at sea before?—No.

Not till you came over to Liverpool?—No.

The vessel put back to Liverpool?—Yes, the same vessel.

Of the Fitzgerald family; how many of them remained alive?—None.

You lost all your clothes?—Yes, everything, and every one that was with me.

Supposing no disaster had happened to the *E.Z.*, and your passage had been completed successfully, should you have had reason to complain of not being carried in the *Commerce*?—I had a great deal to complain of; nearly every day you would have the water up to your knees.

Was the weather so rough?—Yes, it was no sooner in it than out of it; the water would come in and go out. If we were under deck, we should not have had that; we should be saved from it; it used to come under the bedclothes; they used to be wet at the bottom, under us.

How large was this place where the fourteen lived; how many feet long, and how many feet wide?—I could not tell that.

When it was washed away, was there nothing over your head but the sky?—Nothing in the wide world, nothing but the sky.

Were you all in this place at the time that the sea washed away this house where you lived; were you all inside at the time?—All the passengers but me; at the time of the accident, I was outside.

And that was the reason you were saved?—Yes, I believe so.

When you got back to Liverpool, did you tell anybody there that they had not put you on board the vessel they had promised to put you in?—I do not think I did say anything; I did not care, if I could come home.

Did he [the captain] tell you whether you were nearer to America or to England when this accident happened?—We did not ask him.

Have you given up all notion of going to America?—I have nothing to carry me there.

Has the danger you went through on board this vessel prevented you thinking any more about it?—I should not like to go there.

You would not like to go to sea again?—Not if I could help it.

9
1847, The Plague Year

Three young Irish emigrants of 1847, having reached St. John, New Brunswick, wrote home to their parents: 'Dear Father & Mother there is a disorder verry numorous in this Country what the Call the tipes fevir there is thousands of people Dieing . . . No more at present from your Dearly Beloved Children John Mary & Margret Mullowney till Death Weare all highered in one house.'[1]

Tipes was typhus. The potato crop had failed in Ireland in 1845 and 1846. The Irish had fled from starvation and disease, but had brought the disease with them. In the winter of 1846–7 the Canadian newspapers were reporting the famine more fully than the English press. The Roman Catholic Archbishop of Quebec asked his parish priests to collect for the Irish poor, 'subjects like ourselves of the British Empire'. The collection in Quebec exceeded £4,000, and that in a city where many were still ruined from the fire of the previous year. Father Bernard O'Reilly, parish priest of Sherbrooke, said, 'In the backwoods, there is no money. You may have produce, but cash you cannot get. My poor scattered people were quite unprepared: in some places, they had heard nothing about distress *at home*, as they say. I got about thirty or forty dollars in cash—it was all they had. But there is not a man who is not selling some article to give his mite.' One correspondent, signing himself 'Q', wrote to the *Quebec Mercury* regretting that the plan put forward by more than one philanthropist had not been adopted. This was to reserve at least half the collection as a fund to provide food, clothing, and shelter for the crowds of destitute people that the coming spring would assuredly bring to Canada. He said this plan had been called that of a cold-blooded calculator, unfitted for the present emergency when thousands were dying; but these critics should remember that it would take at least six weeks for the money to get to Ireland from Quebec, and by that time large numbers of emigrants would be on their way to Canada, probably destitute.[2]

Almost certainly destitute. Ireland was a country of starving and homeless paupers. It was noticed that the skin of starving human beings became rough to the touch, very dry like parchment. The shoulder blades were thrown up high. The hair became thin on the head, but in children a new growth of downy hair appeared on the brow. Sores grew between the fingers. Men were cheerful just before their deaths. They crawled into workhouses in the last stage of famine, but then seemed to recover, sat up in bed, talked, ate between sentences, and fell dead. At Kilrush workhouse a doctor told one visitor: 'If you wait a quarter of an hour, you will see that man [pointing to one of these cases] die.'[3] Priests thought it ominous that young people stopped marrying. In three parishes in the west of Ireland, containing 30,000 people, there were only three marriages in the fortnight before Lent in 1847, when usually there would have been thirty or forty in each parish.[4]

In Skibbereen a widow was caught in a potato garden with a few stalks, and taken before the magistrates. Her defence was that she was dying of hunger. She was fined £1 with the option of four weeks' hard labour. At Castlebar people lay in the streets with green froth at their mouths from eating soft grass. Inquests brought in verdicts of 'Starvation', 'Hunger and Cold', and 'Died of famine'. Members of the nobility promised to eat less. Very early in the year, famine news became ordinary. Newspaper headlines like 'The Prevailing Scarcity' and 'Progress of Starvation' became commonplace, and the famine was often not considered the most important news. On January 9, 1847, the *Galway Vindicator* carried a column of 'Condensed News'. A circus elephant had bitten the tail of another elephant. M. Soyer had made a monster pie for the King and Queen of the French, containing twenty-two head of game. Wolves had appeared in extra-ordinary number in Luxembourg. Under the report of these events, as the twenty-sixth item in the column, it was mentioned that the mortality in Tralee workhouse had become so great that the guardians had ordered that no more should be admitted. The thirty-second and last item said that in Limerick there were 2,513 paupers in the workhouse. 'As to holding more inquests,' said the paper later the same month, 'it is mere nonsense. The number of deaths is beyond counting.'[5]

In the parish of Kilgless, Roscommon, seven skeleton bodies were found in a hedge, half eaten by dogs. The police shot seven dogs. In the mouth of one of them was a heart and part of a liver. In Tipperary one of the few prospering trades was in the sale of coffin mountings and hinges. At the May Fair in Nenagh, to the disgust and astonishment of all, a man drove up in a cart and offered for sale a load of badly made coffins. *The Freeman's Journal*, of Dublin, thought this was inhuman, and the first time coffins had ever been offered for public sale at a fair. In the same town a man carrying in his arms the body of his child tried to beg enough money for a coffin, but most of those he begged from were themselves beggars, he collected only eightpence, and buried his child himself without coffin or shroud.[6] In Dublin the *United Irishman* reported that the season continued— epauletted puppyism in every fashion, wigged debasement fresh from a public hanging, girls in gay dresses, and no shadow of desolation. This newspaper and its revolutionary successor the *Irish Felon* printed recipes for home-made gunpowder, and called the Lord Lieutenant Her Majesty's Executioner-General and General Butcher, High Commissioner of Spies and General Suborner, Chief Legal Murderer and Jury-Packer General of Ireland.[7]

The *New York Times* said that in Kilkenny even the dogs had deserted: also the legal profession had been annihilated, because where there were no people left, there could be no litigation.[8] In 1841 the population of Ireland had been 8,175,124, and Disraeli said it was the most thickly populated country in Europe. According to the 1851 census the population was only 6,552,385. The commissioners of the census remarked that at the normal rate of increase the population should then have been over nine millions, so the real loss was about two and a half million people in ten years. And in the years between 1851 and 1854 another 822,000 left.[9]

Many sailed directly from Irish ports. In starving Limerick most ships were advertised as sailing not just for New York or Quebec but 'for the flourishing city of New York'; 'for the flourishing city of Quebec'. But most people went first to England and sailed from Liverpool. Others stayed in England, not because they had any love of that country but because they had no money to go further. They were not welcome. One family got as far as Cheshire and camped near the house of Thomas Murdoch, chairman of the emigration commissioners. The moment his servants noticed the Irish they considered them a pestilence to be driven away. Murdoch went down to the camp and found a poor family of four children, and their mother, father, and grandmother. The mother said they used to live fifteen miles from Athlone. They had brought over a tattered blanket with them, took sticks out of a hedge and propped the blanket up, like a tent, and slept under it on the bare ground. Murdoch saw smoke, and a kettle boiling, and asked what they had there. They said nettles. For three years before this, they had existed on three acres of potatoes, in Ireland, but this year they had none to plant, the workhouse was overflowing, so their master said there was nothing for them but to leave, and if they did leave he would give them a pound note. With this they begged their way to Dublin and paid their fare to Liverpool, and then walked to Murdoch's place, thirty-six miles from Liverpool.[10]

In 1847, by the end of June, more than 300,000 Irish had landed in Liverpool. The medical officer of health calculated that 60,000 to 80,000 had settled in the city, in corners of the already overcrowded lodging houses and in cellars which had been closed under the Health Act of 1842. Fifty or sixty destitute Irish were found in one house of three rooms, and more than forty sleeping in one cellar. The doctor said that if the entire population of the surrounding towns of Blackburn, Bolton, Bury, Chorley, Lancaster, Ormskirk, Prescot, Preston, Warrington, and Wigan had decided to take up residence in Liverpool, they could not have increased the death-rate more than the Irish did. They brought fever with them. In the Vauxhall Wood district 2,810 people, nearly one-seventh of the ordinary population, died from fever. Ten Roman Catholic priests died, a missionary minister, ten doctors, and many hundred English residents who might have lived if Liverpool had not been turned into a 'City of the Plague'. They brought smallpox, diarrhoea, and fever.[11] In June there were twenty times as many fever deaths as usual. The missionary minister, the Rev. John Johns, died of fever in June, and £2,552 was collected for his widow and invested in railway stock for her. In his last report, published after he died, Mr. Johns said that around the sufferers he heard many complaints, but *from* them none. They seemed resigned beyond natural resignation: whoever saw them could scarcely fail to ask himself whether life which could be so negligently left could have been that blessing to them which it should be to every subject of a Christian and civilised empire. He said the cellars must be shut up. They were 'the causes and concealment of scenes incompatible with the well-being of society'. There were many Black Holes out of Calcutta.[12] A month after Mr. Johns's death the *New York Tribune,* reporting the deaths of Catholic priests in Liverpool, said, 'There is much greater courage required to face Death in a cellar, hut or garret, than on the battlefield, and the Catholic clergy of Liverpool possess that superior bravery.'[13]

The Irish did not want to stay in Liverpool or anywhere in England. They wanted to go to America, and those that did not have the fare tried to beg it. Many sent petitions to the government in London. Among them was this one sent from Listowel on July 2, 1847.

'I Micheal OBrien Corperal of the royal affrican Corps Service $17\frac{9}{12}$ years, Discharged at 8 pence per day which is not sufficient to support me and my family and by Trade a labourer, and fit able bodied in any Part of the world that I may be employed in and is Now applying for a passage to north America for Myself and family, Wife 30 years eldest son 17 years Second son 15 years, third son 7 years, and one female Girl five years, I would wish to go to a place where I could Support them, I Micheal OBrien in a State of the Greatest Distress . . .'

He said that if he was not granted a passage he would have to go into the workhouse, which would be a great hardship on him after his long service to Her Majesty in foreign lands. He ended the letter, 'An answer is required', and addressed it to 'Right Honorable Colonial Secretarie Horse Gards London'. Lord Grey wrote on the letter that there should be some uniform procedure about such requests, because some of the candidates might be eligible for Australia.[14]

The most eloquent petition was sent to Lord Monteagle, an Irish landowner, formerly Chancellor of the Exchequer in Melbourne's administration of 1835–9, and chairman of the 1847 Lords Committee on Colonisation from Ireland. It is written in the language of the King James Bible, and it says:[15]

'Petition from poor Irish
To the Right Honourable Lords Temporal and Spiritual.

'Honoured Gentlemen,
We, the undersigned, humbly request, that ye will excuse the Liberty we take in troubling ye at a Time when ye ought to be tired, listening to our Cries of Distress; but like Beggars we are importunate. We the undersigned are the Inhabitants of the Parish of Rattibarren,

Barony of Liney and County of Sligo. It is useless for us to be relating our Distress, for ye too often were distressed by hearing them,—for none could describe it; it can only be known by the Sufferers themselves. We thank ye, and our Gracious Sovereign, and the Almighty for the Relief we have, though One Pound of Indian Meal for a full-grown Person, which has neither Milk nor any other kind of Kitchen, it is hardly fit to keep the Life in them; but if we got all that we would be thankful. But if we have Reason to complain, there is others has more Reason to complain, for in the Parish Townagh they are getting but Half a Pound, and several of them are not able to buy One Pennyworth of Milk. I fear the Curse of the Almighty will come heavier on this Country, the Way they are treating the Poor, but Distress stares us in the face more grim than ever, for we have no Sign of Employment, for the Farmers is not keeping either Boy or Girl or Workman they can avoid, but are doing the Work by their Families though they are not half doing it. In Times past the Poor of this Country had large gardens of Potatoes and as much Conacre as supported them for nearly the whole Year, and when they had no Employment from the Farmers they were working for themselves, and when they had no Employment they had their own Provision; but now there [are] Thousands and Tens of Thousands that has not a Cabbage Plant in the Ground; so we hope ye will be so charitable as to send us to America, and give us Land according to our Families, and any thing else ye will give us (and we will do with the coarsest Kind). We will repay the same, with the Interest thereof, by Instalments, as the Government will direct. And if any refuse or neglect to pay the same, the next Settler to pay the Money and have his Land. And we will bind ourselves to defend the Queen's Right in any Place we are sent, and leave it on our Children to do the same. So we hope for the sake of Him gave you the Power and England Power, and raised her to be the Wonder of the World, and enabled her to pay Twenty Millions for the Slaves in India, that ye will lend us Half the Sum, which we will honestly repay, with the Interest thereof, for we are more distressed than they; and hope for the sake of Him that said, "He that giveth to the Poor lendeth to the Lord, and He will repay it," that ye will grant our Petition. And may He grant ye heavenly Wisdom, with temporal and spiritual Riches also, is the earnest Prayer of your Petitioners.

[Eighty-six Names.]

'We think it useless to [bother?] ye with Names, as we could get as many Names as would nearly reach across the Channel.

'We hope your Lordship will excuse the Liberty we take in troubling you. We know that you have Irish Poor at heart, and that you are their best Friend, which is the Cause of us making so free.

'We hope ye will make Allowance for Deficiencies for this, for the Writer is a poor Man that knows little about Stiles and Titles, for we are not able to pay a Man that could it right.

'To Lord Monteagle,
House of Lords, London.'

The reply is not recorded.

In 1847 as in every year since 1834, many more emigrants landed in the United States than in Canada—140,000 as against 110,000—but in 1847 the Canadian immigration did increase enormously. More than three times as many emigrants entered Canada that year than in the previous three years put together, and the year's disasters took place not at New York but in the St. Lawrence.[16] There was no sudden preference for British America. Those Irish who had any notion at all where they were going—and some barely knew in what direction America was or whether Canada was a British possession—preferred the United States as a free republic, and thought of Canada as just another England across the sea, with the same queen and the same oppression. The Irish had no reason to love England. But in 1847 they had to go to British North America for two practical reasons— the new and more severe Passenger Acts passed early that year in the United States, and the trouble taken in New York and Boston to keep emigrants out.

The two Acts of Congress of February and March 1847 provided that in all emigrant ships each passenger should have not less than fourteen superficial feet of deck space, and that for each passenger carried over the proper number the master of the vessel should be liable to a fine of $50 or one year in prison. The British Act then in force allowed only ten feet to each passenger. The American law, as amended by the March Act, counted each child however young as one full passenger: the British Act allowed two children under fourteen years of age to be calculated as only one statute passenger. The U.S. Act also specifically said that no matter how many passengers the calculation of fourteen square feet each would allow the vessel to carry, she should not in any case carry more than two to every five tons of the vessel's tonnage: the British allowance at the time was three to every five tons.[17]

As it happened, the new United States laws were not properly enforced, but the masters and owners feared that they might be, and for a while this had the same effect as enforcement. In May the *Amelia Mary*, an English ship, cleared out of Donegal bound for New York, but then the master discovered he had more passengers than the new American acts would allow, so he just landed seventeen of them on the beach and sailed again.[18] The American packets from Liverpool found that their capacity had been reduced by about one fifth, and for this reason, but mainly because there were more passengers that year than the ships could carry anyway, fares rose very high. Brokers extorted what they could get. As early as April the chief emigration officer was reporting that fares to New York had risen to £7, double the ordinary fare, and that brokers were setting aside passengers who had already booked at the old, lower fares, in favour of newcomers ready to pay more.[19] The result was that only the better-off emigrants were able to sail to the United States. The poor emigrants, and the emigrants of the Irish famine were mostly poor, had to take passage in British ships which were sailing for British North America and were therefore not touched by the United States Acts. They carried as many emigrants as they had before, and charged the usual fares of £3 10s. or so.

Even those passengers who did get to the United States were sometimes turned away. In 1847 Massachusetts became alarmed by the import of pauperism and disease and began to enforce to the letter a law of 1837 that any passengers who were lunatics, idiots, maimed, aged, infirm, or had been paupers, should not be permitted to land until the master, agent, or owner of the vessel had given a bond in the sum of one thousand dollars, with good security, that no such passenger should become a public charge within ten years. This was a bond of $1,000 for *each* passenger, and that year it was only too likely that most Irish emigrants had been paupers before they left home.[20] In August the acting British consul in Boston wrote to the Foreign Office in London saying he had found bonds for two ships, but that two other vessels from Cork had had to sail on to New Brunswick. He much regretted the enforcement of such a law, particularly since sick passengers would now have to suffer even more while the vessel looked for other ports, but he could suggest no remedy.[21] Thomas Murdoch said the demanding of these bonds amounted to a virtual prohibition of emigration.[22]

The size and character of the Canadian immigration of 1847 took nearly everyone by surprise, but it ought not have done. There was known to be famine in Ireland. The effect of the new United States

Acts could have been guessed. The kind of vessels that struggled into the St. Lawrence when the destitute Irish could get nothing better should have been known. The year before, the barque *Elizabeth and Sarah* arrived at quarantine downriver of Quebec City on August 5, having cleared from Killala on May 26. She had thus taken forty-one days across the Atlantic which, considering the state she was in, was a fortunate passage. She came in with bad water and starvation. No food had ever been given to the passengers, who had to rely on their own sea-stock, and never more than a quart of water a day. All the water casks were unfit, and the water in some was putrid. The master and seventeen passengers had died of fever. She had been cleared by the customs officer at Killala with 212 passengers, some of them children who only counted as halves, making 183½ statute passengers in all. At quarantine in Canada she was found to have 259 passengers, so taking into account the seventeen who had died, she must have left with 276, making 241½ statute adults. But she could legally have carried only 155 statute adults, so there was an excess of 86½. For all these people there were only thirty-six berths, all the starboard berths having fallen down after a few days at sea. The medical officer at quarantine said the vessel was the oldest in the north of England, having been built eighty-three years before, in 1763.[23]

But little was done. At the end of January, 1847, Lord Grey, the Colonial Secretary, wrote to Lord Elgin, Governor-General of Canada, saying he thought it unnecessary to prepare villages for the reception of emigrants, as had been suggested, because in 1846 there had been 'little if any distress, among the emigrants, unless the consequence of their own fatuity'. Grey said that no free passages would be given, because this would only encourage those who now saved up for the fare, or had money given to them by relatives, to apply for government aid: no more would emigrate in the end, and even those wanting to go to the United States might go by way of Canada on a free government passage. If it were free, infirm people might go. It would cost, at an estimated £10 a passage, about £2,000,000. This estimate was high and must have included every-thing, not just the Atlantic passage, but also the journey to Liver-pool, food and clothes for the voyage, and the steamer trip upriver in Canada. And, said Grey, what was worse, the system of voluntary emigration, which was now working so satisfactorily and on so large a scale, would be entirely deranged, and might not again without great difficulty be restored.[24] If Lord Grey's figure of £2,000,000 was anything but a guess, he must have been calculating that 200,000 people, at £10 each, would have taken any offer. But only 43,000 people had emigrated to British North America in 1846, and in 1847, which was to be by far the busiest year ever, only 110,000 went, so either his figure of 200,000 was a wild exaggeration, concocted to demonstrate falsely how much free passages would cost, or he believed that 200,000 might really go, which means that he could not have believed what he had just stated, that free passages would not increase emigration in the end.

The Colonial Office had also declined an offer from James Buchanan to set up in Canada a depot to receive pauper emigrants from England. Buchanan had previously been British consul in New York, and his son, A. C. Buchanan, was the chief agent for emigration in Canada. The older Buchanan said he might be seventy-six years old, but he was active in mind and body, and he offered, without salary, to set up the depot he proposed. The letter was addressed to Grey, who sent it to the emigration commissioners, who sent it back with an endorsement saying the project of a 'depot in upper Canada with a view to receive the Pauper Population of England' was one which from its designation would not be found to admit of adoption. Of course this was right, the Canadians were naturally touchy about any suggestion of pauper immigration, and Buchanan was told his offer was not accepted.[25] Still, as it happened, his depot, which could have been given some more tactful name, would have been very useful that year. But nothing special was prepared in Canada. In April, a meeting of residents was held in Toronto to determine how an Emigrant Settlement Association could set up an office in the city to help emigrants and get them work when they arrived;[26] and at the beginning of May, Dr. George Douglas began to set up the quarantine hospital at Grosse Isle.

Grosse Isle is thirty miles below Quebec City, in the St. Lawrence. To the south it faces the village of Montmagny, and to the north the huge panorama of Cap Tourmente and the Laurentians. The island is nearly three miles long and, at its broadest point, one mile across. It is rocky and well-wooded, but with small valleys here and there. Before 1832 it was uninhabited, but in that year, when cholera came with emigrants from Ireland and England, it was first used as a quarantine island. In 1834 there was another cholera epidemic, and then, in 1847, typhus. The quarantine hospitals there were last used in 1937. About 11,000 bodies are buried there.[27]

In 1847 Dr. Douglas had been medical superintendent of the island for ten years. Lord Elgin thought him knowledgeable, experienced, and humane.[28] That spring, when it became obvious that the emigration was a calamity, the emigration commissioners in London said that no man could be better fitted than Dr. Douglas, by his public spirit, decision, and humanity, to cope with it.[29] Unfortunately for Douglas, he also had a farm on the island, which he rented from the government for a nominal sum of $100 a year,[30] and every now and again it would be suggested that he profited from this farm by selling provisions to the quarantine patients. There was never much evidence of this, Douglas himself vigorously denied it, and no one ever had anything but good to say of him as a doctor, but the innuendoes remained.

In 1847 there was ice on the St. Lawrence until late April, and it was not until May 4 that Douglas opened up the hospitals on Grosse Isle. He had his usual medical staff—one steward, one orderly, and one nurse. They took with them fifty new iron beds and double the usual quantity of straw. The hospital had enough room for 200 patients.[31] The first vessel of the season, the barque *Syria* from Liverpool, arrived on May 14 with 243 passengers. Nine had died on the voyage and fifty-two were ill. The first death, on May 15, was that of Ellen Keane, aged four years and three months.[32] On May 19 the barque *Perseverance* and the ship *Wandsworth* arrived, both from Dublin. On the *Wandsworth* there had been forty-five deaths. The masters of both vessels said the sickness had been brought on by their passengers having embarked starving at Dublin, and then having ravenously devoured the breadstuffs given them on board.[33] But it was not the breadstuff that was killing them. They had typhus.

An emigrant's tract of the time described the disease in ordinary language: 'This is a complaint which comes on when many persons are crowded together in a small space. Recollect that this, like all fevers, is a complaint that will last its own time; that there is no such thing as cutting it short; and that the game you have to play is to get the patient to *live on* till the fever leaves him.'[34] It was a game not best played on board an emigrant ship. Typhus is a disease of the blood vessels, the brain, and the skin. The onset is sudden. The symptoms are shivering, headache, congested face, bloodshot eyes, muscular twitchings, and a stupid stare, as if the sufferer were drunk. The disease takes its name from the Greek *tuphos* (mist) which describes the vague mental state of the patient. The pulse goes as high as 130 and as low as thirty-five. The skin becomes dark, and sometimes the illness was called *fiabhras dubh*, or

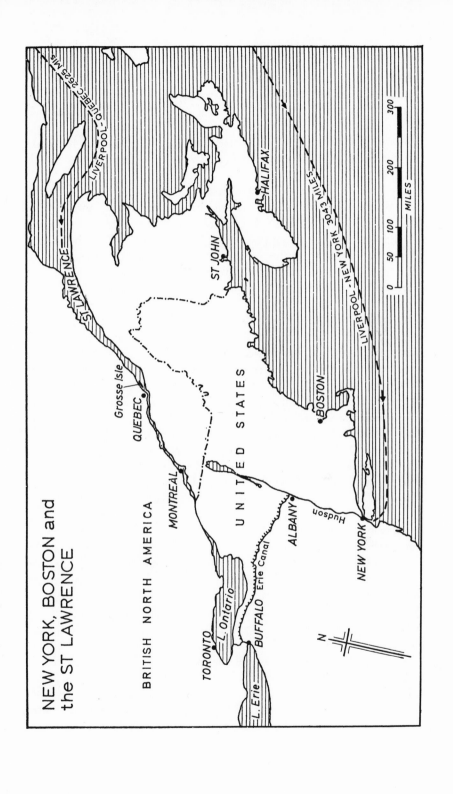

NEW YORK, BOSTON and
the ST LAWRENCE

BRITISH NORTH AMERICA

UNITED STATES

TORONTO

L. Erie

L. Ontario

BUFFALO Erie Canal

ALBANY

Hudson

NEW YORK

BOSTON

MONTREAL

QUEBEC

Grosse Isle

ST LAWRENCE

ST JOHN

HALIFAX

QUEBEC 2625 MIS

LIVERPOOL –

LIVERPOOL - NEW YORK 3043 MILES

N

0   50 100   200   300

MILES

black fever. About the fifth day a rash comes out, and the delirium becomes a stupor. It is a disease greatly encouraged by starvation, dirt, and overcrowding. What no doctor of the day knew was that it is a disease carried in the faeces of lice. The faeces dry to a light dust, and a man may be infected through a scratch on his hand or by breathing the dust in, even though he has no lice on his body.[35]

By May 28, Douglas had 856 cases of fever and dysentery on the island, 470 more waiting on board ships in the roads, and another thirty-six vessels, with 13,000 passengers, waiting to be inspected. He had received extra supplies of eight marquees and 266 bell-tents. These had come from the Army, but the officers had decided not to risk the health of their men by sending a party to pitch them. Everybody in the island was worn out from attending the sick and dying, and so the tents could not be put up for some days. In the only places where tents could be pitched, the ground was either gravel, from which the pegs loosened in windy weather, or soft alluvial soil, into which a man sank after a shower of rain. Before the week was out, Douglas expected to have 20,000 people in quarantine, 'the population, in fact, of a large city'.[36] By May 30 he had managed to get four large marquees pitched, and put sixty-four beds in each. Many bell-tents were also pitched and filled with beds, but still there were thousands waiting in the ships, falling ill and dying. All his staff were ill or exhausted, so he could hardly find enough people to dig graves and bury the dead. Dr. Benson, who had come in on board the *Wandsworth* from Dublin, had helped at first, but then died. Douglas said that the lower orders of the Irish were so afraid, that they were leaving their nearest relatives without the least compunction, making no attempt to help them.[37] In London, when the emigration commissioners received a despatch saying that at the end of May there were still more than 12,000 emigrants waiting even to be inspected, they wrote to the Colonial Office saying that much as they lamented the sufferings of the season, they were anxious that these sufferings should not for a moment be supposed to afford any evidence of ordinary experience, 'not merely because this would not be consistent with the facts, but also because it would of course seriously prejudice that annual emigration of the humbler classes which on the whole we believe is so beneficial to their interests'.[38]

By June 5, shanties were being erected, and more tents were made from the sails of waiting ships.[39] On June 8 Douglas wrote a hasty letter to the younger Buchanan, chief agent at Quebec.

'Grosse Isle, Tuesday, 9 a.m.
Out of the 4,000 or 5,000 emigrants that have left this island since
Sunday, at least 2,000 will fall sick somewhere before three weeks are
over. They ought to have accommodation for 2,000 sick at least at
Montreal and Quebec, as all the Cork and Liverpool passengers are
half dead from starvation and want before embarking; and the least
bowel complaint, which is sure to come with change of food, finishes
them without a struggle. I never saw people so indifferent to life;
they would continue in the same berth with a dead person until the
seamen or captain dragged out the corpse with boat-hooks. Good
God! what evils will befall the cities wherever they alight. Hot
weather will increase the evil. Now give the authorities of Quebec
and Montreal fair warning from me. I have not time to write, or
should feel it my duty to do so. Public safety requires it.'[40]

By June 10, 1,800 sick were crowded into hospitals, sheds,
shanties, and tents, and into the church. Five new hospital sheds
were being put up—and these still stand on the island. Douglas said
the accumulation of so many fever cases had generated a miasma so
violent and concentrated that few who came into its poisonous
atmosphere escaped. Clergymen, doctors, attendants, servants, and
policemen fell ill one after another. On average it was eighteen to
twenty-one days before a doctor caught the disease. Out of twenty-
six doctors and attendants working on the island up to the middle of
June, only three people, including Douglas, escaped the fever, and
they were severely affected in general health from breathing the foul
air of the ships and tents.[41]

It was difficult to keep servants. Douglas compelled some to stay,
but they neglected their duty to the sick and tried their best to
provoke Douglas to dismiss them. New servants sent down from
Quebec were often 'the vilest and most profligate of both sexes, and
were influenced by the most sordid motives'.[42] From June 19 to 26
it rained and was hot and foggy, and during the rain it was impossible
to wash or dry the vast quantities of hospital bedding.[43] The island
had become a hospital in a swamp. As a quarantine, it had ceased to
be in the least effective. While the ships waited at anchor, passengers
who were still well rapidly took the infection from those already ill.
On the island the separation was by no means complete, as it could
not be. Those who landed fit had to sleep in open tents on the bare
ground in the mid-summer heat, humidity, and rain, and fell ill
themselves. Those who were allowed to leave the island, because

they were able to walk to the steamers, and because some had to go to make way for others, carried the infection to Quebec and Montreal, so they might as well have been allowed to go straight there without stopping at quarantine. At this point, all that Grosse Isle achieved as a quarantine was to delay the spread of infection by the few days the vessels were kept there. Stephen de Vere, who arrived in June, said the medical inspection on board was slight and hasty. Hardly any questions were asked. The doctor walked past the passengers lined up on deck, selected for hospital those who did not look well, and ordered them on shore. Some who were not ill were detained, and many who had fever were allowed to go. On the island the sheds were very miserable, and so slightly built as to exclude neither the heat nor the cold. No sufficient care was taken to disinfect and clean a shed after the removal of the sick to one of the new hospitals. Many poor families preferred to burrow under heaps of loose stones than sleep in the infected sheds.[44]

July was calm and sultry. In some places the graves could be dug only three feet deep because there was solid rock beneath. In these grave-trenches the coffins were placed in two layers, and covered with a few shovelfuls of earth. Rats came ashore from the ships at anchor, found the graveyard, dug down, and began to gnaw the bodies. To prevent this, cartloads of earth were brought from the hills around, and dumped on the graves.[45]

In mid-July the provincial government set up a committee to inquire into the management of the quarantine.[46] The Rev. William Moylan, Roman Catholic priest and vicar of St. Patrick's, Quebec, said the sick were sadly neglected. He had given water to two people who had been left in a tent for eighteen hours without help. In the old sheds the sick were in bunk beds. The planks of the upper tier were not close together, and the filth of the upper patients fell on the lower ones. Then Father Moylan grumbled that Douglas had made the government boatmen work on his farm. As to the money belonging to the sick and dying emigrants, it was the general opinion of all the clergymen on the island that some of the nurses and orderlies were not overscrupulous, and took it for themselves.

Douglas himself gave evidence. He said he kept six men constantly digging graves. He praised Cullingford, his chief orderly, who had formerly been a sergeant in the British Army. He said that at least two of the boatmen received more pay from him than from the government. He had no doubt at all that the dead and dying were sometimes robbed by the nurses and attendants. He was tired. He said he was broken in health.

Captain Edward Boxer, Royal Navy, captain of the port of Quebec, agreed: when he had seen Douglas on the island on May 28 he already appeared nearly worn out. On June 1 Boxer had recommended to the provincial secretary that sheds for 2,000 patients should be erected, and a steamboat hired to carry the sick from the ships to hospital, and this had been done.

The Rev. Bernard O'Reilly, parish priest of Sherbrooke, had been on the island from July 6 to July 14. Both in the sheds and in the tents, the sick were lying on bare boards or on the ground because there was no straw. He went on board the *Avon* and the *Triton* and administered the last rites to 200 passengers. On the island there was no spring water and no lime juice for the sick, or at least he saw none. The clergymen had no boat to take them on board the waiting emigrant vessels, so unless some sailors sent a boat out of kindness, the wretched emigrants were allowed to die in sight of their clergy without the supreme consolation of an Irish Catholic, the last rites of his church. He thought Douglas was making superhuman exertions, and doing the work of more than three men, but things should be organised in quite a different way. 'I was eight days on Grosse Isle, and during that period I could convince myself that, if things continue as they now exist, very few of those who land on its rocky shores, shall ever leave them.' Sooner or later the government ought to provide sheds where emigrants who had recovered from fever could convalesce. There the wretches who came up daily from quarantine, without health, home, friends, or money, could recover their strength and then continue their journey without endangering others. This had to be done if the government did not choose to consent to the wholesale murder of thousands who were then crossing the Atlantic, or about to leave home for Canada. He wished to blame none, because he did not know who was to blame, but he had to express his grief that so many thousands of his fellow creatures, fellow countrymen and subjects of the empire, should have been sacrificed to neglect and improvidence. As long as they were crammed on board emigrant ships, they would die in hundreds, and the remnant, on landing at Grosse Isle, would find a very slight change for the better in their condition. Most would sink under fever and dysentery. Many who were healthy and went to Montreal would fall ill there; and of those who were able to leave Montreal and go on further, the large majority were 'pre-doomed to expire on the wharves of Kingston or Toronto, and carry with them whithersoever they direct their steps, the dreadful malady that now hangs over the country like a funeral pall'. Father O'Reilly was asked whether Dr. Douglas had omitted to board all vessels arriving at the quarantine station. He replied that he understood it was Douglas's responsibility alone to board ships. From every person who had visited Grosse Isle he had heard the highest praise for the zeal Douglas had displayed in attending to incessant calls, and it was a wonder to all that he could withstand the horrible fatigue, especially as he had lately been unable to walk. O'Reilly knew that some ships had waited several days at anchor before they were visited. He knew that after the inspection the sick had been left on board for days without medical attendance. He thought Douglas would soon sink under the weight of his labours, and that for his own sake and that of the emigrants, his duties should be shared by others.

Another Roman Catholic priest, the Rev. Jean Baptiste Antoine Ferland, said that in Grosse Isle one long ditch extended into the middle of a row of tents, and received the corrupted matter which flowed from the grave-trenches. When a burning sun shone on this pestilential mud, the smell was heart-sickening. He too had had trouble getting aboard ships to administer the last rites. To deprive Irishmen of a priest at the moment of death, if one could be got for them, was a cruelty. Many had died without the consolation of religion and for a Roman Catholic that was a heavy affliction. Where did the fault lie at Grosse Isle? Certainly not with the officers employed there. Emigration had come like a torrent and overthrown everything.

In defence of Douglas, the Bishop of Montreal sent a letter saying that very few men indeed would have been found capable of the same energy, collectedness, attention to a multiplicity of calls, and power of methodical arrangement in the face of accumulated and harassing difficulties. The bishop was aware there had been surmises and suspicions about Douglas's looking after his own interests, and gossiping stories about his making a trade of milk. Of this he knew nothing, but he did happen to know that there were instances when Douglas had sent milk on board ship as an act of charity, for infants who had lost their mothers. When he was on the island, there had not been enough nurses. Douglas had been delighted to be told that sixteen were being sent from Quebec, but when they saw the hospital, ten of them refused to stay there and returned. 'Upon the whole,' said the bishop, 'the impression produced upon my mind was of the hopelessness of doing anything effectual to stay the consequences of such a visitation from the hand of God.'

August was sultry too. The *Virginius* arrived from Liverpool with 476 passengers, fever, and dysentery. On the voyage 158 had died, including the master, mate, steward, and nine sailors. The remains of the crew, with the aid of the passengers, could only just moor the ship and furl the sails at quarantine. Three days after her arrival only the second mate, one seaman, and a boy were fit for duty, and 106 people were ill with fever. Douglas said the few who were able to come on deck were ghastly, yellow-looking spectres, unshaven and hollow cheeked, and without exception the worst-looking passengers he had ever seen. Not more than six or eight, out of 634 who had sailed from Liverpool, were really healthy. While Douglas was writing his report on the *Virginius,* another vessel came in. He looked at her and then added to his despatch: 'Another plague ship has just dropped in, the *Naomi,* from Liverpool . . . the filth and dirt in this vessel's hold creates such an effluvium as to make it difficult to breathe.'[47] Soon five more vessels came in, with 2,235 more passengers: 915 were able to continue their journey, but Douglas was convinced most would fall ill. Those who landed at the tents in comparatively good health sickened from the changes of air and diet, and many died suddenly.[48]

One of the vessels to arrive at the end of July was a brig from Dublin carrying about one hundred passengers, among them Robert Whyte. He kept a diary of the voyage, which he published under the title of *The Ocean Plague.*[49] Although he was an emigrant himself, he was an opponent of mass emigration, and printed this quotation on the title page of his book: 'To throw starving and diseased paupers under the rock at Quebec, ought to be punishable as murder.—Lord Sydenham.' Sydenham was a former Governor-General of Canada. Whyte's fellow passengers had been induced to emigrate, believing that they were bound for a land of milk and honey, and thinking any change from Ireland would be for the better. One passenger told him: 'Ah! Sir, we thought we couldn't be worse off than we war; but now to our sorrow we know the differ; for sure supposin we were dyin of starvation, or if the sickness overtuk us, we had a chance of a doctor, and if he could do no good for our bodies, sure the priest could for our souls; and then we'd be buried along wid our own people, in the ould church-yard, with the green sod over us; instead of dying like rotten sheep thrown into a pit, and the minit the breath is out of our bodies, flung into the sea to be eaten up by them horrid sharks.'

The brig left Dublin on May 30. Fever soon appeared. The moaning and raving of patients and the cries of 'Water, for God's sake some water,' kept Whyte awake. Much of the water was in foul casks. He saw a woman dying. She had been of a clear complexion, and contented, but now her head was deformed and swollen and the face leprous white. The swelling had started in her feet and crept up her body. Her husband stood by her with a 'blessed candle' in his hand as she died, and said amen as her body was lowered into the Atlantic. They arrived at Grosse Isle towards the end of July. While they were waiting to be inspected, a woman died, and the ship's boat took her ashore for burial. The sailors could not find the burial ground, so they dug a grave on another island and were about to bury the woman when they were discovered and had to leave, taking the body with them. Eventually they found the burial ground by following several other boats. The husband was desperate. He was disfigured by smallpox and blind in one eye. After the grave was filled up he took the shovels, placed them crosswise on the grave, and said: 'By that cross, Mary, I swear to revenge your death; as soon as I earn the price of my passage home, I'll go back, and shoot the man that murdered you, and that's the landlord.'

Vessels were arriving with every tide, the German ones neat and healthy, the Irish and English vessels full of disease. By the evening of July 31, more than thirty vessels were waiting in the roads. Boats plied all day long between ships and the hospitals. The sea was high, the miserable patients were drenched by the spray, and then had to clamber ashore over the slimy rocks, or be carried by sailors. An almost unbroken line of boats carried the dead for interment. The doctor's boat shot unceasingly about, besides several others carrying captains of ships, many of whom had handsome gigs with six oars and uniformed rowers. The rigging of many vessels was covered with the passengers' clothes hung out to dry. The state of the clothes showed from which country the ships came. The rags of most vessels showed they were Irish.

Throughout the season the Roman Catholic priests distinguished themselves. The youngest was the Rev. Bernard McGauran, who had been ordained only the year before and sent to be chaplain of the small church at Grosse Isle. He was a big, strong man who spent whole nights and days administering the last sacraments to the dying and then burying the dead. He said, 'I have one day seen thirty-seven people lying on the beach, crawling in the mud, and dying like fish out of water.' Eventually he too caught typhus, and though he recovered, was never the same afterwards.[50] Another young French-

Canadian priest, the Rev. Elzéar Alexandre Taschereau, was taken from his parish and sent to Grosse Isle because he spoke excellent English. He was there only eight days, giving the last sacraments to hundreds in the holds of emigrant ships, before he fell ill. He survived to become Archbishop of Quebec and a cardinal.[51] Another priest was Charles Félix Cazeau, who went to Grosse Isle to look after the many orphans. He became a domestic prelate to the Pope, and Vicar-General of the arch-diocese of Quebec, but he was remembered mostly as the foster-father of hundreds of the 'orphans of '47', whose careers he followed. Both he and Father Moylan looked after the children, and placed them in the care of Catholic lay-women at Quebec. All these women caught typhus.[52]

The Roman Catholic Church cared for 619 orphans.[53] They were washed, clothed, and fed, and the priests tried to discover what their names were, and which were related to each other, so that families should not be broken up. If the childern were too young to talk it was difficult to discover which were brothers and sisters. If one infant ran to meet another, or held its hand, or smiled at it, or kissed it, or showed pleasure in its company, that was a clue. The orphans were found foster-parents. A country priest showed one child in his arms to his congregation, and said there were many others: 'Go quickly to Quebec. There you will find these orphan children—these gifts offered to you by the good God—go quickly—go tomorrow, lose not a moment—take them and carry them to your homes, I say go tomorrow without fail, or others may be before you.' Next day there was a procession of waggons to Quebec, and 200 children were taken into new homes.[54] Father Thomas Cooke, Vicar-General of Trois Rivières, wrote to the Archbishop of Quebec on June 17, 1847: '*Les personnes charitables disputent la possession des orphelins irlandais.*'[55] There were more people willing to receive orphans than there were orphans to receive.

Not only priests, in the certainty of their religion, behaved courageously. So did two inventors, in the certainty of their disinfectant. They were M. Ledoyen and Colonel Calvert, who had devised a disinfecting fluid, and sailed from England to Grosse Isle in July to test it. They tried it in two vessels, the *Douce Davie* and the *Emigrant*. They also used it to remove effluvium from a bell-tent in which thirty-two containers filled with excrement had been placed for twenty-four hours. 'This,' said Douglas, who appeared to be sceptical, 'was effected by M. Ledoyen, who sprinkled the fluid, and waved a wet sheet with the same throughout the tent for about an hour.' But, he said, both these gentlemen contracted fever themselves, and one had died, so he thought it fair to infer that the fluid did not afford the protection claimed for it. Later, Ledoyen wrote to Lord Grey saying his lordship would have observed that he and Calvert had succeeded in disinfecting enormous quantities of nightsoil. He felt confident that if his fluid had been in use when the fever first started in Canada its ravages would have been altogether stopped. He made one reference to the late Colonel Calvert, whose death, he said, arose from 'the immense fatigue, anxiety and exertion'.[56]

From Grosse Isle the fit, or at any rate those not obviously dying, went up river to Quebec and Montreal by river steamer. The biggest of these steamers were very elegant, with saloons 150 feet long, Persian carpets, armchairs and sofas, cut-glass chandeliers, vases of flowers, mirrors, door-handles of gilt or porcelain, and handsomely bound Bibles reposing on centre tables.[57] But all this was not for steerage passengers, who were bundled together in the between decks with children, bedding, boxes, tin kettles, and a bar selling liquor. In 1842 Charles Dickens had travelled from Quebec to Montreal in a steamer full of emigrants, whom he admired. He said it was very much harder for the poor to be virtuous than it was for the rich, and the good that was in them shone the brighter for it. Bring a rich and worthy man from his mansion to that crowded deck, strip from his fair young wife her silken dress and jewels, stamp early wrinkles on her brow, array her faded form in patched attire, let there be nothing but his love to set her forth or deck her out; so change his station in the world that he should see in the children who climbed about his knee not records of his wealth and name, but little wrestlers with him for his daily bread; let the children's prattle be not of engaging fancies but of cold, thirst, and hunger; and who should say what kind of man he would be then, if such realities were his? Looking at those emigrants, far from home, houseless, indigent, wandering, weary with travel and hard living, and seeing how patiently they nursed and tended their young children, Dickens thought what ministers of hope and faith the women were, how the men profited by their example, and how very seldom even a moment's petulance or harsh complaint broke out among them; and he felt a stronger love and honour of his fellow men come glowing on his heart.[58]

That was 1842, and the emigrants were nearly all English, from Gloucestershire. They were poor, and they had had a long passage out, but they suffered nothing compared with the Irish of 1847. That year the government, seeing it had to move the emigrants from Grosse Isle somehow, made a contract giving one man the monopoly of carrying them at so much a head, with no restrictions or regulations. The consequences, according to Stephen de Vere, were frightful.[59] He saw small and ill-ventilated steamers arriving at the quay in Toronto after a forty-eight-hour passage, freighted with fetid cargoes of 1,100 or 1,200 'Government Emigrants' of all ages, the healthy who had just arrived from Europe mixed with the half-recovered convalescents of the hospitals, unable during the passage to lie down or almost to sit. In almost every boat there were clearly marked cases of fever, and in some there were deaths. The dead and the living were huddled together. Sometimes they were stowed in barges and towed behind steamers, 'standing like pigs upon the deck of a Cork and Bristol packet'. It was the unhesitating opinion of every man he spoke to, including government agents and doctors, that much fever throughout the country had been generated in the river steamers. Father O'Reilly held the same opinion, and just as strongly: emigrants were crammed on board the steamers, exposed to the cold night air or to the burning summer sun, and the most robust constitution soon gave way. Montreal and the whole province had learned the consequences of permitting up to 1,000 dirty, debilitated people to be huddled together for forty-eight hours on the deck of a steamer.[60]

It was the steamer trip from Dublin to Liverpool all over again, smoother in the St. Lawrence than across the Irish Channel, but a longer voyage, and this time endured by people broken down by the long Atlantic crossing, hunger, and disease.

Some emigrants fell ill at Quebec, others stayed to settle there, but most went on to Montreal and Toronto. Montreal was then a city of 44,093 people, of whom 15,268 were English, Scotch, or Irish. It was a city of twenty-three colleges, academies, and convents, sixty-eight elementary schools, two cricket clubs and one quoits club, and imported from England large amounts of farming implements, clothing for the armed forces, and copies of the Holy Scriptures. The emigrants from Grosse Isle inevitably brought typhus, and in the end more died there than at quarantine.[61] One citizen of Montreal wrote an angry letter to Lord John Russell, the Prime Minister, in London, describing how he had visited the fever sheds. After passing through nearly 2,000 adults in all stages of the disease, he came to two or three hundred infant orphans, some only fifteen or twenty days old, many taken from the side of their dead mothers. 'Is this', he asked, 'the work of the Almighty? No, my lord; I believe that blasphemy hangs on that assertion.' He preferred to blame the rapacity of Irish landlords.[62]

Back at Grosse Isle, in September, the number of deaths increased. At one time, as many as 14,000 emigrants waited at anchor. In one vessel, the *Sisters* from Liverpool, Captain Christian had to bring up the bodies of the dead from the hold on his shoulders. Neither passengers nor sailors would help. Christian was a humane man, whose attention to sickly passengers was said by Douglas to be beyond all praise, but he caught typhus and died at Quebec. In another vessel, the *Erin's Queen*, the master could only get the dead brought up by paying his seamen a sovereign for each body.[63]

By mid-October, only a few days before the first snow, patients were dying of cold.[64] Those who remained were sent to Point St. Charles, and the Grosse Isle quarantine was closed on November 3. At the beginning of the season the island had room for 200. At the end there was room for 2,300 in newly built hospitals. The tents had not been needed since the end of August. Dr. Douglas still wanted a steam apparatus to wash clothing saturated in the ejecta of the sick and dying. When the station closed there were 4,000 pieces of bedding to be washed, and this was being done by a washerwoman and two assistants who stayed on the island all winter.[65]

On December 27, 1847, Douglas sent in his formal report on the year at quarantine.[66] He had inspected 400 vessels—later this was amended to 442—and had taken 8,691 emigrants into the hospitals, sheds, or tents on the island. All had typhus or dysentery or both, except for ninety-two with smallpox and twenty-five with other diseases. Altogether 3,238 died—1,361 men, 969 women, and 908 children. He tabulated the average number of sick daily:

May 15–31	451	September	1330 1/30
June	1508½	October 1–21	346 9/21
July	1454¾	Daily average	
		for season	1307 8/159
August	2021 1/3		

Of those who looked after the sick on the island, four Roman Catholic priests had died; two clergymen of the Church of England; four doctors; three stewards; twenty-two nurses, orderlies, and cooks; three policemen; two carters employed to remove the sick, dying, and dead; and four others.

From the Roman Catholic archdiocese of Quebec five priests (including Douglas's four) had died, and ten others had caught typhus and recovered. In Montreal the vicar-general to the Catholic bishop died, and in Toronto the Catholic bishop.

It is impossible to know how many died altogether that year in British North America. A few months afterwards the Imperial government in London gave out the following figures:[67]

	Canada	New Brunswick	Total
Embarked	89,738	17,074	106,812
Died on voyage	5,293	823	6,116
Died at quarantine	3,452	697	4,169
Died at hospitals	6,585	595	7,180

So, 15,330 died on the way to Canada, or at Grosse Isle, or at the hospitals (which means at Quebec, Montreal, and other places other than quarantine); and 2,115 emigrants to New Brunswick died. This means 17,465 emigrants to British North America died in 1847, or one in six of all who sailed.

But these figures are certainly incomplete. No proper list of those who died on the voyage was kept. In the chaos of Grosse Isle, no proper check was kept either: the doctors had better things to do. And what figures there are disagree with each other. The number of emigrants to Canada was stated not only as 89,738, as above, but also, by A. C. Buchanan, as 97,953. And the total of 106,812 emigrants to the whole of British North America in 1847 later became 109,680, and this is the figure usually quoted in public documents.[68] The most puzzling figure of all is that given for deaths of Grosse Isle. No figure is at all likely to be accurate. A hopeless epidemic of typhus, with the medical superintendent so exhausted that he was at times unable to walk, and with his staff dying around him, does not make for statistical accuracy. But the two figures coming from Douglas himself are nothing like the same. In his annual report he says 3,238. But a monument on Grosse Island which has carved on its east face the statement that it was erected by Dr. Douglas and eighteen assistant medical officers on duty on the island in 1847, says on its west face that 5,424 immigrants are buried there.

There is no knowing. The figures, such as they are, only show how many died, according to the captains' statements, on board ship; and how many were recorded to have died at quarantine or in other hospitals. Of how many died travelling to other parts of Canada, or crossing into the United States, there is no record at all. Douglas himself thought that nearly half of those who left the island apparently fit, would die somewhere. Robert Whyte, when he parted from his fellow passengers after Grosse Isle, said a still more horrible sequel was to come. The survivors had to wander out and find homes, and who could say how many houseless, famished, and half-naked wretches would die in the snow as a Canadian winter set in?[69]

And all this considers only the voyage and the later troubles in Canada. Before the emigrant even left Ireland he would have been weakened by hunger and disease, and perhaps would also have had to withstand the steamer trip to Liverpool and the wait there in a dirty cellar. It can only be a guess, but taking all the hardships and dangers into account, it is hardly likely that more than half of those who started out, survived.

In December, 1847, Grey wrote from Downing Street to Elgin, serenely justifying himself and saying he need scarcely assure the Governor-General that the calamities of the year had caused the most sincere and lively sorrow, but upon looking back at the melancholy history of these sufferings, it was at least some consolation to them that these sufferings did not appear to have been produced or aggravated by their measures, or by their having neglected any precaution it was in their power to adopt. It was no slight gratification to him to remember that, strongly as he had been urged at the beginning of the season to increase the multitude who flocked unaided to America, by providing at the public expense for the conveyance across the Atlantic of a large additional number of those who were anxious to fly from distress in Ireland, he had steadily refused to do this, and abstained from giving any artificial stimulus to the tide of emigration, while, at the same time, he had taken such precautions as were in his power to mitigate, as far as possible, the sufferings to which he foresaw that even this spontaneous emigration would naturally give rise. So, he was saying in effect, he had done nothing and it had all turned out for the best.[70]

The Mayor of Toronto had other views. In a letter to Elgin, which Elgin passed on to Grey, the mayor said that if the widespread sufferings of the past year had been a dispensation from the chastening hand of Providence, unaffected and unaided by human agency, then the city of Toronto would willingly or at least silently have borne its portion of the general loss and misery. But sincerely believing the suffering to have arisen in a very serious degree from neglect, indifference, and mismanagement, he respectfully ventured to press on His Excellency the Governor-General the absolute necessity of remedial measures. 'Above all, the fact cannot be too widely promulgated in Great Britain and Ireland, that the throwing of a half-clad and penniless emigrant on the shores of the St Lawrence may be the means of ridding an estate of a burdensome tenant; but it is an almost hopeless method of providing for a fellow-Christian.'[71]

The Imperial government continued to do substantially nothing, but this did not matter so much, since the Canadian immigration returned to normal. Less than half as many emigrants arrived in 1848, and the average for each subsequent year up to 1855 was about a third the emigration of 1847. In 1848, Canada doubled the emigrant tax to 10s. a head, and ship masters were required to give bonds of £20 to save public expense on any emigrant certified by a doctor as likely to become a permanent public charge.[72] The Imperial government, which in 1847 had paid only a £10,000 Parliamentary grant and an extra £20,000 from the military chest, eventually found the whole expense of the season, about £150,000.[73] It also repaid to the Catholic Church the cost of looking after orphans, and the expenses of the priests who went to Grosse Isle.[74]

Years later Dr. Douglas, who had done so much, was still defending himself against little innuendoes. Writing to the provincial government in Quebec, he said he was impelled in justice to himself to show how little he had merited the accusation of having profited from the management of the quarantine station. He had saved the government money by buying firewood at 2s. 6d. a load from the island as against 8s. to 13s. from the mainland. He had taken over the lease of the farm on Grosse Isle only when the previous tenant defaulted, and he had been out of pocket by doing so. His economies on the island had excited much ill-will, mostly from the canteen keeper whose profits fell when Douglas prohibited the sale of liquor on the island. He said he knew no one ever gained by parading himself as an injured man, but it was hard that, though he had saved the province so much, he should now lie under suspicion of having sought his own interest. He said that the money and effects of those who died in hospital without friends had been used to help pay the general expenses of the station. He gave a list of the money left, over five years, by dying patients. It came to £24 15s. 11d. 'And most of this', he said, 'was left by Emigrants to be transmitted to their relations, and was so transmitted.'[75]

There are a few memorials to the emigrants of 1847. In 1859 the navvies, mostly English and Irish, who built a railway bridge in Montreal erected a stone on the old site of the emigrant sheds at Point St. Charles. It says:

TO
PRESERVE FROM DESECRATION
THE REMAINS OF 6,000 EMIGRANTS
WHO DIED OF SHIP FEVER
A.D. 1847–8
THIS STONE
IS ERECTED BY THE WORKMEN
OF
MESSRS. PETO, BRASSEY & BETTS,
EMPLOYED IN THE CONSTRUCTION
OF THE
VICTORIA BRIDGE
A.D. 1859

In the grounds of the old general hospital at Kingston there was a mound, not very high, on which the grass was said to be always green, because of a peculiar richness of the soil: 1,900 emigrants were buried beneath it. [76]

On Grosse Isle there are two memorials.[77] The first that a visitor sees as he approaches across the St. Lawrence stands 140 feet above the level of the river on Telegraph Hill, the highest point of the island. It is a Celtic cross in granite, erected in 1909 by the Ancient Order of Hibernians in America. On its north side it names the priests who ministered to the emigrants of 1847, and on its south, west, and east sides it bears inscriptions in English, French, and Gaelic. The English inscription says:

Sacred to the memory of thousands of Irish immigrants, who, to preserve the faith, suffered hunger and exile in 1847–48, and stricken with fever ended here their sorrowful pilgrimage.

Beneath Telegraph Hill, in a valley which was the principal cemetery of the island, is the earlier monument erected by Dr. Douglas and his assistants. On the south face, it commemorates Doctors Benson, Pinet, Malhiot and Jameson, who died there in 1847; and on the north face two doctors who died earlier, in 1834 and 1837. The inscription on the west face says:

In this secluded spot lie the mortal
remains of 5424 persons who
flying from Pestilence and Famine in
Ireland in the year 1847 found in
America but a Grave

10

New York

New York by 1850 was the third largest city in the western world, after London and Paris, and the largest port and most thriving city of the United States. 'Those who fancy New York a mere busy provincial and commercial city—a sort of Liverpool—will be surprised', said the London *Times*, 'to find it a great metropolis.' This opinion was picked up and reported in America, and so was the next bit, in which *The Times* went on to say that the city was not so much like London either, but was rather Paris with a dash of Hamburg.[1]

New York was an ostentatiously rich city. At 563 Broadway old master paintings by Titian, Rubens, Raphael and others were for sale; and at 189 Broadway, Ever Pointed Gold Pens. Gold bird-cages were also to be bought. Fine French calf-boots were $1.50. H. S. Beal, at his Daguerrian Rooms at 183 Broadway, would take your photograph for a dollar.[2] Each year New York consumed $68,000 worth of fresh salmon shipped in from St. John, New Brunswick.[3] There were 132 principal eating houses, from Delmonico's, with its very fashionable Italian and French cuisine, to Gosling's in Nassau Street where Mr. Gosling dined more than 1,000 people a day, very cheap.[4] The hotels were more splendid, and very much larger, than any in Europe at the time. The grandest was Astor House, opposite the City Hall. Rathburn's Hotel could sleep 300.[5] The United States Hotel, proprietor H. Johnson, advertised that it had installed at great expense, 'an extensive range of water closets, not equalled by any similar Establishment in the United States'.[6]

The new emigrant could look in shop windows, or he could buy a copy of a paper-bound booklet called the *The Wealth and Biography of the Wealthy Citizens of the City of New York*,[7] an alphabetical list of the most prominent capitalists whose fortune was estimated at $100,000 or more, with the sums appended to each. By present-day values they would be millionaires. An introduction said the booklet's aim was to 'hold up to view some of the brightest examples of prosperity in this *touch-stone* land as beacons for those ambitious of fortune's favours'. An emigrant could read this and think there was hope. *Adams, John* ($300,000) was of Irish descent, and known for integrity in the dry-goods line. *Conger, Abraham B.* ($100,000) had simply 'married Miss Hedges'. *Cavanna, Augusta* ($100,000) was the distinguished hairdresser. *Collins, E. K.* ($100,000) owned packet ships. *Goodhue, Jonathan* ($100,000) also owned packets, which showed that this was one way to get rich. *Drew, Daniel* ($250,000), 'a shrewd keen money-making man', ran a line of steamboats up to Albany and would have got most of his money from emigrants too. *Pease, John* ($100,000) was 'the famous horehound candy man'. *Slocum, Daniel* ($100,000) was the famous maker of pins, whose Yankee ingenuity was said to have superseded the dull, plod-on-your-way principle of the English manufacturers. The most splendid example of all was *Astor, John Jacob* ($25,000,000), born near Heidelberg and an emigrant himself, who had beaten skins in Gold Street, New York, in early life, and then made his money in the fur trade. His income alone was $2,000,000 a year—$41,500 a week, $5,760 a day, $240 an hour, or $4 a minute. And he had come as a steerage passenger. 'On one occasion', so the booklet said, 'young Astor ventured beyond the limits assigned to the steerage passengers, and appeared on the quarter deck: Captain Stout, observing it, came up, and in a very peremptory manner, asked him how he *dared* to intrude there! *ordering* him instantly to retire! This poor steerage passenger is now the richest individual in the Western Hemisphere.' The *Wealth and Biography* also had a good story about *Fish, Preserved* ($100,000), owner of packet ships, who was said to have been given this name by sailors who found him as a baby adrift on a raft at sea. It is a pity the story is untrue. Preserved Fish came of an old family, the name was an old family name, and he was born and baptised at Portsmouth, Rhode Island.[8]

The booklet ran to thirty-two pages, and listed about 600 possessors of more than $100,000. This was in 1846. By 1855 there would have been many more. New York City was growing fast.

In 1840 the population was 313,000; in 1845, 371,000; in 1850, 516,000; and in 1855, 630,000.[9] By the end of 1855 the city had grown rapidly up to 34th Street.[10] Some fine houses had been built on Fifth Avenue, and no longer in the red-brick and two-storey English style which had previously been common in New York, but in brownstone. Streetcars were just coming into use, Central Park was scarcely begun, and Harlem was a quiet country town. The first world fair had been held in 1853, in the New York Crystal Palace, which was a smaller copy of the London one. But the City Hall fountain was believed to be larger than anything in England. It had a basin 100 feet broad and sent a jet of water sixty feet into the air, a jet, moreover, which could be made to assume the shapes of a vase, a dove, or a sheaf of wheat. There had been a wonderfully rapid commercial growth. Apart from cotton and emigrants, the China and East India trades thrived. The telegraph had just come to the city, and so had the railway. The first main line was the New York and Erie, which in 1851 was opened all the way from New York to Dunkirk, on Lake Erie. New York was a great shipbuilding city. The yards along the East River launched whalers, clippers, and packets made of white oak, live oak, hackmatack, locust, yellow pine, and white pine. By 1855 the city had $323,000,000 worth of foreign commerce a year, and her ships docked at 113 piers on the Hudson and East River waterfronts. In fifteen years the population had more than doubled. Here are a few entries, taken from the 1855 census, showing what New Yorkers did. There were:[11]

Actors 231	Gold and silversmiths 403
Apothecaries and druggists 521	Hotel and inn keepers 709
Authors 34	Jewellers 1,099
Ax makers *nil*	Junk-shop keepers 213
Bar keepers 565	Laborers 19,748
Billiard makers 4	Lace makers 35
Bird-cage makers 7	Laundresses 2,563
Boatmen and watermen 1,004	Lawyers 1,112
Bookbinders 1,315	Librarians 1
Botanists 1	Looking-glass makers 34
Brewers and distillers 360	Midwives 20
Clergymen 393	Milliners 1,585
Confectioners 704	Musicians 746
Custom house officers 212	Patent-medecine manufacturers 22
Editors 129	Photographers 88
Embroiderers 169	Physicians 1,252
Gamblers *nil*	Piano makers 760
Gold beaters 100	Policemen 1,164

Porcelain makers 5
Professors 80
Publishers 74
Reporters 36
Runners 57
Sculptors 46
Soldiers and military officers 78

Speculators 199
Tailors 12,609
Teachers 1,268
Tobacconists 1,996
Umbrella makers 270
Wine and liquor dealers 619

These figures can be read in many ways—but with care. A city with more bookbinders than policemen, and three times as many actors as soldiers, may be taken for a bookish and theatre-loving place— but it is more likely to have been just a very badly under-policed city in an unmilitary country. No gambler and only fifty-seven runners does not suggest an honest and uncorrupted city so much as a city where no one would admit to being a gambler, and where runners probably either evaded the census altogether or called themselves agents or hotel-keepers. Still, a city with lace, porcelain, and bird-cage makers, and with many more confectioners than clergymen, sounds a sophisticated place, not too unlike Paris. But it was Paris with 10,000 scavenging pigs which lounged round the streets[12] but were not mentioned in the census. New York was rough, and not a European city. In 1850 a boy from London, who had been sent out to America and got himself a job in a store, wrote home promising to send a guinea to his mother, and then went on:

'Now I will tell you something about the country, that is to say, about New York. Provisions are very cheap; plenty of work to be had; clothes are dear, but men paid well for their work; house rent is very dear in New York, it is a very healthy place; guns and pistols are very cheap . . .'[13]

It was a violent and dangerous city, and the police force was agreed to be of no practical value. The mayor congratulated them on their efficiency and spirit, but men were still attacked and murdered within sight of their own doors. 'We have long since become accustomed', said *Frank Leslie's Illustrated Newspaper,* 'to the incapacity of Mayor Wood and his army of idlers, and therefore expect nothing.'[14] And the *New York Herald* called the city police the worst in the world.[15]

It was a city in which, to English eyes, democracy was everywhere; and so were piles of rubbish. There was no titled aristocracy or College of Heralds, but a shop on Broadway devised and sold coats of arms as a matter of business; and in the booksellers' works on the British peerage and baronetage were as common as in England.

The $250,000 a year spent on clearing away rubbish in 1,500 carts
did not prevent Broadway from being ankle-deep in mud and refuse.[16]
Hordes of dogs as well as pigs roamed the streets, and the dogs were
feared to be mad, and were hunted. In fifteen days in June 1847,
400 dogs were killed by four Negroes employed by the city at $2 a
day.[17] A New York city directory for the same year advertised Colt's
revolvers, and listed twenty-eight banks, 192 churches from
Abyssinian Baptist to Zion's, and no fewer than 440 people who had
had to move in the previous year because their houses had burned
down.[18] In 1846 seventy-four New York newspapers, and by 1855 no
fewer than 223 newspapers and magazines, reported the doings of the
metropolis of the New World. Dr. Elmore of Grand Street advertised
that he could cure cancer, saying his treatment was milk but the cure
certain.[19] O. S. Fowler advertised his lectures on the Sexual Science of
Masculine Perfection: admission 25 cents.[20] In 1851 the Long Island
Railroad was already running late, but for good reason: 'A portion of
the track . . .' said the *New York Times,* 'has been torn up near River-
head (which is several miles beyond civilisation), by some villainous
scoundrels, which detained the morning train of Monday by about
two hours.'[21] John Conklin and James Cullum were arrested in
Atlantic Street by Officer Cox, for 'trying to sell some old duds'.[22]
In December that year 'A Celt' wrote to the paper calling the Irish
immigration a Hejira, a term the Roman Catholic Irish would not
have liked, and said Providence was ordering the matter;[23] and the
same day the Hungarian rebel Kossuth was entertained to a cere-
monial dinner at Irving House, with terrapin stewed in port wine,
oysters fried in butter, and 101 other items on the menu.[24]

New York was, of course, and had been for thirty years, easily the
most important port for emigrants. The trade was there, so the ships
followed the trade. In turn, more trade followed the ships, and
New York became the American metropolis. No other American
port even approached New York in the emigrant trade. Here are the
State Department figures in thousands, showing emigrants entering
at the chief American ports, for three sample years:[25]

	Total	New York	Boston	Philadelphia	Baltimore	New Orleans
1846	158	98	13	7	9	22
1851	408	294	25	18	8	52
1855	230	161	17	7	6	20

New York's share, in these three years, was thus 62 per cent,
72 per cent, and 70 per cent.

Newly arrived emigrants, without the sense or the money to get out of the city and travel inland for work, wandered aimlessly about the city. The Almshouse Commissioners reported that large numbers of them, as soon as they had landed, having no idea where to go or what to do, just roamed round in utter desolation until someone guided them to the almshouse board. 'And here is exhibited so sickening a picture of human destitution and suffering as no pen, however eloquent in the sad gloom of misfortune's description, could well paint in illustration of the dark and solemn truth. The deplorable infirmity of their desolate unhappiness must be *seen and felt* to be appreciated; and then, to often find amid the motley groups some with the last gasp of expiration issuing from their cold and blanched lips, forms a scene of dismay and distress too agonising to look upon with any other than feelings of horror and overwhelming sympathy.'[26] The Rev. Moses Marcus, Rector of the Church of St. George, 406 Broadway, and a member of the British Protective Emigrant Society, said many emigrants experienced 'the very reverse of those dreams of golden streets'. 'Alas,' he said, 'we have seen the sturdy Laborer,—England's pride and boast—who had left his own country to improve his circumstances and enable him to provide the better in another for a young and increasing family, wherewithall God had blessed him, wandering with his wife and children about our city, not knowing where now to wend his way.'[27] Some of them were robbed. Anne Steele arrived in the barque *Thetis* from Belfast, and lodged in Washington Street at a house kept by Francis Knowles. She had to sleep in a room with three men and four girls, and next morning found the lock of her chest picked, and a sovereign and 9s. taken.[28] Another emigrant, a woman from southern Ireland, had lost her husband on the voyage, her mother was ill, and she and her six children were destitute. Some hackmen on the wharf collected $12 or $13 for them, and the police took them off to hospital where they were said to be comfortably lodged.[29]

Some of the women emigrants were taken in by the New York Magdalen Female Benevolent Society at its asylum between 88th and 89th Streets, but they had a hard life there. In summer they had to get up at five in the morning, and in winter at six. Rule IV said each female should give up all her clothes to the matron, who would permit her to keep only those which were suitable to the custom of the house. Rule V said inmates' apartments should always be open to inspection by the matron, 'and no key shall at any time be turned against her'. Rule IX forbade snuff, opium, ardent spirits, nicknames, and loud laughter, and said: 'Each one is to avoid the telling of indelicate stories [and] the relation of sinful adventures.' In 1850 forty-six 'degraded females' were taken in. In 1851 the ladies of New York made the degraded females a gift of twelve Bibles, twelve hymn-books, and some cake. In 1852 the society spent $2,057.65 on its seventy inmates. In 1853, when the society moved to a new building on 88th Street between Fourth and Fifth Avenues, there were fifty-four inmates; six had been discharged at their own request, three sent to hospital, four expelled, seven placed in service, eight restored to friends, and four had left of their own accord. A Mrs. Pond gave the females two divans. In 1855 the society advertised the prices of work done at the asylum. Gentlemen's night-shirts, long, would be made for 44 cents, and short for $37\frac{1}{2}$; ladies' dresses, double gown, $1; drawers, scalloped, $37\frac{1}{2}$ cents; chemise, yoke and sleeves scolloped, 75 cents.[30] The year before, the pauper inmates of Bellevue Hospital made 252 nightgowns and 696 shrouds, not for sale but for use.[31]

One place from which some of the degraded females came, and the place to which some of them went back, was the Old Brewery, said to be unparalleled in the lowest sinks of vice in the most abandoned quarters of any European city. More murders and robberies were traced to it than to any other house in New York. The upper part was principally inhabited by females of the vilest stamp. In the lower half, beds in partitioned-off stalls were let by the night to all comers. This building was then bought by the New York Ladies' Home Mission Society of the Methodist Episcopal Church, who used it for other purposes. Soon they collected enough money to build a new mission on the site, but before the Old Brewery was torn down, in December 1852, it was illuminated, and visited by thousands of people of all classes.[32] By the next January a bestseller called *The Old Brewery or The New Mission House at the Five Points* had been written by the ladies of the mission. An advertisement called it 'A second Uncle Tom's Cabin', and said the deep interest exhibited by the public and the book trade since the announcement of this truly charming volume was unparalleled in the history of literature. Orders for 20,000 had already been received.[33]

The records of the New York Association for the Improvement of the Condition of the Poor[34] give a detailed account of the way many of the destitute managed to live. In 1845 it sent out a 'Circular on Cold Victuals'. This said that there were several thousand families in the city, the refuse of whose tables would, if gathered up and carefully dispensed, relieve an equal number of poor families. But with few exceptions food was given away at the door by servants to people they did not know, and it was notorious that this charity was abused. Sometimes the food was fed to pigs or sold by servants to the keepers of low boarding houses. The rich were asked to allow the association to come and collect the bits regularly, to give to the real poor. In 1847 one of the association's inspectors found a Scotswoman, a widow with four children, in a small attic. She had seen good days, but now she was destitute, and one of her daughters, aged seventeen, was a cripple. 'This widow, reduced by coughing and raising blood almost to a skeleton, lay in one corner of her desolate chamber, on the floor; without any thing in the shape of a bed under her! (O ye sons and daughters of wealth, who recline on your couches of velvet and down.)' She was intelligent and virtuous, but had had to pawn everything. The inspector gave her a bed, procured an excellent cough remedy, and soon had the satisfaction of seeing her so far restored that she was able to return to her daily toil. He had little doubt he saved her life.

In 1849 the association relieved 29,844 people from 6,672 families, but was disturbed to find a good deal of what it called voluntary destitution, chiefly among persons of foreign birth, who seemed to regard labour as the greatest of evils. They lived in indolence, intemperance, and filth. If they were once helped they would certainly apply again; and if helped through a winter, would not only look for help as long as they lived, but probably train their children to expect it after them. The association, though it was benevolent, often complained about the 'debased poor', who loved to clan together in some out-of-the-way place, content to live in filth and disorder with a bare subsistence, provided they could drink and smoke and gossip and frolic without molestation. They sent their children out to sweep crossings and to steal, and sold the very bodies and souls of those in whom their own blood circulated, in order to live lazily on the proceeds. This is puritan Yankee incomprehension of a feckless bunch who sound very like the Irish: the same report of the association was indignant that so many Roman Catholic derelicts should be supported by Protestant funds.

The 1852 report noticed that the labouring population, who made up most of the community, were not getting a proportionate share of the growing prosperity all round them. But this, the report said it scarcely need add, was not the result of a combination among the wealthy to oppress the poor for their own advantage: to think that would be untrue and unjust. It was just the result of those irresistible laws of supply and demand which no body of men, however sagacious or philanthropic, was competent to control. The trouble was that labour was preying upon itself by surfeiting the demand. The association then tried to work out exactly the number of paupers in New York City in 1851, by adding together the number of people who had been relieved at the city's various hospitals and prisons in that year. These are the figures arrived at:

Almshouse	2,782	78%	foreigners
Bellevue hospital	5,342	82%	,,
Penitentiary	3,450	75%	,,
City prison	21,279	71%	,,
Lunatic asylum	441	72%	,,
Randall's island	2,087	75%	,,
Out-door poor	42,872	73%	,,
Workhouse	965	75%	,,
	79,732	75%	

Those were the paupers helped by the city. In the same year 27,022 were helped by the association, which was a voluntary organisation. Half of these had been to the city almshouse as well, so the total number of paupers in New York City could be worked out in this way:

City relief	79,732
The Association	13,511
Other charities	20,000
Total paupers	113,243

Again, three-quarters of these were foreigners, that is to say, recent emigrants.

When they were out of the workhouse, or the hospitals, or the penitentiary, these emigrants lived in cellars and hovels. Downtown they were huddled together in yards so vile that they could 'hardly be stepped into without contracting filth of the most offensive kind'. Rents downtown were usually 25 to 30 per cent higher than uptown, and the charge for a single room on a second or third storey was $8 to $12 a month. Rooms were usually sublet to tenants by an Irish or German liquor seller, who occupied the best apartments free, at his sub-tenants' expense, and still showed a big profit. 'Crazy old buildings—crowded rear tenements in filthy yards —dark, damp basements—leaky garrets—shops, out-houses, and stables converted into dwellings though scarcely fit to shelter brutes

—are the habitations of our fellow-beings, in this wealthy Christian city.' In Oliver Street, in a rear building 16 by 30 feet, two storeys and a garret, ten rooms in all, fourteen families lived. The rent of a room was $1.50 a week, making $750 a year for the premises, which was at least 30 per cent of their whole value. In the same ward, the fourth, one six-storey building held fifty-six families, 250 persons in all. Another tenement house, in Cherry Street, with five storeys, held 120 families, more than 500 people altogether, and this was a building of the better class. In one block, ceilings were so low that the occupants could not stand. In Monroe Street two rear, rough-built, clapboard tenements had four rooms each, and each room held a whole family. These two houses were let for $312 a year, and the landlord made more in rent in a year than the houses would have fetched if he had sold them outright. According to the 1853 report of the association, 18,456 people were crowded into 3,472 cellars. 'They probably now rival the cellar population of Liverpool.'

Emigrants in New York did have their own societies which tried, not at first very effectively, to help the newly arrived, and also acted as patriotic clubs for those who had settled in the city. In the early 1850s the Irish Emigrant Society was at 4 Congress Square, just off Broadway, and the British Protective Emigrant Society at 86 Greenwich Street.[35] In 1853 a Children's Aid Society of New York was formed.[36] A select committee appointed by New York State to look into frauds on emigrants was doubtful about some societies. It thanked them for their kindness and courtesy, but added that duty compelled the observation that some societies did not give emigrants the substantial aid they might expect, and that some officers and agents of the societies had a more tender regard for the money of the emigrants than for their safety and comfort.[37]

It was true that the Irish Emigrant Society was supported by the profit it made on the money its members sent home.[38] If an Irishman in New York wished to send back to Ireland enough money to bring out his wife the society would arrange her passage through its Irish offices, taking the husband's money in advance at New York, in dollars, and charging him a commission of $12\frac{1}{2}$ per cent. The society kept what was called its Bill Fund at the Bank of Ireland and paid the Irish or Liverpool broker out of this fund, which was 'held sacred to that purpose alone, and never entrenched upon under any circumstances—thus offering a perfectly safe channel to poor Emigrants for remitting the few pounds their filial piety or noble hearted generosity prompts them to send to their familys or friends'.[39]

The many activities of Irish societies in New York are clearly shown in the papers of Charles P. Daley, chief justice of the Court of Common Pleas for the City and County of New York.[40] Daley (1816–1899) was born in New York, his parents having come there from Galway in 1814. He was poor, as a boy ran away to sea, was later apprenticed to a carpenter, in 1839 was called to the Bar, in 1843 was elected to the New York Assembly, and in 1844, at the age of twenty-eight, became a judge. He was said to be care-worn and saddened, but honest and fearless, and a very talkative judge. As a judge and a well-known Irishman he received all kinds of solicitations, invitations, and requests. In 1846 he received a letter saying 'Do you ever buy ball tickets?' and enclosing one for the third annual ball of the Irish Emigrant Society to take place at the Coliseum Room, 450 Broadway: ticket $3, to admit one gentleman and two ladies. Next year the United Irish Repeal Association and the several charitable and benevolent societies of the city favourable to the emancipation of Ireland invited him to the obsequies for the Irish patriot Daniel O'Connell. In 1851 he was respectfully invited to attend the anniversary dinner of the Independent Sons of Erin, and later to a dinner to welcome Kossuth. Eliza Flynn wrote asking for help, saying that he had once given her a cheque for $15 and that now her mother was dead. Andrew Ellard wrote saying he had been in America eighteen months, that he was now dollarless and his wife at the point of confinement, and asking for help in finding a job as an attorney's clerk. In Daley's possession were the papers of the Friendly Sons of St. Patrick, who met at the City Hotel in 1846, where 'after many good speeches songs etc. the hilarities of the evening were kept up until a late hour'. When the friendly sons met to celebrate St. Patrick's Day in 1854 the speaker said there would be, that night, more wearing of the green along the Mississippi than along the Shannon or the Foyle. (Applause.) He had Mother Ireland in mind, but their meeting was not a coroner's inquest upon the corpse of their mother. He was not a coroner, his audience were not a jury, and he believed it would not conduce to the main object of the meeting, which he took to be the promotion of good will and humour, if he should undertake to make out a case for the ghastly prosecution. He would let the case stand over. He believed it must one day be heard, and then he would pray for the guilty, that God might have mercy on their souls. (Cheers.)

The Irish Emigrant Society, which had been formed in 1839, did concern itself almost entirely with emigrants, offering free advice where to get work and how best to travel inland. But most of the Irish societies were political as well as Roman Catholic, and Edward E. Hale, a writer on emigration, thought they were religious as a matter of politics. 'I have never', he said, 'had reason to believe that the mass of Irish are attached to the Roman Catholic religion as a matter of faith. It is a matter of national pride, and of the gallantry of those who lived where it has been persecuted. A Catholic congregation here, under the charge of an English or French priest, is almost always restless. They want an Irish priest, for their interest in their faith is, that it was their faith in their oppressed home.'[41] This resolute nationalism of the Irish, even in America, got on the nerves of some American Americans. In 1855 a society was formed with the object of freeing Ireland by force. Of this, *Frank Leslie's Illustrated Newspaper*, New York, said: 'Eccentric as is the constitution of the Irish mind, we doubt if any idea ever occurred to it more paradoxical than that upon which the new league is based. To re-assert a distinct nationality after voluntarily renouncing it, is, unfortunately, too familiar a phase of Celtic humour to excite any surprise here; but to propose an invasion of the mother country for the purpose of imposing upon others this ultra-nationalism, and of liberating a people who protest not only that they are not enslaved, but that they will cordially assist in repelling their invaders, is something so disinterested and uncommon, that we are lost in admiration at the fervour of patriotism which it displays.'[42]

The English were not in the least political, and gave no such trouble. Indeed, the Rev. Moses Marcus, of St. George's, Broadway, thought the English too lukewarm in their Englishness. He said Roman Catholics had always taken care, at least more than the Protestant English had, that the consolation of Divine Truth should not be wholly lost to emigrants of their faith, even in the wilderness. In 1847 he wrote from New York to Lord John Russell, in London, saying he was a clergyman of the Church of England, but about twelve years previously had been received into the diocese of New York. There he had witnessed the lamentable condition, spiritual and temporal, of his poor fellow countrymen in the city, who through bad companionship and evil counsellors were almost immediately drawn off from their Mother Church and soon lost amid the haunts of infidelity, profligacy and vice. So he had taken up his mission; and now he asked for some money to keep it going. This letter was sent to the Colonial Office, though why to the Colonial Office rather than the Foreign Office is not clear, since New York matters cannot for some time have been regarded as colonial, and across the back of it Benjamin Hawes, Colonial Under-Secretary, wrote his opinion:

'For the support of Anglican Congregations in Foreign Countries, Parlt. places funds at the disposal of the Fo: Office. But the writer, who officiates to British Emigrants and others at New York, declines (as I understand it for the following reasons) to avail himself of this resource. As he finds a Protestant Episcopacy in New York, he thinks he wd be guilty of the Sin of Schism, by opening a new Episcopal place of worship there, disconnected from the Bishop of that City. But if he puts himself under that Bishop, he must use the American, not the English Liturgy, unless indeed, the Bishop wd give him express license to do so. But the Bishop it seems is suspended from his function, (I believe for supporting what is vulgarly called Puseyism) and so is not in a condition to give any such indulgence. By this circuit the writer reaches the conclusion, in which so very many lines of argument terminate, *viz* that the British Treasury ought to help him. I should deny the legitimacy of the inference. It may be very right for him to obey his own conscience, by refusing to accept money on terms, which he thinks wd make him a Schismatic. But why the British Treasury shd advance money to aid him, in thus abstaining from what he esteems an unrighteous source of gain, it would I think be hard to discover . . .' Having read all this, Lord Grey the Colonial Secretary, wrote at the end: 'State quite shortly that I cannot accede to his request.'[43]

For want of Treasury money, a few British emigrants may have turned infidel in New York. But some Englishmen, even so far away from home, did not neglect their cricket. There were at least two cricket grounds in New York. In Harlem in 1851 the St. George's Club beat New England by an innings and 31 runs, scoring 180 against the Americans' 78 and 71.[44] The same year the Hoboken cricket ground, a convenient open space, was the scene of a riot between emigrants and gangs of New York rowdies.[45] By 1853, American cricket had improved. In a two-day match between St. George's (all emigrants) and New York (all born in America), New York made 125 for the loss of only two wickets, and St. George's were 61 all out. *The New York Illustrated News* was very pleased, and said: 'A knowledge of cricket is considered, by Englishmen, essential to a complete education, mental and physical, and their love thereof being early implanted, it may be considered a national custom. It tends to muscular development and is one of the healthiest pastimes known.'[46] The United States were rapidly assimilating this mentally and physically beneficial game and that summer beat Canada at Harlem.[47]

A city which had two cricket grounds, and whose census revealed that it had no ax makers but 1,585 milliners, was on its way to civilisation. It was also a city which could fairly be called, as *The Citizens' and Strangers' Pictorial and Business Guide*[48] did call it, the commercial metropolis of the Western hemisphere, and the second maritime city in the world. 'London only bears away from it the palm of commercial activity and importance. Neither Canton, nor St. Petersburgh, nor Constantinople, cherished by imperial munificence and power, can boast, in their harbours, of an equal display of shipping impelled by steam and wind, to every part of the habitable globe.' Solyman Brown, the editor of this guide-book, reckoned that if the entire property of New York City were shared out it would come to $354 for everyone who lived there. Not that he, or many other New Yorkers, would have suggested or approved of this socialist idea, because, as Mr. Brown went on to say, the master passion of New York was the love of wealth, which was prevented from degenerating into avarice only by an antagonistic passion, which was the love of display.

New York also had, according to Mr. Brown's calculations, 261 miles of streets. It was an old superstition, sometimes half believed by the simplest emigrants, that the streets of New York were paved with gold. When they got there they learned three things: first, that the streets were not paved with gold; second, that the streets were not paved at all; and third, that they were expected to pave them.[49] Still, in New York, there was hope even for an emigrant who had to do that. *Smith, Peter* arrived from Ireland, at first worked as a paver and then as a contractor, then 'won large sums on the election of 1844', and by 1846 was one of the 600 New Yorkers who possessed at least $100,000.[50]

11

Quarantine, Runners, and Rackets

June 2, 1848—'Half past four. Land seen from the mast-head: much joy and rejoicing; drank my last bottle of beer; most of us had a peer through a glass. At ten, made out a beacon, and the sailors had an extra allowance of grog. At eleven, went below for a little rest; made up my bed for the last time, and wished for the morrow.'[1]

The landfall was America, and the ship was coming into New York at night, thirty-seven days out from England. The diary is that of an unknown English steerage passenger. Next morning the emigrant ship was in the bay.

June 3—'Glorious morning! To the right is Long Island; to the left is Jersey State. What a fine country! Here at last is America. Yonder is Sandy Hook, with a lighthouse. What neat wooden cots by the water's edge! Observe those forests of trees, with a house here and there peeping through the foliage. The sight now before us compensates for all our toil and trouble.

June 4—'Up on deck by four in the morning. Arrived opposite Staten Island. What a number of windows the houses have! No tax, as in England. Eight o'clock—Two men came on board; these were custom-house officers. Then the doctor. Each passenger's name was called over, and every one had to pass in review before him. Then all below was examined; and the ship being pronounced healthy, was permitted to pass. The passing and repassing of steamboats enliven the scene. Almost all are on deck: the women and children much diverted with seeing the fishes play.

June 5—'Most on board providing their last meal. Biscuits by wholesale trod under foot. My kit sold to the captain for two shillings and fourpence. Near upon half-past eleven our ship took her station at what is called Elephant Wharf. Carmen, visitors, and inquirers stepped on board; and at the end of forty days, once more I trod on terra firma, quite well, grown much stouter, and in full health during all the voyage. Repaired to an eating-house; dined off various dishes, including green peas, and paid a shilling. Considered this not a bad specimen of America, and looked forward to days of comfort.'

This was a cleaner and more cheerful arrival than most. When Dr. John H. Griscom, general agent to the New York Commissioners of Emigration, went through the steerage of another ship, the *Ceylon*, just in from Liverpool, he saw emaciated, half-nude figures, many of them with petechial eruptions disfiguring their faces, crouching in the bunks, strewn round the decks, or encumbering the gangways. Broken utensils and a debris of food was spread recklessly about. Some emigrants were just leaving their bunks for the first time since leaving England, having been allowed to lie there all the voyage. And when a ship had typhus aboard, said the doctor, the miasmatic poison would cling to her sides, ceilings, and floors. It was impossible to eradicate it without the most thorough airing, ablution, and disinfection such as he presumed no vessel in the European passenger trade had ever received.[2]

Ships were generally cleaned for the first and only time as they entered the bay, before the doctor saw them. Emigrants were made to scrub the steerage with sand, sluice it down, and then dry the timbers with pans of hot coals from the galley, so that in a few hours no one would have imagined, from the ship's appearance, that she had made anything else than a tidy and prosperous voyage.[3]

In the summer of 1851 the packet ship *Kossuth* put into New York and landed her 592 steerage passengers at the foot of Rutger's Slip. An artist from *Gleason's Pictorial Drawing Room Companion* was there to draw the passengers as they disembarked. He made his sketch, and described what he had drawn. On the left was a woman emigrant hearing of the death of a relative; nearby a man and his wife met again after a long separation; a son supported an aged father; in the background two lovers greeted each other; one man was supervising the loading of a dray, and a dock loafer was picking his pocket. This, said the artist, was an epitome of the scenes witnessed on the arrival of emigrant vessels.[4] The *Kossuth* was one of 1,712 emigrant ships arriving in New York that year. Thirty or forty sometimes came in on one day. The confusion and uproar as they landed their passengers could be heard a great distance off. You did not have to be close; you could hear it if you were yachting in the bay.[5] In 1847, 1,879 emigrants died on the voyage to New York, and 534 babies were born. At quarantine, 319,000 passengers were inspected by the doctors.[6]

New York was afraid of the ship fever, smallpox, and cholera coming in with emigrants, and the city was lucky to escape with no great epidemic, at any rate nothing like the Canadian disaster of 1847. That year there was typhus at New York, but the New York Academy of Medicine tried to reassure the citizens by saying that although 570 people had died of typhus in the city from January 2 to June 26, this was a trifling mortality in a population of more than 400,000.[7] But the manufacturers of patent medicines did well. The wise were recommended to commence purifying their blood immediately with Dr. Sweetzer's Panacea, and those already attacked by the sickness should hasten to do the same. Sweetzer's Panacea, at $5 for half a dozen bottles, was the greatest purifier and strengthener of the system yet discovered.[8] Brendreth's Pills, to be taken four or six times every six hours with toast and water, were said to be truly the safety valve of the disease. The advertisement tossed in some mumbo-jumbo about sulphuretted hydrogen gathering in ships' holds, and how one part of this noxious ingredient in 500 parts of pure air meant instant death, and then gave the symptoms of typhus, including lowness of spirits, pain in the head, occasional vomiting, tongue furred and sometimes mahogany coloured, great thirst, and foreboding of some calamity.[9] Dr. Townsend's Sarsaparila was more bluntly advertised: the manufacturers pointed out that there had been 432 deaths in New York the previous week (though they did not say from what cause), that this proved the city was far from healthy, and that Townsend's Sarsaparila would prevent disease—at any rate, 10,000 bottles a day were sold, and had never been known to injure anyone.[10]

An effective quarantine was a better preventive than Townsend's Sarsaparila, and there had been a quarantine of sorts at New York for many years. The first quarantine law was passed in colonial times, in 1758. In 1799 the State legislature empowered health commissioners to set up a marine hospital on Staten Island. By 1846 all vessels coming into New York had to anchor in the quarantine ground and wait for an inspection by a doctor. The quarantine ground was a stretch of the bay marked by two buoys, one three-quarters of a mile to the south of the marine hospital and the other a quarter to half a mile north of the hospital.[11] The quarantine, such as it was, was probably essential to the health of the city, but there were those who did not want it at all. James Tapscott did not. He said the law acted oppressively, and that it would be perfectly safe for ships, if found healthy, to come up to the city at any time of the year.[12] Of course it would have been, if the ships were healthy; but Tapscott, as an emigrant broker, had every interest in getting his passengers off the ships as soon as possible, without quarantine delays, so his views were hardly surprising. But some of the views expressed to a special committee set up in 1846 were surprising. The eminent Dr. Scouttenen said it was terrible for men to be kept in a lazaretto for ten to fifty days at the caprice of an inspector. 'The interests of commerce and of the nation require, that *every precaution* not indispensable should be abolished; for to fetter industry is to ruin the artisan, and it is perhaps as well to die by the plague as by famine.'[13] He did not make it clear how the quarantine would fetter industry or starve artisans.

That was in 1846. Three years later the typhus and cholera brought to the city on board emigrant ships, especially the typhus of 1847, had changed people's minds. There was no longer any doubt that there should be a rigorously maintained quarantine. The two questions in the minds of the investigating committee of 1849 were, 'Was the quarantine rigorous enough?', and 'Should the quarantine be moved further out than Staten Island?' As one doctor put it, large evils required large remedies, and New York, being the greatest clustering point for emigrants, required, above all cities in the world, 'the amplest provision against the introduction of all the unclean things that characterise foreign pauperism, and grow the ranker in the process of importation'.[14] Another doctor, from the marine hospital, said an offensive effluvium arose from dead bodies buried at quarantine. The dead were buried in trenches nine feet deep and the coffins were placed in tiers three deep. The ground was soapstone rock, which was dug out by pick and broken in pieces to cover the coffins. This made a very porous covering, and in warm weather the effluvium escaped freely.[15]

The quarantine did not work anything like as well as it should. Two days a week were set aside on which friends could visit patients, and on those days hundreds came and went on ferry boats between the island and the city. 'The extraordinary spectacle is presented', said the committee's report, 'of an unlimited and restrained inter-course, with an establishment whose great aim and end, is to prevent that very intercourse.'[16] A resident on the island said the gates of the hospital were a complete thoroughfare, and that the gatekeeper never stopped anyone going in at all.[17] Another witness said it was a burlesque and a farce, and that the quarantine might as well be placed on the Battery, at the southern tip of Manhattan. Of course, none of the island residents liked the marine hospital. Benjamin F. Dawson lived there during the summer, in a house five or six hundred feet north of the hospital, which he thought decidedly a nuisance. 'I consider it so from the abominable smells from the burying ground and from the lately erected buildings being too near the wall, so near we can look into the windows and observe the patients on the piazzas. The smell seems to proceed from the putrid flesh. I cannot describe the smell. It is horrid. . . . I think I have heard cries from patients in this hospital and [I remember] one case in particular when the cries were so distressing that I closed my windows.'[18]

The proposals were that the hospital should be removed to Coney Island or Sandy Hook or to two other places. The committee de-scribed Coney Island as a sand beach only used as a fishing station and as a watering place for bathing, much frequented in the summer months, but suggested that the hospital should be removed to Sandy Hook, sixteen miles from the city. But the main quarantine hospital, throughout the period 1846–55, remained where it had always been, at Tompkinsville, near the north-east point of Staten Island, south of New Brighton, and just north of the narrows, where the Verrazano bridge now joins Brooklyn and Staten Island. There were thirty acres of hospital grounds, and a thousand beds. The place was often full. Year after year, about 1,600 vessels arrived at quarantine. All passengers were supposed to be examined and if any sick were discovered they were sent to hospital and the ship was quarantined for thirty days, but the examination off Staten Island was not much more thorough than that at Liverpool. Often there were more than 1,000 passengers on a single ship, so a rope was drawn across the vessel, leaving between the health officer and his assistant a passage just wide enough for one man at a time to walk through. 'If the quick eye of the health officer detects a blind, deaf, dumb, or idiotic person,—or one who has any aspect of sickness, he stops, him, questions him,—and if he does not pass such questioning satisfactorily, he is reported.'[19] It did not always work well. The ship's master did not want to be quarantined for thirty days, and so his officers did whatever they could to assist emigrants to pass the inspection, if necessary by hiding them, or by landing sick passengers, or sometimes all of them, illegally on the New Jersey shore. Or if a vessel was quarantined, those passengers who were not taken off to hospital sometimes took themselves off in boats and lighters to the city. Even if the emigrants did remain on board, their infected rubbish did not. When an emigrant ship came in the passengers threw bunks, bedding, and filth of every description overboard. This was washed up on the island inside an hour, and rag pickers came to collect and sort it, and take the saleable bits into the city to sell. The quarantine might be for thirty days, but infected rags got into the city in twenty-four hours.[20]

From May, 1847, each emigrant entering the port had to pay hospital money of $1.50 and was thereafter entitled to treatment not only if he was ill when he arrived but also if he fell ill within a year. Those who found themselves not doing so well in New York as they had hoped, or found themselves starving there, could either present themselves as paupers at the almshouses, or, if they knew how to go about it, could say they were ill, which they probably were anyway, and present themselves at the emigration com-missioners' office and ask to be taken to the commissioners' hospital. Dr. James Johnson came across one destitute emigrant who had paid his $1.50 and knew his rights and asked to be taken into hos-pital. Johnson told the man he was not ill. 'The emigrant then began crying, and refused to leave the office, insisting that the Com-missioners of Emigration were bound to take charge of him, as he was sick and unable to work. I then advised him to enlist, when he replied that he had had enough of that, as he had been with the British army for a short time!'[21] He was lucky not to be taken in. That year, 1847, there were 600 cases of smallpox at the marine hospital, more than 30,00 of typhus, and sixty or seventy of cholera; these diseases had spread through the hospital, killing many who, with only some mild and temporary illness, had asked to be taken in, as they were entitled.[22] The commissioners said their tickets of admission had proved their death warrants. In 1852, another bad year, more than one in six of the patients died. Whole families were taken in, and if the parents died the emigration commissioners took charge of any money they left, if it was more than 25 cents, and held it for the benefit of the children. John Hall, who came to New York from Liverpool in the vessel *India*, died at quarantine on February 19, 1848, leaving $190 and a gold watch, and five daughters

—Sarah (aged 17), Elizabeth (13), Jane (11), Mary (age unknown), and Hannah (2½). The commissioners paid out $95 for clothing and nursing of the children, and put the rest on deposit in the Seamen's Bank, for savings. Andrew Hannon, from Liverpool in the *Virginia*, died on May 1, 1848, leaving three children, Anderoga (8), Michael (7), and Edward (4), and $1.25, which was put in the bank for their benefit.[23] Orphans were familiar. *The English Orphans: or, a Home in the New World* by Mary J. Holmes was advertised in New York as the most popular book of the day, 50 cents paper or 75 cents cloth.[24]

To accommodate the orphans and convalescents, and to take in emigrants who were ill but not with infectious diseases, the commissioners opened another hospital on Ward's Island, where the East River meets the Harlem River at Hell Gate. The island is opposite 101st Street to 114th Street and was then as far from the populated part of the city as the Staten Island quarantine was. Hospitals to take a thousand people, and an emigrants' refuge for convalescents, were set up on the island. These institutions were supposed to be separate, but they were nearly always crowded and became one vast hospital. Generally, there were twice as many patients there as at Staten Island, and sometimes five times as many.[25] It was not a pleasant place. The New York doctors refused to give their services free there as they did at the city poor hospitals, and so six visiting physicians and surgeons were paid $600 a year each. There were also six resident doctors, young graduates who got no pay, just board and lodging, and did it for the experience.[26] And there was a warden of the island, Joseph Westerfield, who was paid $1,200 a year. Before he went there he had been steward at Staten Island, before that a captain of police for three years, and before that a butcher by trade.[27]

On July 1, 1851, Henry Lloyd, aged thirty-three, arrived as an emigrant in New York, was ill for two weeks, asked to go to hospital, and was sent to Ward's Island. He was put with 150 or 200 people in a barracks. The place was infested with vermin, so that he had to throw away his clothes after he left. He protested about the smell, and was told, 'If the place is not sweet enough for you tell the other men not to fart too much.' This was the night of a doctors' ball. In the morning, when he went to wash himself, he met a group of doctors, all drunk, and one of them threatened to throw him in the river. 'I then asked them', said Lloyd, 'whether I was in a hospital or a prison; they replied that I was in a lunatic asylum; I answered that from their actions I should suppose that I was.'[28] Dr. Thomas Emmet, who was one of the doctors Lloyd saw after the ball, said he remembered the party, but not making those remarks to Lloyd, whom he had thought either drunk or crazy. He and the other doctors parted about four in the morning, after daybreak, and no one was drunk. 'There were ladies present,' he said, 'whom we respected, at the boat house, that night, and I do not think we were under the influence of liquor so as to be boisterous . . . one or two of the gentlemen may have been a little excited.'[29]

One of his colleagues, Dr. William Thompson, said he knew of no cases where wine or brandy was ordered for patients and drunk by the nurses.[30] If it had been, it would have been nothing new. Three years before, the emigration commissioners had thought it necessary to pass a resolution saying that wine, brandy, porter, and beer furnished at the marine hospital were for the patients only.[31]

But whether the doctors were drunk or not, there was no denying that Ward's Island was a dreadful hospital. The doctors who worked there said so themselves. Dr. John Griscom said the shanties on the island were filthy.[32] The same Dr. Emmet who thought one or two of his colleagues were perhaps a little excited said he had at times put five patients in three beds: fever patients were generally put in separate beds, though sometimes on the floor.[33] Dr. Alexander Hosack said many patients were discharged in a worse condition than when they came. After a snowstorm he had seen several beds covered with snow because the windows were so badly fitted. People were dying of typhus in those beds.[34] And the food was bad. 'The meat, when landed, was frequently thrown into the dirt cart, and when delivered to the cook was found covered with dirt and horse manure.'[35]

Charles Webb, superintendent of the British Protective Emigrant Society, avoided sending English people to Ward's Island at all. 'Women having children constantly complained of being separated from their children. Many emigrants begging assistance, dread going to Ward's Island; . . . many complained of their children's names being changed. So they could not find them when they went for them. I recollect a case where an Englishman had a wife and five children, who were destitute; his wife and children were sent to Ward's Island; before they had been there many days, the woman and four of the children died of a fever they took there . . .; the man went there and found his only remaining child, then sick, carrying wood; he took him away from the island; the child is still living.'[36]

Then there was the affair of the exhumed body which got into the

New York newspapers. Three of the emigration commissioners were sent to Ward's Island to investigate the story. One of them was Gregory Dillon, who as president of the Irish Emigrant Society was an *ex-officio* member of the commission. He said the emigrant hospital was treated as a school of experiment for mere medical students, and that three-quarters of the emigrants who had died lately had been subjected to post-mortems. They were treated worse than prison dead. 'In one of these cases, even after the children had been buried, one of the young physicians so far forgot the rights of the father and his own duty, that in the dead of night he, in company with two other house physicians, went to the grave yard at Potter's Field, and with his own hands dug up the remains of the child and carried them to the dead house for dissection.' He said that sometimes, after dissection, the bodies were not buried entire, but parts were taken away by the physicians as it pleased them, and parts of different bodies were thrown into the same coffin and buried together. He concluded that the newspaper reports were strictly true.[37]

His was a minority opinion. The two other commissioners sent to investigate thought the charge either groundless or grossly exaggerated. Post-mortems were common in private practice when there was any doubt about the cause of death, and took place, said the commissioners, in the wealthiest families, and 'sometimes upon the bodies of the most distinguished members of the community'. According to the sexton's book, only thirty emigrants who died between October 1 and November 14 had been cut open: they did not say how reliable the sexton's book was. They could not find any ground to ensure what had been done, except in the one case of the boy, which might, if it was overlooked, lead to abuses.[38] The three commissioners went to Ward's Island on November 27. Three weeks later a grand jury of New York County also investigated the charges of malpractice, but concluded that the commissioners merited the highest commendation for the correct and humane way in which they managed their affairs. A minority of two jurymen dissented, and protested against this commendation.[39] The balance of evidence seems to show that the young medical men, who after all did the job for nothing, took the opportunity to increase their medical knowledge, and treated the emigrants' bodies as they would probably not have treated the bodies of the most distinguished members of the community. Nobody denied that a boy named Bennett had been treated at the hospital for an abcess across the abdomen, affecting the liver and stomach, that he had died on

November 7 and been buried, and that Dr. Ely, determined to get the body, crossed to the cemetery at midnight and dug it up. When the story got about, Dr. Ely left the island suddenly.[40]

The commissioners' servants were at times not exactly gentle in their treatment of live emigrants either. In 1850 they hired numbers 25 and 27 Canal Street, and the following year number 23 too, to be used as a general inquiry office and labour exchange.[41] Matthew Brennan, captain of police for the 6th district, inspected these houses and found that the dirt on the first floor was half an inch thick in places and caked down.[42] The commissioners' man at Canal Street whipped the women with a little stick like a riding whip, treating them like cattle.[43] William P. Quin, one of the commissioners' men there, replied that he never used a whip: 'I carry a cow-hide or rattan when I am going through the ranks; whip my own shins, but never hit any of them to my knowledge unless by accident.'[44]

Robert Bowne Minturn, who was a commissioner of emigration as well as a shipowner, thought the place worked well, and had found work for fifty to 150 people each day. If there had been any distress there, it had never come to his knowledge. He considered the superintendent of the place a very humane and judicious man. The superintendent's name was Fagin.[45]

One day in January 1852 Elizabeth Daly went to Canal Street to ask for help. She and her husband had settled in New York and done well, but then they had to escape in their night clothes when their house burned down. At the commissioners' office the officers said they could do nothing for her. 'And I finally was turned out of the place; one of the officers there reflected on me in some way, said something in a reflecting way about my being an old woman or such like; I did not hear exactly, but I burst out crying and was turned out.'[46]

The emigrants were undoubtedly a mob, and Quin and Fagin at Canal Street even if they did, accidentally, treat the women like cattle, did at least find jobs for more than 18,000 emigrants in that year, 1851.[47] The real menace to the emigrants, if they escaped hospital, came from the runners, and New York had the racket infinitely better organised than Liverpool.

Robert Garnham, English gentleman, thought the behaviour of these runners most shameful: he was shocked that they used violent language too. As soon as the ship had passed the medical inspection, she was surrounded by a whole swarm of them. It was far worse than the arrival of a vessel at a French port. The Americans were of a much lower character than the French. They would walk off with a box and it was never heard of again. And there was an enormous overcharge for porterage. One porter charged £5 11s. 9d. for moving boxes which had cost 30s. to move in London. Mr. Garnham was evidently a strong-willed man because he summoned the porter before the magistrates, and though he was insulted and threatened by a whole gang of fellows in such a way, he said, that few people would have persevered with the case, he did, and the decision went against the porter, who threatened him with all sorts of personal vengeance.[48]

He was lucky to get away with it. Dr. Henry Van Hovenburgh, one of the health officers who inspected the passengers while the ships lay off quarantine, said it was not uncommon for eight or ten boat loads of runners to surround a ship. 'They are desperate men', he said, 'and can be kept off only by armed force.'[49]

Up to 1847 it was usual for emigrant ships to disembark their passengers immediately after clearing quarantine. The emigrants would not stay on board until the vessel docked, but would be unloaded on to open lighters. In bad weather they suffered so much from exposure in the last trip across the bay, that later the bigger shipping companies either brought the loaded vessels directly into dock, or unloaded their passengers not into lighters but into steamships. Then the runners did one of two things. Either they hid on board the steamships, and revealed themselves as soon as the steamer had left the emigrant ship, and began pushing their tickets, or they chartered steamships themselves, took on board cargoes of emigrants, and sold them whatever they could on the way in to the city. The steamer *Cinderella* was in the employ of runners, and if an emigrant had sense enough to refuse to buy the tickets offered, and the strength to persist in his refusal, he was put ashore three or four miles above the Battery, on the East River, when it would cost him as much to get his baggage brought down into the city as to take the offered passage to Buffalo.[50]

Sometimes the captain of an emigrant ship was a party to the whole deal and sold his passengers to the runner offering him the biggest bribe. This was a refinement of the system, and was not being generally worked until 1854. Then the runner would give a captain anything from $100 to $300, and receive in return a monopoly of the whole shipload of emigrants.[51] Another refinement of the trade was to send a runner from New York to Liverpool where the man passed himself off as an emigrant and came back on the same vessel, getting to know which of the passengers were most worth fleecing. Then, back in New York, he told his employers, so that they could be ready to pounce upon the emigrants, knowing what amount of robbery they could bear.[52]

Before the system of buying shiploads grew up, the various gangs had a gentlemen's agreement to take emigrant vessels in turn,[53] but honour-among-runners sometimes broke down, and there were petty squabbles and fights among racketeers, with the emigrants in the middle being defrauded by all comers, sometimes by the police and customs officers as well. The purpose of the runners was to rob the emigrants, which they did in four ways. First, by simply stealing whatever luggage could be stolen, whenever the opportunity offered. Second, by seizing luggage, carrying it willy-nilly to a boarding house, and there demanding with menaces a great fee for a service which the emigrant had not wanted and could have done for himself. Third, by taking a cut from the boarding-house owner for bringing him customers. Fourth, by selling river, canal, or railroad tickets to take emigrants to the interior. This was much the most profitable line of business, much more so than stealing heavy trunks containing rags. Sometimes the sale of tickets was pure profit, as when they were forged and worthless. Sometimes it was almost all profit, as when the emigrant was sold a ticket to, say, Detroit but found at Albany that his ticket would not be honoured beyond that city. Always it was largely profitable. Before the railway came in 1852, almost all emigrants going inland travelled by the Erie Canal, first going up the Hudson river to Albany by steamboat, then changing to boats of sixty-five to eighty-five tons and travelling by the canal to Buffalo on Lake Erie, 360 miles from Albany. Once on the canal, an emigrant thought himself out of difficulties, but soon found he was mistaken. 'They are crowded like beasts into the canal boat, and are frequently compelled to pay their passage over again, or be thrown overboard by the captain.'[54] The fare from New York to Buffalo was normally $2.50. The superintendent of the British Protective Emigrant Society said runners charged $7.[55] The runners of course denied this, but in denying it they admitted that they nevertheless made huge profits. Porter Adams, describing himself as a passenger forwarder, which meant runner, said that he asked $5 to send a passenger from New York to Buffalo. Of this, the river fare to Albany was 50 cents, profits to the office in New York 50 cents, and canal fare from Albany $1.50, leaving the emigrant stranded at Albany and the runner with $2.50 for himself.[56] Henry Vail, another runner, was even franker. He said: 'It is a fact that I and others engaged in the business get all we can from the passengers, except that I never shave a lady that is travelling alone; it is bad enough to shave a man; I have all I get over a certain amount which is paid to the transportation companies. $6.50 is the highest amount I ever received from a passenger.'[57]

Two accounts, one by a poor Scottish emigrant called James Heeslop, and another by a crooked passenger broker called George W. Daley, show how the racket was worked. Heeslop arrived in New York on his way to Port Washington in Ohio. In New York he gave four sovereigns to an agent, who agreed to arrange the passage of Heeslop and three members of his family to his destination, and gave him tickets. Another agent then told him the tickets were good only as far as Buffalo and asked for another three guineas, which Heeslop gave him. But when he had got only as far as Albany, Heeslop was told at the office of Smethurst and Co. that he would have to pay another eight sovereigns for his family's passage, and another fifteen for his luggage. By then Heeslop was driven almost crazy by these repeated plunderings, but he paid the extra twenty-three sovereigns demanded, and was put on board a canal boat. There he was found by the St. Andrew's Society and brought back to New York, where the society on his behalf asked for a warrant against 'the notorious Smethurst'. The police justice issued a warrant for Henry D. Smethurst's arrest, but he was not to be found. When Smethurst did appear again, the Scottish emigrant was missing, 'the instruments and associates of Smethurst having in the meantime cajoled or sent him from the city'. So, thirty sovereigns, or $145, had been extorted from Heeslop for fare. The ordinary fare to his destination was $2.78 a passenger, or $8.61 for the man and his family, thus leaving the runners a swindling profit of $136.59.

With Heeslop spirited away—and this is a very early example of a familiar hoodlum technique—there was no evidence, and nothing to be done. This story was told in 1847 to a committee of New York State looking into frauds on emigrants, who said that until they came to investigate them they would never have believed the extent of the frauds and outrages.[58] The same committee also heard the sworn testimony of George W. Daley, known as One-Eyed Daley. He was himself one of the principal racketeers, and had been in partnership with the notorious Smethurst and with James Roach, but had fallen out with them and was thus ready to vilify them, just as Roach was later to vilify him. He said that in July 1846 he had left the partnership on account of the imposition practised on emigrants by his partners, and had then opened an office of his own in New York in opposition to Roach and Co., who then, not wanting competition, paid him a bribe of $1,000 to give up the business. They paid him this $1,000 in weekly instalments, and also gave him back another $200 he had spent opening his office. But before this he had been in partnership with Roach and Smethurst, and estimated there had been a hundred men in their employ. Smethurst and Daley stayed in Albany, and Roach managed the New York end. When a vessel was reported Roach generally sent down three or four men to board the ships: they carried books of tickets with them, and sold the emigrants tickets there and then.

Anyone who bought a ticket from Smethurst or his partner was likely to regret it. At Albany the neatly printed ticket would be worthless, a second fare would be demanded, and, as the 1847 committee put it, 'the only evidence he can furnish of the fraud committed on him is to exhibit his ticket with a picture of three horses, when the [canal] line boats are only drawn by two'.[59]

Daley also said that the night watch at the custom house connived at the frauds, by putting the passengers in the way of the runners, and were paid for this service. And 'stooling' was a frequent practice. A runner would board an English vessel at quarantine, single out a passenger of influence, and offer him a gold watch and chain if he would persuade his fellow passengers to go by a certain line. The passenger would agree, on condition he could have the watch in advance, and the runner would take the watch, put it in the man's pocket, and throw the gold chain round the man's neck. The passenger then went to work and got all the other passengers booked according to the agreement, the luggage was taken to the river boat, and then the runner and stool would go to the forwarding office. There a third man would seize the stool, saying 'Then you are the man that robbed the man of his watch, are you?' By then the runner would have vanished, and the stool, taking the third man for a policeman, would not only give up the watch but pay over a handsome sum besides. The supposed officer was in fact just another runner.

Having told the committee this story, Daley then produced a letter written by Roach in New York to his partner Smethurst in Albany, and dated May 20, 1847.

'Mr. Smethurst:

'Sir—There is three hundred emigrants on the Rochester tonight. There is three families on her that are booked by Brish; they are friends of Mr. Swarts, and their friends in Buffalo are people of standing, and you must put them on a boat where they will be comfortable, for Brish has been to see me about them, and also Mr. Swarts. You must be easy with them about their luggage, and weigh it straight. All that have my tickets put them through; the head man is a "Stool"—make him jump. Send down Van Toble's tickets. I shall not send you any money till I come up. I think that I shall make some arrangements with Noyes, so that he will not be opposition here. Run the O.P. line strong this week.

Yours,
JAMES ROACH'

[The *Rochester* was a river steamboat. Henry Brisch was a New York runner, and so perhaps was Mr. Swarts. Nothing is known of Van Toble. Noyes was evidently a competitor to be bribed out of the way as Daley himself later was.]

Daley was questioned about some of the points in the letter.

He said, 'The "O.P. line" means rob the passengers all you can and divide the profits with me.' He did not explain exactly what the initials stood for.

The stool referred to in the letter had been promised a passage for himself and three members of his family, and $100. He got the passage but not the money. Stools seldom got off as well as that. 'They are generally charged more than other passengers. They submit to it rather than be exposed to their companions as traitors to their interests. The Stools are not paid what they are promised one time in twenty. When they demand their pay they are threatened with exposure to their companions, whose interests and rights they have so grossly violated, which is generally sufficient to silence them.'

As for weighing the luggage straight, he said that great frauds were usually practised. At Albany the man who did the weighing for Smethurst aimed to increase the real weight by about a third. Sometimes he did better than that. Daley said he weighed himself at 274 lb. on Smethurst's scales when his real weight was 170. In spite of his repentance Daley continued in the passenger trade. Five years later he was admitting to another investigating committee that he did not always charge the rates printed on tickets, but saying, 'We never take more but oftentimes less than these rates.' That was in 1852, and though he may have become an angel by then, he was probably not one in 1847, even though he had fallen out with his former partners. One of these was Roach, and he too had left the partnership, also for what he tried to represent as conscientious reasons.[60] He said he was sick of it. His partners had not been men he liked to do business with, particularly Daley, whose treatment of the passengers he called uncivil and brutal. Having made his money out of emigrants, Roach then explained he was leaving the business because *too much* money had been made from them. He said the partnership was employing too many runners at high wages to make the business profitable unless extortion was resorted to. He also added this reason, which rings true: '. . . I concluded that men who would cheat the emigrants in the way they did, would cheat me; and that I stood no chance of making anything at the business.' This was the man who had written to Smethurst saying, 'Run the O.P. line strong this week,' or, in other words, rob the passengers all you can and divide the profits with me.

The reformed Roach was also condemned by Charles Cook, who worked as book-keeper for a passenger agent, selling canal tickets. He said Roach kept a mob called The Sixteen, or Fighting Men, to encourage the emigrants to pay up, and quoted him as saying that 'there was no use of talking about being honest while in the passage business; all he wanted was to get hold of the cattle . . .'[61] But to this Roach replied that Cook himself had been paid $1,200 a season.

The two investigating committees of 1847 and 1852 are full of dubious witnesses exonerating themselves and accusing the others. William P. Paff, who kept a German public house at Albany and forwarded passengers from Albany not by canal but by railroad, said he was paid $50 a month by Smethurst, but then went on piously to say that in almost all cases passengers were displeased when they were called upon to pay for their luggage. 'Smethurst exacts pay of them,' he said, 'and in some cases detains their luggage until he is paid.' Paff described himself as 'an out door agent in this city to protect passengers'. He must have protected them in much the same way as the association of Liverpool lodging-house keepers protected their customers. An anonymous letter put in evidence to the 1847 committee saw Paff differently, and called him 'a tool that they [Smethurst's] use to cheat thousands'. Friedrich Kapp, who was later to become one of the commissioners of emigration, called Paff 'one of the meanest runners' and Roach 'one of the lowest'.[62]

Charles Gallagher was another up and coming man. In 1845 he was a customs officer on the night watch, slipping tips to Smethurst and Roach. The next year he was a full-time runner for that firm. Then he started up on his own, whipping in passengers for Harnden and Co., who conveyed emigrants not only across the Atlantic but also inland. William Harnden, the founder of the business, had died in 1845, but his partners were continuing the business under his name. By 1852 Gallagher had prospered, was calling himself proprietor of American Passenger Express Lines, and making allegations of corruption against all and sundry—against William S. Root, a city weighmaster who he said was in the employ of Wedeken and Daley (who had also prospered); against Regan, a clerk with the emigration commissioners; against Irwin and Katen at the Irish emigration office; and against Judge Drinker.[63]

The chief villain of the whole business was the notorious Smethurst. The crooked scales belonged to him or his men. When Benjamin D. Quigg, deputy sergeant-at-arms of the New York house of assembly, went to serve a subpoena on Smethurst to appear before the 1847 committee he took the opportunity of weighing himself on these scales, which gave his weight as $163\frac{1}{2}$ lb.: then he weighed himself on some honest scales elsewhere, which gave his weight as $142\frac{1}{2}$ lb. Josiah Clarke made the same comparison: his proper weight was 169 lb., but on the Smethurst scales he was more than 200.[64] When Smethurst did appear before the committee they got nothing out of him. He said he had offices both in Albany and New York. (As it happened, his home address in New York, at 54 Barclay, was practically next door to the British consul's, at number 58.)[65] As to overcharging for tickets, his clerks might have charged more, but if they had, they had never given the extra to him. He had sometimes taken luggage as far as Milwaukee for nothing. He said he had nineteen runners in New York, whom he paid anything from $12.50 a week to $600 for the season. In Albany he had seventeen men. He had paid Roach $2,000 for three months, and the others from $30 to $500 a month. These figures do not agree with Daley's, who said that while he was with Smethurst they employed about 100 men. Did he ever use fraudulent weights? What answer can the committee have expected to this, other than the innocent reply they got: 'I never do . . .' he said; 'my men may have done so.'

Smethurst had a malign wit. The gentlemen of the State investigating committee asked him: 'Did you ever give passengers a ticket marked ST, and tell them it meant state room?'

He replied: 'It has been done frequently. I have seen it done, and by men in my employment. It is done as a joke. ST means steerage.'

Smethurst was probably untouchable by the law as it was. If things got too hot he could always spirit a witness out of the way, as he did the Scotsman Heeslop. He did not hustle the emigrants himself, or even fix the weights himself. His runners did that.

The *New York Tribune* supplied a definition of a runner: he must be a man, or rather a brute, that fire would not burn, rope hang, nor water drown; with a fist like a sledge-hammer, and muscle enough to overthrow a bull. With such qualifications, in proportion to his smartness, he would receive from $50 to $100 a week from his employer the broker.[66] The second investigating committee, in 1852, was told by George Wilkie, a passenger agent for the New York and Erie Railroad, that emigrants were being taken by the runners almost by force: 'It has become so profitable, that the fighting and fancy men are employed as runners, and the house having the largest gang are the most successful.'

Two of the fancy men were Awful Gardner and John Morrissey. Awful Gardner was first named as one of George Dayley's runners before the 1852 committee. Then in October 1853 the *New York Times*[67] carried a headline ARREST OF AWFUL GARDNER and an account of how Orville Gardner, described as a prizefighter, had come before Judge Bogart on a charge of maiming William Hastings, known as Dublin Tricks. The complainant exhibited to the magistrate his injured ear, which was frightfully mutilated. He said Gardner struck him with his fist in the face, knocked him down, threw himself on him, seized his left ear between his teeth, and feloniously bit a large piece entirely out of the lower part of the ear. Gardner also hit Hastings severely about other parts of the body, and tried to gouge his right eye out. A warrant was issued for Gardner's arrest, and he was brought to court and given bail of $1,000. The *Times* has nothing more about this case, but almost two years later, in September 1855, it reported that that 'interesting gentleman' generally known as Awful Gardner, who seemed to have withdrawn from public life for the few months previously, had turned up again the day before, having gone into the California trade, selling tickets to California to emigrants. A man had declined to buy a ticket from Gardner, who had hit him on the face and broken his lower jaw. 'We have not heard', said the *Times*, 'of Gardner's arrest.' Two weeks later there was another headline, CAUGHT AT LAST. The *Times* was glad to hear Gardner had been arrested for assault on William Henry.

In October Hezekiah Orville (alias Awful) Gardner was convicted in the Court of Special Session. The judge sent him to prison for six months.[68]

John Morrissey was a much more successful hoodlum, who rose to be Congressman and State senator, and to have his biography written by the sporting editor of the *Police Gazatte*.[69] This amounted to a eulogy and at one point said of Morrissey that though the beginning of his career was as nearly hopeless as a man's could be in a civilised society, he had fairly worked himself out of the mire into which he had been born and bred, and, from the condition of a creature of brutal instincts and disreputable habits, had transformed himself into a reasoning and courteous gentleman, and a conscientious observer of decorum and good manners. He was born in Templemore, Tipperary, in 1831, his family emigrated to Canada when he was five years old, and, after a few destitute months there, moved south over the border to Troy, New York. Morrissey was a big boy for his age, good at rough-and-tumble fighting, and became a gang leader. When he thought he was rough enough he went up to New York, walked into the Empire Club run by Dutch Charley, and announced he could lick any man there. Tom Burns, Mick Murray, and half a dozen others pitched into him with clubs, chairs, and bottles and laid him out. He kept his feet for a long time, fighting with earnestness until he was struck behind the ear by an earthern spittoon, and then his admiring opponents picked him up, put him to bed at the club, and sent him home to Troy. He had found his vocation, and when his health was fully recovered he returned to New York City and became a runner. Big Tom Burns and General Billy Wilson, brother runners and prizefighters, tried to drive him from one ship with belaying pins, but Morrissey routed both of them. He afterwards used to say that Awful Gardner had been present at the fight and had agreed to see fair play. 'But as soon as the fight began he ran up the rigging like a squirrel and stayed there until it was over.' From then on Morrissey's progress was steady. He wanted Kate Ridgely, who was already the mistress of Tom McCann, and had to fight him for her. A stove overturned, some hot coals fell out, and McCann forced Morrissey on to them and held him there until the smell of burning flesh filled the room. Bystanders threw water on the coals, gas and steam rose in McCann's face and choked him, Morrissey rose and won, and was afterwards known as Old Smoke all his life. In 1853, before an immense crowd, he met Yankee Sullivan in an illegal prizefight for a purse of $2,000. After thirty-seven rounds the crowd rioted, revolvers were drawn, and Sullivan, who had prudently got away, was unable to make his way back through the mob, consequently failed to get to the scratch for the thirty-eighth round, and Morrissey was declared the winner.

Next year, in what was more a brawl than a prizefight, he met William Poole on Amos Street dock, and lost. Poole was later killed by Morrissey's gang. In 1858 he fought John J. Heenan, the Benficia Boy, for the heavyweight championship, beat him, retired from the ring, and went into gambling, saloon-keeping, and politics. He made a friend of Commodore Vanderbilt, the financier, by giving him a racehorse, married a Miss Sally Smith of Troy, and tried to move into the fashionable quarter of that town. The residents disapproved of him and bought up the plot of land he had intended to build on. He took his revenge by buying the land behind their elegant houses and erecting a loud smelling soap factory.

As a gambler he won and lost several fortunes, and once lost $124,000 in one night. In 1867 he was elected to the United States Congress for the 56th Congressional district of New York, in 1869 he bought a gambling casino in Saratago (now Schuylerville), New York, and in 1877 was elected State senator. But in May 1878, after a long and painful illness, he died at the age of forty-six. The State legislature passed a resolution praising the 'energy which marked his life-long struggle against formidable obstacles, and, above all . . . his rare and unquestioned integrity'. Eulogies were spoken by six senators, his vacant chair and desk were draped in mourning, and a basket of flowers was placed on his desk, by order. At his funeral the Governor and eight State senators were pall-bearers, and 15,000 people followed his body to the cemetery in the rain. At his death he still owned the gambling casino, and a part share of a race-track.[70] It only shows what a respectable runner could come to.

I2

Colonising and Shovelling Out

'It strikes me', said Samuel Cunard, founder of the steamship line, 'that as the government have a great many steamships which they want to have employed for the purpose of exercise, they might be employed to take trips occasionally with emigrants: they could take a thousand people over at very moderate expense. The ships are kept continually employed running round the coast for exercise, and why not send them for that eight day voyage ... It would be wrong in me, perhaps, to suggest that the Admiralty might not like it.'[1]

Cunard was speaking in 1847, and meant that the steamships should take emigrants to Canada, and not to the United States, which would not have welcomed British naval vessels. It was an obvious suggestion, and could have changed the whole character of Canadian emigration for the better. Eight days in a steamship of the Royal Navy out of Limerick or Tralee or some other port on the west coast of Ireland, rather than forty days in some ancient brig from those ports, or rather than the steamer crossing to Liverpool and then the sailing packet across the Atlantic, would have saved a lot of suffering and many lives. But the Admiralty would not have liked it. Lord Grey at the Colonial Office would not have liked it. The British government could never have considered interfering with commerce in such a way. There were also good political reasons why naval ships could not be used. So the idea was unthinkable. It was well beyond the scope of mid-nineteenth-century government. The Colonial Land and Emigration Commissioners could never have conceived of such a thing. It would never have entered their heads.

The board of emigration commissioners was created in 1840 to be responsible to the Colonial Office for overseeing emigration of all kinds, both assisted and voluntary. The chairman was a civil servant of long standing. The first was Thomas Frederick Elliot, a barrister, who entered the Colonial Office in 1825, had been to Canada as secretary of a commission of enquiry, and in 1840 became chairman of the new board. In 1847 he left to become assistant under-secretary at the Colonial Office, and was succeeded as chairman of the emigration commissioners by T. W. C. Murdoch.[2] The commissioners' first concern was with the colonies, and they instinctively talked not of emigration but of colonisation. They had complete control over the granting of free passages to the Australian colonies, which were paid for by those colonies from sale of Australian land. The commissioners chartered the ships, and selected intending settlers. Emigrants generally had to be labourers, shepherds, miners, or female domestic servants, though a few blacksmiths, wheelwrights, and carpenters were also taken. 'Reduced tradesmen' resident in workhouses would not be considered. The most acceptable candidates were young couples with no children. No family would be accepted with more than two children under seven, and the parents could not be older than forty. Good character was indispensable, and 'decisive certificates' of this were required. They had to be vaccinated against smallpox. Single women under eighteen without their parents were not admissible unless they were engaged as domestic servants to ladies going out as cabin passengers in the same ship. Single men could not be allowed except in a number not exceeding that of the single women in the same ship.[3]

This last proviso simply meant that the commissioners were interested in good breeding. They explained that, obvious though it was, it was not always kept in mind that for the permanent growth of a colonial population, every single man sent out in excess of the number of single women was absolutely useless. He was a mere sojourner, leaving nothing behind him when he died. As for the morality of the colony, they hardly needed to observe that an overwhelming excess of single men was fraught with the greatest danger. To this danger the colonies were keenly alive, and had urgently pressed the British government that in order to counterbalance the spontaneous influx of males a female immigration was not only a convenience but a moral necessity. Briefly, the girls were needed for breeding, and for morality, and in the meantime they would make useful domestic servants. The commissioners succeeded so well in counterbalancing spontaneous males, and shipped so many girls out that the South Australia government eventually went so far as to complain of the 'unnecessary and embarrassing' number of single women, who, it seems, presented another kind of moral danger.[4]

The commissioners' wide responsibilities included not only the selection of girls for Australia but also the colonisation of the Falkland Islands, the shipping of 13,000 Indian coolies to Mauritius, and, in 1853, the carrying of 1,040 Chinese labourers from Hong Kong to Panama to work for an American railway company. From Hong Kong a Mr. White wrote to the commissioners saying this first experiment in emigration from Hong Kong could be considered successful. The vessel had got under way amid the firing of crackers and the uproar of gongs and drums as a token of the emigrants' satisfaction. When they reached Panama they were not so happy. Wang-te-Chang, Chinese interpreter, wrote in his journal that the labourers' clothes were filled with wet and yellow dirt as they worked, that they were flogged, and given no vegetables to eat, and had not enough fresh water to drink and so drank salt water, and then they cried, and began to hang themselves. Thirty or forty committed suicide, and many died of disease, until only 400 were left. The dead were buried naked in ditches, which was an affront to their religion. The interpreter found one coolie dead 'on the dirt and wet sun shining of one pond'. Wang asked the survivors if they would like to go on to Jamaica to farm. They said no matter where, as long as it was out of the hands of the American company. Wang began to look for someone to take them, saying such a person would be a second Moses. When they left China these coolies had thought they were going to California to dig gold, not to Panama to die making a railroad. Eventually, 205 were taken to Jamaica, but few survived there either.[5]

The commissioners also concerned themselves with the theory and principles of good colonisation. For instance, said Elliot, he heard almost daily that colonisation was a lost art, and that they should imitate their forefathers, and so forth. He supposed the old American colonies were alluded to, but more beggarly and calamitous settlements than they had been he could not conceive. People fell into the error of imagining that because these were now great countries they had originally been great colonies, but this was not so: Virginia had perished four times before it took root, and in New England four successive attempts were made before the land was finally settled.

He also thought, without going into any deep discussion, that the ancient Greek colonies could bear no useful comparison with modern settlements, and nor could the Romans'.[6]

Apart from this learned discussion of principles, and attending to the successful emigration of coolies, and inducing a fecund settlement of Australia, the commissioners found that they also had to deal with the rapidly increasing North American emigration. It was different. They could never control it directly as they did the Australian emigration. It was huge, and they never had the resources to begin to control it as they should have done. The commissioners never received more than £25,000 of government money in one year. That was in 1851, and their average annual grant from the Exchequer was only about £17,000.[7] This had to pay the upkeep of offices in London and at the ports, the salaries of the commissioners, clerks, and emigration officers, and the occasional expense of relieving the passengers of ships which put back.

The North American emigration was not considered colonisation proper, which was what the commissioners felt to be their real business. Even the Canadian emigration could hardly be called colonisation because so many entered Canada and then crossed straight away into the United States, sometimes as many as six people out of ten.[8] In the middle of the century the situation was still much as the Durham Report had described it in 1839: '. . . on the American side all is bustle and activity . . . On the British side of the line, with the exception of a few favoured spots, where some approach to American prosperity is apparent, all seems waste and desolate. The ancient city of Montreal, which is naturally the commercial capital of the Canadas, will not bear the least comparison in any respect with Buffalo, which is a creation of yesterday.'

Canada wanted British emigrants, as long as they were not paupers. A report in 1849 to the governor general from the inspector general of Montreal said it was doubtful if the mother country had considered the great value to itself of colonisation as opposed to mere emigration. It was to be assumed that Britain was interested not only in getting rid of her surplus population but also in selling her manufactures. The commercial policy of the United States was protective, and a duty of 30 per cent was levied on British imports. Canada on the other hand was a free market for English goods. There was no duty. The average annual consumption of British goods in the United States was not more than $3 a head, but in Canada it was $8. Surely this should convince the English government and manufacturers of

The screw steamer *City of Glasgow*, 1,610 tons, at Philadelphia. This ship, run by William Inman for Richardson's of Liverpool, was the first steamer to carry steerage passengers regularly to America. She disappeared in the Atlantic in 1854 with 430 souls on board.

Panorama of New York, 1852. The circular building is Castle Garden, not yet
used as an emigrant depot. The wide street running up the centre of Manhattan
is Broadway. The spire at centre left is that of Trinity Church. City Hall is on
the far left. The Liverpool packets docked in the East River along South Street
(stretching from the centre to the left of the picture).

The quarantine grounds and hospital at Staten Island, 1856.

Castle Garden, New York, before it was converted
into an emigrant depot. Here Jenny Lind is
singing at a concert in 1851.

South Street, New York, where the packets docked, in the 1850's.

Monument at Grosse Isle quarantine in the St. Lawrence, thirty miles downstream from Quebec City. The inscription on the side says: 'In this secluded spot lie the mortal remains of 5425 persons who flying from Pestilence and Famine in Ireland in the year 1847 found in America but a Grave.'

Above left: Paddy O'Dougherty, who left Ireland a pauper in 1845, worked in America as a bridge builder at forty cents a day, and within eight years was worth $100,000 and owned a country seat.

Above right: 'Paddy's Ladder to Wealth in a Free Country.' A more likely story than O'Dougherty's. In New York labouring was about all an Irishman could get.

Left: Emigrants landing at a New York quay, having transferred in the bay from their sailing packet to a small steamboat, 1858.

Arrival of the packet *Kossuth* at Rutger's Slip, New York, in 1851 with 592 emigrants. On the left, a woman emigrant is told of the death of a relative; next to them, a man and his wife meet again after a long separation; left centre, a man supports his aged father; behind them, two lovers greet each other; centre right, a man superintends the loading of a dray has his pocket picked by a dock loafer.

A RUNNER'S PROGRESS

John Morrissey was born in Ireland and
brought to America when he was five.
When he grew up he became first
a successful emigrant runner, beating
up rival runners.

Then a prizefighter and heavyweight champion of the world.

Baggage smashers at New York
in 1853, separating a passenger
from his bags.

And finally a New York State Senator.

hen a gambler with a casino at Saratoga,
New York.

Runners at New York.

Canal barges on the North River, New York, 1852. Many emigrants went to the west via the Hudson River and the Erie Canal to Lake Superior.

A pair of engravings, "As I Was" and "As I Am," a very hopeful idea of what emigrating could do for a man, from an emigrant's pamphlet sold in London in 1855.

The emigrant's Christmas dinner in
the Far West—Effect of the Smell of
roast beef. An American cartoon of 1853.

the importance of encouraging emigration to Canada, so that the emigrants there could buy more British goods.[9] But nothing of the sort happened. In the same year, 1849, a committee set up by the Legislative Assembly of Montreal said its painful task was to report that the emigration of Her Majesty's subjects to places out of Her Majesty's dominions—just by walking across the Canadian border—was much more considerable than had been believed, and threatened to become a calamity.[10] The commissioners in London knew that they could do nothing to stop this, and explained that Canada and New Brunswick, with a population of 1,750,000, did not have work for an average annual immigration to them of 29,000, and that many of these people naturally went south to the States, which had a population of 23,000,000, and much more work to offer. The commissioners were not astonished at this; nor did they think that the stream of emigration could now be turned aside from the United States, even if this were desirable. Anyway, so far as emigration was looked on as a relief to the mother country, that relief was the same whether the emigrants went to the States or to the British colonies.[11]

Emigration to the United States, direct and indirect, though it was by far the most important movement the commissioners had anything to do with, could not be called colonisation at all. The United States was no longer a colony. The commissioners had no power even to regulate the north American emigration, and did not try.

There were good reasons for this, practical reasons as well as reasons of principle, and these are openly stated by Grey in his memoirs, which he published in 1853, the year after he went out of office.[12] They amount to an apologia for Lord John Russell's colonial policy. Grey says, going back to 1847, that it was only with difficulty that the government was then able to resist the very general wish that it should promote and in part pay for the Irish emigration of that year.

He said government help would have paralysed the exertions of individuals. This was cant. But then he went on to say, in effect, that the emigration managed itself better than it could have been managed by the government. This was undoubtedly true. He said that had the government undertaken the removal of the distressed Irish, it would have had to select which people should go: this was a small but a practical objection, because the government had at that time no means of selection—no organisation, and not enough officers to do it. Then he came to his crucial point, which was undeniable. If the British government had organised the emigration the United States would immediately have passed laws preventing a destitute multitude from being cast on its shores by a foreign government, and Canada could not have been prevented from doing the same without, as Grey put it, producing an alienation of Canadian affections fatal to the authority of the British Crown. 'As it was, there were great complaints as to the description of emigrants that went to the North American Colonies, and it was only by showing that the Government had neither the power nor the right to interfere as to the selection of emigrants, that these complaints were met. If the emigrants had been sent out by the Government, it would have been universally felt that the Government could not possibly repudiate the responsibility of providing for them on their arrival in the Colonies.'

Then Grey came to his last reason, which is a very strong one. The spontaneous emigration had been far bigger than anything the government could have thought of. This is true. The government which in the last nineteen years had taken only 123,000 people to Australia, could not have begun to think of taking 250,000 in one year to North America. It would no more have occurred to Her Majesty's government to take that many, than it would have occurred to them to carry emigrants in naval steamboats which were doing nothing but hurrying around on exercises.

Grey's reasoned argument that the government could do nothing to organise the North American emigration, and indeed should do nothing, shows how very little the opinions of Edward Gibbon Wakefield ever affected this emigration. Wakefield's is one of the biggest names in the history of nineteenth-century emigration, and in the early 1830s Grey (then Lord Howick) had shared many of his views, but by the time Grey was Colonial Secretary not a shadow of them remained. Broadly, Wakefield proposed a state-organised emigration, and believed that sound colonisation would be better achieved not by giving land away to emigrants but by selling it at a fair price. The buyers of land would then have to be either men of some substance, or would first have had to work in the colonies to earn the price of the land, to the colony's general good. But though these views had their effect on emigration to Australia, where land was sold at a fair price, they never had anything to do with America. They could, of course, never have had any application to the United States. As for British North America, dear land there would only have driven yet more emigrants south to the cheap lands of the States.

A most revealing example of government timidity in the late 1840s was the proposed emigrant depot at Liverpool where emigrants would have been able to lodge while they waited to embark. The idea came from the government emigration officers at the port, was supported by the mayor, and even, at first, liked by Grey himself. It would have kept emigrants away from the town while they were waiting to go aboard their ships, out of the hands of the runners and touts, and out of the boarding houses. It would have saved the emigrants from extortion and distress, and from the diseases of the boarding houses and cellars. By keeping the emigrants in one place, it would have made the medical inspection and the mustering of passengers easier. It would even have made a profit. It is difficult to think of any one thing the commissioners could have done which would have helped the emigrants more. It was obviously practical. John Bramley Moore, Mayor of Liverpool, thought a depot as necessary for emigrants as sheds were for bales of merchandise, and said he could only look upon emigrants as live merchandise: vessels were being constructed with the sole object of carrying emigrants, and it had become the most profitable carrying trade.[13]

But the idea failed. It was at first planned that the emigration commissioners should lease the building. Bramley Moore told Grey that in a year 134,000 emigrants passed through the port, and that if they stayed there two nights at 6d. a night, this would bring in £6,700 a year and the place would pay for itself. Nothing was required except bare walls, gas, and water: no ornament of any kind. The depot would cost £20,000 to £25,000 to build.[14] The Dock Committee had even gone so far as telling a civil engineer to draw up plans for a building to sleep 4,000. His estimate for this was £42,900. This was considered too much, so he drew up a new plan for a building to house 1,200 adults, or 1,500 with children. This would have been built of bricks from old demolished houses. If the emigrant trade had fallen off it could have been turned into a warehouse. The plan was that steamers from Ireland or Scotland should disembark emigrants at a dock by the emigrants' home, and a day or two later the ship to take them to America should come alongside the same dock and take on its passengers.[15]

The commissioners approved. In the end the Colonial Office did not. The objections were that the government would be placing itself in the position of a great lodging-house keeper; that there was a possibility of making a loss; that if it were made compulsory for emigrants to enter the depot (and this was necessary if the scheme was to work), then the charge would amount to a tax levied only on those emigrants who went from Liverpool, and would thus discriminate against that port; and that such a depot should anyway be managed not by the central government but by the corporation of Liverpool.[16]

The corporation, as the mayor said, represented 'those parties whose object and business it is to live upon these emigrants by plundering them', and so nothing was done.[17] It was a brave idea. As it happened, since 200,000 emigrants passed through Liverpool in 1851, the depot, far from making a loss, would have made a profit of £3,300 that year. That would have been just from the charge of 6d. a night for bed. If the commissioners had been able to steel themselves to interfering with trade—knowing that the trade they interfered with was mostly an evil racket—they could, on a calculation based on the mayor's estimate, have sold £300,000 worth of clothes and provisions each year, and made a fair annual profit of £50,000.[18] The salaries paid to the emigrant officers at Liverpool were never more than £1,000 a year altogether. With £50,000 to play with, the commissioners could have improved emigrant protection at Liverpool out of all recognition. Perhaps this is unfair speculation. Perhaps the idea of a government taking a monopoly of boarding and provisioning 200,000 people a year in one depot was much too bold to succeed. But it nearly was adopted, and six years later the New York Commissioners of Emigration did put into practice an almost identical scheme.

The British government needed to be convinced before it did anything extraordinary. The remedies required to put the emigrant trade right were extraordinary. Sometimes the instinct to do nothing was right, as with Grey's instinct not to intervene in the 1847 emigration, but sometimes it was manifestly wrong, as with the failure to build the Liverpool depot.

The one way to convince the government, or at least a Parliamentary select committee, that reform was necessary was to appeal to the Christian conscience. It was necessary to show that a state of affairs was intolerable, that is to say inhumane to the point of being unchristian, or else immoral. The state of affairs discovered by de Vere on his 1847 voyage to Quebec—disease, starvation, filth, death—was intolerable. His letter came to the attention of the Colonial Office and of Parliament, and some attempt was made to legislate against some of the worst evils.[19] But the inhumanity did really have to be intolerable. It was not enough for the emigrant to be merely wretched. As the commissioners said, they were not insensible to the deficiencies and the dangers of emigration, but 'after every allowable degree of regulation, poverty will inevitably have its ills; and it is impossible that the poor should not be without some of the advantages and securities on their passage which it might be wished they should possess'.[20]

There were a few private attempts to organise emigration. The Ragged School Union, whose chairman was the Earl of Shaftesbury, ran schools for the children of the destitute poor, and sent a few boys overseas—twelve on one ship, eleven on another, but never in any great numbers. The boys' previous pitiable history was contrasted, in the *Ragged School Union Magazine*, with the prospects before them of starting a new life where the finger of contempt would not be pointed at them. Of the eleven on the ship *Ava*, to Canada, three had been in prison, two for theft, and one for tearing up his clothes in a casual ward.[21]

A few parties of mechanics went out together too; and one charity sent out needlewomen. The *Illustrated London News*, reporting the embarkation of a shipload of girls, said that one of the striking characteristics of the past London season had been that, amid so much, some of the most fashionable women had employed themselves in works of active benevolence on behalf of distressed needlewomen, many of them rescued from the very depths of poverty and suffering; on board ship they were addressed by Sidney Herbert, who as war secretary in the Crimean War was to send Florence Nightingale to Scutari. The report said the personal interest taken in the fate of the needlewomen by the noble ladies who were sending them out was most touching.[22]

The Mormons' emigration was well managed. In the 1840s and 1850s they were vigorously gathering converts in Great Britain. They called themselves the Poor Man's Church, and made much of the Archbishop of Canterbury's stipend, which they said was £27,705 13s. 6d. a year, and of the amount the late Bishop of Cashel left in his will, which they said was £400,000.[23] In Liverpool they sold 17,000 to 20,000 copies a week of their own newspaper, *The Latter Day Saints' Millennial Star*, at 1d.[24] In 1850 they were reported to have an emigration fund of three and a half tons of Californian gold, and to be carrying on emigration on a larger scale than was ever attempted in modern times by any political or religious society.[25] Mormon emigrants left England in companies, and each company came to Liverpool in the charge of a president and six committee men. They were famous for their discipline. When one man, not a Mormon, asked Samuel Sidney, the writer on emigration, for advice whether he should emigrate in a party with fifty others, the reply was: 'Can you make fifty men, without other law than their own will, move like the Mormons, or a military machine?'[26] In 1849, 2,500 Mormons emigrated, and in 1853, 2,700.[27] The Mormons' president in England was Samuel Whitney Richards, who was also an authorised passage broker, and editor of *The Millennial Star*. In 1854 he gave evidence to a select committee who were very curious to know how the Church's emigration was organised.[28] He said they chartered ships themselves, charging £3 12s. 6d. to New Orleans. Then they went up the Mississippi, and then west overland into Utah Territory. The fare all the way was £20. They had about 60,000 members in Britain, mostly in Birmingham, Manchester, Merthyr Tydfil, London, Glasgow, and Liverpool, and the year before the Church in Britain had spent £4,000 to help its members emigrate. No declaration of religion was required, no emigrant had to sign anything, and they would even take people whom they knew to be not of their faith. When Richards was asked if he preferred to take mechanics or agricultural labourers, he said: 'We prefer either who are honourable men.'

'Have you any proselytising agents in this country?—I might say we are nearly all so.

'Have you any particular instructions or desire to have more females than males in this emigration?—No, not any.'

Compared with needlewomen and mechanics, the Mormon emigration was large, but easily the biggest emigration schemes were those undertaken by Irish landlords. This was commonly known as shovelling out. In England each parish fed its own paupers out of a parish rate levied on owners of land within the parish. In 1847 this Poor Law was for the first time applied to Ireland, and landowners were called upon to feed whole populations of starving peasants, from whom they were no longer even getting rent. This would quickly have ruined the landlords, who found it cheaper to induce their tenants to leave by paying their passages to America, and often by chartering whole ships. Economy, or the wish to avoid bankruptcy, was naturally the landowners' principal motive, but many did also act out of a generous desire to give the people a new start in America.

But the details of shovelling were not pleasant. As the people went, their houses were tumbled. Some, seeing that they had to go, would wreck their own houses for 5s. Others had to be evicted by soldiers, and then the 'destructives' pulled the roof down. A good gang of destructives could break down thirty houses in a morning.[29] Earl Fitzwilliam was a better landlord than most, and 'a man of chivalrous honour, high moral courage, and perfect independence and disinterestedness'.[30] In 1847–65 his estates were disencumbered of their peasants. In 1847 more than 300 families were sent to America, about 1,600 people in all. His agents kept ledgers listing the people and their ages, and the amounts spent to send them out; often there are scrawled comments against the names.[31] Some tenants made a reasonable bargain for themselves. John Lambert, aged forty, had a wife and eight children aged from fifteen to eighteen months: he had twelves acres of land and was willing to give it up if 'allowed something in addition to passage and support'. Sarah Welsh of Killinure held one acre but 'would give it up on getting encouragement to go out to America'. John Hinch, aged thirty, of Killibeg, lived with three sisters on a holding of five acres, but gave this up in exchange for their passages, money for food, and an extra £16 5s., amounting to £40 in all. Mary Murphy, a widow aged forty-eight, is written down as having been ordered by Fitz-william to be emigrated. This sounds strange. He could undoubtedly evict her, but he had no power to deport her. She said she had nine children, but three of these were struck out by the agent because they were only stepchildren. Betty Carney was described as a widow it 'would be desirable to get rid of . . .' Betty Byrne was written down as 'rejected', but no reason is given. One tenant brought a letter from her parish priest, which is pinned inside one of the ledgers. It certifies that 'the bearer Anne Lynch has been nursing a deserted child, named John, these four years to the 16th September next, whom she wishes to bring with her to America if she were enabled to pay his passage'. Against almost all entries is the note, 'Cabin to be thrown down.' Some refused to go, preferring the Irish workhouse to emigration. Here are some examples:

Mat Doyle, wife and three children: 'Cabin to be thrown down. Declines going.'

John Appleby, aged twenty-two, one of a family of six: 'Did not go.'

Daniel Doyle, aged twenty-one: 'Will not go.'

William Byrne, aged fifty-six, with wife and eleven children: 'Declines going to America'.

Simon Byrne, aged sixty-four, and seven dependants: 'Won't go.'

Most did go. The landlords, whether they acted out of self-interest or generosity, got little thanks for it, particularly in British North America where they shipped most of their tenants.

Early in June, 1847, the *Aeolus*, 817 tons, a new ship, arrived at St. John, New Brunswick, carrying 500 emigrants from the Sligo estate of Sir Robert Gore Booth. The master, Michael Driscoll, wrote to Sir Robert saying his passengers were 'scattering fast' and getting good employment, and that the health officer considered Sir Robert's tenants 'could not be classed as Common advintururs, or Emigrants', nor the ship 'classed among the dirty old Emigrant hired Vessels', as she was superior to any of Her Majesty's transports. He also said: 'Sir Your Kind acts at hoam to privint famine and to Elivate the Condition of the Poor is as well nowen here as in the Town of Sligow, Your Ever Thankful Tennants were Highley Respected on being landed in this town.'[32]

The Hon. John Robertson, who appears to have been Sir Robert's agent in St. John, wrote to him at the same time, slightly less enthusiastically. He said the Irish had been difficult to manage because they were utterly unused to the work they had to do. He acknowledged a letter from Sir Robert, which must have come on the *Aeolus*, saying that two more ships, the *Yeoman* and the *Lady Sale*, would be bringing emigrants from Sir Robert's estate. 'I wish for your sake as well as my own', said Robertson, 'that she might bring some other Cargo. I will however do the best in my power for them poor Creatures on their arrival.'[33] Moses Perley, government emigrant agent at St. John, was less enthusiastic still, saying the tenants had been exported to disencumber Sir Robert's estate, and that it was a shovelling out of hopeless paupers.[34]

The *Yeoman*, 950 tons, came in August, in good order with no fever. The 500 passengers had been given tea and sugar every day, and had been generally well cared for. She was a good ship. The master had been a physician, and his wife, who was literate, wrote home to Lady Gore Booth saying the fiddler on board had made happy faces and nimble feet, and that the ship had its own little church on board, rigged up with sails and flags.[35] Perley reported that the passengers had yielded their holdings on Sir Robert's estate in return for their passage and expenses. Three gentlemen of the province, writing to the Lieutenant Governor, described the passengers as miserably squalid.[36] Any Irish were squalid that year, but the *Yeoman* was not overcrowded, her passengers had been fed, and they were not diseased.

Sir Robert's third load came in September on the *Lady Sale*, 736 tons, and this time eighty-five out of 340 did have fever. The doctor at quarantine called them a freight of paupers, chiefly widows, orphans, and old people. One old man had sixteen young children with him, probably his grandchildren, dependent on him alone. The doctor said all this displayed the heartless character of the person sending them.[37] Perley reported that he had never seen such abject misery. They did not have enough clothes for decency, and the master had bought a quantity of red flannel shirts and blue trousers so that they could land without exposure.[38]

The Irish landlord most execrated in St. John that year was not Sir Robert Gore Booth but Lord Palmerston, who was Foreign Secretary at the time. He too exported his tenants from Sligo. The *Eliza Liddell* arrived in July with a cargo of old men and children. Many were taken to the hospital, and one wrote this letter to a local magistrate:

'I beg you will consider our deplorable condition here; we are poor patients in great destitution, bordering on starvation. Now, worthy magistrate, we humbly beg that you will preserve our lives a few days longer, and we shall sound your praises through all the old country as our best benefactor, and the Lord will bless your salvation. —Owen Gilgan.'[39]

Gilgan, his wife, and four children all later recovered.

Then on November 1, late in the season, when the St. Lawrence was frozen, the *Aeolus* returned to St. John, this time bringing not Gore Booth's tenants but another 428 cottiers from Palmerston's estates, making about 2,000 of his who had been shipped away that year. She was a fine ship, the food was plentiful, and the master 'kind hearted and excellent', but the emigrants were ragged and diseased. Many of the boys and young girls had no clothes, and had to tie blankets and other bedding round their waists with rope. One boy came on deck naked in the bitter cold, and a sailor wrapped him in a bread sack. Many died. Perley said few would survive until the spring. 'And the unpleasant reflection arises, that some of the emigrants by the *Aeolus*, who have departed this life, would now in all human probability be alive, had they been allowed to remain in Ireland.'[40]

Palmerston was asked to explain, and sent to Elgin a letter from his agents. This agreed that most of the passengers were paupers, since it was unlikely that Lord Palmerston would have spent so much to remove from his estate people who could pay their rent. Their entreaties to be sent to America had been so urgent that some of them knelt in the roads praying to be sent out.

This was a poor explanation. Gore Booth gave a much longer and better one when he appeared the next year before a Lords committee on Ireland.[41] He said the cost of keeping paupers in the workhouse was £2 12s. a year. It had cost him £4 15s. a head to emigrate them, £5,999 in all. On the whole the committee was sympathetic to him. One member asked:

'Do you not consider that in proportion as you remove to America you lessen the Temptation to come to England?—Of course that must be the consequence.'

He also thought that emigration was good for trade. One emigrant had written saying he had bought £7 worth of clothes. If that man had stayed in Ireland he could not have bought seven shillings' worth. The implication was that the £7 worth of clothes would have been made in England and exported to Canada, and that this was good for English manufacturers. Gore Booth produced a letter from the Roman Catholic priest of his parish saying he (Sir Robert) was deeply rooted in the affections of his grateful peasantry. He produced accounts showing that during the famine he had bought bread, oats, and anything he could get for his people, and set up soup kitchens. In all, including the cost of emigration, he had spent £15,499 16s. 9½d. on his tenants, and could not have done this unless he had also owned property in Lancashire on which he had been able to borrow money. He was frank about the kind of people he sent out: 'Supposing on my property was a man who was an indifferent character, or being in the habit of making whisky, or of a doubtful character, I would prefer the emigration of such a man from the country to getting rid of a good responsible tenant.'

So there is the picture of a shoveller-out. He had sent out his tenants on ships far above the average. Nevertheless, when they landed, the tenants looked like paupers. This was because they were paupers. That is why Sir Robert had got rid of them. At the same time, they had wanted to go, and Sir Robert, although he had avoided ruin by shipping them off, and although he had brought back cargoes of timber on his emigrant ships so that the voyages could not have been a dead loss, had still spent £15,000 on his tenants—a sum fifteen times as great as that expended annually by the government on the salaries of its emigration officers at Liverpool.[42]

But the greatest encouragers of emigration were not the British government, nor the Mormons, nor any charitable ladies of fashion giving up their time to collect for distressed needlewomen, nor shovelling landlords, but people who had been emigrants themselves. Sir Robert Gore Booth spent £15,000, which was a fortune. But in one year, 1854, at least £1,730,000 was sent back to Britain and Ireland by emigrants who had prospered, to bring out their friends or families.[43]

It was a tradition to send or sometimes bring money home. The navvy Paddy O'Dougherty, who became a propertied gentleman, sent back the first money he saved to bring over his wife and children. A Ragged School boy who saved £250, sent £100 of it home.[44] Michael Foley, dying in mid-Atlantic on the brig *Trafalgar* from Cork, gave the master £4 1s. to send back to his family in Killarney, and this was done.[45] A Cork policeman who emigrated wrote from America offering to send money to bring out any of his former colleagues who wanted to come, and five of them went.[46] A doctor inspecting emigrants at Liverpool frequently saw young girls with tickets marked 'Paid in America', which had been sent by a brother or sister who had gone over twelve months before.[47]

In a ballad of the day Mary pleads with her sweetheart William not to go. He replies that he must, but then says:

> My Love, I'm bound for foreign nations,
> If the Lord be pleased to send me o'er,
> To seek for promotion and look for labour,
> Since all things failed on the Shamrock Shore.
> But if you have patience 'till fortune favours,
> To crown my labours believe what I say,
> I'll come home love with golden store
> And bring you off to America.[48]

There is no knowing exactly how much was sent back, though a few shipping houses gave out figures. Tapscotts' in 1850 received the money for 7,500 prepaid passages.[49] In the same year the Black Star packet line received £400,000 for this purpose.[50] Train's packet line did $1,000,000 worth of business a year sending drafts from America back to families at home.[51] In 1850 a reporter of the London *Chronicle* collected figures from five shipping firms, the biggest of which had received drafts for more than 40,000 passengers. Baring Bros, the bankers, received £500,000 for passage money each year.[52]

The emigration commissioners tried to collate the figures from all shipping and banking houses, and arrived at these yearly totals:

1848	£460,000
1849	£540,000
1850	£957,000
1851	£990,000
1852	£1,404,000
1853	£1,439,000
1854	£1,730,000
1855	£873,000

These sums were sent back through brokers or bankers. There was no way of knowing how much was sent back by post.[53]

The commissioners said the figures showed a generosity and self-denial probably unparalleled in the world.[54] Grey approved too, considering it highly creditable that such feelings of family affection, and such fidelity and firmness of purpose, should exist so generally among the lower classes.[55]

13
The Breaking of Lieutenant Hodder

The laws by which the British government purported to control the embarkation and passage of emigrants were called the Passenger Acts. The first was passed in 1803. The Act which was in force for most of the disastrous season of 1847 had been passed in 1842, and that was the tenth Act to get on the statute book. By 1855 six other Acts were passed. (Details of all these Acts from 1842 on will be found in Appendix A.) Anyone innocently reading these statutes would have thought that the State had taken a detailed grip on the passenger trade, and had, if anything, rather overstepped itself. Sacred principles of the English common law had been abandoned left, right, and centre. Privacy of contract was completely set aside. Neither a shipper nor an emigrant could make a contract which gave a passenger less than six feet of headroom in the steerage, and the cargo, if any, had to be stowed in such and such a way. No shipper could depart from these conditions, or from a hundred others, and no emigrant could offer to accept less, in exchange for a lower fare. William S. Lindsay, ship's master, later shipowner, and Member of Parliament, protested that the right to make a free contract was violated 'simply to carry out an idea', and he saw that idea as 'the too zealous, misdirected efforts of, we fear, a spurious humanitarianism'. He would say that, of course. He was an M.P. in the shipping interest. But that was the law, and freedom of contract had gone, at a time when Sir Henry Maine, the celebrated jurist, was about to publish a classic treatise whose whole theme was that the basis of societies, as they develop from the primitive to the modern, moves from status to contract, from the early Roman system where not only a citizen's slaves, but also his wife and children, were within his power, to the modern English society where relationships were determined by agreement between persons equal in the sight of the law. Of course, an illiterate emigrant was not the equal, in any sense, of the rich and crafty broker, and that is why the principle had, in the Passenger Acts, been abandoned. But it was a legal principle still much cherished—in principle.[1]

The sacred tenet that the State should exercise no arbitrary powers was also set aside. The State, in the person of the half-pay naval officers who inspected emigrant ships before they sailed, could arbitrarily decide, among other things, on the merits of the crew, the lifeboats, the cook, the kitchen ranges, the water-casks, and the surgical instruments carried. He even had to decide whether the ship's doctor was a competent physician, and there was no appeal from his decision.[2]

The principle that only Parliament could legislate was set aside, because the emigration officer had such vast discretions to determine whether the vessel was stowed, crewed, and provisioned 'to his satisfaction'[3] that he could in effect make and state the law on the spot: he was a uniformed delegated legislator. And if this officer prosecuted a ship's master or a broker, even the burden of proof was often shifted from the officer to the broker, who, if his defence was that the section of the Act under which he was prosecuted did not properly apply to him, had to prove it: the onus was on him to show he was not caught by the Act, not on the prosecution to show that the Act caught him.

The Passenger Acts, in short, were a fully developed branch of administrative law, at least eighty years ahead of their time in their arbitrariness, with the common law as good as abrogated, and large judicial powers given to a junior executive officer. This arbitrariness was quite justified by the helplessness of the emigrants and the corruptions of the passenger trade, and if the Acts had worked the emigrant would have been well protected. But the Acts did not work. To enforce them, if they had been wisely drafted and enacted, would have taken a vast corps of government officers, but there were never more than twenty-four officers for the whole of Great Britain and Ireland. In the season of 1847, when report after report showed that vessel after vessel had broken or completely disregarded the whole substance of the Acts, there were only seven prosecutions in the United Kingdom.[4] And not only were the Acts unenforced, but parts of the passenger code were manifestly unenforceable.

The most hilarious example of this was an Order in Council made by the emigration commissioners in 1848, which laid down detailed rules for conduct on board North American passenger ships.[5] Rule 1 legislated all emigrants out of bed by seven in the morning, Rule 6 caused all decks to be dry holystoned or scraped at nine, Rule 9 gave each family a regular turn at the cooking fire, Rule 13 made Tuesdays and Fridays washing days but allowed that this should be 'with reference to weather', Rule 14 assembled all passengers in clean linen and decent apparel at half past ten on Sundays, Rule 16 prohibited gunpowder and Rule 19 gambling, Rule 20 placed all passengers' swords in the care of the captain, and Rule 21 strictly forbade swearing and improper language.

This Order in Council was promulgated by the commissioners, printed, placed in their annual report, placed before a House of Lords select committee on colonisation, and ordered to be hung up in at least two conspicuous places between decks in all emigrant ships. It is difficult to believe that anyone who had a hand in its preparation can ever have been to sea, or read with understanding any one of the many reports of seasickness, overcrowding, and disease aboard emigrant ships. Aboard a ship of the Royal Navy, with the officers and sailors devoting most of their time to the discipline of their steerage passengers, it is possible that the Order might have been enforceable—in fine weather. Aboard an English merchant vessel, with no discipline and no one in authority to attempt to enforce it, the Order was an impossibility. Aboard an American packet, out of British waters, the Order would not only have been impracticable but would not have carried the slightest authority.

It was worthless, and the commissioners must have known it was worthless. If they did not, they cannot have known their business. Murdoch, who was chairman of the board at the time, must have realised this: when he was confronted with Vere Foster's account of daily life aboard the *Washington*, where the Order in Council was not exactly religiously enforced, he replied: 'We hear very little of what takes place on board American ships.'[6]

But to be fair to the commissioners they had been trying for years to put government agents on board emigrant ships at sea, to make at least a show of enforcing the Passenger Acts. This came out in the commissioners' reply to the articles of Dr. Custis, who, besides making his charges of bribes, brutality, and rape, and talking of floating brothels, also said that in his opinion the sooner the Emigration Commission and the Passenger Acts were abolished the better, because they only served to delude passengers into a false security which prevented them looking out for themselves. He said the nation was bound to look into the matter and purge itself from a sin (he was back to immorality again) which cried out for vengeance and might well call down a national judgment on them all.[7]

The commissioners mildly replied that Custis's statements bore the appearance of being highly coloured, but nevertheless must not be assumed to be without foundation. They suggested placing a government officer on board each ship, something which had been 'repeatedly proposed during the last seventeen or eighteen years'. The commissioners saw that there were difficulties. On foreign ships the officer could have no legal authority and would be regarded as a government spy, and 'such means of annoyance might be brought to bear upon him as would give him the strongest motive for conciliating the master and officers of the ship rather than scrutinizing their conduct towards the emigrants'. That the commissioners should fear a government agent might be intimidated, shows they knew perfectly well how an ordinary emigrant might be treated. But they went on to suggest that the agent should sail secretly, as an ordinary steerage passenger. The cost would be between £40 and £50 a ship, and if agents sailed on up to twenty ships a season, this would make £1,000 a year. The Colonial Office could not countenance anything so ungentlemanly. T. F. Elliot endorsed the commissioners' letter as follows: 'I confess that I should feel almost an insuperable dislike to employing secret Government Agents . . .' And so on. He thought Custis had an excitable imagination and a gift for fine writing, and had grossly exaggerated. If complaints on board ship were trifling, it was natural that passengers should be unwilling to prosecute on arrival, but he could not believe that a remedy would be wanting if such gross outrages occurred as Custis had imagined in his letter. It was decided to 'make enquiries', and no more.[8]

Now Custis certainly had been excitable in his charges of rape and seduction, but his articles were mostly concerned with common brutality. If Elliot could not imagine that such outrages were often without remedy, then he must have forgotten the case of the *Washington*, and he must have forgotten the evidence of witness after witness to three Parliamentary select committees.

But even though large parts of the Passenger Acts were not enforceable, there were other parts that were. It should have been possible to determine at Liverpool how much steerage space a vessel had, and how many passengers this entitled her to carry, and to check that she carried the quantity of foodstuffs and water that the law demanded. Until the case of Lieutenant Hodder in 1851 it was expected and assumed that this was done.

Thomas Eyre Hodder was an Irishman, a distant relation of the Earl of Leitrim, and his brother was Deputy Lieutenant of County Cork. Hodder entered the navy as a boy in 1811, was promoted lieutenant in 1824, and served in the West India station. He was put on half-pay in 1829, and except for a brief attachment in 1836 to the *Vanguard*, eighty guns, which was fitting out at Portsmouth, he had not been to sea since.[9] In 1834 the Colonial Office formed the corps of emigration officers, and recruited half-pay naval lieutenants to oversee emigration at Liverpool, Bristol, Dublin, Belfast, Cork, Limerick, and Glasgow. Hodder was one of these, and went to Dublin. In 1845 he transferred to Liverpool as chief officer, and he and one assistant dealt with the famine emigration of 1847 from that port. He was an honest and courageous man, whom the commissioners trusted. In 1851 he was still only a lieutenant, and was receiving £308 5s. a year, plus his naval half-pay.[10]

Liverpool was by far the busiest emigration port, and 1851 was its busiest year. A shipping agent remarked that hardly any number of emigration officers could have done the job. Sometimes, after the winds had been unfavourable for a while, as many as twenty or thirty ships would go out of dock on one tide. Ten or twelve officers would not have been enough. There were then only three at Liverpool, and it was their duty to inspect ships leaving at the same time from different docks as much as three miles apart.[11] They did not even have a cutter to get from one vessel to another.

In March, 1851, the British ship *Blanche* out of Liverpool, Thomas Duckitt master, on her first voyage, arrived at New Orleans. Twenty-five of her passengers died on the voyage, the second mate and thirteen of the crew caught the fever too, and so did the master. At one time there were only four seamen left to work the ship. The master thought only a merciful Providence had enabled him to bring the ship in. At New Orleans 140 passengers were taken off ill. The *Blanche* had been carrying 470 emigrants, and when the port health officer measured her he found that this was eighty-four more than her lawful complement.[12] The master defended himself, saying that he had done his duty and that his feelings had been deeply wounded at finding himself, arriving in a strange country and a foreign port, arraigned before the world as an inhuman monster and a murderer. Fifty passengers had come forward and signed a testimonial certifying that he had done all he could for them. As for the overcrowding, he had nothing to gain from taking more passengers than was legal, since the between decks had been chartered for a round sum, and he had not been paid so much each. At Liverpool the ship had been surveyed by a sworn government officer, and if there was any blame it was that officer's and not the master's.[13] The British consul at New Orleans complained, the complaints reached the emigration commissioners, and Hodder was summoned to London to explain himself. He said he had been in the habit of accepting American customs officers' measurements of ships, and not measuring them himself. He excused this neglect by saying the increase of emigration had thrown very laborious duties on the officers at Liverpool. The commissioners asked more questions, and the case became even worse. Because this was the *Blanche*'s first voyage she did not even have certificates signed by United States customs officers, and the captain's own statement of her capacity had been accepted. 'And this,' said the commissioners, 'appears to have been for some time the established practice at Liverpool with regard to ships proceeding to the United States.' So with pain and regret they suggested that Lieutenant Hodder, who had been seventeen years in the department, eleven at Dublin and six at Liverpool, an officer of high integrity and conciliatory manners, who had done much to protect emigrants against fraud, should be moved to a less arduous post at Glasgow.[14]

The commissioners' report went to the Colonial Office, where Elliot, who had formerly worked with Hodder for many years, decided that the commissioners were too lenient. Grey agreed, saying the result had been to throw a just discredit on the British officers, and told the commissioners to dismiss Hodder.[15]

Hodder protested. He said he had done his duty with faithfulness and zeal. 'The *great* increase of Emigrants introduces a much larger number of brokers and others employed in the trade, who are for the most part chiefly interested in devising modes of evading the intentions of the law.' It had been a physical impossibility to carry out the letter of the law, although he hoped he had fulfilled the spirit. 'I do now, indeed, most deeply regret that I had not officially stated the total inadequacy of the staff at this port, but the extreme reluctance which was always shewn when I *spoke* on the subject to make any addition to the force, induced me to proceed in the face of all difficulties, trusting that the tide of Emigration would soon begin to slacken . . .' If he was dismissed a stigma would be cast on his character which could never be eradicated. If he had been guilty of any dishonourable conduct he would not have dared to offer one word in extenuation, but he could not believe that the commissioners would visit so heavily the offence of having been found unequal to cope with the frauds and devices of people united against him.[16]

Grey still insisted on his dismissal.

In the meantime, Hodder's successor at Liverpool, Captain Charles Patey, R.N., had been instructed to find out what had been happening in the port. His report is a sad document. He said ships' water-casks had not been inspected, and passengers had not been counted. It had been the custom merely to take the passenger list and see that there were no more on it than the ship was supposed to carry, and to collect the tickets of any passengers who happened to be on board. Ships had been cleared before the passengers, or sometimes even the cargo, had been taken on board, sometimes a week or ten days before the ship was due to sail, sometimes when the vessels were leaving dock in a state of confusion with the passengers and their luggage still being hurried on board. In Patey's opinion the clearing had been a mere matter of form.[17]

He asked for an extra officer to help him, and a cutter. The commissioners gave him both. They said that the practice of not measuring the ships 'had rendered nugatory the supervision of the Emigration Officer over the numbers carried'.[18]

A petition signed by the Mayor of Liverpool and 248 other people was sent to the Colonial Office, saying Hodder was able, humane, and perfectly impartial, had been conspicuously benevolent in years of famine and pestilence, and was probably too unobtrusive to have fully explained the mitigating circumstances of the case. The petition asked Grey to reconsider.[19] He refused. Hodder's brother also wrote, but he too was refused.[20]

Hodder was unlucky. He had dealt with the 1847 emigration with only one assistant, while the London officer, having only one-twelfth of the number of emigrants to inspect, had two assistants. By 1850 Hodder had two assistants as well, but he had to cope with more than fifteen times as many emigrants as his colleagues at London.[21] The emigrants at Liverpool were also of much the worse kind, and the rackets there much better organised. He had quite the most arduous post in the department, and yet his counterpart at London was promoted captain on the recommendation of the commissioners, while Hodder was dismissed. He had neglected the letter of his duties, because they were impossibly heavy, but the commissioners were guilty of neglect too. If they did not know the work at Liverpool had become impossible, then they could have had no idea of the size and condition of the emigration from that port. And even if they had not known, they should have woken up earlier that year when Hodder, in public, dropped a great deal more than a hint of what was happening.

Giving evidence to a parliamentary committee at Westminster, Hodder said he could not count the passengers, because there was no possibility of getting them together. 'We only muster those going to the colonies,' he said. The members of that select committee, being sharper than the commissioners, wrote in their report: 'Without a muster of the passengers there can clearly be no effectual check on the number put on board; and so strongly has this been felt at Liverpool by the emigration officers, that they appear to have given it up as hopeless.'[22]

Hodder did make one more unsuccessful attempt, through William Brown, one of the Members of Parliament for South Lancashire, to induce Grey 'to open some other door of occupation'. He said that after forty years in Her Majesty's service he was thrown upon his only resource, his half-pay.[23] The half-pay of a naval lieutenant in 1851 was 7s. a day.[24]

Patey, who succeeded the disgraced Hodder at Liverpool, became a rear-admiral. Commander Charles Schomberg, who took over at Liverpool in 1853, went on to command a ninety-gun warship, and became a vice-admiral. Thirteen years after he left Liverpool, when he must have been over sixty, Hodder was given his only promotion, to commander, and he died in that rank in 1873.[25]

It follows from Hodder's own admissions, and from Patey's report, that in the years 1847 to 1851 the Passenger Acts had been enforced at Liverpool only upon vessels sailing to British North America, that is to say, on one vessel in thirteen. At by far the most important British emigration port, vessels bound for the United States had done as they pleased. The Passenger Acts had been enforced only if the ships' masters had chosen to enforce them themselves. Neither food nor water had been inspected, and the passengers had not been counted. For all the good they were, the Acts might as well never have been passed. Yet while this was going on, in the heaviest years of the mid-century emigration, the commissioners in London were so deluded that they were determining by Order in

Council the hour at which emigrants on board foreign vessels at sea should rise in the morning, and at what hour they should scrape or holystone the decks.

It also follows that the British government figures for emigration from Liverpool for these years, apparently so precisely recorded, are plainly false. They are nothing more than an adding up of the masters' own statements. There is no saying how inaccurate they are. The *Blanche* was carrying eighty-six passengers in excess of her lawful complement of 386. This was probably an unusual excess: it was that and the fever that made the New Orleans health officer suspicious. But it does seem reasonable to suppose that in the years from 1846 to 1851 ships out of Liverpool bound for the United States may have carried 10 per cent more passengers than they were allowed. After 1851 the new emigrant officers at Liverpool, with their cutter and no doubt a little added zeal, tried to be more exact, but even then they cannot have succeeded to the letter. Even with the new assistant Patey was granted when he took over, there were still only four officers, and if eight vessels often left on one tide, they could not possibly have done their duty.

The United States Passenger Acts were simpler and a lot shorter, and as they did not legislate for the impossible they stood a better chance of being enforced. At least they were more enforceable. (They are also summarised in Appendix A.) They were without the trimmings of the English Acts, but provided for ventilation, and privies (one for each hundred passengers), and gave emigrants more room. American Acts were less precise about food. The 1848 Act did specify that each passenger should receive each week one and a half pounds of navy bread, one pound each of oatmeal and peas, three and a half pounds of potatoes, a pound of pork, and six gallons of fresh water, but this clause was repealed the next year when the master was simply required to provide a 'sufficient supply of good and wholesome food'.

The limits of legislation were better realised than in England. As one witness told an American committee on cholera in 1850, if legislation aimed at the removal of the disease it would first have to give the poor not only airy and comfortable dwellings but an abundance of wholesome food. 'But this is a great work, beyond the ordinary range of legislation.'[26] Also, strangely enough, the same suggestion was made to a United States Senate committee as Samuel Cunard had earlier made in England. It would be better, said a witness, for the United States to give emigrants free passage in its own naval vessels, selecting the best of those who wanted to come.[27] But this too was beyond the ordinary range of legislation.

The interests of Great Britain and of the United States in the regulation of the emigrant trade were not altogether the same. The British interest was to get them away—though this was to be achieved with humanity—and as far as possible to soften the hardships of the voyage. The American interest was to receive the emigrants in good health, and strong enough to work. Therefore the passage had to be regulated, but, more immediately important, the arrival had to be managed so that emigrants did not bring disease or cost too much in poor relief.

Immigration at New York was handled by two authorities. The Passenger Acts were a federal matter, for the United States collectors of customs, but the health and welfare of immigrants was the responsibility of the Commissioners of Emigration, who were appointed by New York State. The commissioners were much the more efficient of the two organisations. The commission was set up by the State on May 5, 1847, from motives of humanity and self-defence, when it was obvious that the year's emigration was going to be very heavy. The commissioners were the mayors of New York and Brooklyn, the presidents of the Irish and German emigration societies, and six other citizens. They were empowered to collect $1.50 from each passenger arriving, and to spend this money on the quarantine and other hospitals, and on finding jobs for emigrants. If an emigrant became ill or destitute in any county of New York State, that county could recover his keep from the commissioners. So the commission not only provided a quarantine but was also the means of making the emigrants pay for their own poor relief, which they did, since the $1.50 tax covered all costs incurred by the State and city.[28]

The New York commissioners, unlike the emigration commissioners in England, were not paid civil servants. They worked voluntarily. The most active of them were Gregory Dillon, president of the Irish society, Minturn, and Gulian C. Verplanck, who was chairman.

Verplanck came of an old Dutch family which settled in America in the seventeenth century, and he was a very various man. He became a lawyer in New York, then he travelled for two years in Europe, then for three years he was professor of theology at an episcopal seminary in New York City. He was elected to the United States House of Representatives in 1824 and remained a member for the rest of his life. For a few years he was a New York State senator.

He helped to obtain a copyright law for authors, he wrote satirical verse, and in 1847, the same year as he took over chairmanship of the emigration commission, published his own edition of Shakespeare's plays.[29]

In 1855 he claimed that the commissioners had saved the State $4,000,000 and the city $2,000,000, had looked after 100,000 emigrants in its hospitals, and found jobs for a million others. But some of the New York press was hostile, one paper described the commissioners as useless and expensive,[30] and there were frequent accusations of corruption. Dr. Van Hovenburgh, the port health officer, was said to be bribable, and to sell steamer loads of emigrants to runners.[31] Smethurst the broker was said to have at least one of the commissioners in his pay, and the commissioners' officers and their boatmen were reputed to work with brokers who made it worth their while.[32] Most of these accusations were made by runners or brokers themselves, so they cannot be taken at face value, but there were enough complaints to justify a State inquiry in 1852. This found that there was nothing in the charges of bribery, but that some of the commissioners' buildings were very dirty.[33]

Even if there was no corruption, the law the commissioners were supposed to administer did not always work. In 1847 runners were obliged to take out licences, but this only made things worse. Runners remained the same men, their calling remained what it was, their honesty was no better than it had been, and the badge which they now were obliged to wear gave their villainy a certain degree of authority and credit. 'He points to the badge, "Licensed emigrant runner", and soon satisfies the perplexed emigrant that he, the licensed runner, is the person specially appointed to look after the stranger, and protect him from the danger of being imposed upon; he often even succeeds in making the emigrant believe he must do as the licensed runner tells him.'[34] The framing of some of the laws regulating runners was sloppy. One clause of a State law of 1848 required boarding-house keepers to have a licence, but imposed no penalty if he did not. Another clause said that every person who solicited alien passengers *without* a licence should *forfeit* his licence.[35] Henry Smethurst did not even have a licence, and said publicly that he did not, but he was for years the most successful crooked broker in the port.[36] In 1852 a runner called George Andrews said he had heard of no frauds on emigrants that season; at any rate, he did not know of a solitary case of a runner being prosecuted.[37] What prosecutions there were were unsuccessful. George (One-Eyed) Daley

boasted that he had been in the emigrant business fifteen years and
tried for frauds more than a hundred times, but had never been
convicted.[38] The law against soliciting was hardly enforced at all.
In 1852, when 3,967 men were convicted of vagrancy in New York
City, only three were imprisoned for soliciting emigrants, the same
number as were convicted of the exotic crime of mutiny. The following year 7,435 men were committed to the city prison for 'intoxica-
tion', 2,678 for assault, 1,415 for disorderly conduct, thirty-eight for
'bastardy', seven for sedition, but only one for soliciting emigrants.[39]

By a law of 1819, the United States customs officers were given the
duty of checking that vessels entering American ports were not
carrying more emigrants than they could legally carry, and of making
quarterly returns to the Secretary of State,[40] but neither this nor subsequent Acts imposed on the customs officers or on anyone else the
duty of prosecuting for breaches of the Acts. When the Black Star
packet *Washington* arrived in 1851 her master, if the very strong
evidence against him is believed, was liable to fines of $105,000, but
even in this flagrant case no prosecution was brought.[41] It was not a
system likely to work well. When, before 1834, the British customs
were formally responsible for enforcing the British Passenger Acts,
little was done, and it was not until a specialist corps of British
emigration officers was appointed that a real attempt was made to
carry any part of the law into effect. In the United States there was
no special corps, and the customs officers had other and more profitable duties to perform. It is doubtful whether they even properly
performed the duty of counting passengers on incoming vessels.
There is no known evidence that they did, and some that they did
not. The returns to the Secretary of State were incomplete. Minturn
said in 1848 that the statistics were 'imperfect', and that the law was
'not carefully attended to'.[42] He was not only an emigration commissioner but also an owner of emigrant packets, and he should
have known whether his own vessels were properly inspected or not.
Herman Melville, who knew the emigrant trade, said it was hardly
to be believed that vessels were examined.[43] Murdoch, chairman of
the British commissioners, said: 'If there have been a great number
of deaths, or if any loud complaints are made, the [American] law I
believe is put in force; but practically speaking, I believe the law is
not put in force.'[44]

Custis, the surgeon who made much of the evils of the trade, told
the story of one ship's master entering New York. According to him,
the master said: 'The person deputed to measure the ship came to me

and said, "You have more than you ought to carry, and I will have you fined." I took him into the cabin and—shook hands with him, and requested him to try again as he might have made a mistake. He did so, and, on his return, told me I could have carried sixteen more.'[45]

This is not incredible. Charles Gallagher was a customs officer at New York until he went on to better things and became one of the most successful runners.[46] The customs officers, who were the first to board vessels coming into the harbour, notoriously touted for runners and passenger brokers. As one broker told a State committee,[47] those employed by the government were more valuable as runners in consequence of their official station, and a man connected with the custom house had an advantage over other men.

14

America for the Americans

His Excellency Henry J. Gardner, Governor of Massachusetts, addressed the State Senate and House of Representatives on January 9, 1855.[1] He began by remarking that the Gracious Being who had permitted them to assemble that day had also through his providential care enabled their ancestors to establish religious freedom on the shores of Massachusetts, and, later, permitted their revolutionary forefathers to secure the added boon of civil liberty. He earnestly and fervently trusted that they should now be aided by His wisdom so to deliberate and act that 'these unspeakable privileges may be transmitted unimpaired to those who shall come after us'. They ought to be profoundly grateful that while the Ruler of the Universe had permitted calamities such as the Crimean War to befall others, Massachusetts had been spared, and had again been vouchsafed peace and plenty. The Senate, Representatives, and governor had now met according to time-honoured custom, to enact—for the common good—honest, wise, and thoughtful legislation. Honest, and therefore not for a party but a people: thoughtful, and therefore protecting the rights of the whole and invading the privileges of none: wise, and therefore not for a year but for generations. Having got through this, he plunged straight into what he called the most prominent subject before the State and Nation—emigrants, the duty of republicanism towards them, and the dangers from them. He said it was an astonishing statistical fact that nearly four-fifths of the beggary, two-thirds of the pauperism, and more than three-fifths of the crimes, sprang from emigrants. The people demanded of their statesmen that this should be controlled. The times were propitious for the development of this great American movement by the united action of the whole people. The flood of emigrants tended to bind the people together 'in one united national, not party, movement'. The movement, not a party, was in fact the Know-Nothing, or American, party. The governor could not bring himself either to name it or call it a party, but he belonged to it, and so did all the senators he was addressing, and all but two of the representatives, and the principle which united them was that of America for the Americans. They did not like emigrants, and particularly they did not like Irish Catholic emigrants, and they were sure they had God on their side. In his address the governor frequently called on God, and also brought in to support his argument not only the Bible but the splendour of Athens, the early Caesars, Plymouth Rock, George Washington, and the battlefield of Lexington.

The dominant race, he said, meaning his own, must regulate the incoming class, meaning emigrants. This was political destiny, and history proved it. So, they should dispel from popular use all foreign languages; discourage imported political demagogues, among them the leaders of 'continental red republicanism'; purify and ennoble the franchise; 'adopt a carefully guarded check-list throughout the nation'; and Americanise America. By continental red republicans he probably meant the political refugees who had come to America after the failed European revolutions of 1848: there were few of them, but they were a nuisance. By a purified and ennobled franchise he meant one which excluded emigrants. He went on to say that the prodigality with which citizenship and the franchise were lavished upon foreigners clearly tended to 'lower the tone of American feeling'. In Athens citizenship had been bestowed only as a distinguished favour. In early Rome the Caesars had given citizenship with a sparing hand, but the line of degenerate emperors had corrupted, extended, and destroyed citizenship, 'until the national blood was tainted, the distinctive national prejudice and spirit were dissolved, and the state perished under a horde of foreign barbarians, whose warlike invasion affords almost the only historic parallel in number to the peaceful and insidious foreign influx to our shores in the present day'. Every additional naturalisation tended to denationalise and Europeanise America. George Washington had warned them to beware of foreign influence. The alien, however honest and well disposed, who had lived among foreign customs and institutions, could not enter into the spirit and comprehend the genius of American institutions like a man born and educated among them, and even a native citizen could not vote until he had lived twenty-one years under the blessings and influences of the American system.

This is a dubious argument. It was true that no native-born American could vote until he was twenty-one, but it is uncertain how much even an American child, in its babyhood and infancy, could have appreciated the influences and blessings of the American political system. Nevertheless, this argument was used by the governor to justify his proposal that no naturalised emigrant should have the vote until he had lived in America twenty-one years, and this was later enacted by the State legislature.

The governor complained that emigrants reduced the pay of American labour, which was true; and that nine-tenths of the gold recently found in California, the golden gift of Providence, had been shipped off to Europe to pay for imported luxuries, when it should instead have stayed at home and been used to make gold coins to take the place of paper money. Then he suggested that alien paupers should be returned with humanity to their own countries. The annual cost of supporting a pauper in the almshouse was nearly sixty dollars a year: 'The cost of sending them to Liverpool, whence most of them come, would not exceed twenty dollars each, including a comfortable outfit.'

A little later the United States House of Representatives Foreign Affairs Committee was using much the same language, saying that if it was the duty of government to protect America from foreign aggression with ball and cannon, it must surely also be its duty to protect the country 'from an enemy more insidious and destructive, though coming in another form'. The committee, like the governor, went to the Bible for spiritual help, and quoted Ezekiel 28:7: 'Behold, therefore, I will bring strangers upon thee, the terrible of the nations, and they shall draw their swords against the beauty of thy wisdom and they shall defile thy brightness.'[2]

This violence of political feeling and language was nothing new. Samuel Morse, the inventor of the Morse code, was also an all-American pamphleteer. 'Up! Up! I beseech you,' he beseeched in 1845: 'Awake! To your posts! Shut the open gates. Your enemies, in the guise of friends, many thousands, are at this moment rushing in to your ruin through the open portals of naturalisation.' The American character had within a short time been badly degraded:

emigrants were the conspirators against it. He would not hear talk of American Irish or American English. One might with as much consistency say *foreign natives* or *hostile friends*. And then, to show the beauty of his wisdom, he said that Roman Catholic priests could compel Protestants to submit to Rome by punishments, and that these punishments could be CONFISCATION OF PROPERTY, IMPRISON-MENT, and DEATH.[3]

The anti-Catholicism was nothing new either. Stories like *The Stolen Nuns* and *The Haunted Convent*, about Protestant girls spirited away by priests, were very popular.[4] One illustration showed a priest's confessional, with a kneeling girl making her confession to a priest, whose bed waited on the other side of the room. When Kossuth came to America in 1851 he was welcomed not only as a patriot and a struggler against European tyranny but also as a Protestant, and on the first Sunday he was in New York a Baptist minister preached on 'The Coming of Kossuth. Illustrative of the Second Coming of Christ'. Later during his visit Kossuth's welcome wore thin, perhaps because he came to be seen as a continental red republican.

The nobility of Americanism was a very suitable pretext for a diverting riot. The Astor Place riots of 1849 were really anti-foreign, as most of the rioters probably had no settled opinions on how to play Macbeth. What happened was that Edwin Forrest, an American actor, and William Charles Macready, an Englishman, were due to play Macbeth in two different theatres in New York one night in May, 1849. Forrest was said to have been publicly hissed in London, so in reply his supporters broke up Macready's performance at the Astor Place opera house. The performance was postponed until May 10. Posters appeared saying: 'Workingmen! shall Americans or Englishmen rule this country? The crews of the British steamers have threatened all Americans who shall dare appear this night at the English aristocratic Opera House. Workingmen! freemen! stand up to your lawful rights.' On the night of the proposed performance 300 rowdies were ejected from the theatre, and then attacked the police outside. The Seventh Regiment charged the mob: 141 soldiers were hurt and thirty-four civilians killed or wounded.[5]

In San Francisco, where Americanism was very strong in the mid-fifties, the lynching of Joseph Hetherington very likely had some-thing to do with his being English. He was hanged in July 1856 before a crowd of 15,000 spectators, and after no trial at all. Earlier that month he had met a Dr. Randall in a San Francisco hotel. He was in dispute with Randall over some land, and when he met him he pulled the doctor's beard, which was big and flowing. The doctor pulled out his revolver and fired three times at Hetherington, who fired back twice, killing the doctor. Vigilantes seized Hetherington, and on July 29 he and another man, Bruce, with whom Hetherington had no connection, were brought out to be hanged. The newspaper reporting the hanging says Hetherington behaved like a coward, but its own account shows he did nothing of the sort. On ascending the gallows, he said: 'I am now about to meet my Maker. To the best of my knowledge, I have not lived a day in my life that I was afraid to meet my Maker that night.' (To the reporter: 'Have you got that?')

Bruce kept on interrupting, saying, 'Go on, old hoss,' and saying he was drunk, and didn't care a damn, gentlemen.

Hetherington said he had shot Randall to save his own life. 'And will die a gentleman, though on the gallows.'

Bruce: 'Dry up.'

Hetherington: 'I was going to make a remark that few people . . .'

Bruce: 'Go it, old hoss.'

The executioner drew on the white cap. Hetherington said: 'I should like to have seen Fletcher Haight, but it was denied me. Remember me to Fletcher Haight and Henry Haight. Lord have mercy on my soul.' He was about thirty-five, and spoke in a strong Cumberland accent.[6]

Extreme Americanism had its opponents. There were many who saw that this fear of the foreign emigrant was excessive and unreasonable. A Methodist minister, preaching in New York in 1848, answered the America-for-the-Americans with a text of his own from the Bible, 'And if a stranger sojourn with thee in your land, ye shall not vex him' (Leviticus 19:33–4), and said there might be many Roman Catholics among the emigrants, but Romanism never had conquered liberty. To make Catholicism justly an occasion of alarm, one would also have to transfer to America the social and political systems of Europe, its serfdom, titled aristocracy, and monarchy. What if the less educated emigrants should think that the potatoes and cabbages of the old country were larger and better than those of the New World? Should this make Americans suspicious and hateful? This would be inconsistent with American principles. Home prejudices might cling to the emigrant while he lived, but they would be buried with him, and his children would be as great lovers of liberty and as strong enemies of unrighteous aristocracy as present native Americans, whose fathers had been emigrants only a few years ago. True, the great majority of groggeries, and especially Sunday groggeries, were in the hands of those born out of the United States, but generally the picture was radiant with hope and promise.[7]

A select committee of New York State said in its report the same year that if there was anything of which Americans ought to be proud, it was their noble and free institutions; and the fact that the country was now becoming so generally the resort and resting place of the downtrodden and oppressed of the world should only increase that pride.[8] Herman Melville felt the same: '. . . if they can get here, they have God's right to come; though they bring all Ireland and her miseries with them.'[9] Bostonians would have disagreed, not only in the mid-1850s, when Americanism was suddenly powerful everywhere, but for many years before. In 1848, after the disease and expense of the year before, a Massachusetts Senate committee said it was frequently asserted that America had become the Botany Bay of all Europe, and its poor-house too, as if it were the moral cesspool of the civilised world. Boston had spent nearly $50,000 in legal costs, prosecuting emigrants. One day the previous June there had been sixteen cases in the police courts, all against foreigners. Unless something was done, throngs of foreign paupers would get a permanent foothold on the soil of the State, and how to raise money to look after them would be an intolerable source of perplexity. Britain was making an effort to send her paupers out of the kingdom. Those who landed in British North America found few charitable institutions of any kind, and so came south to New England to be at once provided for at the public charge far better than they ever had been at home. After the hardships of the voyage, the undermining of health, and the death of friends, even those who had not been paupers in their native land became, in the agony of disappointment, paupers in the truest sense of the word when they touched the soil of Massachusetts, begged for food on the day of their arrival, clustered about the city, and refused to travel west. During 1847 a few over 25,000 emigrants arrived in Boston by sea, and more by rail from St. John, by way of Portland. Half the children in Boston schools were of foreign parentage. Between 1,200 and 1,300 citizens had petitioned the legislature to ensure that the State in future should spend less public money on emigrants. To finish, the committee asked this question: 'If a single vessel freighted with emigrants from the United States, particularly those from the almshouses of the seaboard,—aliens by birth,—were carried into any port in Great Britain, with a view to throwing them upon the community there for support, what

would be the probable result? A sensation, unlike the ordinary mercantile transaction, would be manifested at once by the civil authorities, and if they could not be kept away by gentle means, we should
be made to feel the indignation of an insulted government. Yet that
very indignity is heaped upon Massachusetts from the beginning of
a season to its termination. . . .'[10]

The governor of 1852, in his address, was concerned to make what
profit could be made out of emigration.[11] New York permitted, in
all cases, the payment of a lump sum in commutation of the sureties
against their becoming a public charge which were otherwise
required of all emigrants, though the commutation money was much
greater when the emigrant was aged, insane, or sick. The laws of
Massachusetts did not permit this, requiring a bond of $1,000 for
paupers or sick emigrants. The result was that emigrant vessels preferred to go to New York, and the commutation money went into
the treasury of New York State, though afterwards many emigrants
who had entered at New York came to Massachusetts and became a
charge there. The evils of foreign pauperism could not be avoided,
so the governor thought it wiser to take advantage of direct
emigration, which increased the business of the State, and would in
some degree replenish the treasury.

By 1855 the line was altogether harder, and soon after Governor
Gardner had delivered his speech yet another committee on emigrants[12] was saying that magnanimous vapouring and philanthropic
profession had lately been the fashion, but it would be hard to find
any motive, of duty or expediency, for welcoming unreservedly the
poverty, degradation, the vice of Europe. Pauperism was a curse to
the pauper as well as to the community. Mere sentiment and showy
philanthropy should not be suffered to trifle with real interests and
permanent good. 'It should be remembered that even simple comfort
and decency are an unwonted luxury to most of the unfortunate
inmates of these receptacles [workhouses].' To improve emigrants,
morally, intellectually, and physically, was a true economy as well as
a sacred duty, but the almshouse should offer no charms to the idle,
perverse, and demoralised. More foreign paupers should be sent
back. This would eventually discourage some emigrants from coming in the first place, and it would, moreover, 'act *in terrorem* upon all
who had any remnant of energy and ambition, or who retained any
hope or purpose of a life of respectability and self-dependence, to
avoid more carefully and dread more cogently the seeing themselves
reduced to such a strait'. Sympathy would be wasted on the matter;

the confirmed paupers were almost purely animal, and only physical deprivation and suffering affected them; there was nothing approaching persecution or injustice in sending them back. The report did not say so in as many words, but the whole sense and tone of it was that if paupers were going to be paupers, they might as well be paupers back home where they would be no charge to the Commonwealth of Massachusetts. 'To them it matters little or nothing.'

Through the reports and addresses of the time runs the conviction that Great Britain was, as a matter of policy, deporting to America her paupers and convicts. Many emigrants were paupers, and some had no doubt been convicts, but the government had nothing to do with sending them, directly or indirectly. Grey's memoirs show that the government was very careful and anxious *not* to have the slightest connection with the sending out of emigrants. Thousands of Irish were, of course, privately shovelled out by English landlords, but they were almost always sent to British North America, if only because shovelling landlords, partly out of natural inclination, and partly to justify their actions, preferred to talk of colonisation rather than emigration, and preferred to see Canada rather than the United States get the benefit of their generosity. And it was altogether an American delusion that English parishes were engaged in 'a fraudulent conspiracy to relieve themselves, not only of the obligation of humanity, but of the expense of supporting their own helpless population'.[13] It was true that the English Poor Law of 1834 did empower poor law guardians to pay the fares of emigrants from their parishes, but this power was rarely used. In the late 1840s only about 200 a year were sent out in this way. In the early 1850s the figure did rise quickly to 3,000 or so, but then dropped off again.[14] Three thousand, among an American emigration, in 1850, of 258,000, hardly mattered.

The accusation that Britain was making the United States a Botany Bay is nonsense. To dump convicts in America would have been, to say the least of it, an unfriendly act towards a more or less friendly government. A few English ex-convicts were helped to emigrate by a private organisation, but this caused a small scandal in England when it was discovered. In September 1848 the London *Times* published a leading article, intended to be witty, which said that a Mr. Jackson had been carrying out an extensive felon emigration from the City Mission.[15] ('Extensive' later turned out to mean thirteen men.) To entitle himself to the benefits offered by Mr. Jackson, said *The Times*, the only court at which a man had to have been presented was the Central Criminal Court. The longer the sentence, the better the claim on the Felon Emigration Society. Fourteen years was better than seven. If the men were being sent to Australia that would not be so bad, because that country was inhabited only by kangaroos, but Mr. Jackson was despatching his emigrants, untidy morals and all, to the United States—into the very heart of a populous commercial community, where the authorities were coy at receiving a perennial stream of English blackguardism. Some time back the wives of two emigrants had gone to a police officer saying their husbands had received free passages to America from an association with which the name of Lord Ashley (who later became Earl of Shaftesbury) was said to be connected, and of which Mr. Jackson was the principal manager. It came out that Mr. Jackson had met with great success in 'throwing thieves of various degrees of standing in the profession upon the United States'. It was an essential qualification for these men to have led the life of often convicted criminals. But two men had been so eager to qualify that they had invented suitable convictions, one really having none, and the other only one under the Hackney Coach Act. The newspaper went on to say that a free passage to America was a signal boon to be conferred upon the honest and industrious, and had been the daily and nightly thought of hundreds of thousands who, in the midst of infinite temptations, had never swerved from the path of rectitude and honesty, but it would be in vain for such men to present themselves to Mr. Jackson. Next day a letter appeared in *The Times* from the secretary of the City Mission, who said that in the spring a few gentlemen had collected £56 to help some men to a fresh start. Thirteen men were sent. They were selected not because they were criminals, but because although they had been such, they had seen the folly and wickedness of their course.[16]

Massachusetts had been not exactly deporting passengers, but having them sent back, since 1846. Forty-two of the passengers who came on board the ship *Maguinticock* from Liverpool were bonded, and when three of them became a charge on the State the bondsmen were called on to fulfil their obligation, and arranged instead to return the three to Liverpool. The records for 1847 and 1848 contain occasional notes about passengers landed in Boston: 'Bridget McKenna, 4 yrs, Dead.' 'Stephen Sullivan, 20 yrs, Demented.' 'Many of these persons have died in the house of industry'—this of passengers from the ship *Albatross*, Liverpool. 'Peter Malone, 26 yrs, Gone back go England.' Others were just seen off over the State line, like some of the emigrants from the ship *Washington*, from Liverpool, into Boston on December 14, 1847—'The captain has sent many to New York.'[17]

By 1855 there were formal deportations. On May 15 of that year the packet *Daniel Webster* sailed for Liverpool, taking with her Mary Williams and her infant child Bridget, whose passages were paid by the State. She went against her will, begged not to be sent, and cried. The *Boston Daily Advertiser*[18] said: 'The offence of this poor woman, for which she was thus violently and ignominiously expelled from Massachusetts, was the fact that she was born in Ireland and called a pauper. Her infant daughter, who unconsciously shares her mother's sad fate, is a native of the Commonwealth of Massachusetts; but she too partakes of that hard lot of poverty which it has been reserved for Massachusetts to make a crime, and a crime which Massachusetts punishes as no other crime is punished in America, by banishment—banishment from one's native land.' About thirty-five emigrants were sent back at the same time. The *Boston Atlas*[19] said Mary Williams had not been a pauper abroad. She came with an aunt who was still living in the State. The girl had been seduced abroad and came to America to have her baby. At the time of her confinement she was sent to the almshouse, and then before she could ask anyone for help, or get work to keep herself, she was driven out. 'And all this,' said the *Atlas*, 'cost the State of Massachusetts just $12 passage money.'

In 1855, 295 emigrants were sent back to Liverpool, and 341 to other places. The Know-Nothing governor remarked: 'Christian philanthropy should be exercised in every thing relative to their return; but they should be sent back systematically, uniformly and speedily.' He said nearly everyone shipped to Liverpool consented to go.[20]

The Know-Nothings, as a national party, had come up rapidly in 1854, but American nativism of the Samuel Morse kind had flourished for years. In 1844 the Mayor of New York had been elected on a nativist ticket. The Irish were always there to be complained of. 'They bring the grog shops like the frogs of Egypt upon us,' said the *American Protestant Magazine*. The Order of United Americans was formed, and the Order of the Star Spangled Banner, and the United Daughters of America.

In 1852, many emigrants voted Democrat to help elect Franklin Pierce to the presidency, and he appointed foreigners to diplomatic posts, and a Catholic Postmaster-General. True Americans were dismayed. Anti-Catholic orders and gangs were formed: The Order of the American Star, the Wide Awakes, the Black Snakes, the Thunderbolts, the Rip Saws, the Screw Boats, the Live Oak Club. All-American gangs fought Irish Catholic gangs in New York. Bill the Butcher, whose real name was William Poole, the man who beat John Morrissey on a dock-side brawl but was then killed by Morrissey's gang, was a prominent Know-Nothing. His last words were reported to be, 'Good-bye boys. I die a true American.' More than sixty patriotic secret societies existed in New York. Know-Nothing toothpicks were sold. The letters KN were daubed on walls. A clipper ship was named the *Know Nothing*. The *North Carolina Weekly Standard* printed a Know-Nothing menu:

Catholic broth   Jesuit soup

Roasted Catholic   Broiled priest

The Pope's Big Toe, broiled

Fried nuns, very nice and tender

(Dessert) Rich Irish Brogue   Sweet German Accent

The Know-Nothings claimed George Washington as their first member, from his supposed words at Valley Forge, 'Tonight let none but native-born Americans stand guard.' The party's name derived from its members' typical reply when asked about their aims —'I know nothing', or, 'I know nothing in our principles which is contrary to the constitution'. They had special handshakes and secret signs. One was supposed to be this: Close one eye, place the thumb and forefinger, formed into an O, over the nose.

Eye	Nose	O
I	Knows	Nothing

They called meetings by distributing heart-shaped bits of white paper, or red bits if there was danger.

Indignation against foreigners and Catholics was coming to a head at a very fortunate time for the Know-Nothings. The old party lines were broken by the passing in 1854 of the Kansas–Nebraska Act, which permitted the extension of slavery to these two new territories if their inhabitants wished it. The old Whig party, lacking in any firm policy on the issue, fell apart. Not caring either for the pro-slavery Democrats, or for the new Republicans, who vigorously opposed the extension of slavery, many voted for the Know-

Nothings who from 1854 on styled themselves the American Party. Abraham Lincoln said that the progress in degeneracy seemed to him pretty rapid. As a nation, the United States had begun by declaring that all men were created equal. This was now read to mean that all men were created equal except Negroes. When the Know-Nothings got control it would read that all men were created equal except Negroes and foreigners and Catholics. If it came to that he would prefer to emigrate to some country which made no pretence of loving liberty, Russia for instance, where despotism could be taken pure, without the base alloy of hypocrisy.

Horace Greeley—who opposed drink, slavery, the Mexican war, and female suffrage, but supported the Irish cause—derided the Know-Nothings in his *New York Tribune*. It was this paper that first used the title of Know-Nothings to describe them. In 1854 Greeley said the party would seem to be as devoid of the elements of permanence as an anti-cholera or anti-potato-rot party would be. And in the summer of 1855 the *Tribune* carried an article about the Upa tree, or Ailanthus, which stank, particularly when the temperature was 92 degrees, and befouled the air like a volcanic swamp. 'Where are the Know-Nothings?' the newspaper asked. 'Here is a legitimate field for them; let them rid us of this foreign tree, and in its place we will have one that does not stink—one of American growth.'[21]

William Chambers, writing from Scotland, derided the party too.[22] He said it had not been spoken of when he was in America early in 1854, and had sprung up in twelve months. That the United States, which had been entirely settled by foreigners of various races and religions, where every white man could trace his origin to European ancestors, and where immigrants were essential to national progress, could do anything to repel foreigners, seemed to him like national insanity. They called their lodges wigwams, held night meetings, administered illegal oaths, and resembled the dark and mysterious societies of the Middle Ages. The cry of America for the Americans was just meant to draw attention away from 'certain delicate questions—slavery, for example'. He could not really believe there was a dread of Catholicism, when in 1850 there had been 35,711 churches in the United States, only 1,112 of them Catholic. Chambers said one of the Know-Nothing demagogues called himself the Angel Gabriel, wore a long white robe, and summoned meetings by blowing a horn.

The Angel Gabriel was John S. Orr, sometimes known as Hector Orr. In May 1854 he preached around Boston and provoked riots with Irish labourers. On June 11, 1854, he addressed a crowd from the steps of the City Hall in New York, and then crossed to Brooklyn with a thousand followers and addressed a crowd of 10,000. He preached, and there were riots, at Nashua, New Hampshire, and Bath, Maine, where the Roman Catholic church was burned. He was jailed in Washington D.C., then announced that freedom was dead, and left for British Guiana, where it came out that this 200 per cent native American was a mulatto, half Scottish and half Negro.

The party was very successful in local elections. By 1855 it controlled all but one New England State, and also Maryland, Delaware, Kentucky, New Jersey, Pennsylvania, and California. After the 1854 elections in Massachusetts the governor and all the State officers were Know-Nothings, and so were all the State senators. The State House of Representatives was made up of one Whig, one Free Soiler, and 376 Know-Nothings. In his address to the members of both houses, the State governor said, 'Coming, as you do, fresh from the people, your deliberate conclusions will doubtless be a fair criterion of their wishes.' The legislators were certainly fresh. Only thirty-four had served in the assembly before, and most were mechanics, labourers, clerks, and schoolteachers. It was suggested that the text for this legislature might be Job 8:9: 'For we are but of yesterday, and know nothing.' They voted themselves extra pay, but apart from that did little except, on the last day of the session, pass two amendments to the State constitution, excluding from the franchise all naturalised citizens who had not lived twenty-one years in the country, and allowing only native-born Americans to hold office.

The Know-Nothing party ended as suddenly as it had begun. Part of its charm was secrecy, and as soon as it went into national politics, and had to hold conventions and announce policies, this secrecy vanished. In city and State elections it did brilliantly, but nationally the issue of slavery, which had indirectly helped the formation of the party, in the end destroyed it. A pro-slavery resolution put through the 1855 Know-Nothing convention by Southern delegates caused a lasting breach. In 1856 the party's presidental candidate carried only Maryland, and the new Republican party swept the Know-Nothings out of the North.

It is easy to condemn fanatical nativism. The Angel Gabriel, the riots, the mumbo-jumbo, and the other excesses of the Know-Nothings condemn themselves, and so do the bigotry and hypocrisy of Governor Gardner, who was so sure that ancient Athens, George Washington, and the Ruler of the Universe were on his side. But there were honest grievances. In 1855 more than half the inhabitants of New York City were emigrants—326,089 out of 629,810.[23] Emigrants were not on the whole the most intelligent or the most industrious or the best educated of their nationality, because the intelligent, educated, and industrious could do well enough back home. Many of the English emigrants, and nearly all the Irish, were poor. Many of the Irish were drunken, and some must have seemed dirty savages. A Yankee go-aheadism was not part of their nature. They brought disease with them, and they filled the poor-houses and prisons. In 1854 the warden of the New York city prison reported that a large number came to him in a miserable and most filthy condition, and that many might owe their lives to the benefit of a bath under the supervision of the doctor.[24] That was Yankee cleanliness. The same year, 5,228 people out of the 6,213 admitted to Bellevue Hospital were emigrants. So were 3,248 of the 3,744 patients admitted to the hospital on Blackwell's Island, and of them, a third were suffering from 'debauch and delirium tremens', and a third from syphilis.[25]

The policy of the United States government remained what it had been in 1817 when John Quincy Adams said that America invited none to come but would not keep out those who had the courage to cross the Atlantic. In the middle of the century the federal government *was* in a sense proud that America, with her free institutions, was the resort of the downtrodden and oppressed people of the world. More important, and, of course, a better reason, the United States needed population; native Americans alone could not increase fast enough to fill the continent, so there had to be emigrants. This was many years before the Statue of Liberty was erected, inviting the tired, the poor, the huddled masses, and the refuse of other countries' teeming shores, but America was open to all. The policy of the United States was well put by the Supreme Court justices in the Head Tax cases of 1849.

These were *Smith v. Turner* (Health Commissioner of the Port of New York), and *Norris v. City of Boston*.[26] By 1847, both New York and Boston were levying head taxes on each emigrant entering. At New York this was $1.50, and at Boston $2. Both had previously demanded bonds of surety that sick or aged passengers would not become a public charge, and the power to do this was not challenged. Both, indeed, continued to demand bonds for sick or aged passengers, but, apart from this, both began to demand a head tax on all healthy passengers as well. Their right to do this was challenged, and the cases came to the Supreme Court. The plaintiffs argued that the tax had the effect of regulating foreign commerce, and was a duty levied on trade, which under the constitution was a federal matter. The defendant cities replied that the head tax did nothing of the sort, and was a mere police regulation under the pauper laws of the two States.

Mr. Justice McLean, giving judgment in *Smith v. Turner*, said that to encourage foreign emigration was a cherished policy of the United States. As a branch of commerce, the transportation of passengers had always given profitable employment to American ships, and in the past few years had required an amount of tonnage nearly equal to that of imported merchandise. The tax on passengers, in the discretion of the (New York) legislature, might have been $5 or $10, or any other sum, amounting even to a prohibition of the transportation of passengers. The principle was vital to the commercial power of the Union. In the Boston case the same judge said that the plaintiff Norris had arrived at Boston with nineteen passengers, and had paid under protest the $2 demanded for each. A Massachusetts Act of 1837 gave power to demand bonds of $1,000 for each sick or infirm emigrant, and this was an exercise of an unquestioned power in the State to protect itself against foreign paupers. But as for the head tax demanded under the same Act, that was a regulation of commerce, and not within the power of the State. Both the New York and Boston head taxes were held to be void.

Mr. Justice Grier, concurring, gave his reasons at greater length. He said it had been assumed as a fact that all the foreigners who arrived at New York and Boston, and afterwards became paupers, remained in those cities and there became a public charge; and that therefore the tax was for the emigrants' own benefit, or for that of their class. But hundreds almost daily left those cities and went by rail or steamboat to the western States. And paupers, as such, were not allowed to land without a bond being given anyway. By the stringency of these bonds, the aged, the poor, and the infirm were compelled to continue their journey, or to migrate to other States. And yet, after the two States had driven off all paupers, and obtained an indemnity against loss by them if they remained, it was still complained of as a hardship that the States should not be allowed to tax those who, on examination, had been found *not* to be paupers or likely to become so. A right to tax amounted to a power to exclude, and it followed that those States in which the great ports were situated had a right to exclude, if they saw fit, all immigrants from access to the interior States, or to prescribe the conditions on which they should be allowed to proceed on their journey, whether by the payment of $2 or $200. Twelve States were without a seaport, and within and beyond those States were many millions of acres of vacant lands. It was the cherished policy of the general government to encourage and invite 'Christian foreigners of our own race'* to seek an asylum in America, and to convert those waste lands into productive farms, and thus add to the wealth, population, and power of the nation. Was it possible that the framers of the American constitution should have left it to the discretion of some two or three States to thwart the policy of the Union and dictate the terms upon which foreigners should be permitted to gain access to the other States?

Plainly it was not. And plainly the head taxes had to be held unconstitutional. The real issue, as Mr. Justice Grier made clear, was whether New York and Massachusetts should be allowed to act in their own self-interest and against the interest of other States, and against the cherished policy of the Union to encourage immigrants. But this large issue was decided on a legal nicety. For a maritime State to demand a bond was legal. For it to demand a flat tax was not. The inevitable happened. The States of New York and Massachusetts worked a dodge demanding not the payment of a tax but the execution of a bond for all passengers, but kindly permitting the amount of the bond, say several hundred dollars, to be commuted by a once-for-all payment to be made on entry. It so happened that the commutation money was the same as the old, and illegal, head tax. The result was precisely the same, the internal States suffered as before, and the system continued until 1875 when the Supreme Court held, in another case,[27] that the commutation money was unconstitutional too; but by then the U.S. government was soon to make immigration a federal matter, removing it from State jurisdiction.

The interests of the Union were as they had been defined by the judges in the head-tax cases, and the policies of the Union were generous to emigrants. Still, it was hard, particularly on Boston, that it had to receive so many diseased and impoverished emigrants. New York City was much larger and richer, and could look after itself. In 1847, for instance, the impact of emigration was much heavier, proportionately, on Boston than on New York. That year, 25,000 emigrants arrived in Boston by sea from England, Ireland, or British North America. There are no figures for the numbers who came

* This is the judge's own phrase, though why immigrants needed to be white or Christian is not apparent, and the judge did not explain.

south by land from the British provinces, walking, or by the Eastern Railroad, but it was 'a great number'. If this great number was only 5,000, which is to put it at its lowest, then 30,000 poor emigrants, many of them diseased, came to Boston which was then a city of about 120,000 people. It was a fair complaint made by the special committee of the Massachusetts Senate the following year, that emigrants were heaped upon the State all season; and it was a fair question to ask what would have happened if Massachusetts had tried to dump paupers on a European port.

Not, of course, that Boston minded all emigrants. In October 1852 a group of Swedish emigrants from Gothenburg landed in the city, and marched through the streets on the way to the railway station, past the offices of *Gleason's Pictorial*, which said: 'They are what is called Jenny Lind Swedes, being from the better class of agricultural labourers in their own country. . . . All Protestants, hale, hearty. There is room and to spare in our western country for all such emigrants as these. We grieve to see paupers, and such like, arriving from abroad; but when we behold a body of intelligent and well-found emigrants like these, arrived on our shores, we rejoice to extend to them the honest hand of welcome.' The Swedes went by the Western Railroad, via Albany and Buffalo, to the west.[28]

Most emigrants to America were not Jenny Lind Swedes. The Irish and English were not so healthy, not so used to extremes of climate, not so willing to take trains immediately to the west, not much good at pioneering. They were poor, but most of them were not in any legal sense paupers. This was passionately and convincingly argued by Gregory Dillon, president of the Irish Emigrant Society in New York and *ex officio* a member of the Commissioners of Emigration. In 1850 he was one of the three commissioners who investigated reports that doctors on Ward's Island had been improperly dissecting the bodies of patients. He said in a written opinion:[29] 'The late scandalous proceedings at Ward's Island may be traced to [a] cause, which penetrates through all our establishments, and works quietly but with baleful effect. I refer to the opinion entertained by many that emigrants are paupers and are, therefore, entitled only to pauper consideration. This is a radical error. It is a mistake of fact which leads to serious consequences, and I am sorry to say that the gentlemen associated with me on the committee are of the same opinion. They are not paupers in any just sense of the term. . . . Every emigrant that comes to our shores pays a dollar and fifty cents to this Commission. Those who have health, spread over the country, and increase our wealth and prosperity; those who are sick are relieved by the fund to which all, both well and sick, have contributed, and the fund is sufficient, and in my opinion more than sufficient under proper management. The whole class therefore, are, as it were, underwriters for each of their number, and by their own aggregate contributions alone relieve the misfortunes of one another. It is true that we, the members of this Board, render our services gratuitously; but a fund, to which no citizen of this State contributes a farthing, and which fund is found sufficient to pay upwards of $5,000 per annum to a resident physician at the quarantine, and $3,000 to a general agent and his private secretary, cannot with any propriety be called a pauper fund. . . . But so long as your general agent, physicians and other employees shall consider the emigrants to be paupers, and their fund to be a pauper fund, so long shall we fail in securing to the sick and wretched emigrants that consideration which not only humanity, but his rights, demand.'

15

Steamships and Castle Garden

By 1850 steamships were nothing new on the Atlantic. For ten years
Samuel Cunard had been carrying the American mail in steamships
subsidised by the British government, and by 1850 he had ten such
vessels. That year E. K. Collins started his line out of New York,
carrying the United States mail to Liverpool and receiving a subsidy
from Congress. His ships and Cunard's were required by the subsi-
dising governments to be fit for use as armed cruisers in time of war.
There was great rivalry between them. The Collins ships did the
westbound crossing in an average of eleven days eight hours, a day
faster than the Cunarders. The Cunarders were pretty and rakish, but
shipped water. The Collins liners were ugly, but drier.[1] When the
Washington, a new Collins steamer, made her first voyage to England
the English press was severe on her, saying she did not so much sail
as roll along. The American press retorted that she could whip any
British steamer afloat, and that there was no use arguing about it.[2]
The ships of both lines were paddle steamers. Both lines carried
mail, cabin passengers, and fine cargo. Neither wanted much to do
with the emigration business.[3]

In 1850 William Inman was twenty-five, and a partner in the
Liverpool merchant house of Richardson Bros., where he had for-
merly been a clerk. He had been managing Richardson's line of
Philadelphia sailing packets, but in the summer of 1850 he saw the
Clyde-built steamship *City of Glasgow* (1,610 tons gross), liked her,
and persuaded his partners to buy her. On December 17 she made

her first voyage for Richardson's, out of Liverpool for Philadelphia with 400 steerage passengers.[4] An American magazine, reporting her arrival, said: 'Time and space are annihilated, and one goes to sea with as much actual comfort, and surrounded with as many luxuries and elegances as . . . in the most princely mansions ashore. Ten days from land to land, across that immense watery waste, the Atlantic, what a miracle!'[5] Next year Inman bought the *City of Manchester* (2,125 tons gross; 274 feet long), and she made a profit of 40 per cent in her first year. The company called itself the Liverpool and Philadelphia Steamship Line, made regular fortnightly sailings, and by 1856 had bought three more ships. All the fleet were iron-hulled screw ships: the Cunarders were wooden paddle boats. In 1857 Inman separated from Richardson's, took the steamers with him, and renamed the line after himself. When Collins was ruined, Inman took over the United States mail contract, but his first business always was, and remained, steerage passengers. He and his wife made one voyage to see how the discomforts of an emigrant ship could be made more bearable. Talk of comfort, luxuries, and elegances was nonsense, but it was fair for Inman to say, as he did, that he carried emigrants 'in so much shorter a period and in so much better a way'.[6]

He was not the only man to see the advantages of iron screw steamers. The year Inman started, one of the partners in the Black Star Line, the biggest line of emigrant sailing packets, with twenty ships, said the screw steamer would eventually carry away the trade by cutting the passage time in half.[7] But the steamer lines were used to mail-subsidies and cabin passengers, did not see the demand for steerage passages, and conservatively preferred the known paddle-wheel to the unknown propeller. So Inman had no strong competition for several years.

His ships more than halved the passage time. The sailing packets took thirty-five days, the Inman liners only fourteen or fifteen, not so fast as Collins or Cunard but a sudden and very big improvement on the long and uncertain passages of the packets. The steamers were in every way better. In the steerage each adult had a separate berth. The women were berthed in a compartment by themselves. A doctor was carried, and, more than this, the company refused to allow sick people to board the ship. Passengers were given cooked breakfasts, dinners, and suppers. They had to bring with them a tin plate, a quart mug, a knife, fork, spoon, and bedding.[8] Inman did not provide these remarkably better conditions out of the goodness of his heart. The sailing packets he had managed had not been more humane than anybody else's, but for the steamships he wanted the better-off emigrants who could afford to pay eight guineas, more than double the sailing-ship price, for a steerage passage to Philadelphia, and £8 16s. to New York, and he had to offer something besides the shorter passage.

As for the Passenger Acts, Inman did not like them, and persistently represented to the emigration commissioners in London that he ought to be exempt. He said that speed was the essence, and he should be able to sail at the advertised time without having to wait for the emigration officer's inspection. This request was denied. He also wanted to carry more passengers than he was allowed. In a letter addressed to the commissioners' secretary, and beginning 'Esteemed Friend', he complained that the *City of Glasgow* was restricted to 645 passengers, but had room for 1,000.[9] Getting nothing out of the commissioners, he took to writing direct to the Colonial Secretary of the day, the Duke of Newcastle. He claimed the *City of Glasgow* had been delayed because an emigration officer insisted on inspecting her three times in one day, keeping 'respectable females with infants at the breast, standing on a damp quay in a north wind'. One passenger threatened to write to *The Times* about this, and Inman, who was waiting with the respectable females on the damp quay, said he wished the man would. His complaint did not stand examination: he was irritated because the officer had refused to clear the ship while only seven of her crew were on board. Inman explained that the rest would join the ship in the river, and though this was very likely the custom, the officer, after the example made of Hodder, insisted on carrying out his duty to the letter and made the steamer take on all her crew in dock.

The commissioners assured the Colonial Office that they had every confidence in the correctness and respectability with which Inman ran his vessels, but Elliot, dismissing the complaint, wrote: 'When Passengers are lying in a comfortable Dock, they fret at every delay, but after they have got to sea, and the storm rages or a fire breaks out, they would not feel obliged to the Government Officer who had

---

Opposite: Advertisement by Richardson's for their emigrant steamships, 1853. The rates of cabin passages are in large print, but from the start Richardson's were more interested in steerage passengers, whom they carried to New York for £8 16s. The ship on the poster is the *City of Manchester,* sister ship of the *City of Glasgow.*

STEAM COMMUNICATION

MONTHLY FROM

LIVERPOOL

TO

NEW YORK, BALTIMORE,

PITTSBURGH, CINCINNATI, CHARLESTON, HAVANA, &c.

BY WAY OF

PHILADELPHIA.

THE LIVERPOOL AND PHILADELPHIA STEAM SHIP COMPANY

INTEND SAILING THEIR NEW IRON SCREW STEAM SHIPS AS FOLLOW:—

CITY OF GLASGOW,	- - - - -	Captain K. MORRISON	- - - -	1610 Tons.
CITY OF MANCHESTER,	- - - -	Captain WILLIAM WYLIE	- - -	2125 ,,
CITY OF PHILADELPHIA,	(building) -	Captain ROBERT LEITCH	- - -	2189 ,,
CITY OF BALTIMORE, -	(building) -	Captain R. LEITCH	- - - - - -	2472 ,,

FROM LIVERPOOL.

CITY OF MANCHESTER	..Captain LEITCH	,,	.. 1st February, 1854.
CITY OF GLASGOW	......Captain WYLIE....	,,	.. 1st March, ,,

FROM PHILADELPHIA.

CITY OF MANCHESTER	..Captain LEITCH ....Saturday		7th January, 1854.
CITY OF GLASGOW	......Captain WYLIE....	,,	.. 4th February ,,
CITY OF MANCHESTER	..Captain LEITCH ....Thursday	..	2nd March ,,

RATES OF CABIN PASSAGE

FROM LIVERPOOL.

After Saloon State-rooms, (2 berths in each,) - -	21 Guineas each berth.	
Ditto, and Midship, (3 berths in each,) - -	17 ,,	,,
Ditto, Ditto, Forward State-rooms -	15 ,,	,,

Including Provisions and Steward's Fee,

ALL HAVING THE SAME PRIVILEGE, AND MESSING TOGETHER.

A limited number of Passengers to Philadelphia will be taken at Eight Guineas; to New York at Eight Pounds Sixteen Shillings, and supplied with Provisions of a superior quality, properly cooked, and as much as is required; and these Passengers are hereby informed, that, in order to satisfy the requirements of the Government Officers, the Date filled into their Contract Tickets will be, in every case, the date of the day preceding the fixed day of sailing, and those Passengers booked for New York, will, on their arrival in Philadelphia, be provided by the Agents of the Steamers with a Ticket entitling them to a Free Passage by Steam-boat or Railway to New York.

THESE STEAMERS CARRY PHILLIPS' PATENT FIRE ANNIHILATORS,

AN EXPERIENCED SURGEON IS ATTACHED TO EACH STEAMER.

Passengers will find PHILADELPHIA the most central Port, BEING ON THE DIRECT MAIL ROUTE from New York to the Western and Southern States.

RATES OF FREIGHT.

Freight £4 per ton, with 5 per cent. Primage, with the exception of Unmanufactured Produce, &c. which will be taken, subject to agreement, payable here or in Philadelphia, at 4 dols. 80 cents per pound sterling. Private arrangements have been made by the Agents to transport fine goods to New York, by Steam-boat (including insurance) and Canal, at four cents per foot, or about 6s 6d per ton measurement, and by steamer to Charleston eight cents, and to Norfolk and Richmond Va., at six cents per foot.

Goods intended for the interior of the United States, if consigned to the Agents at Philadelphia will be forwarded without charge for commission. Dogs at Three Pounds each.

Apply in Philadelphia, to SAMUEL SMITH, 12, Walnut-street; in Belfast, to RICHARDSON BROTHERS and CO.; in Dublin, to CORNELIUS CARLETON; in London, to EDWARDS, SANFORD and CO. for Passengers, and PICKFORD and CO. for Goods; in Paris, to FRED. REDFERN, 8, Rue de la Paix; in Havre, to W. DAVIDSON; in Manchester, to GEO. STONIER; and to

RICHARDSON BROTHERS & CO.

Liverpool, 12 Mo. 10th, 1853.　　　　　　　　　12 13, Tower-buildings, LIVERPOOL.

J. MAWDSLEY & SON, PRINTERS, LIVERPOOL.

240 Going to America

violated his duty of seeing that the ship had every requirement demanded by law.' Inman might be the only steamship owner carrying steerage passengers, he said, but other less respectable companies might come along.[10]

Another company did, and in early 1854 Inman wrote persistently to the Duke complaining about the new Canadian Navigation Company. This company was taking its steamships, the *Sarah Sands* and the *Charity*, out of dock without clearing at all, which gave it an advantage over Inman who, as he repeatedly declared, declined to break the law in this way. According to Inman, the Canadian company, which in spite of its name was sailing to Portland, Maine, and not to Canada, employed two devices to escape the emigration laws. First, it stated that all emigrants on board were cabin passengers, and cabin passengers did not come within the Acts. Inman was sure they could not all be in the cabin, and became certain when 120 steerage passengers he had no room for transferred to the Canadian company, which declared them to the customs officers as cabin. Second, and this offended Inman deeply, the competing company would sail with one bag of mail, which turned its ship into a mail steamer, which as such was exempt from the Passenger Acts. After another complaint the Colonial Office decided to prosecute the Canadian company, but then withdrew because it turned out that one bag of mail might well constitute a legal defence, and the company did have a mail contract with the Canadian government. Inman did not then have a mail contract, though he had offered to carry the mail for nothing.[11]

Newcastle tired of the correspondence, and twice told Inman to write to the commissioners and not to him, but he took no notice. This was in February, 1854. On March 1 the *City of Glasgow* sailed from Liverpool with 430 souls on board.[12] She should have berthed at Philadelphia about the middle of the month, but did not appear. On April 21, when the steamer was already hopelessly overdue, the sailing vessel *Baldaur* in mid-Atlantic (lat. 45.30, long. 32.54) sighted a large steamer two miles off with a strong list to port. She was making no smoke and no people were seen on board. The *Baldaur* steered towards her, but she vanished, and the *Baldaur* found only large quantities of biscuits and some boxes in the sea. When first seen, the steamer had a barque alongside her, but this steered away south. The reported position was 500 miles north of the Azores, and it was conjectured and hoped that a barque had rescued the passengers and taken them there.[13] But no passengers were landed in the

Azores. In May, Inman wrote to the commissioners about the 'probable loss' of the *City of Glasgow*, and sent a chart showing where floating ice had been seen in the Atlantic the previous month. The commissioners regretted that in their opinion no vessel that could be despatched to the place where the ice had been seen could any longer be any help in saving life.[14] Ice had come further south than usual that year. The American mailsteamer *Franklin*, on passage to Le Havre, reported many icebergs. The sailing packet *Yorkshire*, on a westward passage, encountered ice far south in April. In Liverpool the only hope was that if the *City of Glasgow* had found ice, she had not struck a berg but had just been frozen into an ice-floe. If this were so, she might still be safe, but she had been provisioned for only sixty days, until the end of April.[15] Inman kept her name in newspaper advertisements of forthcoming sailings until June 2, when he abandoned hope and took her out.[16]

A rumour went about that she had been seen run aground on the Massachusetts coast. This was not true. Then it was said she had foundered, but that her crew and passengers had been saved and taken to Africa. This new rumour was based on a letter supposed to have been received in Londonderry from one of the steamer's passengers. Inman said there was no truth in this.[17] A story was printed in Philadelphia and London newspapers about an Englishman who had gone ahead to Philadelphia earlier in the year and was waiting for his wife and other children to come over on the *City of Manchester*. He received a letter from his wife saying she had missed the *Manchester* but would come on the *Glasgow*, and then nothing more. After the *Glasgow* was evidently lost the man still waited for letters at the post office, and was taken off to the asylum, a raving maniac. Inman denied this, saying the man was much distressed but perfectly sane.[18] On August 18 the barque *Mary Morris* from Glasgow to New York, weather very thick, fell in with the hull of a large iron vessel, apparently Clyde-built and painted black with a red bottom, like the lost steamer, with machinery in her but all the woodwork burned out; but then lost sight of her. As Inman pointed out, this was more likely the *Shandon* of Glasgow, which burned out in August and was abandoned.[19] There was nothing conclusive. The *City of Glasgow* was never heard of again.

It was a bad time for steamships. In the autumn of the same year two others were lost. The *City of Philadelphia*, belonging to the Pennsylvania Steam Ship Company, whose ships sailed alternately with Inman's and in association with his, was wrecked off Cape Race,

Newfoundland, though all passengers and crew were saved;[20] and the Collins steamer *Arctic* foundered after a collision, and most of her passengers drowned. There was not room for all in the lifeboats; one passenger offered £30,000 if the boats would put back to save him. They did turn back, but the man sank before they reached him.[21] Two years before, the West Indies mail steamer *Amazon* (2,256 tons) burned out at sea and only one man and a woman escaped.

But in spite of these disasters the superiority of the steamship was plain, and by 1855 the last of the sailing packets were built—the *Neptune* (1,406 tons), Black Ball Line; The *Phoenix* (1,487), Red Star; *Aurora* (1,639), Blue Swallowtail; *Ellen Austin* (1,626), Dramatic; *Amazon* (1,771), Black Star.[22] All were very big, and the *Amazon* was the largest packet ever built. The packets carried emigrants for another ten years, but all the time they steadily lost to the steamers. Many of the improvements which legislation had failed to bring about were achieved all at once by the steamers. As soon as the voyage was more than cut in half, the emigrant's chance of arriving fit was more than doubled. The steamer had steam and fire to cook with, and could offer regular cooked food with no trouble. As soon as Inman refused, no doubt in his own interest, to accept sick passengers, he was imposing a medical test much stricter than the government ever had. Everyone who could afford to go by steamer did, and as the demand increased so the fares got lower. By 1856 more than 5,000 emigrants arrived at Castle Garden, New York, in steamships, and by 1865 more than three-quarters of all emigrants came by steam.[23]

Castle Garden was at the southernmost tip of Manhattan. At the same time as the steamship made the Atlantic passage tolerable for the first time, Castle Garden made the emigrants' arrival in New York less of an ordeal. It was an emigrant depot, rather like the one that had been proposed for Liverpool some years before. All emigrants had to land at the depot, which was run by the emigration commissioners. Only emigrants were allowed in, and runners were kept out. It worked, and the commissioners were very gratified, saying that the benefits were four: the depredators were limited to the emigrants' fellow passengers, and there was little chance of successful pillage by them; the public funds were relieved, because there was less distress and sickness; for the first time the emigrants could be exactly counted as they entered the depot; and there was an advantage to the community in general 'in the diminution of human suffering, in the reduction of calls on the benevolent throughout the country, and in the dispersion of a band of outlaws attracted to this port by plunder, from all parts of the world'.[24]

Castle Garden was built as a fort in 1807-9, and as Fort Clinton was one of the city's defences in the war of 1812. From 1823 on it was used as a place of entertainment, and was claimed to be the largest auditorium in the world. It was 600 feet round and its capacity was put at anything from 6,000 to 15,000. Lafayette was received there, and so was Kossuth.[25] Jenny Lind gave her first American concert there in 1850. P. T. Barnum put on the show, Genin the hatter paid $225 for a ticket, and Miss Lind gave her fee of $10,000 to charity.[26] When the commissioners proposed to take the place over, a howl went up that this was unlawful appropriation of public property for the purposes of questionable charity. Mobs gathered, and their demonstrations were garnished by public speeches and illustrated by the American flag. But these were seen to be mobs of runners, baggage-smashers, grog-shop keepers, and crooked brokers, protecting their own miserable interests, and in spite of their protests the city leased the place to the commissioners.[27]

Their emigrant depot opened on August 1, 1855, amid threats. The runners could not climb the thirteen-foot wall put up to keep them out, so they dressed in emigrants' clothes and tried to get in that way. They failed. Others earnestly pleaded to be allowed in to see fathers, brothers, or sisters, but that failed too, since the runners were too well known to be able to palm themselves off as anyone's sons or brothers. They began to hoot and throw stones, and John Kennedy, one of the commissioners' men, and known as the Mayor of Castle Garden or the Head General, drew his revolver on them.[28]

As they arrived, emigrants were brought directly from the dock into the Garden along a narrow gangway. Once again the medical inspection consisted of simply looking at them as they walked past one by one. Inside, clerks checked their baggage, asked how much money they had and where they wanted to go, showed them maps, and sold railroad and canal tickets at proper prices. Then they had to bathe. There were two wash-rooms, fifty feet by twenty, one for men and the other for women. In each room was a bath with hot water and big enough for twelve to splash about in at a time, and also a trough in which fifty could stand and scrub. They were made to use soap, and given towels. In cold weather the Garden was warmed, and in hot weather it was cooled by a running fountain throwing a high jet. Emigrants could buy bread, cheese, coffee, and milk there, and cook in the kitchens if they wanted to. Liquor was forbidden, and any found there was poured on the ground before the eyes of its owner. Each head of family had to state his means. This was done partly to sort out the destitute and partly to please the statisticians, who had always wanted to calculate an emigrant's money worth and to know how much cash was brought into the country. In 1855 emigrants brought in $86 a head, which was surprisingly high. The Irish always understated what they had for fear of being robbed and in the hope of getting off cheaper. The English invariably overstated. The Scots told the truth, and willingly pulled out their purses for inspection. There were no beds at Castle Garden, and emigrants were encouraged to go on their way to the interior the same day, and not to go into the city at all. But if they liked they could sleep in the galleries, and 3,000 a night sometimes did.[29] Others could not resist seeing the city, and strolled out and up Broadway, where they were naturally robbed, but they had not nearly so much to lose as before. Their luggage was safe and could not be stolen or carted off to a dismal boarding house, with $5 or $10 charged for the porterage. The runners now had no market for fraudulent tickets, when good ones could be bought cheaper at Castle Garden. The preference of the commissioners was to take the emigrant in, see him fed and bathed, and then get him on the first train or river boat out of the city. But many emigrants had no plans to go further. Some had not even thought of it.

The *New York Times* thought highly of Castle Garden. 'Honoured is that house which for generation after generation has served as an ornament, and in old age commences a new career of practical usefulness. And our venerable Castle Garden is very highly honoured that, after half a century of service as a military rallying place and a fashionable resort for the seekers of amusement, now when its walls are cracked and crumbling and all its early glory departed, it is vouchsafed the privilege of granting a boon to humanity, as well as to the City, of which it is the gateway.' The *Times* went on, in the kind of prose it reserved for edifying occasions, to remark that Castle Garden had received Lafayette and other great men: 'So, after all, the change is not so very great. Instead of one ovation a year to some distinguished foreigner, henceforth there will be a perpetual ovation to thousands of sovereigns. . . . The large hall of the Garden is a capital place for Young Europe to enjoy itself in, during the brief hours of his tarry in our City, in his route westward. A tall fountain feeds a noble basin of water near the spot where the stage was, and cools the air even at the noon of the heated term.' Children sailed paper boats in the basin. The whole of the castle was theirs. The best seats, which at Jenny Lind's concerts sold at great prices, were free and open to the poorest.[30]

There again is this hopeful insistence that Castle Garden was a place to stay briefly on the way west. But the figures collected there showed what must have been a matter of common observation before, that few emigrants were pioneers. Two out of five stated their final destination as New York. Most of those not wanting to stay in the city intended to go only as far as the States of the eastern seaboard. About a fifth were on their way to Illinois, Wisconsin, or Ohio, but very few indeed were going much farther west than that. In the last five months of 1855 only 800 or so were going to Minnesota, Utah, and California put together, and only five to Texas and one to Kansas.[31]

The usual charges were made that the commissioners were fraudulent, and as usual the complainants were runners and brokers. A grand jury found that the runners had become a noisy and utterly lawless crowd round the thirteen-foot fence, continually insulting the commissioners, who had to carry loaded firearms in self-defence. If the police did their job this crowd could be broken up entirely, but the grand jury regretted that this obvious duty of the police was entirely neglected.[32]

The runners did not give up quickly. While so many emigrants stayed in the city there was still a profit to be made from them. But the profits were less than they had been, and one day several hundred runners sailed for California, where many of them fell into the hands of the Vigilantes in San Francisco. Others carried on their old business of defrauding and swindling, only now they sold tickets to California to would-be gold miners. Others died in expeditions to Mexico and central America.[33]

By the time Castle Garden was opened, emigration was already falling off. In London the Colonial Secretary, when he was sent the emigration figures for 1853, said it was now quite unnecessary to lay them before the Cabinet, as had been done since 1847, and the practice had better be given up.[34] In Liverpool only two brokers were prosecuted in the whole of 1854.[35] At the busiest of times the officers had not been diligent in their prosecuting, but this was a new inactivity. The number of emigrants leaving Liverpool and entering at New York in 1855 was much less than half the average of the previous five years. There was work in Ireland, and no longer starvation. In England wages had risen. Those who could find nothing better joined the British Army and went to the Crimean War. In America, particularly in the emigrant ports of New York, Boston, and New Orleans, the Know-Nothings suddenly came to power and commenced their persecutions. The transatlantic fare increased because many British ships left the emigrant trade and went off as transports to the Crimea, and many emigrants could not find the fare to come. In the American west there was drought, and the crops were bad. Railway building stopped. Manufactures slumped. A quarter of the population of New York City was said to be out of work: an independent report to the Colonial Office agreed, putting the number of unemployed there as high as 150,000, and saying the distress in many American cities was so severe that emigrants who had the fare were going back home.[36]

There always had been some emigrants who returned. Some went back prosperous, like the boy from Plymouth workhouse who did well in America, returned to England in 1851 to see the Great Exhibition, and, having by then an income for life, went back to visit the workhouse, told them who he was and what he had been, distributed £5 in silver, and impressed on the inmates the value of honesty, gratitude, and obedience.[37]

Others returned because they could not stand America. One man published a poem about his American anguish:[38]

> Wand'rer! that one am I—and since the time
> That I first 'gan in quest of wealth to roam,
> I have not ceased to hate the fatal clime
> Which tempted me to quit my native home.

One English yeoman, a strong man, went out in the steerage to New York with his wife, eight children, and a large quantity of boxes and packages. He looked at farms within fifty miles of the city, but did not like the farming, the land, the people, the weather, the food, the drink, or anything he saw, felt, or heard. Ten days later he took the first packet back, with his wife, children, and their luggage which had not even been unpacked.[39] One Lancashire man who went out found that he would have to work hard to get on, that his accent was considered half-gibberish, and that he was homesick as well; so he worked his passage back on the same packet that had brought him.[40]

By the mid-1850s men were returning not out of dislike but because they could not get enough work to live. In 1854 more than 12,000 came back to Liverpool from the United States, and in 1855 more than 18,000.[41]

Some, like the Lancashire man, worked their passage home. If they were not seamen, and most were not, that was a foolish thing to do. Edward Moore, a labourer, had emigrated from Ireland because there was a warrant out for him for voting twice in the last election. In America he went to Pittsburgh, and then to New Orleans, where he signed articles to go on board the *Wandering Jew*, for Liverpool. He was drunk at the time. He was told he would only have to coil rope on deck, but when they got to sea he was made to go aloft. He had never been to sea before except for the steerage passage from Ireland. The mate kicked and beat him and fractured his nose. William Harrison, another emigrant, also shipped on board the same vessel; he had been in New Orleans twelve months, was in bad health, and wanted to come home. He was beaten, then fell from the main-top yard, and was insensible for a week. A third man working his passage, whose name no one was sure of, was beaten, kicked, dumped in a barrel of water, left there for half an hour, and then put in the forecastle with his wet clothes still on. He died two days after sailing. He rose from his bunk, got as far as the door of the fore-castle, said, 'I am going to heaven. There was a man came for me last night,' fell down, and never spoke again. An emigrant returning on another ship, a grocer, died of injuries in hospital at Liverpool. Hawthorne, who took statements in Liverpool about all these men, said almost every ship from New York was bringing in former emigrants, incapable as seamen, but working their passage back.[42]

Others would have liked to return, but could not even do that. John Williams, twenty-six years old, arrived in the United States on November 6, 1851, on board the packet *Enterprise*, Black Star Line, Captain Funk. By January 13 he was destitute and told this story. He had served his time as a draper at Wrexham, North Wales. Since he arrived in America he had had nothing to do. He brought with him £6 and a silver watch, patent lever, which cost seven guineas, and a gold chain which cost three guineas in the old country, and his clothes. He had no friends in America. He tried his best to get work, called in tailors' shops and answered advertisements, but found that in some places they objected to an Englishman. He pawned the watch and chain for $12, and then had to sell the pawn ticket for $7. The last thing he earned was 25 cents for carrying a bag for a lady, and that was all the work he had found since he arrived. Two weeks before, his landlord turned him out. He did not know where to go and did not like to beg. He wandered round the streets by day, and at night was hungry and stood in Water Street crying. A policeman in the first district spoke to him and asked him what he was doing there. Williams said 'Nothing', and the policeman asked him what he was crying for. He replied that he wanted something to eat and did not know where to go or what to do. The policeman took him to the station house, where the captain said he would do all he could, but that the only thing was for Williams to go to the Commissioners of Emigration in Canal Street, and took him part of the way to show him. There the clerk said he could do nothing. Williams said, 'What am I to do? I suppose I must starve.' The clerk said they had so many now they could do nothing. 'Well then,' said Williams, 'I must go away?' The clerk said yes. That was Sunday. Next day he went back to the police captain, who said he was sorry. He was turned out of a bar where he went not to drink but to sleep. For five days he walked about, thinking of returning to England. He went back to the police captain again, who gave him a ticket to a city alderman, who sent him back to the commissioners, where the clerk said that if he was young like Williams and could get nothing to do he would commit suicide. Williams tried two other places, was given another 25 cents, but spent that. He had written to his parents in Wales, but they had not replied. He would be willing to go back if he could get back. Before he came over he was getting his board and £40 a year at Gamble, Mamby, and Scragg, drapers, of Liverpool and Birkenhead. Since he arrived in America he had not spent $3 altogether for drink; he had not been in the habit of drinking; he had not gambled a cent; he had lent some money but the people went away; he had not spent any money on lewd women.[43]

Williams does not sound heroic. Most emigrants were neither heroic nor fortunate. They were uprooted and in a foreign country, and only the strong did well. There were few Andrew Carnegies, and many did much worse than Williams, who just wanted to be back with Gamble, Mamby, and Scragg, drapers. The emigration movement, as a movement, is heroic to look back on, and without it America would now be different, but for the individual emigrant it was often a personal tragedy. A man had to survive a lot even to get to America, and then had to start again, mostly from nothing. Many emigrants did not prosper. Their children stood a much better chance than themselves.

Today in Liverpool most of Waterloo Road is still standing, and the same buildings which were once spirit vaults, lodging houses and the offices of M. Dalton (provision dealer) and Harnden & Co. (American packet brokers) are occupied by Eric's café and betting shops, or used as warehouses, or boarded-up and empty. On Grosse Isle the fever sheds still stand; a row of white wooden crosses marks the graves of 5,424 emigrants, and you have to walk carefully through the long grass in the valley because the ground is uneven where the grave trenches have sunk. The monument at Montreal, which was once on the site of the fever sheds there, is now next to the site of Expo 67 and in the centre reservation of a motorway. South Street in New York City, where the emigrant packets docked, is now tatty, half-derelict, and overshadowed by the East Side Express Highway which runs overhead; where the Black Star Line of Liverpool packets came in, at the old pier 19, Louie's Grill offers Hero Sandwiches as a house speciality. On the Battery the shell of Castle Garden still stands, and from it there is a good view of the Statue of Liberty.

More than 2,300,000 people came through these places in ten years in the middle of the last century. Among them were John Ryan, labourer, who crossed the Irish Sea at night on the steamer in a storm, having no shelter 'except as a man can shelter himself'. There was Ellen Keane, aged four years and three months, of the barque *Syria*, who was the first to die of fever at Grosse Isle in 1847; and T. Hibbert Ware, barrister of the Middle Temple, who found female domestics hard to keep in Canada, and went home. There was the Ragged School boy who wrote to his schoolmaster in London saying he would tell them something about New York, how guns and pistols were very cheap; and the emigrant from Bristol, very cheerful, who exclaimed as he sailed into New York bay, 'Glorious morning! . . . What a fine country! Here at last is America.' And Thomas Garry, in Sligo a beggar by profession, but in the United States working to bring his family over and writing home to his wife saying he loved her and the children as his life, and if God spared them they would shortly be together in the lands of promise.

Sources and Bibliography

All sources are listed, chapter by chapter, in the notes which follow. All manuscripts, State papers, documents, newspapers, magazines, guides, and books are fully named and described the first time in each chapter that they appear. The whereabouts of manuscripts and unpublished documents is always stated, and so is that of newspapers and books which I had trouble in finding, or found in unexpected places. The page numbers of printed British Parliamentary Papers are those of the copies in the British Museum State Paper Room. The pagination is sometimes different in other copies.

Notes for Chapter 1: The Lands of Promise

1. *Sidney's Emigrant's Journal*, December 1849. Published monthly in London by Samuel Sidney.
2. Advertisement in *Gore's Directory* of Liverpool for 1847.
3. *The Emigrant Churchman* by a Pioneer of the Wilderness (perhaps the Rev. A. W. H. Rose), edited by the Rev. Henry Christmas, London, Richard Bentley, 1849.
4. *The Settler's New Home* by Sidney Smith, London, John Kendrick, 1850.
5. *Chambers's Edinburgh Journal*, February 11, 1854.
6. *Emigrant Tracts*, 1850–2, Society for Promoting Christian Knowledge, London. Tract IX.
7. Cartwright's evidence is in the *Report of the Select Committee of the Senate of the United States on the Sickness and Mortality on Board Emigrant Ships*. Washington, 1854, 33rd Congress, 1st Session. Senate. Rep. Com. No. 386.

8. *Redburn: His First Voyage* by Herman Melville, London, Richard Bentley, 1849. (This is a novel, and the remarks are those of its hero Wellingborough Redburn, but Melville had crossed the Atlantic as a seaman and was drawing on his own experience.)

9. *Letters on Irish Emigration* by Edward Everett Hale, Boston, 1852.

10. Evidence of Captain Schomberg, emigration officer at Liverpool, in the *First Report of the Select Committee on Emigrant Ships*, H.C., 1854, Vol. 13.

11. *Thirty-third General Report of the Colonial Land and Emigration Commissioners*, Appendix No. 1, H.C., 1873. Vol. 18.

12. *Immigration into the United States* by Jesse Chickering, Boston, Little, Brown, 1848. *History of Immigration into the United States . . . from September 30, 1819 to December 31, 1855; compiled entirely from official data . . .* by William J. Bromwell of the Department of State, New York, Redfield, 1856. *Special Report on Immigration* by Edward Young, Chief of Bureau of Statistics, U.S.A. Washington, 1871. (Bromwell's and Young's figures are identical, and often differ from Chickering's.)

13. *Fourteenth Annual Report of the Colonial Land and Emigration Commissioners*, H.C., 1854, Vol. 28. In 1853, 31,459 foreigners sailed from England to America.

14. Evidence of R. B. Minturn in H.C., 1847–8, Vol. 17.

15. Bromwell (see note 12 above), pp. 132, 156 and 172.

16. Quoted in *Hints to Emigrants, Addressed chiefly to Persons Contemplating an Emigration to the United States of America, with copious extracts from the iournal of Thomas Hulme, Esq.*, Liverpool, E. Rushton, 1817.

17. In a letter to Baron von Fürtenwarther, *Niles Weekly Register*, XVIII (1820), pp. 157–8, quoted in *The Atlantic Migration, 1607–1860* by Marcus Lee Hansen, Harvard, 1940.

18. *Thirty-third General Report of the Emigration Commissioners*; Appendix No. I, H.C., 1873, Vol. 18.

19. Chickering (see note 12 above).

20. The letters of Henry Johnson and his wife Jane are from the Letters of the McConnell family in the manuscripts department of Toronto Public Library (Jane Johnson's maiden name was McConnell). The letters are typewritten and endorsed, 'Copied from the original by Edwin Seaborn, M.D., F.A.C.S., LL.D.'

21. *Autobiography of Andrew Carnegie*, Garden City, New York, Doubleday, Doran, 1933. Also *Dictionary of American Biography*.

22. *Illustrated News*, New York, November 5, 1853, p. 261.

23. Despatch from the Governor General the Earl of Elgin to Earl Grey, Colonial Secretary, from Montreal, May 28, 1847, in *Papers Relative to Emigration*, H.C., 1848, Vol. 47.

24. Both Waters and Campbell from the *Report of the select committee to examine into the condition, business accounts, and management of the trusts under the charge of the commissioners of Emigration*, etc., State of New York, Assembly Document, 34, 1852.

25. *New York Tribune*, April 17, 1847.

26. Garry from evidence of Sir Robert Gore Booth, Bart, in the *First Report of the Select Committee of the House of Lords on Colonization from Ireland*, H.C., 1848, Vol. 17. Garry's letter is printed in Appendix X to minutes of evidence before the *Select Committee on Colonization from Ireland*, H.C., 1849, Vol. 11.

Notes for Chapter 2: Who Should Go, and Why

1. *Cobbett's Weekly Political Register*, New York, May 8, 1817.

2. *Sidney's Emigrant's Journal*, London, March 2, 1849.

3. The same. January 25, 1849.

4. The same. November 23, 1848.

5. The same. November 2, 1848.

6. The same. Discontented dispositions, wits, and drunkenness, November 2, 1848; governesses, August 1849; draper's assistant, and two youths, October 1849; Tennessee sheepdogs, July 1849; sadler, November 1849; town wives, October 1849.

7. *Chambers's Edinburgh Journal*, Edinburgh, price 1½d., began on February 11, 1854, to run a series of articles by William Chambers (1800–1883), who with his brother, Robert Chambers the elder, had founded the magazine and the publishing house of W. & R. Chambers. The reference to the aristocracy is from the last article of the series on October 14, 1854.

8. *Punch*, London. Dukes, 1846, Vol. I, p. 62. Peers advised to buy spades and emigrate, 1848, Vol. 15, p. 73.

9. *Chambers's*, 'A Word to Genteel Emigrants', February 28, 1852.

10. *Sidney's Emigrant's Journal*, London, November 2, 1848.

11. Evidence of Captain Charles Patey, R.N., to *Select Committee inquiring into the operation of the Passenger Acts*, H.C., 1851, Vol. 19.

12. *Illustrated London News*, December 22, 1849.

13. *Niles Weekly Register*, Baltimore, 1816, p. 419, quoted in appendix to Chickering. See note 12 for Chapter 1.

14. *Chambers's*, August 26, 1848.

15. *Punch*, London, 1850, Vol. 18, p. 15.

16. *Emigration; its advantages to Great Britain and her Colonies* . . . by P. L. Macdougall; London, T. & W. Boone, 1848. Toronto Public Library.

17. *Work and Wages; or, the Penny Emigrant's Guide to the United States and Canada, for Female Servants, Laborers, Mechanics, Farmers etc* . . . by Vere Foster, London, W. & F. G. Cash, 1855.

18. One of a collection of original and proof broadsheets, this one undated but from references in broadsheets in the same collection likely to be *c.* 1854: *Poetical Broadsides* etc., British Museum catalogue number 11621 k 4 (Vol. I). 'Sons of John Bull' bears the imprint 'E. Hodge's (from Pitt's) Printer, wholesale Tay and Marble warehouse, I, Dudley-street, 7 Dials'.

19. Evidence of Hon. Dudley Mann, who wrote from Bremen to the *Select Committee of the Senate of the United States on the Sickness and Mortality on Board Emigrant Ships*, 1854, 33rd Congress, 1st Session, Senate. Rep. Com. No. 286.

20. *The Emigrant's Manual*, Edinburgh, William and Robert Chambers, 1851. In Chambers's Instructive and Entertaining Library, Series of Books for the People. 1s.

21. *The British Colonies Described, with advice to those who cannot obtain employment at home* by William H. G. Kingston, London, S.P.C.K., 1851. This was the fifteenth of eighteen emigrant tracts published by the Society for Promoting Christian Knowledge in 1850–2.

22. *Emigration: an address to the clergy of England, Ireland, Scotland and Wales, on the condition of the working classes, with a few suggestions as to their future welfare* by Thomas Rawlings, New York, George Trehern, 1845.

23. *The Emigrant's Reverie and Dream. England and America* [Anon.], London, Saunders and Otley, 1856.

24. *Emigration and Superabundant Population Considered, in a Letter to Lord Ashley* by Amicus Populi, London, Pelham Richardson, 1848. 6d.

25. *The Emigrants' Penny Magazine*, Plymouth, J. B. Rowe; London, T. Saunders, 1850–1.

26. Young. See note 12 for Chapter 1.

27. Evidence of Thomas Frederick Elliot to 1848 Committee. See note 26 for Chapter 1.

28. *Emigration and Colonization* . . . *including a correspondence with many distinguished noblemen and gentlemen, several of the governors of Canada, etc.*, by Thomas Rolph, London 1844, Toronto Public Library.

29. Minturn's evidence to the 1848 Committee. See note 26 for Chapter 1.

30. Address of the Irish Emigrant Society of New York to the People of Ireland, quoted in *Sidney's Emigrant's Journal*, London, July 5, 1849. British Museum.

Notes for Chapter 3: America in the Mind of the Time

1. *Illustrated London News*, January 20, 1849.
2. Information about Tupper from biographical sketch to the fiftieth edition of *Proverbial Philosophy* by Martin F. Tupper, London, Moxon, Son, and Co., about 1880.
3. *On the Penitentiary System in the United States, and its Application in France*, Philadelphia, Carey, Lea and Blanchard, 1833.
4. *American Notes*, London, Chapman and Hall, 1842, and many later editions. Also *Martin Chuzzlewit*, first published 1844 and countless subsequent editions.
5. *Society in America*, 1837, and *Retrospect of Western Travel*, 1838.
6. *Domestic Manners of the Americans*, London, Whittaker, Treacher and Co., Ltd., 1832, and many later editions.
7. *North America*, London, Chapman and Hall, 1862.
8. *The Emigrant* by Sir Francis B[ond] Head, Bart., New York, Harper, 1847.
9. *Illustrated London News*, December 22, 1849.
10. *Harper's New Monthly Magazine*, Vol. 2 (December 1850 to May 1851), p. 47.
11. The same. Vol. 4 (December 1851 to May 1852), p. 616.
12. *Redburn: His First Voyage* by Herman Melville, London, Richard Bentley, 1849.
13. 'Records of an Irish-American Organisation kept before 1864', in the Daley Papers, New York Public Library Manuscript Room.
14. Letter of Harvey to Monteagle, dated May 31, 1847, Monteagle Papers, MS 13400, National Library of Ireland. (Most of this group of papers consists of letters from emigrants to Australia, but there are a few to do with American emigration.)
15. *Work and Wages; or, the Penny Emigrant's Guide to the United States and Canada, for Female Servants, Laborers, Mechanics, Farmers, etc . . .* by Vere Foster, London, W. & F. G. Cash, 1855.
16. *Chambers's Edinburgh Journal*, last article in series of articles 'Things as They are in America', October 14, 1854.
17. *America as I Found It* by Mary Lundie, London, Nisbet, 1852.

18. *The British Colonies Described, with advice to those who cannot obtain employment at home* by William H. G. Kingston, 1851. This was tract 15 of a series of eighteen published in 1850–2 by the Society for Promoting Christian Knowledge, London.

19. *Sidney's Emigrant Journal*, London, October 1848.

20. *The Emigrant's Guide; or a Picture of America: exhibiting a view of the United States, divested of democratic colouring . . . also a Sketch of the British Provinces; delineating their native beauties and superior attractions* by an Old Scene Painter, London, W. Simpkin and R. Marshall, 1816.

21. *The Backwoods of Canada: being letters from the wife of an emigrant officer*, London, Charles Knight, 1846. [By Catherine Parr Strickland, afterwards Traill.]

22. *Shamrock*, New York, July 6, 1811, quoted in *The Atlantic Migration, 1607–1860* by Marcus Lee Hansen, New York, Harper and Row, 1961.

23. *Sidney's Emigrant's Journal*, London, November 2, 1848.

24. *Chambers's Edinburgh Journal*, October 3, 1846, British Museum.

25. The same. June 10, 1854.

26. *Punch*, London, 1847, Vol. 2, p. 154 for the rotten eggs, and *Punch*, 1851, Vol. 20, p. 246, for the American treasures.

27. *Chambers's Edinburgh Journal*, June 10, 1854.

28. *The Emigrant Churchman* by a Pioneer of the Wilderness, edited by the Rev. Henry Christmas, London, Richard Bentley, 1849.

29. *The Emigrant and Other Poems* by Alexander M'Lachlan, Toronto, Rollo and Adam, 1861. Montreal City Library.

30. *The Emigrant's Reverie and Dream: England and America* [Anon.], London, Saunders and Otley, 1856.

31. Diary and Drawings of T. Hibbert Ware, in the manuscript room of the Toronto Public Library.

32. *The Canadian Emigrant Housekeeper's Guide* by Mrs. C. P. Traill, Toronto, 1862, 'Published by authority', Montreal City Library.

33. *The English Notebooks* by Nathaniel Hawthorne. Based upon the original manuscripts at the Pierpoint Morgan Library and edited by Randall Stewart, New York, Modern Language Society of America, London, Oxford University Press, 1941. Entries for August 20, 1853, and August 17, 1855.

34. *Frank Leslie's Illustrated Newspaper*, September 20, 1856. The book was *Perversion; or, The Causes and Consequences of Infidelity* by W. J. Conybeare, London, Smith, Elder, 1856.

35. *The Emigrant Ship and Other Poems* by James Lister Smith, London, Hope and Co., 1851.

36. The broadsides quoted here are originals, sometimes uncorrected proofs, pasted into volume I of *Poetical Broadsides*, etc., in the British Museum, catalogue number 11621 k4. Many are undated, but from internal evidence seem to be *c.*1854.

Notes for Chapter 4: Leaving Home

1. *Illustrated London News*, December 21, 1844.
2. *The Emigrant's Manual*, Edinburgh, William and Robert Chambers, 1851.
3. *Gleanings in the West of Ireland* by the Hon. and Rev. S. Godolphin Osborne, London, T. and W. Boone, 1850.
4. *Ireland in 1862* by the Rev. Father Adolphe Perraud, Dublin, James Duffy, 1863. Translated from *Etudes sur L'Irlande Contemporaine*, Paris, C. Douniol, 1862. Father Perraud, in his quotation from Corinthians, gives the Latin of the Vulgate. I have given the English of the Authorised Version, though, of course, the English form of words would not have been familiar either to Father Perraud or to Irish emigrants.
5. Cobden in a speech at Drury Lane Theatre, London, on March 30, 1843, quoted from Perraud (see note 4), p. 240.
6. John Duross, in *First Report of the Select Committee on Emigrant Ships*, H.C., 1854, Vol. 13.
7. John Besnard, from the same report.
8. Sylvester Redmond, from the same report.
9. This is the steamer company's estimate.
10. William Watson, from the 1854 report (see note 6 above).
11. Recommendations from the *Select Committee on the Passengers' Act*, H.C., 1851, Vol. 19.
12. Manuscript letter of H. Montamis of Quebec, 1852, but not otherwise dated, 'To the agricultural office'. In Record Group 17 III.I. Immigration 1842–55. Canadian National Library and Archives, Ottawa.
13. Frederick Sabel, in report of *Select Committee on the Passengers' Act*, 1851. H.C., 1851, Vol. 19.
14. *Morning Chronicle*, London, July 22, 1850. Article on 'Labour and the Poor: Departure of Emigrant Vessels—The Stow-aways—The Roll-Call. Letter X.'
15. *Tenth Annual Report, Addressed to the Committee of the Liverpool Domestic Mission by their Minister to the Poor*, March 1847. Liverpool Record Office.

16. *Liverpool Mercury* and Supplement, March 5, 1847.

17. *Realities of Irish Life* by W. Steuart Trench, London, Longmans, Green, 1868.

18. Mrs. Caroline Chisholm in *First Report from the Select Committee on Emigrant Ships*, B.P.P., 1854, Vol. 13.

19. *Pauper Immigration*, Commonwealth of Massachusetts, House No. 255, April 24, 1855.

20. *Alien Passengers and Paupers*, Commonwealth of Massachusetts, Senate No. 46, February 1848.

21. *Immigration and the Commissioners of Emigration of the State of New York* by Friedrich Kapp, one of the Commissioners, New York, the National Press, 1870.

22. Samuel Sidney in *First Report from the Select Committee on Emigrant Ships*, B.P.P., 1854, Vol. 13.

23. *The Emigrants' Penny Magazine*, Plymouth; and London, T. Saunders; May 1850.

24 *The Canadian Emigrant Housekeeper's Guide* by Mrs. C. P. Traill, Toronto, 1862. Montreal City Library.

25. Advertisements in *The Emigrant's Manual*, Edinburgh, William and Robert Chambers, 1851.

26. *Chambers's Edinburgh Journal*, March 3, 1855. 'American Jottings, Emigrant Trappers.'

27. Frederick Sabel in report of the *Select Committee on the Passengers' Act*, 1851, B.P.P., 1852, Vol. 18.

Notes for Chapter 5: Liverpool and the Last of England

1. *Gore's Liverpool Directory*, 1855. From the 1851 census.

2. *Encyclopaedia Britannica*, eleventh edition.

3. *Encyclopaedia Britannica*, eleventh edition. Also *Liverpool* by Quentin Hughes. City Buildings Series, London, Studio Vista, 1969.

4. *Gleason's Pictorial*, Boston, June 17, 1854.

5. All the references to Melville are from *Redburn: His First Voyage* by Herman Melville, London, Richard Bentley, 1849. *Redburn* is a novel, but Melville had worked as a sailor in the Liverpool trade, and his hero Redburn often reflects Melville's own views.

6. *History of the Commerce and Town of Liverpool*, etc., by Thomas Baines, London, Longman, Brown, Green, and Longman, 1852. Liverpool Record Office.

7. *Gore's Directory of Liverpool and its Environs*, Liverpool, J. Mawdsley, 1847. Liverpool Record Office.

8. The same.

9. *Life of Nathaniel Hawthorne* by Moncure D. Conway, London, Walter Scott, undated but *c.* 1880.

10. *The English Notebooks* by Nathaniel Hawthorne, ed. Randall Stewart, New York, Modern Language Society of America; London, Oxford University Press, 1941.

11. *Redburn*, see note 5 above.

12. *M'Corquodale's Annual Liverpool Directory*, Liverpool 1848. Liverpool Record Office.

13. Evidence of Samuel Sidney in *First Report from the Select Committee on Emigrant Ships*, H.C., 1854, Vol. 13.

14. Evidence of John Duross, constable at Cork, from the same report.

15. Lieutenant Thomas Eyre Hodder to *Select Committee on the Passengers' Act*, H.C., 1851, Vol. 19.

16. William Tapscott, to 1851 Committee, above.

17. *Gore's Liverpool Street Directory*, 1855. Also other directories named in notes 7 and 12 above.

18. James T. Tapscott in *Communication from special committee on Quarantine laws at New York*, State of New York, No. 60. In Assembly, January 22, 1846. Also Tapscott in *Report of Select Committee into . . . Commissioners of Emigration*, State of New York, Assembly document 34, 1852.

19. Letter to *New York Sun* of February 3, 1846, put in evidence to 1852 New York State committee, cited in note 18 above.

20. Letter in evidence to same committee.

21. Anne Doyle, in evidence to same committee.

22. *M'Corquodale's Annual Liverpool Directory*, 1848, see note 12.

23. Colonial Office papers, C.O. 384/79, item 306. Public Record Office, London.

24. Letter of Harnden's in C.O. 384/79, September 25, 1847.

25. Letter of Hodder's, C.O. 384/79, September 25, 1847.

26. *Pauper Immigration*, Commonwealth of Massachusetts, House No. 255, April 24, 1855.

27. George Saul to 1851 Select Committee cited in note 15.

28. *Redburn*, see note 5.

29. William Fitzhugh to 1851 Select Committee, see note 15.

30. Sir George Stephen, to same committee.

31. Lieutenant Thomas Prior to 1851 Committee.

32. Sylvester Redmond to 1854 Committee. See note 13.

33. *Morning Chronicle*, London, July 15, 1850.

34. Lieutenant Prior to 1851 Committee. See note 15, above.

35. T. W. C. Murdoch to 1851 Committee. See note 15.

36. Maurice Dalton to 1851 Committee.

37. Liverpool directories of 1848 and 1855, as in notes 12 and 17, above.

38. John Bramley-Moore to 1851 Committee.

39. Lieutenant Prior to 1851 Committee.

40. The Rev. John Welsh, in *The Port and Docks of Birkenhead. Minutes of Evidence and Proceedings on the Birkenhead and Liverpool Docks Bills in Sessions of 1844 to 1852* [of House of Commons] by Thomas Webster; London, J. Newman, 1873. Liverpool Record Office.

41. Frederick Sabel to 1851 Committee.

42. *Gore's Liverpool Directory*, 1851 and 1853. Liverpool Record Office.

43. The clergyman was perhaps named by Sabel in his evidence, but the printed report leaves the name blank.

44. Lieutenant Hodder to 1851 Committee.

45. Frederick Marshall to 1851 Committee.

46. *Morning Chronicle*, London, July 8, 1850.

47. The same.

48. Sir George Stephen to 1851 Committee.

49. *Morning Chronicle*, London, July 15, 1850.

50. Letter from 'Doctor' in *New York Times*, October 15, 1851.

51. Sabel to 1851 Committee.

52. William Fitzhugh to 1851 Committee.

53. Letter from Vere Foster in *Correspondence on the Treatment of the Passengers on Board the Emigrant Ship 'Washington'*, H.C., 1851, Vol. 40, p. 434.

54. *Fourteenth Annual Report of the Colonial Land and Emigration Commissioners*, H.C., 1854, Vol. 28.

55. Lieutenant Lean, to 1851 Committee.

56. Lieutenant Hodder, to 1851 Committee.

57. John Lancaster, M.D., to 1851 Committee. The three doctors are named in List of Emigration Officers and Medical Officers at Liverpool in H.C., 1854, Vol. 46.

58. Vere Foster, see note 53 above.

59. *Chambers's Edinburgh Journal*, February 11, 1854. The passenger was William Chambers himself.

60. Melville, *Redburn*. See note 5 above.

61. Sylvester Redmond to 1854 Committee. See note 13.

62. *Ballou's Pictorial*, Boston, Vol. 8. January–June 1855, p. 152.

63. *Morning Chronicle*, London, July 22, 1850.

64. The next paragraph is based on an account in the *Illustrated London News*, July 6, 1850, in an article entitled 'The Tide of Emigration'.
65. Lieutenant Hodder to 1851 Committee. See note 15, above.
66. *Illustrated London News*, as in note 64.
67. *Illustrated London News*, December 21, 1850.
68. *Realities of Irish Life* by W. Steuart Trench, London, Longmans, Green, 1868.
69. *Morning Chronicle*, London, July 22, 1850.

Notes for Chapter 6: Hard-driven Ships and Brutal Crews

1. Lieutenant Hutchinson, R.N., harbour and pilot master at Kingstown, in First Report from the *Select Committee on Emigrant Ships*, H.C., 1854, Vol. 13.
2. *Lloyd's Register of British and Foreign Shipping*, London, 1851.
3. *The Emigrant's Manual* [anon.], William and Robert Chambers, Edinburgh, 1851.
4. Article 'Things Talked of in London', in *Chambers's Edinburgh Journal*, February 26, 1853.
5. Sylvester Redmond, journalist, from First Report from the *Select Committee on Emigrant Ships*, H.C., 1854, Vol. 13.
6. *Liverpool Mercury*, July 30, 1847.
7. *Liverpool Mercury*, May 21, 1847.
8. *Liverpool Mail*, May 24, 1851.
9. *Liverpool Chronicle*, September 20, 1851.
10. *The English Notebooks* by Nathaniel Hawthorne, ed. Randall Stewart. Published in New York by the Modern Language Association of America, 1941. Entry for November 22, 1855.
11. *Chambers's Edinburgh Journal*, June 7, 1851.
12. Robert Bunch, British vice-consul in New York, from *Select Committee on the Passengers' Act*, H.C., 1851, Vol 19.
13. Evidence of John Bramley Moore in the Minutes of Evidence and Proceedings to Birkenhead and Liverpool Docks Bills in Sessions of 1844 to 1852, quoted in *The Port and Docks of Birkenhead* etc. by Thomas Webster, London, J. Newman, 1873. Liverpool Record Office.
14. Captain Charley Patey, R.N., to *Select Committee on the Passengers' Act*, H.C., 1851, Vol. 19.
15. Murdoch from First Report of the *Select Committee on Emigrant Ships*, H.C., 1854, Vol. 13.

16. Most of the information in this chapter about Atlantic packets comes from newspapers and newspaper advertisements of the time, from the annual *Lloyd's Register of British and Foreign Shipping* for the period, and from evidence given to many United States and British committees of enquiry. *Merchant Sail*, by William Armstrong Fairburn, published in six volumes from 1945 to 1955 by Fairburn Marine and Educational Foundations Inc., Center Lovell, Maine, is a detailed history of the American mercantile marine and gives an account of many packet ships. Information on the cost of packets is from *Square-Riggers on Schedule* (see note 17 below).

17. Information on shipowners from *Dictionary of American Biography*. Ship-shares owned by Minturn from *Square-Riggers on Schedule* by Robert Greenhalgh Albion, Princeton University Press, 1938, Appendix II.

18. *Liverpool Mercury*, May 21, 1847.

19. *A Descriptive Catalogue of the Marine Collection at India House* [New York City] privately printed at the sign of the Gosden Head, New York, 1935.

20. Colonial Office papers, C.O. 384/88; 1850. Public Record Office, London.

21. *Annual Reports of the Commissioners of Emigration of the State of New York, 1847–60*, New York, 1861, Table A, p. 289.

22. Return of ships sailing from Liverpool in 1850, given in the evidence of Lieutenant Thomas Eyre Hodder, R.N., emigration officer at Liverpool, to the *Select Committee on the Passengers' Act*, H.C., 1851, Vol. 19.

23. Evidence of Thomas Murdoch, chairman of the Emigration Commissioners, to the *Select Committee on Emigrant Ships*, H.C., 1854, Vol. 13.

24. Robert Carter to the Lords *Select Committee on Colonization from Ireland*, H.C., 1847, Vol. 6.

25. *Liverpool Chronicle*, September 20, 1851.

26. Captain Charley Patey, R.N., to the 1851 *Select Committee on the Passengers' Act*, H.C., 1851, Vol. 19.

27. Bunch, to the same committee as in note 24 above.

28. Evidence of William Hadfield, secretary to Birkenhead Dock Co., to same committee as in note 24 above.

29. Entry of October 5, 1854, in journals. See note 10 above.

30. Entry of September 16, 1855. See note 10 above.

31. Samuel Cartwright of New Orleans in letter to *Select Committee of the Senate of the United States on the Sickness and Mortality on Board*

Emigrant Ships, Washington, 1854, 33rd Congress, 1st Session, Senate. Rep. Com. No. 386.

32. *A Word in Season; addressed to the Sailors on Emigrant Ships*. No. 18 of Emigrant Tracts, Society for Promoting Christian Knowledge, London, 1850–2.

33. *The Rise of New York Port [1815–1860]* by Robert Greenhalgh Albion with Jennie Barnes Pope, New York, Charles Scribner's Sons, 1939. Reprinted 1971 by David and Charles, Newton Abbot, England.

34. Thomas Murdoch in First Report of the *Select Committee on Emigrant Ships*, H.C., 1854, Vol. 13.

35. Captain W. H. Walker, R.N., to same committee as in note 34 above.

36. J. Custis, in article of September 30, 1857, in *Mona's Herald*. From a cutting in Colonial Office papers, C.O. 384/99. Public Record Office, London.

37. Evidence to *Select Committee on the Passengers' Acts*, 1851, H.C., 1851, Vol. 19.

38. Letter of Hawthorne from Liverpool to the Secretary of State, Washington, dated April 16, 1857, National Archives, Washington D.C.

39. *English Notebooks* (see note 10 above) for September 22, 1853.

40. *English Notebooks* (see note 10 above) for August 12, 1855.

41. The clipping fron the *New York Evening Post* was sent by Hawthorne with his despatch No. 55 of 1855. National Archives, Washington D.C.

42. Despatch No. 37, sent from Liverpool on May 18, 1855. National Archives, Washington.

43. Special Report of the Managing Committee to the Members of the Society of Friends of Foreigners in Distress sent by Hawthorne with despatch dated February 13, 1857, from Liverpool. National Archives, Washington.

44. Letter of Hawthorne from Liverpool to the Secretary of State, Washington, dated April 16, 1857. National Archives, Washington.

Notes for Chapter 7: The Voyage

1. Letter of Stephen de Vere in *First Report from the Select Committee of the House of Lords on Colonization from Ireland*, H.C., 1847–8, Vol. 17. Also *Emigration, North America*, 1847, Colonial Office papers, C.O. 384/79. [Letter 364 in this volume says that before de Vere

went to Canada he was asked to have the goodness to communicate any information on emigration to T. F. Elliot who was at the time chairman of the emigration commissioners but who had become assistant-under-secretary at the Colonial Office by the time de Vere's letter was received.] Public Record Office, London.

2. *Aubrey de Vere: a memoir* by Wilfred Ward, Longmans, Green, London, 1904. Aubrey was the younger brother of Stephen.

3. *Redburn: His First Voyage* by Herman Melville, Richard Bentley, London, 1849.

4. Evidence of Robert Edward Garnham to the *Select Committee on the Passengers' Act*, H.C., 1851, Vol. 19.

5. *Correspondence on the Treatment of the Passengers on Board the Emigrant Ship 'Washington'*, H.C., 1851, Vol. 40, p. 433. Also C.O. Papers 384/88, item 351. Public Record Office, London.

6. The same.

7. The same, p. 439.

8. Letter of Hodder to Walcott of February 4, 1851, and letter of Walcott to Lord Hobart of February 8, both in H.C., 1851, Vol. 40.

9. 1851 *Select Commmittee on the Passengers' Acts*, H.C., 1851, Vol. 19. Evidence of Murdoch.

10. The same. Evidence of Robert Bunch.

11. Manuscript letter of Martin Donald Macleod to Harry Macdonald of Portree, Scotland, September 5, 1845. Toronto Public Library.

12. *The Young Emigrants*, anonymous, but perhaps by a Miss Willyams (see the reference to the *Emigrants' Penny Magazine* in Chapter 2 of this book), London, Routledge, 1853; New York, Scribner, 1851.

13. Mr. Custis contributed four anonymous articles entitled 'Floating Brothels of England and America' to the *Mona's Herald*, of Anglesey, Wales, from September 16 to October 14, 1857. He was named in a fifth article, which consisted of editorial comment, on October 21. Cuttings of the articles are in Colonial Office papers, C.O. 384/89. Public Record Office, London.

14. Letters of emigration commissioners to Mr. Labouchère, Colonial Secretary, November 11, 1857; endorsement of T. F. Elliot on Colonial Office memorandum of November 16; letter from emigration commissioners to Colonial Office communicating Labouchère's decision. All in C.O. 384/99. Public Record Office, London.

15. 'A Steerage Emigrant's Journal from Bristol to New York',

anonymous article in *Chambers's Edinburgh Journal*, October 21, 1848, Edinburgh.

16. Evidence of Captain Schomberg, R.N., emigration officer at Liverpool, in *First Report from the Select Committee on Emigrant Ships*, H.C., 1854, Vol. 13.

17. *Report to committee of the Common Council of the City of New York*, quoted in United States 29th Congress, second session, House Document 54. The quotation given here is from a letter from the Almshouse Commissioners' Office, New York, January 20, 1847.

18. Evidence of the Rev. John William Welsh, chaplain to the emigrants of Liverpool, in the *Report on the Select Committee on the Passengers' Acts*, H.C., 1851, Vol. 19.

19. Evidence of Lieutenant Hutchinson, R.N., in *First Report of the Select Committee on Emigrant Ships*, H.C., 1854, Vol. 13.

20. Stephen, to *Select Committee on the Passengers' Acts*, H.C., 1851, Vol. 19.

21. Saul, to same Select Committee.

22. Murdoch, to same Select Committee.

23. Redmond to 1854 Select Committee (see note 19 above).

24. Captain Schomberg, 1854 Select Committee (see note 19 above).

25. The Rev. John Welsh to 1851 Select Committee (see note 20 above).

26. Lieutenant T. E. Hodder to 1851 Select Committee (see note 20 above).

27. Evidence of Thomas Wm. Clinton Murdoch to 1854 Select Committee (see note 19 above).

28. Evidence of the Rev. John Welsh (see note 18 above).

29. Letter from 'Doctor' published in the *New York Times*, October 15, 1851.

30. Evidence of Delaney Finch in *First Report of the Select Committee on Emigrant Ships*, H.C., 1854, Vol. 13.

31. Evidence of Frederick Marshall in report of *Select Committee on the Passengers' Acts*, H.C., 1851, Vol. 19.

32. *Chambers's Edinburgh Journal*, February 11, 1854, from an article in the series 'Things as They Are in America'.

33. Evidence of Dr. William O'Doherty in *First Report from the Select Committee on Emigrant Ships*, H.C., 1854, Vol. 13.

34. Report of G. M. Douglas on the year at Grosse Isle, in his letter dated December 27, 1847. Printed in *Papers relative to Emigration*, H.C. 1848, Vol. 47. British Museum State Paper Room.

35. Evidence of Robert Garnham in *Report from the Select Committee Inquiring into the Operation of the Passenger Acts*, H.C., 1851, Vol. 19.

36. Article 'Labour and the Poor: Emigration—Emigrants and Man-Catchers' in the *Morning Chronicle*, London, July 15, 1850.

37. Evidence of John Duross in *First Report from the Select Committee on Emigrant Ships*, H.C., 1854, Vol. 13.

38. *New York Times*, August 18, 1853.

39. *Papers relative to Emigration*, B.P.P., 1848, Vol. 47, p. 185.

40. Evidence of William Philipps in *First Report from the Select Committee on Emigrant Ships*, B.P.P., 1854, Vol. 13.

41. Evidence of Sylvester Redmond to the same committee.

42. Evidence of Dr. Isaac Wood in *Report of the Select Committee of the Senate of the United States on the Sickness and Mortality on Board Emigrant Ships*, 33rd Congress, First Session, Senate. Rep. Com. No. 386, 1854.

43. Colonial Office Papers, C.O. 384/86, item 362. Public Record Office, London.

44. *Tenth General Report of the Colonial Land and Emigration Commissioners*, H.C., 1850, Vol. 23, p. 59.

45. Evidence of T. F. Elliot, chairman of the emigration commissioners, in report of Lords *Select Committee on Colonization from Ireland*, H.C., 1847, Vol. 6. Also see letters from heads of the British medical schools in *Journals of the Legislative Assembly of the Province of Canada*, 1848, Appendix W. National Library and Archives, Ottawa.

46. Report of the U.S. Senate committee of 1854 (details in note 42 above).

47. Evidence of Garnham (see note 4 above).

48. *Emigrant Vessels*, H.C., 1854, Vol. 45, p. 429.

49. *Liverpool Telegraph and Shipping Gazette*, June 4, 1847.

50. *Emigrant Tracts* published 1850–2 by the Society for Promoting Christian Knowledge, London. Vol. IX is 'Medical Hints for Emigrants'.

51. Evidence of Delaney Finch in *First Report of Select Committee on Emigrant Ships*, H.C., 1854, Vol. 13.

Notes for Chapter 8: Washed Away; Drowned Altogether

1. *Liverpool Telegraph and Shipping Gazette*, Liverpool. Report of wreck, May 5, 1847. Letter, May 7.

2. The same. June 11, 1847.

3. *Fourteenth General Report of the Colonial Land and Emigration Commissioners*, H.C., 1854, Vol. 28.

4. *Fifteenth General Report of the Colonial Land and Emigration Commissioners*, H.C., 1854–5.

5. *Emigrant Vessels. Return to an Address of the Honourable the House of Commons . . . for Copies of Reports to the Colonial Office, in the Six Months ending the 31st day of January 1854, of the loss of vessels carrying Emigrants . . .*, H. C., 1854, Vol. 46.

6. *Illustrated London News*, June 2, 1849.

7. The same, July 16, 1849. Details of both the *Hannah* and the *Maria* from *Lloyd's Register of Shipping*, 1850.

8. The same. July 7. 1849. Also *Nautical and Naval Chronicle*, London, 1849.

9. *Destruction of an Emigrant Ship, the Ocean Monarch, by Fire* [reprinted from the *Liverpool Journal*] 1848. *An Authentic Account of the Destruction of the Ocean Monarch, by fire, off the port of Liverpool, and loss of 176 lives, with an engraving*, Liverpool, William McCall, 1848. *The Ocean Monarch. A Poetic Narrative, With an Original and Authentic Account, in Prose, of the Loss of this ill-fated vessel . . .* by James Henry Legg, Liverpool, Deighton and Langton, London, Smith, Elder, 1848. All these are in the Liverpool Record Office.

10. Details of the *Annie Jane* wreck from *Emigrant Vessels*, H.C., 1854, Vol. 46 (see note 5 above). Walters's story from *Ragged School Union Magazine*, London, Partridge and Oakey, April, 1854.

11. *New York Times*, October 31, 1853.

12. Letters of the McConnell Family, Toronto Public Library (see note 20 of Chapter 1).

13. Evidence of John Ryan, in *First Report of the Select Committee on Emigrant Ships*, H.C., 1854, Vol. 13.

Notes for Chapter 9: 1847, the Plague Year

1. This is one of the letters from emigrants and others to Sir R. Gore Booth, Bart., in *Third Report of the Select Committee on Colonization from Ireland*, Appendix X, H.C., 1849, Vol. II.

2. *Quebec Mercury*, February 18 and 21, 1847.

3. *Gleanings in the West of Ireland* by the Hon. and Rev. S. Godolphin Osborne, London, T. and W. Boone, 1850.

4. Letter of J. R. Godley to Lord Monteagle, dated March 16, 1847. National Library of Ireland, Monteagle Papers, MS 13397(3).

5. The widow fined—*Irish Felon*, July 8, 1848. Castlebar—*Irish Felon*,

July 1, 1848. Inquest verdicts—*Galway Vindicator*, months of January and February, 1847. Nobility promising to eat less, *Vindicator*, February 6, 1847. Other items, *Vindicator* for January 9, 19, and 27, 1847.

6. Dogs, hinges, and sale of coffins—*Freeman's Journal*, Dublin, May 13, March 11, and June 3, 1847. Man with child's body, *United Irishman*, Dublin, February 12, 1848.

7. Puppyism—*United Irishman*, Dublin, February 12, 1848. Recipe for gunpowder—*United Irishman*, April 8. The Lord Lieutenant's various styles and titles, *United Irishman* of March 25 and April 8, 1848, and *Irish Felon* of June 24, 1848.

8. *New York Times*, November 28, 1851, article headed 'The Depopulation of Ireland'.

9. *Sixteenth General Report of the Colonial Land and Emigration Commissioners*, 1856, H.C., Vol. 24.

10. Evidence of Thomas William Clinton Murdoch in *First Report from the Select Committee on Colonization from Ireland*, H.C., 1847–8, Vol. 17.

11. *Report of the Health Committee of the Borough of Liverpool on the Health of the Town*, 1847–50, by W. H. Duncan, M.D., Medical Officer of Health; Liverpool, Harris and Co., 1851.

12. *Tenth Annual Report, Addressed to the Committee of the Liverpool Domestic Mission by their Minister to the Poor*, March 1847. Liverpool Record Office.

13. *New York Tribune*, July 9, 1847.

14. Letter from OBrien in Colonial Office papers, C.O. 384/79, 'Emigration, North America 1847', item 418.

15. *Report of Select Committee on Colonization from Ireland*, H.C., 1847, Vol. 6, p. 771.

16. *Thirty-third general report of the Colonial Land and Emigration Commissioners*, H.C., 1873, Vol. 18, Appendix I.

17. *An Act to regulate the carriage of passengers in merchant vessels*, February 22, 1847; and an amending act of March 2, 1847.

18. Colonial Office papers 384/79. Letter of emigration commissioners to Colonial Office, June 9, 1847.

19. C.O. 384/79. Letter of emigration commissioners to Stephen at the Colonial Office, April 23, 1847. Item 660.

20. *An Act Relating to Alien Passengers*, Commonwealth of Massachusetts, 1837.

21. C.O. 384/79, letter of emigration commissioners to Stephen at Colonial Office dated August 16, 1847, item 1404.

22. Evidence of T. W. C. Murdoch, *First Report from the Select Committee on Colonization from Ireland*, H.C., 1847–8, Vol. 17.
23. *Papers Relating to Emigration to the British Province in North America*, H.C., 1847, Vol. 39. Extract from report of Chief Agent for Superintendence of Emigration at Quebec (A. C. Buchanan) to the Governor General, week ending August 22, 1846. The report is dated August 22, 1845, but the 5 is an obvious misprint.
24. *Seventh annual report of the Colonial Land and Emigration Commissioners*, H.C., 1847, Vol. 33. Letter of Grey to Elgin dated January 29, 1847.
25. C.O. 384/79. Buchanan to Grey, February 6, 1847. Emigration commissioners to Stephen, April 7, 1847.
26. *The Elgin-Grey Papers 1846–52*, edited with notes and appendices by Sir Arthur Doughty, four volumes, Ottawa, published by Secretary of State, 1937. Page 1311: Extract from *The Church*, April 23, 1847.
27. Pre-1847 details and estimate of 11,000 burials from *Le Saint-Laurent et ses Îles* by Damase Potvin, Montreal, editions Bernard Valiquette, *c.* 1940.
28. *Papers relative to Emigration*, H.C., 1848, Vol. 47. Despatch from Elgin to Grey, May 28, 1847.
29. C.O. 384/79. Emigration commissioners to B. Hawes at Colonial Office, Item 1227.
30. *Potvin* (see note 27 above), p. 65.
31. *Papers relative to Emigration*, H.C., 1848, Vol. 47. G. M. Douglas, M.D., to Hon. D. Daley [provincial secretary] dated December 27, 1847, being a report on the year at Grosse Isle.
32. *Journals of the Legislative Assembly of the Province of Canada*, 1847, Appendix L. Letter from Douglas to Governor General's office giving weekly report for May 8–15.
33. Douglas's annual report (see note 31 above).
34. 'Medical Hints for Emigrants', being Volume IX of *Emigrant Tracts*, London, Society for Promoting Christian Knowledge, 1850–2.
35. *The Great Famine: Studies in Irish History 1845–52*, ed. R. Dudley Edwards and T. Desmond Williams; Dublin, Browne and Nolan, 1956. Chapter V, 'Medical History of the Famine' by Sir William P. MacArthur.
36. *Journals* (see note 32 above): Douglas to Daley, May 29, 1847.
37. *Journals* (see note 32 above): Douglas to Daley, May 31, 1847.
38. C.O. 384/79. (1847) Emigration commissioners to B. Hawes at Colonial Office, item 1227.

39. *Journals* (see note 32 above).
40. *Papers relative to Emigration*, H.C., 1848, Vol. 47. Letter of Douglas to Buchanan, June 8, 1847. An extract from the letter was sent by Buchanan to the Mayor of Quebec, and this appears in *Journals* (see note 32 above), Appendix R.
41. Douglas's annual report (see note 31 above).
42. The same.
43. The same.
44. *First Report from the Select Committee on Colonization from Ireland*, H.C., 1847–8, Vol. 17, p. 51. Letter of Stephen de Vere. Also in *Papers relative to Emigration*, H.C., 1848, Vol. 47, pp. 319–23.
45. *Les Monuments Commémoratifs de la Province de Québec* by Pierre-Georges Roy, Quebec, Imprimeur du Roi, 1923, Vol. 2, p. 101. (From the Archives of the Séminaire de Québec.) Roy is quoting *Histoire de l'Ile-aux-Grues et des îles environnantes* by A. Béchard.
46. *Report of the Special Committee appointed to inquire into the management of the Quarantine Station at Grosse Isle* in *Journals of the Legislative Assembly of the Province of Canada*, 1847, Vol. 6, Appendix RRR.
47. *Papers relative to Emigration*, H.C., 1848, Vol. 47. Elgin to Grey, December 8, 1847. Also in Douglas's annual report (see note 31 above).
48. Douglas's annual report (see note 31 above).
49. *The Ocean Plague: or a Voyage to Quebec in an Irish Emigrant Vessel. Embracing a quarantine at Grosse Isle in 1847. With notes illustrative of the ship-pestilence of that fatal year*, Boston, Coolidge and Wiley, 1848. No author's name is given on the title page, which states the book is 'By a Cabin Passenger', but the book was entered according to Act of Congress in the clerk's office of the District Court of the District of Massachusetts by Robert Whyte.
50. *Souvenir du Jubilee Sacerdotal de Mgr. C. F. Cazeau, Prélat Domestique de sa Sainteté*, etc., Quebec, *c.* 1880. In the archives of the Archevêché de Québec. An appendix gives the names of the priests who ministered to the emigrants at Grosse Isle. A long passage about Father McGauran appears on pp. 152–3. The quotation attributed to him is from *The Irish in America* by John Francis Maguire, M.P., London, Longman, Green and Co., 1868, p. 136.
51. *Les Evêques de Québec* by Mgr. Henri Têtu, Quebec, 1889. In the archives of the Séminaire de Québec.
52. *Souvenir*, etc. (see note 50 above), p. 158.
53. The same.
54. Maguire (see note 50 above).

55. MS letter, catalogue reference VG XII–40, in the archives of the Archevêché de Québec.

56. *Papers relative to Emigration*, H.C., 1848, Vol. 47. Letter of Douglas, dated December 8, 1847, sent on to Grey by Elgin. Letter from Ledoyen to Grey, received May 6, 1848.

57. *Chambers's Edinburgh Journal*, March 25, 1854.

58. *American Notes* by Charles Dickens, London, Chapman and Hall, 1842, Chapter 15.

59. De Vere (see note 44 above).

60. Father O'Reilly in Report of Special Committee (see note 46 above).

61. *Eighth General Report of the Colonial Land and Emigration Commissioners*, H.C., 1848, Vol. 26.

62. *Thoughts on Emigration, Education, etc. in a letter addressed to the Right Honourable Lord John Russell, Prime Minister of England* by 'A Citizen', Montreal, J. C. Becket, 1847.

63. Douglas's annual report (see note 31 above).

64. MS letter of October 12, 1847, catalogue reference G–I, 1–33, in archives of the Archevêché de Québec.

65. Douglas's annual report (see note 31 above).

66. See note 31 above.

67. *Eighth General Report* (see note 61 above).

68. For example, in Appendix to the *Thirty-third General Report of the Colonial Land and Emigration Commissioners*, H.C., 1873, Vol. 18, which gives emigration figures from 1815 to 1873.

69. *The Ocean Plague*, p. 16 (see note 49 above).

70. *Journals of the Legislative Assembly of the Province of Canada*, 1848, Appendix W, Letter No. 142, Grey to Elgin, December 1, 1847.

71. *Papers relative to Emigration*, H.C., 1848, Vol. 47, p. 327, Elgin to Grey, enclosing address from Mayor of Toronto.

72. Evidence of T. W. C. Murdoch in *First Report from the Select Committee on Colonization from Ireland*, H.C., 1847–8, Vol. 17.

73. *Despatches relative to Emigration*, British North America, 35–8, H.C., 1851, Vol. 40.

74. *Souvenir*, etc. (see note 50 above), p. 158.

75. MS letter of G. M. Douglas to Hon. Mr. Cameron, dated Quebec, December 29, 1853, marked 'Private' and on mourning paper. Record group 17, III, 1. Immigration 1842–55. National Library and Archives, Ottawa.

76. Maguire (see note 50 above).

77. Roy (see note 45 above).

Notes for Chapter 10: New York

1. *The Times*, London, quoted in *Frank Leslie's Illustrated Newspaper*, New York, September 6, 1850.
2. *New York: Past, Present, and Future*, etc., by E. Porter Belden, New York, G. P. Putnam, 1849.
3. According to the Hon. William Wright, Advocate General of New Brunswick at the Railway Convention at Portland, Maine, in July–August, 1850, reported in *Plan for Shortening the Time of Passage between New York and London*, Portland, Harman and Williams, 1850.
4. *A Picture of New York in 1846*, etc., New York, Homans and Ellis, 1846.
5. The same.
6. Belden, as in note 2 above.
7. *The Wealth and Biography of the Wealthy Citizens of the City of New York; being an alphabetical arrangement of the names of the most prominent capitalists whose wealth is estimated at One Hundred Thousand Dollars and upwards, with the sums appended to each name* . . . , New York, Sun Office, 1846.
8. *Dictionary of American Biography*, New York, Charles Scribner's Sons, 1949.
9. The 1840 and 1850 figures are from the United States censuses of those years, and the 1845 and 1855 figures from New York State censuses.
10. Details of New York to the end of the paragraph are from *The Memorial History of the City of New York*, ed. James Grant Wilson, New York History Co., 1893, Vol. III, chapters 10, 11, 12.
11. *Census of the State of New York for 1855*, Albany, 1857.
12. *New York Sun*, August 20, 1847.
13. *Ragged School Union Magazine*, London, Partridge and Oakey. Issue for March 1850.
14. *Frank Leslie's Illustrated Newspaper*, New York, February 16, 1856.
15. *New York Herald*, November 28, 1853.
16. *Chambers's Edinburgh Journal*, Edinburgh, June 3 and June 10, 1854.
17. *New York Tribune*, July 1, 1847.
18. *Doggett's New York Directory*, 1845–6. The number of newspapers in New York in 1855 is from the 1855 census.
19. *New York Tribune*, June 26, 1847.
20. *New York Times*, October 31, 1853.

21 and 22. *New York Times*, October 15, 1851.

23 and 24. *New York Times*, December 12, 1851.

25. Extracted from *Tables showing Arrivals of Alien Passengers and Immigrants in the United States from 1820 to 1888*, Treasury Department Bureau of Statistics, 1889. The years were reckoned from 1 October to 30 September, and so the figures for New York are different from those published by the Emigration Commissioners for the State of New York, whose figures are for the calendar year.

26. Letter from almshouse commissioners, New York City, January 20, 1847, in Report to a Committee of the Common Council of the City of New York, printed in U.S. 29th Congress, 2nd Session, House Doc. No. 54.

27. *Address on the Temporal and Spiritual Condition of British Emigrants*, by the Rev. Moses Marcus, B.D., New York, J. T. Crowell and Co., 1846.

28. Ann Steele's evidence in *Report of the Select Committee appointed by the Legislature of New-York to examine into Frauds upon Emigrants*, Assembly Doc. No. 250, 1847, Albany, Public Printer, 1847.

29. *New York Tribune*, June 24, 1847.

30. *New York Magdalen Female Benevolent Society*, Reports for 1850 to 1855, New York.

31. *Sixth Annual Report of the Governors of the Almshouse, New York, for the Year 1854*, New York, 1855.

32. *Illustrated News*, New York, January 8, 1853.

33. *New York Times*, January 12, 1854.

34. *Annual Reports of the New-York Association for the Improvement of the Condition of the Poor* for the years 1845 to 1853, New York.

35. Addresses from city guides and from *Work and Wages* by Vere Foster, London, W. & F. G. Cash, c. 1855.

36. *Ragged School Union Magazine*, London, July 1853.

37. *Report of the Select Committee to Investigate Frauds upon Emigrant Passengers*, New York, Assembly Doc. No. 46, 1848.

38. Robert Bunch on evidence to Select Committee on the Passengers' Act, H.C., 1851, Vol. 19.

39. Statement on invitation card to Third Annual Ball of the Irish Emigrant Society in New York on December 29, 1846; in the letters of Charles P. Daley, Manuscript Room, New York Public Library.

40. Daley papers, see note 39. These include letters to Daley, cuttings about him and about Irish organisations in New York, 'Records of an Irish-American organisation kept before 1864', and 'Papers of the

Friendly sons of St. Patrick,' minutes 1828–62. See also *Dictionary of American Biography* on Daley.

41. *Letters on Irish Emigration first published in the Boston Daily Advertiser* by Edward E. Hale, Boston, Phillips, Sampson, 1852.

42. *Frank Leslie's Illustrated Newspaper*, New York, December 22, 1855.

43. Letter dated January 27, 1847, from Moses Marcus to Lord John Russell, Colonial Office Papers, 'Emigration, North America 1847', C.O. 384/79, item 404. Public Record Office, London.

44. *Gleason's Pictorial Drawing Room Companion*, Boston, Vol. 1, p. 368, October 4, 1851.

45. *Gleason's*, June 28, 1851, p. 140.

46. *New York Illustrated News*, New York, June 25, 1853.

47. *Frank Leslie's Illustrated Newspaper*, New York, October 4, 1856, p. 261.

48. *The Citizen and Strangers' Pictorial and Business Directory*, Solyman Brown, editor, New York, Charles Spalding, 1843.

49. I owe this anecdote to Mr. Louis Kushnick, of the Department of American Studies in the University of Manchester, England, who told it at a symposium on North Atlantic Emigration held on November 15, 1969, at the National Maritime Museum, Greenwich. He was referring to Russian emigrants to America, but the same was true of Anglo-Saxons and Celts.

50. *The Wealth and Biography*, etc., New York, 1846 (see note 7 above).

Notes for Chapter 11: Quarantine, Runners, and Rackets

1. *Chambers's Edinburgh Journal*, October 21, 1848. Article headed 'A Steerage Emigrant's Journal from Bristol to New York'.

2. Evidence of John H. Griscom in *Report of the Select Committee of the Senate of the United States on the Sickness and Mortality on Board Emigrant Ships*, 33rd Congress, 1st Session, Senate Rept. Com. No. 386, 1854.

3. *Redburn: His First Voyage* by Herman Melville, London, Richard Bentley, 1849, Vol. 2.

4. *Gleason's Pictorial Drawing Room Companion*, Boston, August 9, 1851. This is the date it appears in the copies in Boston Public Library. The British Museum file has the same engraving in a copy dated June 14, 1851.

5. Evidence of Robert Garnham from *Report from the Select Committee on the Passengers' Act*, H.C., 1851, Vol. 19.

6. Annual report for 1851, published in *Annual Reports of the Commissioners of Emigration of the State of New York 1847–60*, New York, 1861.

7. Report on ship fever from the New York Academy of Medicine, in *New York Tribune*, July 13, 1847.

8. Advertisement in *New York Tribune*, July 20, 1847.

9 and 10. Advertisements in *New York Tribune*, July 21, 1847.

11. State of New York Assembly Doc. No. 60, 1846: report of select committee on quarantine. And evidence of Henry Van Hovenburgh in *Report of the Select Committee appointed by the Legislature of New York to examine into Frauds upon Emigrants*: Assembly Doc. 250, 1847.

12 and 13. New York Assembly Doc. No. 60, 1846 (see note 11 above).

14. Evidence of Dr. A. B. Whiting in State of New York Assembly Doc. No. 60, 1849. (The reports of both the 1846 and 1849 committees into quarantine were both printed as Assembly Docs. No. 60 of their years, and it is easy to confuse them.)

15. Affidavit of Dr. Marinus Van Dyke, New York Assembly Doc. No. 60, 1849.

16. Report of quarantine committee, New York Assembly Doc. No. 60, 1849.

17. Evidence of Robert M. Hazard to above committee.

18. Evidence of Dawson to above committee.

19. *Letters on Irish Emigration first published in the Boston Daily Advertiser* by Edward E. Hale, Boston, Phillips, Sampson, 1852.

20. John C. Thompson's evidence to quarantine committee, New York Assembly Doc. No. 60, 1849.

21. Evidence of James B. Johnson in New York Assembly Doc. No. 250, 1847.

22. Annual Report of the Commissioners of Emigration of the State of New York, 1848 (see note 6 above).

23. Table 11 in collected reports of Commissioners of Emigration (see note 6 above).

24. Advertisement in *New York Tribune*, July 7, 1855.

25. General Table on p. 379 of collected reports of Commissioners of Emigration (see note 6 above).

26. Report of Commissioners of Emigration for 1850 (see note 6 above).

27. Evidence of Westerfield in *Report of the select committee to examine into the condition, business accounts, and management of the trusts under*

the charge of the commissioners of Emigration, New York Assembly Doc.
No. 34, 1852.

28. Evidence of Henry Lloyd in above report.

29. Evidence of Dr. Thomas Addis Emmet in above report.

30. Evidence of Dr. William B. Thompson in above report.

31. Resolution of emigration commissioners of May 5, 1848, in report for 1848 (see note 6 above).

32. Evidence of Dr. John H. Griscom, New York Assembly Doc. No. 34, 1852.

33. Evidence of Dr. Thomas Emmet to above committee.

34 and 35. Evidence of Dr. Alexander E. Hosack to above committee.

36. Evidence of Charles H. Webb to above committee.

37. Appendix No. 4 in *Annual Reports of the Commissioners of Emigration of the State of New York* 1847–60, New York, 1861. Also in slightly different form in Annual Report [for 1850] of the Commissioners of Emigration, New York Assembly Doc. No. 37, 1851.

38. Report signed by Adolf Rodewald and G. C. Verplanck, two commissioners of emigration, who with Dillon carried out the investigation, from the same two sources as in note 37 above.

39. Appendix No. 4, etc., as in note 37 above.

40. Two sources as in note 37 above.

41. Emigration commissioners' reports from 1850 and 1851.

42. Evidence of Brennan in New York Assembly Doc. No. 34, 1852.

43. Evidence of Williams, same Assembly Doc.

44. Evidence of Quin, same Assembly Doc.

45. Evidence of Minturn, same Assembly Doc.

46. Evidence of Elizabeth Daly, same Assembly Doc.

47. General Table on p. 379 of Annual Reports of the Commissioners of Emigration (see note 37 above).

48. Evidence of Robert Garnham in report of the *Select Committee on the Passengers' Act*, H.C., Vol. 19, 1851.

49. Dr. Henry Van Hovenburgh in New York Assembly Doc. No. 250, 1847.

50. *Immigration and the Commissioners of Emigration of the State of New York by Friedrich Kapp, one of the said Commissioners*, New York, the Nation Press, 1870, p. 63. Also evidence of John Allen in *Report of the select committee to examine into the condition, business accounts and management of the trusts under the charge of the commissioners of Emigration*, New York Assembly Doc. No. 34, 1852.

51. *New York Tribune* quoted, without any date given, in *Chambers's Edinburgh Journal*, March 3, 1855.

52. Evidence of Robert Bunch, British vice-consul in New York, in report of the *Select Committee on the Passengers' Act*, H.C., Vol. 19, 1851.

53. Isaacs' evidence in New York Assembly Doc. No. 34, 1852 (see note 50 above).

54. R. Schoger's evidence in New York Assembly Doc. No. 250, 1847.

55. Evidence of Robert Bowne Minturn in *First Report from the Select Committee of the House of Lords on Colonization from Ireland*, H.C., Vol. 17, 1847–8. He said the proper rates of passage, without food, were: to Buffalo (500 miles) $2.50–$3; to Cleveland, Ohio (700) $5.50; Detroit (850) $6.00; Milwaukee (1,500) $9.50; Chicago (1,500) $9.50.

56. Porter Adams's evidence in New York Assembly Doc. No. 250, 1847.

57. Vail's evidence in same Assembly Doc. as above.

58. 1847 committee (see note 49 above).

59. Report of 1847 committee (see note 49 above).

60. Roach to 1847 committee (see note 49 above).

61. Cook to 1847 committee (see note 49 above).

62. Kapp, 1870 (see note 50 above).

63. Evidence of Roach and Daley before 1847 Committee, New York Assembly Doc. No. 250, 1847. Evidence of Gallagher in New York Assembly 34, 1852.

64. Evidence of Quigg and Clarke to 1847 New York Committee.

65. *Rode's New York City Directory* for 1850–1, New York, Charles R. Rode.

66. *New York Tribune* quoted, no date given, in *Chambers's Edinburgh Journal*, March 3, 1855.

67. New York Assembly 34, 1852, p. 39, *New York Times*, October 17, 1853.

68. *New York Times*, September 5, 1855, September 18, 1955, and October 3, 1855.

69. *John Morrissey. His Life, Battles and Wrangles, from his birth in Ireland until he died a State Senator. Compiled by William E. Harding, sporting editor of the 'Police Gazette'* [1881]. Published by Richard K. Fox, proprietor of the *National Police Gazette*, New York, as number two in a series called 'Fistiana's Heroes', price 25 cents.

70. All information about Morrissey either from his biography (see note 69 above) or from the *Dictionary of American Biography*.

Notes for Chapter 12: Colonising and Shovelling Out

1. Samuel Cunard to *Select Committee of the House of Lords on Colonization from Ireland*, H.C., 1847, Vol. 6.

2. Evidence of Elliot to *Select Committee on Colonization from Ireland*, H.C., 1847, Vol. 6; and Murdoch to same committee in H.C., 1847–8, Vol. 17.

3. 'Regulations to the Selection of Labourers', p. 645 of *Eighth General Report of the Colonial Land and Emigration Commissioners*, H.C., 1847–8, Vol. 26.

4. See *Sixteenth General Report of the Colonial Land and Emigration Commissioners*, H.C., 1856, Vol. 24, for the commissioners on single men being fraught with danger; and the *Seventeenth Report*, H.C., 1857 (Sess. 2), Vol. 16, on the dangers of too many single women.

5. *Fifteenth General Report of the Colonial Land and Emigration Commissioners*, H.C., 1854–5, Vol. 17.

6. Elliot to *Select Committee of the House of Lords on Colonization from Ireland*, H.C., 1847, Vol. 6.

7. The sums voted annually are listed in *The Colonial Land and Emigration Commission* by Fred H. Hitchins; University of Philadelphia Press, 1931, Appendix 5. The figures were: 1846, £10,364; 1847, £23,815; 1848, £13,451; 1849, £13,654; 1850, £13,296; 1851, £25,331; 1852, £14,083; 1853, £17,396; 1854, £16,840; 1855, £16,720.

8. Evidence of Minturn to *Select Committee on Colonization from Ireland*, H.C., 1847–8, Vol. 17.

9. *Journals of the Legislative Assembly of Canada*, 1849, Appendix EEE, report from F. Hincks to Lord Elgin.

10. *Report of the Select Committee of the Legislative Assembly, appointed to inquire into the causes and importance of the emigration which takes place annually from Lower Canada to the United States*, Montreal, 1849.

11. *Twelfth General Report of the Colonial Land and Emigration Commissioners*, H.C., 1852, Vol. 18.

12. *The Colonial Policy of Lord John Russell's Administration* by Earl Grey, London, Richard Bentley, 1853.

13. Evidence of John Bramley Moore to Commons Committee of 1851 (on docks) in *The Port and Docks of Birkenhead. Minutes of Evidence and Proceedings on the Birkenhead and Liverpool Docks Bills in Sessions of 1844 to 1852*, etc., by Thomas Webster, London, J. Newman, 1873, p. 138.

14. The same. Evidence of J. B. Hartley, civil engineer.

15. Also Hartley, as above.

16. Colonial Office papers, C.O. 384/84, letter dated May 25, 1849.

17. John Bramley Moore's evidence to *Select Committee on the Passengers' Act*, H.C., 1851, Vol. 19.

18. Bramley Moore, in his evidence on the Docks Bill (see note 13 above), said the emigrants spent upwards of £600,000 a year in Liverpool. He was probably speaking of 1849 and 1850, and by 1851 this spending would have increased with the number of emigrants. But still taking his figure of £600,000, and assuming that this was twice the real value of the goods (since the shopkeepers were in league with the runners, and great exploiters), the commissioners, dealing honestly, could have sold these goods for £300,000. A profit of one-sixth of the gross take, which is modest, would have yielded £50,000.

19. Letter of De Vere from *First Report of the Select Committee on Colonization from Ireland*, H.C., 1847–8, Vol. 17.

20. *Seventh General Report of the Colonial Land and Emigration Commissioners*, H.C., 1847, Vol. 33.

21. *Ragged School Magazine*, London, March, 1850; April, 1853; July, 1853; July, 1854.

22. *Illustrated London News*, August 17, 1850.

23. *Latter Day Saints' Millennial Star*; an issue of 1847 but otherwise undated.

24. Evidence of Samuel Whitney Richards to *Select Committee on Emigrant Ships*, H.C., 1854, Vol. 13.

25. *Morning Chronicle*, London, July 29, 1850.

26. *Sidney's Emigrant's Journal*, London, February 15, 1849.

27. *Morning Chronicle*, London, July 29, 1850; and Richards to 1854 Committee (see note 24 above).

28. See note 24 above.

29. *Gleanings in the West of Ireland* by the Hon. and Rev. S. Godolphin Osborne; London, T. and W. Boone, 1850.

30. *Dictionary of National Biography*.

31. There are two ledgers in the National Library of Ireland, catalogued as *Coolatin Emigration Record*, MS 4974–5.

32. Letter of Michael Driscoll to Sir Robert Gore Booth in Appendix X to *Third Report of Select Committee on Colonization from Ireland*, H.C., 1849, Vol. II.

33. Same. Letter of John Robertson.

34. Perley to John Saunders, provincial secretary, July 28, 1847, in *Papers relative to Emigration*, H.C., 1848, Vol. 47.

35. Letter quoted by Sir Robert Gore Booth in his evidence to *Select*

Committee of the House of Lords on Colonization from Ireland, H.C., 1847–8, Vol. 17.

36. Report of committee of three appointed by Lieutenant-Governor to inquire into Patridge Island, dated October 9, 1847. In *Papers relative to Emigration*, H.C., 1848, Vol. 47.

37. *Papers relative to Emigration*, H.C., 1848, Vol. 47. Letter of Dr. W. S. Harding, dated September 13, 1847, to Lieutenant-Governor.

38. Same, pp. 131–2, Perley.

39. In *Papers relative to Emigration*, H.C., 1848, Vol. 47. Letter of Gilgan to Mr. Doran of Shippegan. Also hospital lists of August 24, and September 3.

40. The same. Perley to Saunders, February 23, 1848.

41. *Select Committee of the House of Lords on Colonization from Ireland*, H.C., 1847–8, Vol. 17.

42. This was the amount of salary paid in 1851. Colonial Office papers, C.O. 384/86, letter of emigration commissioners to Merivale at Colonial Office, dated December 17, 1851.

43. *Fifteenth General Report of the Colonial Land and Emigration Commissioners*, H.C., 1854–5, Vol. 17.

44. O'Doughtery in *Illustrated News*, New York, November 5, 1853. The boy in *Ragged Schools Union Magazine*, London, April, 1854.

45. *Papers relative to Emigration*, H.C., 1848, Vol. 47. Letter of Perley, July 29, 1847.

46. Evidence of John Duross to *Select Committee on Emigrant Ships*, H.C., 1854, Vol. 13.

47. Evidence of John Lancaster, M.D., to *Select Committee on the Passengers' Act*, H.C., 1851, Vol. 19.

48. Song, 'New Irish Emigrant', item 206 in *Poetical Broadsides*, etc., a collection of broadsides, some in proof, in the British Museum, catalogue 11621 k4, Vol. 1.

49. William Tapscott to *Select Committee on the Passengers' Acts*, H.C., 1851, Vol. 19.

50. The same. Evidence of William Fitzhugh.

51. Entry for Enoch Train in *Dictionary of American Biography*.

52. *Morning Chronicle*, London, July 15, 1850.

53. *Fifteenth* and *Sixteenth General Reports of the Colonial Land and Emigration Commissioners*, H.C., 1854–5, Vol. 17, and H.C., 1856, Vol. 24.

54. Fifteenth General Report (see note 43 above).

55. *The Colonial Policy of Lord John Russell's Administration* by Earl Grey; London, Richard Bentley, 1853.

Notes for Chapter 13: The Breaking of Lieutenant Hodder

1. Sir Henry Maine's *Ancient Law* was first published in 1861. Lindsay is from his own book, *Our Merchant Shipping*, London, Longman and Co., 1860.
2. There was no appeal from his decisions under the Passenger Act of 1852, 15 & 16 Victoria cap 44. For a Commons debate on the issue, see *Hansard* for June 4, 1852.
3. In the 1847 and later Acts.
4. *Eighth General Report of the Colonial Land and Emigration Commissioners*, H.C., 1847–8, Vol. 26.
5. The same, pp. 644–5.
6. Evidence of Murdoch to *Select Committee on the Passengers' Act*, H.C., 1851, Vol. 19.
7. Custis's five articles 'The Floating Brothels of England and America' appeared in *Mona's Herald* from September 16, 1857 on: cuttings are in Colonial Office papers, C.O. 384/99. Public Record Office, London.
8. C.O. 384/99. Emigration commissioners to Colonial Secretary (Labouchère), November 11, 1857; also Elliot's, Fortescue's, and Labouchère's endorsements, and Colonial Office reply to the commissioners.
9. *A Naval Biographical Dictionary* by William R. O'Byrne, London, John Murray, 1849.
10. C.O. 384/86. 'Emigration. General Miscellaneous 1851'. Letter of emigration commissioners to Merivale at Colonial Office, dated December 17, 1851.
11. Evidence of Robert Carter to *Select Committee of the House of Lords on Colonization from Ireland*, H.C., 1847, Vol. 6.
12. C.O. 384/88. Letter dated June 4, 1851, from emigration commissioners to Merivale at Colonial Office.
13. C.O. 384/88, 1851. The captain's story is in a letter dated April 13, 1851, printed in an unknown newspaper, perhaps the *True Delta*; a cutting was sent to London by the British Consul in New Orleans.
14. Letter of June 4, 1851 (see note 12 above).
15. The same. Endorsement by Grey, dated June 13; and letter of Grey to commissioners, dated June 19.
16. C.O. 384/86. Letter of Hodder to commissioners, dated June 28, 1851.
17. C.O. 384/86. Patey's report to commissioners, dated July 30, 1851.
18. Reply of commissioners to Patey, dated August 9, 1851.

19. C.O. 384/86. Petition in papers for August 1851.

20. C.O. 384/86. Letter of August 7, 1851.

21. Figures in Appendix I to *Twelfth General Report of the Colonial Land and Emigration Commissioners*, H.C., 1852, Vol. 18.

22. Hodder to *Select Committee on the Passengers' Act*, H.C., 1851, Vol. 19. Also see committee's own recommendations and comments.

23. C.O. 384/86. Letter from Hodder to Wm. Brown, M.P., dated August 5, 1851.

24. *Navy Lists*: London, John Murray, 1851.

25. *Navy Lists*: 1865 and 1873.

26. Professor A. C. Clarke quoted in State of New York Senate, Doc. No. 92, 1850.

27. Samuel Cartwright, M.D., in a letter printed in 33rd Congress, 1st Session, Senate Rep. Com. No. 386.

28. See accounts in *Annual Reports of the Commissioners of Emigration of the State of New York*, 1847–60, New York, 1861.

29. *Dictionary of American Biography*.

30. *Frank Leslie's Illustrated Newspaper*, New York, January 12, 1856.

31. Evidence of James Roach in New York Assembly Doc. No. 250, 1857.

32. Percy Holman's evidence in report of the *Select Committee to examine into Condition, Business Accounts and Management of the Trusts under the Charge of the Commissioners of Emigration*, etc., New York Assembly Doc. No. 34, 1852.

33. The same document; findings of committee.

34. *Annual Reports* (see note 28 above); report for 1848.

35. The same 1848 report.

36. Smethurst to 1852 Committee (see note 32 above).

37. George Andrews to 1852 Committee (see note 32 above).

38. George W. Daley to 1852 Committee (see note 32 above).

39. Reports of warden of city prison in *Fifth Annual Report of the Governors of the Alms House, New York, for the Year 1853*, New York, 1854; and *Sixth Report*, for 1854, New York, 1855.

40. *An Act regulating passenger-ships and vessels*, approved March 2, 1819.

41. The *Washington*: see notes 5–10 of Chapter 7 of this book.

42. Minturn's evidence to *Select Committee of the House of Lords on Colonization from Ireland*, H.C., 1847–8, Vol. 17.

43. *Redburn: His First Voyage* by Herman Melville, London, Richard Bentley, 1849, Vol. 2.

44. Murdoch to *Select Committee on the Passengers' Act*, H.C., 1851, Vol. 19.

45. Custis in *Mona's Herald*, October 14, 1856: cuttings in Colonial Office papers, C.O. 384/99, Public Record Office, London.
46. Evidence of George Daley and James Roach to *Select Committee . . . to examine into Frauds upon Emigrants*; New York Assembly Doc. No. 250, 1847.
47. Same document. Evidence of Charles Cook.

Notes for Chapter 14: America for the Americans

1. *Address of His Excellency Henry J. Gardner to the two branches of the Legislature of Massachusetts*, January 9, 1855. Mass. Senate No. 3, 1855.
2. *Report of the Committee on Foreign Affairs of the House of Representatives on Foreign Criminals and Paupers*, U.S. 34th Congress, 1st Session, House Doc. No. 359.
3. *Imminent Dangers to the Free Institutions of the United States through Foreign Immigration*, by an American [S. F. B. Morse], New York, 1845.
4. Information in this chapter about nativism and the Know-Nothings comes, unless these footnotes particularly indicate other sources, from *The Protestant Crusade 1800–1860. A Study of the Origins of American Nativism* by Ray Allen Billington, New York, Macmillan, 1938; from *With the Fathers* by J. B. McMaster, New York, 1896; and from *Brass-Knuckle Crusade. The Great Know-Nothing Conspiracy*, 1820–1860, by Carleton Beals, New York, Hastings House Publishers, 1960.
5. *The Memorial History of the City of New-York*, ed. James Grant Wilson, New York History Company, 1893, Vol. 3, Chapter XI.
6. *Frank Leslie's Illustrated Newspaper*, New York, September 13, 1856.
7. *The Duty of America to Her Immigrant Citizens: a Sermon preached in the Eighteenth-street M.E. Church, November 25, 1848 by Abiathar M. Osbon, of the New York Annual Conference*, New York, Joseph Longking, 1848.
8. New York Assembly Doc. No. 250, 1847.
9. *Redburn: His First Voyage* by Herman Melville, London, Richard Bentley, 1849, Vol. 2.
10. Report of Joint Special Committee on . . . alien passengers and paupers, Mass Senate No. 46, 1848.
11. Address by George S. Boutwell, Governor, to the Legislature of Massachusetts, January 15, 1852.
12. Report to the Massachusetts House of Representatives of the

committee on Pauper Immigration, April 24, 1855, Mass. House No. 255.

13. Arguments of counsel for City of Boston in *Norris v. City of Boston*, 1849, U.S. Supreme Court (48 U.S. 282).

14. *Thirteenth Annual Report of the Poor Law Board*, H.C., Vol. 28, 1861.

15. *The Times*, London, September 20, 1848.

16. *The Times*, London, September 21, 1848.

17. Mass. Senate No. 74, 1848. Account of passengers landed at Boston.

18. *Boston Daily Advertiser*, May 16, 1855, reprinted in the *Citizen* [an Irish weekly edited by the Young Ireland group], May 26, 1855.

19. *Boston Atlas*, quoted in *Citizen*, New York, II, 361. Both this report and that from the *Advertiser* (above, note 18) are taken from *Immigration: Select Documents and Case Records* by Edith Abbott, University of Chicago Press, 1924.

20. Address by Henry J. Gardner, Governor, to the Legislature of Massachusetts, January 3, 1856.

21. *Tribune Almanac and Political Register* for 1855, New York, and *New York Tribune*, July 2, 1855.

22. *Chambers's Edinburgh Journal*, February 3, 1855. Article, 'American Jottings. The Know-Nothing Movement'.

23. *Census of the State of New York for 1855*, Albany, 1857.

24. Report of the warden of the city prison in *Fifth Annual Report of the Governors of the Almshouse, New York, for the Year 1853*, New York, Joseph W. Harrison, 1854.

25. *Sixth Annual Report of the Governors of the Almshouse, New York, for the Year 1854*, New York, William C. Bryant & Co., 1855.

26. U.S. Supreme Court, *Smith v. Turner* and *Norris v. City of Boston*, 1849. (48 U.S. 282).

27. U.S. Supreme Court, *Henderson v. Mayor of New York*, 1875 (92 U.S. 259).

28. *Gleason's Pictorial*, Vol. 3, October 30, 1852.

29. *Annual Reports of the Commissioners of Emigration of the State of New York*, 1847–60, New York 1861. Appendix No. 4: Dissenting opinion by Gregory Dillon.

Notes for Chapter 15: Steamships and Castle Garden

1. Passage times from *History of Merchant Shipping and Ancient Commerce* by W. S. Lindsay, Vol. IV, London, Sampson, Low, Marston,

Low, and Searle, 1873, Appendix 8. Other comparisons between Cunarders and Collins steamers in *Chambers's Edinburgh Journal*, February 11, 1854, and in several other contemporary publications.

2. *Gleason's Pictorial*, Boston, December 24, 1853.

3. Though Cunard did once give free passages to emigrants whose ship had been run down by one of his own steamers. See Chapter 8.

4. Information about Inman from Lindsay (see note 1 above), and from *Dictionary of National Biography*.

5. *Gleason's Pictorial*, Boston, September 6, 1851.

6. C.O. 384/89, 2568. Letter of Richardson's to emigration commissioners dated February 14, 1852.

7. William Fitzhugh to *Select Committee on the Passengers' Act*, H.C., 1851, Vol. 19.

8. Leaflet advertising Liverpool and Philadelphia Steam Ship Company sent to emigration commissioners, in C.O. 384/93, 806.

9. C.O. 384/89, 2568.

10. C.O. 384/91, 3105.

11. C.O. 384/94, items 806, 1167, 1989, and 2605.

12. *Liverpool Telegraph and Shipping and Commercial Gazette*, March 2, 1844. And *Fifteenth General Report of the Emigration Commissioners*, H.C., 1854–5, Vol. 17.

13. *The Times*, London, May 11, 1854. *Liverpool Telegraph*, same date.

14. C.O. 384/92, 4115.

15. *Liverpool Telegraph*, April 22, April 25, and May 4, 1854.

16. *Liverpool Mercury*, June 2 (*City of Glasgow* still advertised) and June 9, 1854 (name no longer in Richardson's weekly advertisement).

17. *The Times*, London, May 19, 1854.

18. *The Times*, London, July 4, 1854, reprinting article from *Jersey Blue*.

19. *The Times*, London, October 12 and October 13, 1854 (quoting *New York Herald*); *Liverpool Mercury*, October 13; see also *Liverpool Mercury* and *Liverpool Telegraph* of August 22.

20. *Fifteenth General Report of the Emigration Commissioners*, H.C., 1854–5, Vol. 17. *The Times*, London, October 2, 1854.

21. *The Times*, London, October 13, 1854. *Liverpool Mercury*, October 13 and October 27, 1854.

22. *Merchant Sail*, by William Armstrong Fairburn, Fairburn Marine and Educational Foundation Inc., Center Lovell, Maine, 1945–55.

23. Quoted in *The Irish in America* by John Francis Maguire, M.P., London, Longmans, Green, and Co., 1868, p. 199.

24. *Annual Reports of the Commissioners of Emigration of the State of New York, 1847–60*, New York, 1861. Report for 1855.

25. *A Picture History of New York in 1846*, New York, Homans and Ellis, 1846. *Gleason's Pictorial*, Boston, Vol. 1, p. 41, 1851.

26. *Illustrated London News*, October 5, 1850.

27. *Frank Leslie's Illustrated Newspaper*, New York, December 29, 1855.

28. *New York Times*, August 4, 1855.

29. *Frank Leslie's Illustrated Newspaper*, New York, December 29, 1854, quoting *Albany Evening Journal*.

30. *New York Times*, August 4, 1855.

31. *Annual Reports* (see note 24 above), Appendix, table D (a).

32. *Annual Reports* (see note 24 above), Appendix No. 7.

33. *Tenth Annual Report of the Commissioners of Emigration of the State of New York* for the year ending December 31, 1856. *Immigration and the Commissioners of Emigration of the State of New York* by Friedrich Kapp, etc., New York, Nation Press, 1870.

34. C.O. 384/92, 678, dated January 19, 1854, and Newcastle's endorsement of January 21.

35. *Fifteenth Report* (see note 20 above).

36. Appendix to *Sixteenth General Report of the Emigration Commissioners*, H.C., 1856, Vol. 24. *Fifteenth Report* (see note 20 above). *Annual Reports* of New York Commissioners (see note 24 above); report for 1855. *Frank Leslie's Illustrated Newspaper*, December 29, 1855, p. 47.

37. *The Emigrants' Penny Magazine*; Plymouth, September 1851.

38. *The Emigrant* [a poem], anon., Dublin, 1855.

39. *Morning Chronicle*, London, July 15, 1850.

40. *Redburn: His First Voyage* by Herman Melville, London, Richard Bentley, 1849. Vol. 1, p. 49.

41. *Fifteenth* and *Sixteenth General Reports* (see notes 20 and 36 above).

42. The stories of Moore, Harrison, and the unnamed man are told in statements by Moore and Harrison, dated February 26, 1857, taken by Nathaniel Hawthorne at Liverpool and sent to Secretary of State, Washington. The grocer is mentioned in Hawthorne's despatch to Washington dated February 13, 1857.

43. Evidence of John Williams in *Report of the select committee to examine into condition, business accounts and management of the trusts under the charge of the commissioners of Emigration*, New York Assembly Doc. No. 34, 1852. In the transcript Williams is reported as saying he came from Wrexham, Devon, but this is an obvious mishearing for Wrexham, Denbigh, in North Wales.

Appendices

The Passenger Acts

What follows is a summary of the Passenger Acts, both British and American, which purported to control and regulate emigration from the United Kingdom to America. A knowledge of the Acts is important, because they show how both the Imperial government in London and the United States Congress in Washington felt compelled, against the spirit of the times, to interfere more and more in the working of the passenger trade. Both Parliament and Congress were moved to pass these Acts by a Christian humanitarianism, and there is no doubt that over the years the conditions of the passenger trade did improve. But it is most important never to take the provisions of these Acts at face value, and never to assume that what Parliament or Congress enacted was put into effect. Some provisions of the British Acts were of their nature incapable of enforcement. Many provisions of both British and American laws, although enforceable, rarely were enforced, because to do so would have taken an army of customs and emigration officers, and there were never more than a few.

At their worst, some clauses of the Acts are laughable. Even the most elementary requirements of the Acts were not dependably enforced.

This is demonstrated in Chapters 12 and 13 of this book.

At the very least, the Acts should always be read sceptically, and it should never be assumed that they are more than statements of a government's well-meaning intentions.

For an extended and most brilliant analysis of the British Passenger Acts and their enforcement, see *A Pattern of Government Growth 1800–60* by Oliver MacDonagh, London, MacGibbon and Kee, 1961. Professor MacDonagh's chief concern is not with emigration as such: it is to demonstrate the development of modern government, and to identify the forces which brought the modern state into existence. To show these forces at work, he chose to study not the Factory Acts, the Public Health Acts, or the Education Acts, but the Passenger Acts; and quite apart from its main purpose, his book is the most fully documented and closely argued account of the real working of these Acts that has been published.

Here, then, are summaries of the main provisions of the British and American Acts which governed emigration in the period 1846–55.

British Acts

1842 (6 & 7 Vic cap 107)

Each passenger to be given weekly seven pounds of bread, biscuit, flour, oatmeal, or rice, or the equivalent in potatoes. This was to be supplied uncooked, and was intended as no more than an insurance against starvation. Passengers were expected to bring their own sea-store.

Emigrants to be paid 1s. a day subsistence money if the vessel did not sail on the date stipulated on the contract ticket.

Passenger brokers and agents to be licensed.

Only three steerage passengers to be carried for each five tons of the vessel's registered tonnage. Each passenger to have at least ten square feet of space between decks.

Two children under fourteen to count as one statute passenger. Children under one year not to be counted at all.

Drinking water to be carried in sweet containers.

Spirits to be neither sold nor drunk on board, on pain of a fine of up to £100.

At those ports where emigration officers were stationed, they and not the customs officers were responsible for carrying the Act into effect—for inspecting water and provisions, assessing the seaworthiness of the vessel, and prosecuting for breaches of the Act.

1847 (10 & 11 Vic cap 103)

This Act was extended to cover all vessels carrying more than one steerage passenger for every twenty-five tons register.

Vessels putting back to British ports were to be provisioned afresh, and the emigrants to be compensated for the delay.

All vessels to be surveyed by two or more surveyors appointed by the emigration commissioners.

The emigration officers were given wider discretion. They could vary the amount and kind of food to be issued to passengers, could determine whether vessels were properly ventilated, and were sole judges of the competence of crews.

1848 (11 & 12 Vic cap 6)

The space for each steerage passenger was increased from ten to twelve square feet.

Each vessel carrying more than 100 passengers to carry a surgeon, whose competence was to be determined by the emigration officer, or to allow each passenger fourteen instead of twelve feet of space.

Emigrants to be certified free of infectious diseases before embarkation by doctors appointed by the emigration officer.

The emigration commissioners were empowered to issue Orders in Council to regulate life at sea.

Each vessel with more than 100 emigrants to provide a cook and cooking places.

Where a broker or other person claimed, in defence to a prosecution brought by an emigration officer, that he was not caught by the Act, the burden of proof was placed on the defendant to prove that he was not caught, rather than on the Crown to prove that he was.

1849 (12 & 13 Vic cap 33)

The berthing together of single men and women was forbidden.

The food ration was increased. As well as the weekly seven pounds of food stipulated by the 1842 Act, oatmeal, tea, rice, sugar, and molasses were to be given out twice a week. (But there was still no meat or vegetables, the ration was still only meant to prevent starvation, and passengers still had to bring much of their own food.)

Brokers had to give sureties of £200 for good behaviour, and magistrates could revoke a broker's licence for any breach of the Passenger Acts.

All vessels carrying more than fifty passengers had either to carry a surgeon or give each passenger fourteen feet of space.

1851 (14 & 15 Vic cap 1)

The Commissioners of Emigration could at their discretion allow steamships (which made much faster passages than sailing vessels) to carry less water and food.

Masters of foreign vessels had to give bonds as sureties that they would carry out the Passenger Acts.

1852 (15 & 26 Vic cap 4)

Vessels sailing without clearance might be forfeit to the Crown.

The number in one berth was reduced from four to two. This meant that each passenger still had only six feet by one foot six inches, but the old six-foot-square berths were now divided into two by a plank.

Single men to be accommodated in a separate compartment.

Sick bays, and at least four privies, to be provided.

The emigration officer could reject any cargo which in his opinion might endanger the life, safety, or health of the passengers.

Food to be issued daily, and already cooked. If there were more than 400 passengers, there had to be two cooks.

All vessels carrying more than 100 passengers had to have a passengers' steward.

All vessels carrying more than 500 passengers to have a surgeon.

Masters to give bonds of £2,000 for good behaviour, and brokers bonds of £1,000.

1855 (18 & 19 Vic cap 119)

All vessels carrying more than thirty passengers, or more than one passenger for every fifty tons register, came within the Acts.

Two children under twelve (as against the old rule of two under fourteen) to count as a statute passenger.

Each passenger to have fifteen square feet.

Each vessel carrying more than 300 passengers to carry a surgeon.

Meat, potatoes, and peas were added to the ship's rations, and meals had to be issued daily, ready-cooked. For the first time passengers could rely on the ship for all their food.

An emigration officer could object to any mode of cargo stowage, and the commissioners, in an epidemic, could prohibit emigration from any particular port.

The subsistence allowance to be paid to emigrants if the vessel's departure was delayed, became 1s. 6d. a day.

United States Acts

1819. An Act regulating passenger-ships and vessels. March 2, 1819.

No more than two passengers to be carried for every five tons of the vessel's register. Two children under eight to count as one passenger.

If the number of passengers carried exceeded the legal complement by twenty, the ship might be forfeit to the United States.

For each passenger the vessel should carry sixty gallons of water, 100 pounds of salted provisions, one gallon of vinegar, and 100 pounds of ship's bread. [This is a strange clause. It is made clear that this food is over and above that provided by passengers for their own use, and it is nowhere stated that the food carried should be given out to the passengers; but at the same time, the clause provides that for every day a passenger is kept short on allowance, a fine of three dollars shall be recoverable from the master or owner and paid to the passenger.]

The ship's captain was required to give a passenger list to the collector of customs at the port of disembarkation, and the collectors were required to make quarterly returns of these lists to the Secretary of State.

1847. An Act to regulate the carriage of passengers in merchant vessels. February 22, 1847.

No more than two passengers to be carried for every five tons of the vessel's registered tonnage, and each passenger to have fourteen square feet of space.

No more than two tiers of berths, each berth to be six feet by one foot six inches.

Two children under eight to count as one adult passenger. Children under one year not to be counted at all.

1847 (An amending Act). March 2, 1847. Repealing so much of the Act of February 22 as allowed two children under eight to be counted as one adult passenger. [So all children over one year now counted as full passengers.]

1848. An Act to provide for the ventilation of passenger-vessels, and for other purposes. May 17, 1848.

Each ship carrying more than fifty passengers to have one ventilator for the between decks, or two ventilators if more than 100 passengers were carried.

Each ship carrying more than fifty passengers to have a cooking range for the passengers' use. Larger ships to have at least one range for every 200 passengers.

For each passenger, the ship had to carry ten pounds of rice, ten pounds of oatmeal, ten pounds of peas, thirty-five pounds of potatoes, a pint of vinegar, sixty gallons of fresh water, and ten pounds of pork. And at least one-tenth of these amounts was to be given weekly in advance to each passenger, commencing on the day of sailing, each passenger being able to recover a fine of three dollars from the master for each day on short rations.

The captain empowered to maintain good discipline and habits of cleanliness among the passengers.

One privy to be provided for each 100 passengers.

The restriction of two passengers for each five tons register was removed. [Each passenger was still entitled to fourteen square feet of space.]

1849. An Act to extend the provisions of all laws now in force relating to the carriage of passengers in merchant-vessels. March 3, 1849.

This act extended nothing. The only clause which related to Atlantic emigration repealed the clause of the 1848 Act which specified that certain amounts of certain foods should be given out weekly, and replaced this by a provision that the owner or master should furnish the passengers, or cause them to furnish for themselves, 'a sufficient supply of good and wholesome food'.

1855. An Act to regulate the carriage of passengers in steamships and other vessels. March 3, 1855.

This is a consolidating statute, and repealed all earlier Passenger Acts.

Each passenger to have fourteen square feet of space, no ship to carry more than one passenger for every two tons register, two children under eight to count as one statute passenger, and the master to be fined $50 with the alternative of six months' imprisonment for every passenger carried over the legal complement.

No more than two tiers of berths, and each passenger to have a separate berth six feet by two.

The 1848 clauses to do with cooking ranges and privies were re-enacted.

Food. Specific rations were again introduced, and in greater quantity. For each passenger, a vessel had to carry twenty pounds of navy bread, fifteen pounds of rice, fifteen pounds of oatmeal, fifteen pounds of peas or beans, twenty pounds of potatoes, a pint of vinegar, sixty gallons of fresh water, ten pounds of pork and ten pounds of beef, a tenth of all these amounts to be given weekly in advance to each passenger, who could recover a fine of three dollars from the master for each day he was put on short rations. Furthermore, if a master wilfully failed to distribute this food he could be fined $1,000 and imprisoned for a year.

The old clauses about discipline and ventilation were re-enacted.

The Act was extended to steamships.

For each passenger over eight years old who died on the voyage, the master was required to pay $10 to the collector of customs at the port of entry.

The American Acts are reprinted in full in *History of Immigration to the United States* by William Bromwell, New York, 1856.

The Forfeiture Clauses

The effect of the forfeiture clauses in both British and American Acts is not clear.

According to the British Act of 1852, a vessel sailing without clearance from the emigration officer might be forfeit to the Crown, but I do not know of any ship which was held forfeit.

According to the American Act of 1819 a vessel carrying twenty more passengers than its legal complement was deemed forfeit to the United States, and that clause of the 1819 Act remained in force until 1855. I do not know how many vessels, if any, were ever taken and *kept* by the United States government under this Act. Many were seized, but it seems to have been the custom to remit the penalty of seizure on payment of a fine. *An Abstract from State Department Records, Pardons Granted from 1794–1853* (National Archives, Washington, Record Group 204) lists many pardon cases. In one flagrant case the British ship *Blanche* entered New Orleans in 1850 carrying eighty-four passengers over her legal complement. (This was the case which led to the dismissal of the chief emigration officer at Liverpool, and is described in full in Chapter 13.) The *Blanche* was seized, together with another British vessel, the *Ottilia*, but according to a letter from the British consul at New Orleans (C.O. 384/88, item 357, dated September 8, 1851) both were 'released by the President of the U.S. from the penalty of confiscation . . . on payment of fifty dollars for each passenger carried by them over the number allowed by Act of Congress'.

The 1855 Act of Congress repealed the 1819 Act, and its forfeiture clause. The 1855 Act relied on heavy fines, and on the threat of up to a year's imprisonment for the captain, but even so expressly retained for the government a large discretionary power of dispensation, allowing the Secretary of State, 'upon such conditions as he shall think proper, [to] discontinue any such prosecutions, or remit or modify such penalties'.

Emigration from the United Kingdom in the Years 1835-60

Year	British North America	United States	Australia & New Zealand	All Other Places	Totals for Each Year
1835	16	27	2	·3	45
1836	34	38	3	·3	75
1837	30	37	5	·3	72
1838	5	14	14	·3	33
1839	13	34	16	·2	62
1840	32	41	16	2	91
1841	38	45	33	3	119
1842	54	64	9	2	128
1843	24	28	3	2	57
1844	23	44	2	2	71
1845	32	59	1	2	96
1846	43	82	2	2	130
1847	110	142	5	1	258
1848	31	188	24	5	248
1849	41	219	32	6	299
1850	33	233	16	9	281
1851	43	267	22	4	336
1852	33	244	88	4	369
1853	35	231	61	3	330
1854	44	193	83	3	323
1855	18	103	52	3	177
1856	16	112	45	4	177
1857	21	127	61	4	213
1858	10	60	39	5	114
1859	7	70	31	12	120
1860	10	87	24	7	128

These figures, expressed in thousands, are taken from Appendix No. 1 to the *Thirty-third General Report of the Emigration Commission-*

ers, H.C., 1873, Vol. 18. They show how much greater emigration always was to the United States than to anywhere else after 1835, and also how much greater the emigration of 1846–55 was than that of the years before and after. But the figures should not be taken as showing more than general trends. They appear to have a precision and accuracy which they do not in fact possess. For reasons explained in Chapter 13, all British government figures are likely to be inaccurate, particularly for the years 1845–50. For those years, the figures for emigrants to the United States are nothing more than an adding together of ships masters' own statements of the number of passengers they had on board. The emigration officers in that time did not count the passengers as they were supposed to, and since no master was going to admit to carrying more passengers than was allowed by law, the figures are certainly underestimates.

The Proportion of Emigrants who were Irish

It is impossible to state the proportion of Irish emigrants to other British emigrants who left the United Kingdom. The statistics for emigrants leaving British and Irish ports did not differentiate between the Irish and the English, Scottish, and Welsh.

As for the proportion of Irish entering the United States, this cannot be stated with any accuracy either, because the U.S. State Department figures only made a half-hearted attempt to distinguish Irish from English. Some collectors of customs in some years did make the distinction, but others did not, so in the same returns there are sometimes two headings, one showing emigrants from Ireland, and the other emigrants from Great Britain and Ireland combined. The only figures which seem likely to be accurate are those of the New York Commissioners of Emigration, who from 1847 onwards did regularly distinguish between Irish and other United Kingdom immigrants. Furthermore, these figures are probably in themselves more accurate than those of the collectors of customs. The customs were corrupt, and had more pressing and profitable duties to perform. The emigration commissioners were solely concerned with emigrants, and moreover collected $1.50 from each, which at least gave them an interest in making a complete count, and collecting from everybody. Of course it might be that the commissioners' officers were corrupt too, and stated that they had collected the $1.50 from fewer emigrants than they in fact had, but although frequent charges of corruption were brought against the commissioners, they were never accused of this fraud.

Here are the numbers, in thousands, of British (English, Scottish, and Welsh), Irish, and Germans entering New York in 1847–55. The Germans are included for the purpose of comparison, because after subjects of the United Kingdom they were the most numerous immigrants of the time. The figures are for New York alone, and not for the whole of the U.S.A. About two thirds of all emigrants to the United States entered at New York.

	1847	1848	1849	1850	1851	1852	1853	1854	1855
British	12	31	39	37	38	42	35	37	28
Irish	53	91	112	117	163	118	113	82	43
German	53	52	56	46	70	119	120	177	53

The figures are taken from Table A to the *Annual Reports of the Commissioners of Emigration of the State of New York, 1847–60.*

APPENDIX D

Occupations of Emigrants to the U.S.A. in 1852

Occupations	Males	Females	Sex not stated	Total
Merchants	12,695	—	—	12,795
Farmers	50,491	—	—	50,491
Mechanics	26,483	—	—	26,483
Mariners	813	—	—	813
Miners	2,605	—	—	2,605
Laborers	88,848	—	—	88,848
Shoemakers	20	—	—	20
Tailors	34	—	—	34
Seamstresses and Milliners	—	309	—	309
Weavers and Spinners	39	6	—	45
Physicians	282	—	—	282
Lawyers	106	—	—	106
Clergymen	129	—	—	129
Clerks	107	—	—	107
Musicians	36	12	—	48
Manufacturers	161	—	—	161
Millers	34	—	—	34
Teachers	21	3	—	24
Engineers	103	—	—	103
Butchers	39	—	—	39
Artists	179	2	—	181
Hatters	3	—	—	3
Painters	5	—	—	5
Printers	1	—	—	1
Bakers	40	—	—	40
Masons	18	—	—	18
Servants	33	3,282	—	3,315
Other occupations	462	10	—	472
Not stated	61,130	160,121	66	221,317
Total	245,017	163,745	66	408,828

These are the U.S. State Department figures for a sample year, 1852. They are probably neither accurate nor comprehensive, but they do give an idea of what persons entering the United States said their occupations were. The figures are for all persons, including U.S. citizens, entering at all American ports. In 1852, 25,740 were U.S. citizens, and the rest aliens. The high number of merchants probably included many such U.S. citizens, and many aliens who came to America to do business and return, and were not therefore emigrants at all. Most of those written down as farmers were more likely labourers. Perhaps the Irish were naturally assumed by the U.S. customs officers to be labourers, but the English and Germans were allowed to call themselves farmers. The unusually high number of miners must have included many on their way to California.

Emigrants Helped by the New York Commissioners

Year	Number of Aliens arrived, for whom Commutation and Hospital moneys were paid, or bonds demanded	Number treated and cared for at Emigrant Refuge and Hospitals, Ward's Island	Number treated at Marine Hospital	Number supplied temporarily with board and lodging	Number temporarily relieved with money, &c.	Number provided with employment	Number of persons forwarded	Grand Total of persons treated, cared for, relieved, forwarded, &c., by and at the expense of the Commissioners of Emigration
1847	129,062	1,629	6,474	—	503	—	798	10,594
1848	189,176	4,057	8,661	—	6,640	—	2,102	27,523
1849	220,791	8,320	6,159	—	16,854	—	2,999	41,258
1850	212,603	10,156	3,411	27,314	—	8,000	2,301	57,386
1851	289,601	14,939	6,343	23,941	—	18,204	7,391	85,026
1852	300,992	15,182	8,887	117,568	—	14,971	4,601	181,005
1853	284,945	14,365	4,796	24,317	20,197	14,334	3,262	91,774
1854	319,223	15,950	4,762	51,569	17,516	13,964	4,608	120,894
1855	136,233	12,901	2,402	59,520	34,405	15,151	4,996	142,357

The last column includes all who received any sort of help, either directly from the commissioners in New York City, or from city hospitals or almshouses, or from institutions in other counties of New York State. In 1847, only one out of twelve was helped; in 1852 nearly two out of three. In 1855 the number of emigrants helped exceeded that of emigrants arriving at the port. This is because 1855 was a year of slump and unemployment, and many of those helped were from the previous year's immigration.

The figures are from the annual reports of the Commissioners of Emigration of New York State.

Emigrants' Stated Destinations

This table, from the annual reports of the Commissioners of Emigration for the State of New York, shows the stated destination of emigrants entering at New York from August 1 to December 31, 1855.

New York	19,489	Vermont	168
Pennsylvania	4,469	Louisiana	60
Illinois	3,444	South Carolina	80
Wisconsin	4,667	Maine	143
Ohio	3,250	Tennessee	72
Massachusetts	2,037	Georgia	70
Canada West	3,346	New Hampshire	71
New Jersey	1,119	Delaware	49
Unknown	957	New Brunswick	2
Michigan	1,648	Texas	5
Connecticut	829	Kansas	1
Iowa	795	North Carolina	11
Missouri	434	Mississippi	6
Indiana	881	Alabama	7
Rhode Island	551	Nova Scotia	80
Maryland	485	South America	25
Uncertain	317	Arkansas	8
California	447	Florida	13
Minnesota	127	Oregon	1
Utah	250	West Indies	2
Virginia	292	District of Columbia	202
Kentucky	183	TOTAL	51,114

The figures are for emigrants from all countries, not only from the United Kingdom. Those going to Wisconsin or Minnesota are likely to have been Scandinavian, and many of those going to Pennsylvania are likely to have been German. The figures are only for the last third of the 1855 emigration season, because they were not collected until the emigrant depot at Castle Garden was opened. They do not purport to do more than state the intentions of emigrants entering in part of one year and only at one port—and it was also an untypical season of little emigration because of war in Europe and slump in America. Nevertheless, the figures are given, for what they are worth, because they were the first of their kind to be collected.

Index

Compiled by Lesley Fox-Strangways Vane

Adams, John Quincy (as Secretary of State),
American policy towards immigrants, 22
Advertisements, 17, 61, 64, 66, 67–9, 86, 90, 91, 92, 117, 130, 171, 239, 241
in American directories, 155, 159
Advice to would-be emigrants, 17
Samuel Sidney's 28–31
Irish Emigrant Society's, 41
a clergyman's, 50–1
William Chambers's, 61–2
Albany, N.Y., 180, 182, 185
Almshouse Commissioners (New York), 160
America and the Americans, 60–1, 65, 93, 101, 193–4, 231–5
Cobbett's view, 28
Chambers's view, 30–1
the food, 32
created for emigrants, 39
profits to, from emigrants, 39–40
views of Dickens, de Tocqueville, Martineau, and Mrs Trollope, 43–4
of Anthony Trollope and Sir Francis Head, 44–5
of *Illustrated London News*, 45
of Melville, 46
St Patrick's Day toast, 46
view of Jacob Harvey, 47
size of, 47
views of Vere Foster, Chambers, etc., 47
described in emigrants' guides, 47–8
place of boasting and sickness, 49
treatment of women, 49–50
slavery, 50
disloyalty 50–1
servants, 52–3
Hawthorne's view, 53
ballads about, 54–5
Passenger Acts, 134–5
first sight of, 169–70
anti-emigrant feeling, 218–30
Castle Garden, 242–9

American Notes (by Charles Dickens), 43
American Protestant Magazine, 227
Amicus Populi, opponent of Malthus, 37–8
Anti-Catholicism, 221, 227–30
Arctic (American steam packet), 88, 93, 242
Arrival, The (a poem), 51
Astor Place Riots, 221
Australia, 190–1, 194, 226
free passages to, 21

Ballads and poems about America and emigration, 33, 34, 37, 42, 51, 52, 54–5, 84, 203, 246
The Ocean Monarch, 122
Baring Bros (bankers), 203
Benson, Dr (of the *Wandsworth*), 140, 154
Bishop of Montreal, 144, 151, 167, 197
Black Ball Line, 67, 86, 88, 90–1, 92, 242
Black Star Line, 88, 90–1, 95, 106, 203, 237
Blue and Red Swallow Tail (packet lines), 88, 242
Boarding of ships, 81–2
Bonds, 70, 135, 153, 224, 231, Appendix E
Booth, Sir Robert Gore (Irish landlord), 200–3 passim
Boston, 223, 226–34 passim, 246
Boston Atlas, 227
Boston Daily Advertiser, 227
Bremer, Frederika (Swedish novelist), on England (1851), 46
British Protective Emigrant Society, New York, 160, 164, 176
Brokers, 67, 135, 186, 198, 206, 243
the Tapscotts, 68–71

Harnden and Co., 71–2
Saul, 72
Byrnes and Co., 86, 92
Bromwell, William (*History of Immigration into the United States*), Appendix A
Brown, William, M.P., 212
Brutality aboard ship, 95–9, 102–8, 247
Buchanan, A. C. (chief agent at Quebec), 137, 140, 151
Buchanan, James, 137
Buffalo, 180, 181, 192
Bunch, Robert (British vice-consul, New York), 92–3
and the *Washington*, 106–7
Burials at sea, 23–4, 105, 118, 146
Byrnes and Co., P. W. (brokers), 86, 92

California, 245
Calvert, Colonel (inventor), 147–8
Canada, emigration to, 21, 22, 24, 40, 44–5, 47, 50–1, 129, 168, 192–3, 212, 225
lack of servants in, 52
collections for starving Irish, 128
during 1847, 134–7
Grosse Isle and typhus, 137–54
Canadian Navigation Company, 240
Canal boats, 180, 181, 182, 192
Canal Street, New York, 178, 248
Captains of emigrant ships, 23–4, 74, 75, 81, 82–3, 90, 91, 96, 98–9, 101–14 passim, 120, 123–7 passim, 134, 135, 136, 138, 145, 150, 156, 179, 200, 201, 206, 209–10, 212, 216–17, Appendix A
American and British compared, 92–4

Cargo, 22, 81, 87, 89, 101, 102, 110, 118, 121, 123, 205
Carnegie, Andrew, 25
Cartwright, Samuel, M.D., letters on hygiene, 19
Cass, Lewis (as Secretary of State), 98–9
Castle Garden, New York, 242–5, 249
Cazeau, Charles Félix (priest), 147
Chambers, William (magazine editor), 35, 229
a voyage, 18
his view of America, 30, 47, 50
advice to gentry, 30–1
advice to emigrants, 61–2
Chambers's Edinburgh Journal, 49–50, 87
Chartists, 33, 37
Chickering, Jesse (writer), on emigrants, 23
Children's Aid Society of New York, 164
Chinese emigrants, 22, 191
Chisholm, Caroline, defence of emigrants, 60
Cholera, 25, 79, 91, 118, 137, 171, 172, 174, 213
Chronicle (London), 203
Citizens' and Strangers' Pictorial and Business Guide, New York, 168
Clippers, 89
Cobbett, William, opinion of America, 28; 37
Cobden, Richard, 57
Collins, E. K., and Collins Line, 65, 88, 93, 236
Colonial Land and Emigration Board, London, 21, 189–96. See also Commissioners of Emigration
Colonial Office, 137, 166, 190 and Inman, 238–41, 245

Commissioners of Emigration, English, 21, 78, 87, 138, 140, 204, 206
their work and policies, 190–6
Order in Council, 207
and Hodder, 207–12
and Inman, 238–41 passim
Commissioners of Emigration, New York, 174, 177, 196, 214–17, 248
and Castle Garden, 242–5
Appendix E
Conditions on voyages, 17–20
from Ireland to Liverpool, 57–9
brutality, 95–9
accounts of de Vere and Melville, 100–2, of Garnham, 102, of Foster on the *Washington*, 102–8
pleasant voyages, 108–10 passim
crowding, 110–12
food, 112–14
surgeons and remedies, 115–18
Coney Island, 173
Convicts, 225–6
Conybeare, The Rev. W. J. (writer of novel *Perversion*), description of an emigrant, 53–4
Corn Laws, repeal of, 34
Cricket in New York, 167–8
Cunard, Samuel, and his ships, 81, 113, 120, 189, 236–7
Custis, Dr. J. (ship's surgeon), 108–9, 207–8, 216–17
Customs, United States, 210, 214, 216, 217

Daley, Charles P. (chief justice, Court of Common Pleas, New York), 165
Daley, George P. (passenger broker), 215–16
broking a racket, 181–6, passim

Dalton, Maurice (runner), 74
Deportations, 227
Depot, for emigrants, Buchanan's
   offer, 137
   proposed, Liverpool, 195–6
   Castle Garden, New York,
   242–5
Destinations of emigrants,
   Appendix F
Destitution, 129, 201, 248
   escape from, by emigration, 31–2
   in New York, 160–4, 176
De Vere, Stephen (landowner and
   philanthropist), on conditions
   aboard, 100–2 passim; 142, 149,
   196
Dickens, Charles, opinion of
   America, 43; 148
Dillon, Gregory (President, Irish
   Emigrant Society, New York),
   177, 214, 234
Disinfectant, 147–8
Doctors, medical inspections, 78–
   80, 169, 243
   dead from typhus, 140, 141,
   150, 154
   in America, 170–8 passim
   also, 203, 206
Domestic Manners of the Americans
   (Mrs Trollope), 43–4
Douglas, Dr. George M. (medical
   superintendent, Grosse Isle), 115
   during 1847, 137–54
Dramatic Line (of packets), 69, 88,
   242
Duke of Newcastle (Colonial
   Secretary), 238–40
Duross, John (Constable, Cork
   Constabulary), 57
Dysentery, 24, 105, 140, 145, 150

Elgin, Earl of (Governor-General
   of Canada), 136, 137, 152, 201

Elliot, Thomas Frederick (chair-
   man, Emigration Commis-
   sioners, and later at Colonial
   Office), 190, 191–2, 208, 210
   and Inman's complaints,
   238–40
Ely, Dr., 178
Emigrant Settlement Association
   (Toronto), 137
Emigrant Ship and other Poems, 54
Emigrant's Dream (poem), 51–2
Emigrants' Employment Associ-
   ation, 38
Emigrants' Penny Magazine,
   (Plymouth), 38
   objects of emigration, 39
Emigrants' individual stories—
   Henry Johnson, 23–5
   Andrew Carnegie, 25
   Paddy O'Dougherty, 25–6,
   203
   Pat Waters, 26
   Maria Campbell, 26
   Catherine Haggerty, 26
   Thomas Garry, 26–7
   Bridget O'Donnell, 31–2
   Harriet Whitmore, 36–7
   Thomas Maguire, 59–60
   Anne Doyle, 70–1
   Eliza O'Neil, 71
   Robert Garnham (cabin
   passenger), 102, 117, 178–9
   Martin Donald Macleod, 108
   R. C. Walters, 122–5
   John Ryan, 126–7
   Robert Whyte, 145–6, 152
   John Jacob Astor, 156
   John Hall, 174–5
   Andrew Hannon, 175
   Henry Lloyd, 175–6
   Elizabeth Daly, 178
   James Heeslop, 181
   John Morrissey, 187–8
   Owen Gilgan, 201

Emigrants' individual
  stories—*cont.*
  Michael Foley, 203
  Joseph Hetherington, 221–2
  Mary Williams, 227
  Edward Moore, 247
  William Harrison, 247
  John Williams, 247–8
Emigrant vessels—
  Wiscasset, 25
  Syria, 26, 249
  Perseverance, 26
  Wandsworth, 26, 138–9
  Yorkshire, 67, 90, 93
  Garrick, 69, 88, 89
  Triton, 71
  Star of the West, 82
  Montezuma, 86
  James Baine, 87
  Constitution, 88, 92
  Washington, 90–1, 102–8, 207,
    208, 216, 227
  Cultivator, 97
  Ocean Monarch, 98, 120–2
  Northumberland, 102
  George Canning, 114
  Fingal, 118
  Exmouth, 119–20
  Powhattan, 120
  California Packet, 120
  Charles Bartlett, 120
  Annie Jane, 122–5
  E.Z., 126–7
  Amelia Mary, 135
  Elizabeth and Sarah, 136
  Virginius, 145
  Naomi, 145
  Sisters, 150
  Erin's Queen, 150
  Ceylon, 170
  Kossuth, 170–1
  Aeolus, 200–1
  Yeoman, 200–1
  Lady Sale, 200–1

  Eliza Liddell, 201
  Blanche, 209–10, 213, 293–4
  Maguinticock, 226
  Albatross, 226
  City of Glasgow and *City of
    Manchester*, 236–41
  Wandering Jew, 247
Emigrant vessels,
  conditions aboard, 17–20, 22–3,
    40
  between Cork or Dublin and
    Liverpool, 57–9, 126
  difficulty of boarding, 81–2
  description of, 85–6
  American and British compared,
    87, 91–2
  packet lines, 88–9
  packets and clippers, size and
    numbers, 89–91
  captains, 92–4
  crew, 94–5
  brutality, 95–9
  in 1847, 146–50 passim
  arriving at New York, 170–9
    passim
  sent by Irish landlords, 200–2
  rules for (1848), 207
  steam, 189, 236–42
  last of the sailing packets, 242
  worked passages, 247
Emigration Commissioners, see
  Commissioners of Emigration
Emigration officers, 21, 95, 202,
  209, 216, 239–41 passim
  their powers, 206
  Appendix A and B
Emmet, Dr. Thomas, 176
English as emigrants, 148, 166–7,
  176, 244, 246, 247–8, Appendix
  C
*English Orphans; or, A Home in the
  New World* (Mary J. Holmes),
  175
Erie Canal, 180

Famine in Ireland, 128–34, 202
Fares, 18, 22–3, 37, 68, 74, 82,
    126, 135, 136
    Cork to Liverpool, 57
    charged by runners, New York,
        180–1, 182, 198, 202, 205
    paid by parishes, 225
    on steamships, 238, 239, 246
Ferland, the Rev. Jean Baptiste,
    144
Fitzwilliam, Earl (Irish landlord),
    his tenants, 199
Food on board ships, see
    Provisions
Forfeiture of ships, 293
Forrest, Edwin (actor), 221
Foster, Vere (philanthropist), 34
    on size of America, 47
    and the *Washington*, 102–8, 207
Frank Leslie's Illustrated Newspaper,
    New York, 158, 166
Franklin, Benjamin, encourage-
    ments to strangers, 22
Freeman's Journal, Dublin, 130
Friendly Sons of St. Patrick
    (Society), 46, 165

Gallagher, Charles (customs
    officer, New York, and runner),
    185, 217
Galway Vindicator, 129
Gardner, Awful (runner), 186–7
Gardner, Henry J. (Governor of
    Massachusetts), 218–20, 224
Garnham, Robert (gentleman), a
    voyage, 102, 117, 178–9
Germans as emigrants, 22, 75, 82,
    102, 146, Appendix C and F
*Gleason's Pictorial Drawing Room
    Companion*, Boston, 170, 234
Grand Jury, (New York County),
    177
Great Exhibition of 1851, 46

Greeley, Horace (of the *New York
    Tribune*), 229
Grey, Earl (Colonial Secretary),
    132, 167, 189, 195, 196, 204, 225
    letters to Lord Elgin, 136–7,
        152
    on Russell's colonial policy,
        193–4
    and the dismissal of Hodder,
        210–12 passim
Grier, Mr. Justice, 232–3
Grinnell, Henry and Moses
    (packet owners), 88
Griscom, Dr. John H. (general
    agent to New York Commis-
    sioners of Emigration), 170, 176
Grosse Isle, 115, 137–54
    today, 249
Guidebooks for emigrants, 103
    descriptions of America, 47–8
    encouragement and recipes, 61
    Tapscott's, 68, 70

Hale, Edward E. (writer on
    emigration), 166
Harnden and Co. (brokers), 71–2,
    86, 185
Harvey, Jacob, 47
Hawes, Benjamin (Colonial
    Under-Secretary), 167
Hawthorne, Nathaniel (novelist
    and American consul at
    Liverpool), view of America,
    53
    description of Liverpool, 64–6
    on ships, 86–7
    on captains, 93–4
    brutality aboard ships, 95–9,
        247
Head, Sir Francis (Lieutenant-
    Governor of Upper Canada),
    view of America, 44–5
Head Tax Cases, 231–2

Herald (New York), 70

Hetherington, Joseph, lynched, 221–2

Hobart, Lord (with Board of Trade, London), 103, 106

Hodder, Lieutenant Thomas, R.N. (chief emigration officer, Liverpool), 68, 71, 72, 80, 83–4, 106
his career and dismissal, 209–12

Hutchinson, Lieutenant, R.N. (harbour master, Kingstown), 111

Icebergs, 90, 120, 241

Illustrated London News, on America, 45; 56, 197

Illustrated News, New York, story of Paddy O'Dougherty, 25–6

Inman, William (shipowner), 236–42

Inspections, medical, in England, 77–8
in Canada, 142
in America, 109, 173–4, 243

Ireland, 20, 56, 67, 120
the potato famine, 128–34, 165, 166, 245

Irish as emigrants, 21, 23–7, 31–2, 35, 76, 84, 100, 111, 113, 125, 126, 244, 247, Appendix C
advice to, 41, 46
from Ireland to Liverpool, 56–62
and the potato famine, 128–34
and typhus (1847), 137–54
in New York, 160–6
shovelling out, 198–202
and remittances, 203–4
feelings against, 219–35 passim

Irish Emigrant Society, New York, address to Irish people, 41; 164–6 passim, 177, 214

Irish Felon, Dublin, 130

Italians as emigrants, 22

Johns, the Rev. John (Liverpool), 131–2

Johnson, Dr. James, 174

Kapp, Friedrich (Commissioner of Emigration, New York), view on treatment of emigrants, 61, 184

Kingston, William H. G. (writer), reasons for emigration, 35–6

Know-Nothings, 219, 227–30, 246

Kossuth, Louis, 159, 165, 221, 243

Lamartine (poet and statesman), on English *proletaires* (1850), 46

Lancaster, J. J., M.D. (medical officer, Liverpool), description of medicals, 80–1

Landlords, Irish, 32, 47, 101, 132–3, 150
and shovelling out, 198–202, 225

Latter Day Saints' Millennial Star, 197, 198

Lean, Lieutenant R.N. (emigration officer, London), on medicals, 78–80

Ledoyen (inventor), 147–8

Letters (by emigrants or about emigration)—Samuel Cartwright, M.D., to Senate Committee, 19
between Henry Johnson and wife, 24
Thomas Garry to wife, 26–7
Hawthorne's to Washington about brutality, 96–9

Letters—*cont.*
    Foster to captain, 103, and to
        Hobart, 106
    from Martin Donald Macleod,
        108
    Micheal OBrien, Corporal, 132
    from 86 Irishmen to Lord
        Monteagle, 132
    Douglas to Buchanan, 141
    citizens of Montreal to Lord
        John Russell, 149–50
    Grey to Elgin, 152–3
    boy in New York writing home,
        158
    Mayor of Toronto to Elgin,
        152–3
    to magistrate from Owen
        Gilgan, 201
    Inman to Colonial Secretary
        and Emigration Commis-
        sioners, 238–41
Limerick, 114, 120, 126, 129,
    130
Lincoln, Abraham, 229
Lindsay, William, M.P., 205
Liverpool, 46, 57, 59, 62, 93, 96,
    102, 114, 120, 122, 155, 164,
    180, 227, 238, 245
    servant girls in, 53
    its trade and buildings, 63–4
    Hawthorne's description, 65–6
    brokers, 67–72
    runners, 72–7
    lodging houses and keepers,
        74–7
    medical inspections, 77–80
    difficulties of boarding ships,
        81–2
    departures, 82–4
    destitute Irish in, 131–2
    emigration officers at, 209–13
    today, 248
Liverpool and Philadelphia
    Steamship Line, the, 238

*Liverpool Herald and Shipping
    Gazette*, 119, 120
Lodging-houses and keepers, 67,
    72, 74–7, 180, 215
Lynching, 221–2

MacDonagh, Professor Oliver
    (*A Pattern of Government
    Growth*, 1800–60), Appendix A,
    288
Macdougall, Captain P. L., view
    of England, 33
McGauran, the Rev. Bernard, 146
McLean, Mr. Justice, 232
Macready, William Charles
    (actor), 221
Mail steamers, 236, 237, 240
Maine, Sir Henry (jurist), 205–6
Malthus, Thomas (clergyman
    and political economist),
    Essay on Population, 37–8
Marcus, the Rev. Moses (member
    of the British Protective
    Emigrant Society), 160, 166
Marshall, Frederick (boarding-
    house keeper), 75–7
Martin Chuzzlewit, 43
Martineau, Harriet, view of
    America, 43
Massachusetts, reports to House of
    Representatives and to Senate
    on emigrants, 60, 135
    Gardner's address, 218–19
    anti-emigrant feeling, 223–7
        passim, 233, 241
Melville, Herman, 107, 216, 223
    emigrant ship in squall, 20
    on America, 46
    comparing Liverpool and New
        York, 64
    on runners, 72–3
    on German emigrants, 82
    a voyage, 101–2

Millionaires in New York, 156, 168

Minturn, Robert Bowne (ship owner and emigration commissioner, New York), evidence to House of Lords Committee, 40–1; also 88, 178, 216

Montamis, H., 59

Monteagle, Lord (Irish landowner), 47, 132

Montreal, 141, 142, 148, 149, 151, 153–4, 192, 249

Monuments, 151, 153–4

Moore, John Bramley (Mayor of Liverpool), 75, 87, 195–6

Morals, 77, 101, 111, 190–1, 208

Mormons, 197–8

Morning Chronicle, London, 59, 73, 77

Morrissey, John (hoodlum, prize-fighter, congressman, senator), 187–8, 228

Morse, Samuel (inventor of Morse code, and pamphleteer), 220–1

Moylan, the Rev. William, 142, 147

Murdoch, Thomas (chairman, British emigration commissioners), 87, 106, 111, 112, 135, 190, 207, 216
and starving Irish, 130–1

Needlewoman at Home and Abroad, The (a poem), 33

Needlewomen, 197

New Brunswick, 26, 128, 135, 151, 155, 193, 200

New Orleans, 19, 209–10

New York, 24, 64, 91, 105, 221, 224, 231–3 passim
Carnegie's view, 25
bonds, 70
description of, 156–9, 168
and destitute emigrants, 159–64
societies, 164–6
English emigrants in, 166–8
an arrival, 169–70
quarantine, 171–8
runners and rackets, 178–80
Castle Garden, 242–5, 246
today, 249

New York Association for the Improvement of the Condition of the Poor, 161–3

New York Evening Post, 97

New York Herald, 158

New York Illustrated News, 167

New York Magdalen Female Benevolent Society, rules, 160–1

New York Sun, 70

New York Times, 78, 114, 124, 130, 159, 186, 244

New York Tribune, story of Catherine Haggerty, 26; 132, 186, 229

Norris v. City of Boston (Head Tax case), 231–2

North Carolina Weekly Standard, The, 228

Numbers, of emigrant vessels from Liverpool to North America (1853), 20
of emigrants (1846–55), 20–1
of emigrants sent out by Tapscott's, 68, and by Byrnes, 86
of emigrants carried by American and British ships, compared, 91
of American and British ships, 91–2
of Irish leaving Ireland, 130–1
of emigrants to Canada and U.S.A. (1847), 134

Numbers—*cont.*
  of emigrants to Canada (1846),
    137
  sick and dead of typhus, 136–
    54 passim
  of emigrants entering at
    American ports, 159
  of paupers, New York, 163
  arriving in New York (1851),
    171
  passing through Liverpool in
    year, 195
  of emigrant Mormons (1849
    and 1853), 198
  shovelled out, 199–202
  emigrants in New York, 231
  emigrants returning to
    Liverpool (1854, 1855), 246

Occupations of emigrants, 28–31,
  Appendix D
Ocean Monarch, 98, 120–2
Ocean Plague (diary of Robert
  Whyte), 145–6
O'Doherty, Dr. William (ship's
  doctor), 113
Old Brewery, 161
*Old Countryman, and Emigrant's
  Friend, The,* 36
Order in Council, regulating life
  on emigrant vessels (1848),
  207
O'Reilly, the Rev. Bernard, 128,
  143–4, 149
Orphans, 144, 147, 149–50, 153,
  175, 201
Orr, John S. (the Angel Gabriel),
  229–30
Overcrowding aboard emigrant
  ships, 110–12, 136, 149, 209–10,
  216
Overpopulation, evils of, in
  England, 36–8

Packet lines and ships, 88–93
  passim
Paff, William P., 184
Palmerston, Lord (Foreign
  Secretary and landlord), 201
Passage, duration of, to America,
  18
  from Cork and Dublin to
    Liverpool, 57–8
  on steamships, 236, 239, 242
Passenger Acts, 21, 57, 71, 108,
  111–13 passim, 116
  United States (1847), 134–5,
    213–17
  arbitrariness of, 205–7
  unenforceability of, 207–12
    passim
  Inman's dislike of, 238
    Appendix A
Patey, Captain Charles, R.N.
  (emigration officer), 87, 211–13
  passim
Paupers, 192, 198–202 passim,
  223–5, 232, 234–5
Pennsylvania Steam Ship
  Company, 241
Perley, Moses (government emi-
  gration agent, St. John), 200–1
Philadelphia, 237, 239
Phillips, William (shipowner and
  broker), 114
Pierce, Franklin (President), 65,
  227
Pigs, 158, 159, 162
Pioneer of the Wilderness, his
  cure for seasickness, 18
Poems, see under Ballads
Poor Law, 198, 225
Population, Liverpool, mid
  nineteenth century, 63
  fall in, Ireland (1841–51), 130
  New York, 157
  of Canada and America (1849),
    193

Posters, 56, 71, 79

Priests, 56, 75, 76, 128, 131, 132, 142–4, 150–1, 153, 166, 202, 221
courage on Grosse Isle, 146–7

Prior, Lieutenant Thomas (assistant emigration officer), 73

Privacy of contract, 225–6

Provisions aboard ship, 17, 18, 23, 57, 71, 101, 103–14 passim, 127, 136, 200, Appendix A
on American ships, 213
on steamships, 237, 242

Punch, emigration for aristocracy, 30
on needlewomen, 33
on slavery in America, 50

Quarantine,
In Canada, 101, 136–54 passim. See also Grosse Isle.
In the United States, 171–8, 179, 214

Quebec, 24, 71, 102, 120, 136, 141, 142, 147–9 passim, 151

Quebec Mercury, 128

Quigg, Benjamin D. (deputy sergeant-at-arms, New York), 185

Quin, William P. (commissioners' man, New York), 178

Rackets, practised by runners in Liverpool, 71–7 passim
by runners in New York, 178–86

Ragged School Union, 122, 125, 197

Rawlings, Thomas (newspaper editor and owner), encouragement of emigration, 36–7

Redmond, Sylvester (journalist), on runners, 73; 111, 115

Remittances, 37, 70, 164, 203–4

Reports—parliamentary (1851), 59
to Massachusetts House of Representatives, 60
Hawthorne's, on American sailors, 95–9
on ship's surgeons, 115
of the Rev. John Johns, 131–2
Dr. Douglas's (1847), 159
of the New York Association for the Improvement of the Condition of the Poor, 161–4
of committee investigating quarantine, New York, 173
emigration commissioners' about Hodder, 210
of select committee, New York State, 223

Richards, Samuel Whitney (president of Mormons in England), 198

Richardson Bros. (Liverpool merchant house), 236–7

River steamers, 148–9, 179, 180, 183

Roach, James (runner), 181–6 passim

Robertson, the Hon. John (agent to Sir Robert Gore Booth), 200

Rolph, Dr. Thomas (surgeon and emigration agent), advantages of emigration, 40

Runners, 62, 67, 68
Liverpool, 72–7, 83–4
their rackets in New York, 178–87 215–16 passim
and Castle Garden, 242–5 passim

Russell, Lord John (Prime Minister), 166, 193

Sabel, Frederick (lodging-house keeper), evidence to 1851 Committee, 59, 62, 75–6
evidence on medicals, 78

Sailors, 66, 83, 110, 121, 124
  brutality of, 94–9, 103–5 passim
St. Andrew's Society, New York,
  181
St. Lawrence, 113, 115, 134–8
  passim, 148, 201
San Francisco, 221–2
Saul, George (broker), 72, 111
Schomberg, Commander Charles,
  R.N., 110, 212
Scots as emigrants, 25, 26, 29, 31,
  108, 162, 181, 244, Appendix C
Scouttenen, Dr., 172
Seasickness, 17–20, 58, 109
Servants, lack of, in Canada and
  America, 52–3
  on Grosse Isle, 141
Ship fever, deaths from, 26, 136
  (see Typhus)
Shipwrecks, 94
  Exmouth, 119–20
  *Powhattan, California Packet,
    Hannah, Maria, Charles
    Bartlett*, 120
  Ocean Monarch, 120–2
  Annie Jane, 122–5
  E.Z., 126–7
  City of Glasgow, 240–1
  City of Philadelphia, 241–2
  Arctic, 242
  Amazon, 242
Sidney, Samuel (writer), advice to
  would-be emigrants, 28–31
  description of emigrants, 61
  on brokers, 68
  on Mormons, 198
Slavery, 50, 228–30 passim
Sligo, 200, 201
Smallpox, 171, 174
Smethurst, Henry D. and Co.,
  181–5 passim, 215
Smith, Sidney, a voyage, 18
Smith v. Turner (Head Tax case),
  231–2

Societies, to help emigrants, 38,
  74, 176, 181
  New York, 164–6
Society for Promoting Christian
  Knowledge, emigrant tracts,
  18–19, 117
Sons of John Bull (a ballad), 34
Staten Island, 171–5
Steamships, 18, 58, 88, 189, 236–42
Stephen, Sir George (barrister
  and philanthropist), on runners,
  73, 77, 111
Stooling, 182, 183
Storms at Sea, 20, 23–4, 110, 123,
  125, 126–7
Stowaways, 26, 75, 83
Surgeons on board emigrant ships,
  19, 94, 95, 103–14 passim, 115–
  18, Appendix A
  on steamships, 237
Swedes as emigrants, 234
Sybil; or Two Nations (novel by
  Disraeli), 34

Tapscott, W. and J. T. (brokers),
  68–70, 86, 92, 203
  against quarantine, 172
Tapscott's Emigrant's Guide, 68, 70
Taschereau, the Rev. Elzéar
  Alexandre, 147
Tents, at quarantine, 140, 150
Thompson, Dr. William (of
  Ward's Island), 176
Times (London), 155, 225–6, 238
Tocqueville, Alexis de, opinion of
  America, 43
Toronto, 32, 108, 137, 149, 151
  letter from Mayor to Elgin, 153
Tracts, 19, 94, 117, 138–40
Train, Enoch, and his packet line,
  82, 88–9, 120, 203
Trollope, Anthony, visit to
  America, 44

Trollope, Frances, view of
America, 43
Tupper, Martin F. (versifier), 42
Typhus, 128–32
in Canada (1847), 137–54, 201
in the U.S.A., 170–7 passim,
209. (See Ship fever)

United Irishman (Dublin), 130

Van Hovenburgh, Dr. Henry
(health officer, New York), 179,
215
Verplanck, Gulian C. (emigration
commissioner, New York),
214–15

Wakefield, Edward Gibbon, 194
Walters, R. C., wreck of the
Annie Jane, 122–5
Ward's Island, 175–8, 234
Ware, T. Hibbert (barrister), 52
Washington, George, 219, 228
Washington (packet ship), 90–1,
102–8, 207, 216
Water on board ship, 101, 103,
110, 112, 114, 136, 146

Watson, William (managing
director of Dublin and Liver-
pool Steam Packet Co.),
evidence to 1854 Committee, 58
*Wealth and Biography of the
Wealthy Citizens of the City of
New York*, 156, 168
Webb, Charles (superintendent,
British Protective Emigrant
Society, New York), 176
Welsh, The Rev. John William
(Anglican chaplain to emigrants,
Liverpool), 75, 110, 112
Westerfield, Joseph (ex-police-
man, ex-butcher, warder of
Ward's Island), 175
Whyte, Robert (writer of *The
Ocean Plague*) 145, 152
Wood, Dr. Isaac (in quarantine
service, New York), 115
Work and Wages, by Vere Foster, 34

Yankees, described, 48, 231
Young, Edward (American
statistician), on enrichment of
U.S.A. by emigrants, 39–40
Young Emigrants, The (children's
book), 38, 108

DESK FOR INFORMATION

EMIGRANT